ONE WEEK LOAN

UNIVERSITY OF GLAMORGAN
LEARNING RESOURCES CENTRE

Pontypridd, Mid Glamorgan, CF37 1DL
Telephone: Pontypridd (0443) 480480

Books are to be returned on or before the last date below

26. SEP 97	1 2 MAY 2001	
	1 9 APR 2002	
2 6 NOV 1997	7 MAY 2002	
	1 1 OCT 2002	
1 0 DEC 1997		
- 8 JAN 1999		
0 5 MAY 1999		
1 5 FEB 2000		
0 1 APR 2000		
1 6 MAY 2000		

Conservative Politics in France

Conservative Politics in France

by MALCOLM ANDERSON

LONDON · GEORGE ALLEN & UNWIN LTD
Ruskin House Museum Street

32?.11
(44)?19"
AND

329.4 (44)
And
324.24404
AND

First published in 1974

ISBN: 0 04 320093 1

Printed in Great Britain
in 10 point Times Roman type
by Alden & Mowbray Ltd
at the Alden Press, Oxford

(19/12/74)

Acknowledgements

I am grateful to the ex-Ministers, Deputies, Senators, party officials, party members, journalists and academics who have generously given me their time and helped me to understand many different aspects of Right-wing politics. I am also indebted to all those scholars and commentators who have furthered the understanding of French politics in the late nineteenth and twentieth centuries. Only the most relevant and the most useful works for the study of the Right have been cited in the footnotes of this book.

I wish to thank the Rockefeller Foundation, the Nuffield Foundation and the University of Warwick, whose generosity has made it possible for me to spend protracted periods in France.

I am very grateful to Dr Jean Charlot, Mr P. M. Williams and Dr V. Wright who read the manuscript and Mr D. M. Shapiro who read the proofs. They do not, of course, bear any responsibility for any errors the book might contain.

M.A.

Preface

This book describes the evolution of the Right in France from a scattering of weak and transitory political associations to a dominating, disciplined national party whose members form the majority in the National Assembly. Other countries too have seen the development of conservative parties from informal systems of clientage, through a number of intermediary forms, to a coherent disciplined organisation with a mass following. In France the transformation was slow and of unusual complexity; it is still only partially understood. Whilst the traditions and ideologies of the Right are treated in numerous books and articles, the organisations and behaviour of the Right, with the notable exceptions of *Action Française* and Gaullism, have not received the same amount of attention. Professor Rémond's elegant account of themes and attitudes in Right-wing politics[1] has not been complemented by a general study of Right-wing parties. This book is, in part, an attempt to fill the gap.

The scope of this study is necessarily wide and its boundaries are imprecise. The main strands of conservatism have never been united in a single organisation, even in the Fifth Republic when the Gaullists have made an almost clean sweep of the traditionally Right-wing electoral bastions. There has also been considerable discontinuity in the organisations of the Right. On the Left, the Radical, Socialist and Communist parties have had histories of over half a century. On the Right, the main electoral parties of the Third Republic, *Fédération Républicaine*, *Alliance Démocratique* and *Action Libérale Populaire*, did not survive the regime as effective organisations. The workings of the Fifth Republic destroyed the *Centre National des Indépendants et des Paysans*, the main conservative electoral party of the Fourth Republic. Numerous less important parties have had shorter histories. Since the late nineteenth century the radical Right of reactionary, nationalist or neo-Fascist inspiration has spawned a multitude of extra-parliamentary organisations variously called parties, leagues, associations and even study groups. They have often had only tenuous connections with the parties engaged in electoral and parliamentary processes. The large number of organisations,

[1] R. Rémond, *La Droite en France*, 3rd edition, 2 vols, 1968, 2nd American edition 1969.

and the lack of contact between them, would make a detailed narra-
tive history of Right-wing parties almost unreadable. The fragmen-
tary nature of the available sources makes the enterprise almost
impossible.

Party archives have been scattered and destroyed. The looseness
of party organisations, paucity of office staff, lack of interest of party
leaders in preserving an historical record, and the transitory nature
of the parties and leagues have combined with the depredations of
two World Wars to reduce to derisory proportions the quantity of
unpublished documents available. For example, although some
papers relating to *Action Libérale Populaire* are conserved by *Action
Populaire* at Vanves, the bulk of the files which survived the First
World War were probably in the hands of the party President,
Jacques Piou. Joseph Denais, as his literary executor, used Piou's
papers to write a biography[1] but the fate of these papers after Denais's
death remains a mystery. Another example of non-availability is the
archive of the *Fédération Républicaine*. In the late 1950s, some papers
of the *Fédération* were held in the offices of the *Républicains Sociaux*,
the small Gaullist party which disappeared shortly after the foundation of the Fifth Republic. Probably the most valuable files of the
Fédération were in the hands of Louis Marin who was for many
years the party President. After his death, the Marin papers were
deposited in the Bibliothèque Nationale and are not available for
consultation. From the description of the papers given to me by
Monsieur Marin in 1959, it seems unlikely, when they become
available, that they will provide major new insights into the working
of the *Fédération*. The situation is very similar for all the parties of
the Right; records have been mislaid or destroyed, or are otherwise
unavailable. Scholars who have written or attempted biographical
studies of leading politicians of the late nineteenth and twentieth
centuries have faced similar problems when trying to find private
archives. The relative lack of archival material makes impossible the
kind of historical scholarship based on the great collections of the
private papers of nineteenth- and early twentieth-century British
politicians. This book is not, however, concerned with the minutiae
of the historical record but with formulating generalisations about a
specific group of political parties. In this sense it is in a humane
tradition of political science, although very much out of harmony
with current fashions for quantification and behavioural research.

The vast quantity of published information in State papers,
newspapers, periodicals, brochures and books compensate to some
extent for the lack of unpublished documents. Oral testimony is

[1] J. Denais, *Jacques Piou*, 1959.

of irreplaceable value in gaining insight and perspective on men and events. I have not administered questionnaires or engaged in standardised interviewing techniques. Over a period of fifteen years I have conversed with a large number of participants in Right-wing politics. These include former *Présidents du Conseil* such as Paul Reynaud and Joseph Laniel, ex-Ministers such as Henri Bergasse and Roger Duchet, Senators such as Jacques Debû-Bridel who began his career as a member of Tardieu's personal staff and is now a Left-wing Gaullist, and Abel Durand who was an important figure in the revival of the conservative interest in Loire Inférieure after the Second World War. I have been received kindly by men possessing *les grands noms français* who have played a certain political role such as the Duke de Rohan, Reille-Soult, the Duke de Dalmatie, longtime Deputy for Tarn, and Count de Grandmaison, former Deputy of Loire Atlantique, and by Deputies who have played an important role in particular incidents such as Michel Raingeard who was a key figure in the passing of the *Loi Barangé*. I have been helped by party officials such as Bernard Le Calloc'h of the *Union des Démocrates pour la République* and Denis Baudouin of the *Centre National des Indépendants et des Paysans* and by Maître Grimaud in Nantes, who had been the electoral agent for an important conservative notable. Journalists, local councillors and ordinary party members in all the main areas of conservative electoral support have been willing to talk to me. Some of the people I have met have shown me letters and miscellaneous documents in their possession. I have met with unfailing courtesy and consideration from men with whose political views I have been in profound disagreement. I am deeply grateful for their assistance.

Most of the information derived from conversations belongs to the *petite histoire* of the Right and is sometimes of doubtful reliability. On both these counts, it is inappropriate to include it in a general study of this kind. I have been specifically asked not to quote directly from some sources. In other cases, I am reluctant to quote material because, as past experience has shown, this can result in informants being besieged by graduate students of several nationalities, who offend only because they are too numerous. This reticence would be difficult to justify if information about sources which could produce major new interpretations of recent history were withheld: such is not the case. The major sources used are published and easily verifiable. The interpretations of the evidence derived from them have been informed by personal contact with a wide range of participants. The work of other scholars has also been of great help.

In recent years, many books and articles have been written which have greatly increased our knowledge and understanding of aspects of the Right or of the environment in which Right-wing politicians have made their careers. This writing has covered a wide range of subjects from detailed local studies, such as those of David Watson on nationalism in Paris at the turn of the century and of François Dreyfus on Alsace between the wars, to general works of interpretation and synthesis, such as the work of René Rémond already mentioned and the books of Adrien Dansette on Catholicism.[1] Falling between these two are the magisterial and very scholarly accounts of Pierre Barral on French agriculture and Philip Williams on the Fourth Republic. Eugen Weber has written a book on *Action Française* which comes close to a definitive work despite the subsequent publication of the Barrès/Maurras correspondence. John Sherwood and Dieter Wolf have written outstanding biographies of Mandel and Doriot respectively; they have given accounts of their subjects which will last more than a generation. It is now impossible to write on Gaullism without being influenced at every turn by the major contribution of Jean Charlot.[2] There are many others, acknowledged in the footnotes of this book, who provide the student of the French Right with information, stimulation and pleasure.

[1] D. R. Watson 'The Nationalist Movement in Paris, 1900–1906', in D. Shapiro (ed.), *The Right in France 1890–1910*, St Antony's Papers, No. 13, 1962, pp. 49–84. F. G. Dreyfus, *La Vie politique en Alsace, 1919–1936*, 1969. A. Dansette, *L'Histoire religieuse de la France contemporaine*, 2nd edition, 1965, English edition, 1961. *Destin de catholicisme français*, 1957.

[2] P. Barral, *Les Agrariens français de Méline à Pisani*, 1968. P. M. Williams, *Crisis and Compromise: the Politics of the Fourth French Republic*, 1964. E. Weber, *Action Française: Royalism and Reaction in Twentieth-Century France*, 1964. M. Barrès, C. M. P. Maurras, *La République ou le roi*, 1970. J. Sherwood, *Georges Mandel and the Third Republic*, 1971. D. Wolf, *Doriot: du communisme à la collaboration*, 1969; first published as *Die Doriot Bewegung*, 1967. J. Charlot, *L'UNR, étude du pouvoir au sein d'un parti politique*, 1967. *Le Gaullisme*, 1970. *Les Français et de Gaulle*, 1971. *The Gaullist phenomenon*, 1971.

Contents

14 CONTENTS

Maps

Introduction

This book describes the evolution of the Right in France from a scattering of weak and transitory political associations to a dominating, moderately well-disciplined coalition whose members have formed the majority of the National Assembly in four successive parliaments. Although the history of revolution and counter-revolution since the end of the eighteenth century is relevant to a study of contemporary conservatism, the point of departure chosen is the 'conquest of the Republic' by the Republicans in the late 1870s and early 1880s. The traditions and attitudes established prior to the last quarter of the nineteenth century were mediated through the new forms of political organisation which slowly came into being under the regime of universal suffrage. At the beginning of the Third Republic, conservatives who remained loyal to the Bourbon, Orleans or Bonapartist dynasties seemed formidably strong. They possessed considerable wealth and social prestige, they enjoyed the support of the Church and, for a time, they had a parliamentary majority. But they failed to restore a monarchy and most could not adapt to the new regime. This 'dynastic' Right was disastrously divided by the Boulangist adventure, diminished by the papal policy in the 1890s, advising Catholics to rally to the Republic, outflanked by nationalists during the Dreyfus affair, and soundly defeated when it attempted to defend the interests of the Church. A long series of electoral setbacks completely discredited it and after the 1880s monarchists and Bonapartists ceased to pose a serious threat to the Republican form of government.

As the old monarchist Deputies and Senators died or were defeated, new groups drifted towards the Right. Almost at the same time as prominent Catholics, responding to the papal initiative, rallied to the Republic, some moderate Republicans, desiring no further social or political change, became alarmed by the rhetoric of the Radicals and by the appearance of the Socialists in the Chamber of Deputies. They became aware, particularly in the first years of the twentieth century, that they had more in common with 'clericals' than they had with many members of the dominant Left-wing coalition, the *Bloc des gauches*. At the same time, nationalism, which was in some respects a new political phenomenon, temporarily rallied additional support for Right-wing candidates in elections in urban areas, and added a new dimension to extra-parliamentary politics. In the first thirty years of the Third Republic, therefore, the Right greatly changed its appearance.

From the 1890s until the First World War there was a fairly rigid distinction in parliamentary politics, between Catholics and anti-clericals. Almost all those who had been on the losing side in the Dreyfus case and over the Separation of the Church and State remained in impotent opposition, although there was much in common between moderate clericals and moderate anti-clericals on issues of economic and social policy. The isolation and impotence of the parliamentary Right was one of the factors which encouraged the great flowering of an extra-parliamentary Right, the most famous example of which was *Action Française*. During the First World War both parliamentary and extra-parliamentary Right rallied to the call for national unity and this, to some extent, modified the post-war situation. The struggle against the external enemy and the comradeship of the trenches helped to diminish the popular prejudices which hindered the co-operation between men who differed on the religious question. Men of the Right participated in government during the war and continued to do so afterwards. In the inter-war period, men such as Poincaré and Tardieu who had become identified with the Right, were among the most notable leaders of government. But parliamentary moderates and conservatives failed to take full advantage of their much improved electoral performance. Ill-disciplined, lacking both common policy objectives and, with the possible exception of Poincaré, generally accepted leaders, they gave the appearance of being indecisive and ineffective. In parliament and government, their only successful years were from 1926 to 1929.

The Republic gained much prestige on the Right of the political spectrum following victory in the First World War but disillusion with the regime soon revived and became particularly acute in the 1930s when government instability, corruption in parliamentary circles and the worsening international situation damaged its credit. This climate encouraged the growth of Right-wing leagues and agitation in the streets. The political forces were, however, fairly evenly balanced: the fear on the Left of a Right-wing coup and the similar fear on the Right of a Communist revolution proved unfounded. Both the Right and the Left were deeply divided by the problems which faced the country in the last years of the Third Republic. The reputation of the Right was gravely damaged by the positions adopted by its leading members. Most of them, although by no means all, supported the policy of appeasement of the German and Italian dictators, and voiced pessimistic assessments about the ability of the country to defend itself. After the defeat of France in 1940, these views led to the acceptance of a subordinate role for France in a German-dominated Europe and to support for the Vichy regime. The political alignments of the late 1930s and early 1940s were, however, very complex. Some men of the Left were involved both in appeasement and in the Vichy regime. Many of the leading exponents of Collaboration with the Germans during the war had Left-wing backgrounds. Conversely, men with careers in the parliamentary and anti-parliamentary Right opted either for the Resistance in France or the Free French movement in London and Algiers. Nevertheless, Vichy had the aura of a Right-wing, indeed reactionary regime, whereas both the internal and external Resistance came to have a progressive and even revolutionary image.

The Right was under a cloud at the Liberation: its organisations were proscribed, most of the newspapers which supported it were confiscated and almost all its former Deputies and Senators were ineligible for elective office because they had voted to give full powers to Marshal Pétain in 1940. The continuity of Right-wing political styles was, however, remarkable. The notables who participated in the new party founded in 1949, the *Centre National des Indépendants et des Paysans* had much in common with their predecessors in the *Fédération Républicaine* and *Alliance Démocratique* in the Third Republic. The Gaullist *Rassemblement du Peuple Français* revived the ambience of the more moderate pre-war league such as the *Jeunesses Patriotes* and the *Parti Social Français*. Moreover, the discredit of the Vichyite Right was short-lived and Vichyites were back in government by the early 1950s. The Right-wing parties of the Fourth Republic were, however, failures. The intractable political problems of the late 1940s and the enormous prestige of de Gaulle produced an impressive surge of support for the RPF. But its discipline broke down when it could not win an immediate and overwhelming electoral victory. Despite the popularity of the best known representative of the *droite classique*, Antoine Pinay, who won a great reputation in 1952–3 as a man who could halt inflation, the notables of the CNIP remained disorganised and faction-ridden. They were incapable of riding out the storms of Poujadism, decolonisation and the progressive discredit of the regime brought about by government instability. Although, in parliamentary terms, they were stronger than ever at the beginning of the Fifth Republic, the divisions within the CNIP over the Algerian question and, later, over attitudes towards the new regime, were so deep that it collapsed as an effective electoral party.

The Liberation until 1962 was a period of confusion and great strain in French politics. The constitutional order was insecure. The constitution of the Fourth Republic had been approved only by a small majority in the referendum of autumn 1946. It was opposed by Communists and Gaullists; the non-Gaullist Right also consistently criticised it. In the first years of the Fifth Republic, the new constitution seemed unlikely to be durable because many regarded 'de Gaulle's Republic' as an interim regime. Disagreements over the constitution were, however, symptoms of deeper political and social conflicts. The Cold War thrust the Communist Party into a political ghetto and compelled politicians of the Right to co-operate with the moderate Left, although they agreed on little other than the maintenance of parliamentary institutions; this weakened their position and damaged their reputation. Economic developments also caused political turbulence: from the early 1950s, strong industrial growth coupled with inflation caused apprehension in a variety of social groups such as the peasants, the small businessmen and the retired, who provided much electoral support for the Right. Above all, involvement in colonial wars, first in Indo-China and then in Algeria, produced a prolonged crisis during which the regime collapsed and its successor was threatened by subversion for almost four years. The factors on which the confused politics of this period were based were fertile soil for Right-wing agitators. Extremist groups proliferated, especially between 1954 and 1962. Although only the Poujadist movement had notable electoral success, these groups were an important element in the political system until the granting of independence to Algeria deprived them of their principal issue.

At the beginning of the Fifth Republic, the old Right was caught in a dilemma. It could either support de Gaulle over Algeria and over the new constitution or oppose him on these issues: if it did the former it risked absorption into Gaullism, if the latter, electoral defeat. It could not resolve this dilemma and the Gaullist coalition emerged victorious in the elections of 1962, commanding an absolute majority in the National Assembly. They have maintained this majority, although with little to spare after the narrow electoral victories of 1967 and 1973. The consequence of these repeated electoral successes was that the government enjoyed greater freedom of action and independence of parliamentary control than ever before under a Republican regime. De Gaulle used the opportunity to pursue a striking foreign policy. In domestic affairs, although much legislation was passed, the government often seemed to be responding to pressure for reform rather than taking the initiative. When it acted with decision, as over the reform of social security in 1967, it caused great offence. After the events of May 1968, major reforms of higher education and trade union rights were sometimes regarded by Gaullists in parliament as barely necessary and rather disagreeable concessions. As the Fifth Republic progressed the conservative characteristics of Gaullism became more pronounced.

A great range of issues and events have to be considered in plotting the main changes in Right-wing politics since 1880. Many parties have been established and have disappeared and the forms of political organisation have changed. The discontinuities of Right-wing politics are more striking than the continuities. The interests, attitudes and perspectives which have lain behind Right-wing parties, and even behind the same party label, have not only evolved with time but varied from locality to locality. The urban Right of Paris, Lyons and Marseilles and the rural Right of the Basque country or the southern fringe of the Massif Central differed greatly in the late nineteenth century and, despite their common present allegiance to Gaullism, remain different. The various manifestations of conservatism in Alsace – regionalist, Christian Democratic and Gaullist – are by no means the same as Breton conservatism which has evolved from monarchism via moderate Republicanism to Gaullism. The French Right has been highly fragmented and the relatively high degree of integration of conservative France in Gaullism is a fragile achievement. An analysis of the local political systems of France is necessary to understand the fragmentation of conservative forces and groups. This is a fascinating and difficult study. Most of the research which bears on it is in the fields of electoral geography and voting behaviour. This research provides only partial insights into relationships between representatives and the electors, networks and associations of interest, social institutions, the nature of political conflict and the issues which are regarded as political in particular localities. Localism has been diminishing slowly over the past century with the spread of education, improved transport facilities, increased social mobility and industrial growth. But the trend towards a greater degree of unity among Right-wing forces has been punctuated by explosive movements showing either that the old particularism is not dead or that new disintegrative factors have emerged. Conservative forces could still divide along geographical lines. In the Fifth Republic, governments have been made acutely aware that new regional alignments based on collective regional economic interests can cause political difficulties. Gaullist electoral domination of the very particularist peripheral provinces of Alsace, Brittany and the Basque country is insecure because there is a latent conflict between the national and local appeals of Gaullism.

Localism and regional differentiation have been compounded by other factors. Amongst the most important of these has been the complex nature of the class system. The lingering influence of a variety of aristocratic groups and the survival of old, deeply entrenched bourgeois societies has helped to maintain peculiar styles of politics. Whilst there remained a large backward or pre-industrial sector of the economy, it was virtually impossible for a single political organisation to aggregate conservative interests because they were so dissimilar. It was only after 1945 that a 'second industrial revolution' brought fundamental alterations in the legacy left behind by the imperfectly carried through industrialisation of the nineteenth century.

There has also been an intricate pattern of relationships between traditions, ideological concerns and social institutions. This has had the paradoxical effect that policy questions on which there has apparently been a large measure of agreement have sometimes helped to maintain divisions between conservatives. At the turn of the twentieth century a national bloc or clerical party was discerned by contemporary political observers, and the Right was certainly agreed on opposing anti-clerical measures. The religious question was, however, perceived in different ways by different groups within the Right and in different parts of the country. The coalition of groups which made up the Right also shared the characteristic of confessional parties, agreed on defending the Church but on scarcely anything else. The persisting importance of the divisions created by the religious question was a hindrance to the establishment of 'rational' political alliances between men who had interests in common.

Political organisations of the Right have tended to lead a precarious existence in a rich and complicated environment. The accidents of political history, the tenacity of political traditions, the complexities of the class structure, the divergent local political systems have all made it extremely difficult for national political organisations to put down strong and durable roots. The local committees which mobilised support for individual candidates and the national committees which tried to limit the damaging effects of a multiplicity of conservative interests in the last quarter of the nineteenth century can hardly be described as political parties in the modern sense of the term. Not until the beginning of the twentieth century were serious and successful attempts made to establish parties of the Right on a national basis. The new twentieth-century organisations were very varied in character. The *Fédération Républicaine*, building on the debris of unsuccessful initiatives, provided a permanent co-ordinating body for the old-style electoral committees and a national platform for a group of prominent parliamentary notables. *Action Libérale Populaire* was a more ambitious attempt at party building, drawing up a detailed programme and attempting to establish branches in all parts of the country. *Action Française*, composed of the followers of Charles Maurras, was committed to direct action and radical political change, but it eschewed electoral activity until after the First World War. The *Ligue de la Patrie Française* was an attempt to combine the activist temper of the extra-parliamentary leagues with the fruits of electoral and parliamentary activity.

The second wave of party building took place in the inter-war period. Although it partly reflected the relative lack of success of the pre-1914 organisations, genuinely original approaches to the problems of political organisation were few. Excepting the armed conspiracy of the *Cagoule* and the drive towards a French Fascism in Doriot's *Parti Populaire Français*, the party organisers of the 1920s and 1930s did little more than offer refinements and variations of the pre-1914 groups. The inter-war parties, like many aspirations of the French Right, were buried during the Second World War through their involvement with Vichy or Collaboration. The third wave of new organisations which followed the war had even less novelty than its inter-war predecessor. Disputatious members with divergent interests, lack of internal discipline and a programme which was vague almost to the point of being meaningless were characteristics which the *Centre National des Indépendants et des Paysans* shared with the *Fédération Républicaine*. The authoritarian structure, the mobilisation of mass enthusiasm and a programme centred on the reform of the State was a combination sought by the *Ligue de la Patrie Française* and several other leagues before the establishment of the Gaullist *Rassemblement du Peuple Français* in 1947. These two major efforts in party building were flanked by minor parties of the extreme Right which ranged from respectable organisation, patronised by well-known names, to clandestine groups of political adventurers with a taste for violence.

In the early part of the Fifth Republic a new movement, claiming to be composed of the most loyal followers of General de Gaulle, but not recognised by him, prospered to such an extent that four years after its foundation it gained, with the help of a subordinate ally, a majority of seats in the National Assembly. This movement, originally called the *Union pour la Nouvelle République*, was successful before it was properly organised; its structure was a response to its success. The electoral fortunes of the UNR were built on de Gaulle's political achievements of solving the Algerian conflict, defeating the old parties of the Fourth Republic, establishing stable government and restoring the international prestige of France. It attracted some support in all parts of the political spectrum but it had particular appeal for moderate and Right-wing voters. Although it captured most of the clientèle of the CNIP and the *Mouvement Républicain Populaire*, the Gaullist Party had a different style and different objectives to either of these parties. Like many conservative parties in other countries, its main purpose was to provide disciplined support for the leadership and the content of its programme was of secondary importance. Its leaders consistently denied that it was a Right-wing party and it was never de Gaulle's declared intention to act as midwife for a disciplined conservative party. The elections of 1962 and 1967, in which de Gaulle was deeply involved in campaigning for his followers, and the circumstances of his withdrawal from affairs have helped to emphasise the conservative character of the UNR and the *Union des Démocrates pour la République*, as it was subsequently known. The union of the Left for the elections of 1973 has further enhanced the identification of the UDR with conservatism.

In a general account of Right-wing politics there is an inevitable tendency to give the impression that the Gaullist Party is the long-awaited culmination, the realisation of the old dream of a disciplined conservative party. But the Gaullist achievement is not indestructible: new problems constantly occur and new problems have to be met. The Gaullist Party faces the consequences of a series of scandals which were revealed during the period when Chaban-Delmas was Prime Minister from 1969 to 1972. Scandal is a traditional feature of French political life and the Gaullist claim to have established a less corrupt regime than its predecessor has been revealed as cant. The significance of scandals has changed and because the UDR has achieved a relatively high degree of discipline, the reputation of the whole party has suffered. Partly as a consequence of this the Gaullists lost many votes in the elections of 1973. They escaped defeat because the electoral system worked in their favour and because those who voted at the first ballot for the moderate *Mouvement des Réformateurs* rallied to them at the second ballot to prevent a Left-wing victory and to preserve some of their own representation in parliament. The UDR has lost its absolute majority in the National Assembly and now relies on its less disciplined allies, the *Républicains Indépendants* and the *Centre Démocratie et Progrès*. The Gaullist leaders seek to bring members of the *Mouvement des Réformateurs* into the majority. The future is quite uncertain. The UDR may integrate its allies into a more broadly-based party but its allies may promote or profit from factionalism within the ranks of the UD. The fluidity of the party system, so immediately apparent in the Fourth Republic, is still present under a different form.

CHAPTER I

The Course of Conservative Politics: Men and Issues, 1880–1958

Right-wing politics from the Third to the Fifth Republics is a history of discontinuities. The collapse of the *ordre moral*, the Boulanger adventure, the Dreyfus affair, the *union sacrée* of the First World War, the period of the riots of February 1934 to the formation of the Popular Front all altered the situation and the perspectives of the parliamentary Right. These crucial episodes changed the way in which its members viewed their prospects of acquiring power and their attitudes towards the existing regime, how they evaluated previous policies and how sympathetic they were to subversion by extra-parliamentary forces. The extreme Right, the Right of demonstrations in the street, of stirring calls for the *coup d'état*, of conspiracies both serious and farcical, was equally stimulated and conditioned by these same events. Like the dramas of defeat in 1940, Collaboration and Resistance from 1940 to 1944, the collapse of the Fourth Republic and the Algerian War from 1954 to 1962, the episodes were destructive of morale and of careers. In the resolution and aftermath of crises, participants became discouraged and discredited: they retired or were pushed aside by new men with different outlooks.

The succession of clans, networks, associations of families, cabals, leagues and parties which made up 'conservative France' in these years, were bound together by many small threads, common experiences, individual life histories and odd personal itineraries. But the Right, taken as a whole, had a different character after every major political upheaval, a different constellation of forces and a different set of perceptions about the political system. The vocabulary of political discussion – of the *relève des générations*, of *années tournantes* – reflects a widely experienced intuitive feeling for the sea changes which punctuated French politics every ten to fifteen years. From time to time Right-wing groups were self-consciously playing an historical role: *nouvelles équipes* have announced 'national revolutions', 'recoveries' and 'revivals' which have not taken place. Sometimes a generation of young men have acquired a sense of identity and purpose, the sources of which are fairly obscure – an example would be the generation of the *années trente* in the years 1930 to 1934, described so evocatively by Jean Touchard and Loubet del Bayle.[1] The feeling that the new generation was living in, or indeed creating, a new political world does not diminish the importance of the previous great battle in setting a major part of the framework in which political action and discussion took place.

The refusal to adapt to the new regime
The first displacement of a generation of Right-wing politicians in the Third Republic was of a particularly decisive nature. The accession of Jules Grévy to the Presidency of the Republic in 1879 marked the culmination of the Republicans' drive for power. The confused period of the Republic of 'the Dukes' and of the *grands Notables* presided over by the ineffectual Marshal MacMahon disappeared, never to be restored.[2] Agonising division over the form of the regime and inability to adapt to the realities of universal suffrage conducted the 'reactionaries' – the Legitimists, Orleanists and Bonapartists – into total and irrevocable eclipse. This eclipse caused a drastic change in the personnel of government, even more decisive than that which followed the collapse of the Second Empire. There was only one transitional ministry based on a compromise between the old and the new men, the Waddington administration from February to December 1879. After the resignation of Waddington, only Freycinet of the sixty-three men who had held ministerial office between 1871 and 1879 continued a ministerial career.[3] The defeat of the men drawn from monarchist and Bonapartist milieux pursued an inexorable course. They had lost control, in 1876, of the Chamber of Deputies when President MacMahon dissolved it in an attempt to find a new conservative majority. The majority in the Senate was reversed in 1879. Control of local government passed out of conservative hands: as a result of the 1881 elections the Republicans controlled the mayoralties of 20,000 communes against 9,500 held by the monarchists and Bonapartists, and 'conservatives' had a

---

[1] J. Touchard, 'L'Esprit des années trente', in *Cahiers de la civilisation*, No. 1, 1960, pp. 89–120. J. L. Loubet del Bayle, *Les Non-conformists des années trente*, 1969.

[2] D. Halévy, *La Fin des notables*, 1930. *La République des ducs*, 1937.

[3] J. Ollé-Laprune, *La Stabilité des ministres sous la Troisième République 1879–1940*, 1962, pp. 11–12, *passim*. L. Teste, *L'Anatomie de la Troisième République, 1870–1910*, 1910.

majority in only twenty-one *conseils généraux*, the Republicans in sixty-five. There was a purge of the prefectoral corps in 1877, the upper ranks of the army in 1878, the Council of State in 1879 and the magistrature in 1883 to remove anti-Republican elements. Despite these measures the traditional elites remained strongly represented in some parts of the State machine – notably the army and the diplomatic corps. The Council of State after the purge was certainly less reactionary in a political sense, but may have become less sensitive to the claims of the industrial working class and less sympathetic to social legislation. The effects of the purge were therefore complex and inconclusive. The Republicans won a decisive political victory by their conquest of an unassailable majority in the Chamber of Deputies but, despite the purge, their control of certain parts of the State apparatus was much less secure.

The position of the anti-Republican Right in the country certainly remained strong enough to alarm their opponents. The wealth of the Right was considerable although (excepting the Orleanist families and some Bonapartists) it was not associated at this time with the new commercial and industrial wealth of the nineteenth century. Conservatives owned most of the newspapers and dominated the provincial press. They had, in almost every corner of France, the powerful support of the Church. But these assets did not compensate for the strategic weaknesses of the Right. In the first place, composed of aristocrats and notables, it was ill-adapted to organise effectively to fight elections in a regime of universal suffrage. It seemed incapable of even a minimum understanding that only one candidate of the Right should put forward his candidature in each constituency. The Right only once came near to an agreed list of candidatures before 1914: this was in 1885 when the system of single member constituencies was temporarily abandoned in favour of multi-member constituencies based on the *département*. The second weakness was that the Right was united only on one very general aim, the revision of the constitution, and there was considerable disagreement over the nature of this revision. The death of the Imperial Prince in 1879 whilst serving in the British army in South Africa, weakened the Bonapartist cause because of the lack of a generally acceptable successor. The monarchists were divided in their allegiance between Legitimist and Orleanist pretenders. Much of the *élan*, the simple faith and loyalty went out of the monarchist cause with the event which brought most of them together, the death in 1883 of 'Henri V', Count of Chambord. Most monarchists thereafter supported the Orleanist pretender but factionalism had already damaged their cause beyond repair.

The third weakness of the Right was the absence of any legislative programme which had the agreement of more than small groups of members of parliament. The majority of the Right could see little purpose in having a legislative programme under a Republican regime. But the great rallying cries of their opponents had specific legislative implications. In the celebrated Belleville programme of 1869, the majority of the Republicans had a credo and a comprehensive list of social and political reforms (including separation of Church and State, abolition of a standing army, election of judges, introduction of income-tax, abolition of institutions inherited from the monarchy such as a Senate and Presidency) which could be supported by the most advanced Radicals and assented to by many Opportunists who had no intention of assisting their enactment. 'Liberty' was translated into the laws of freedom of the press and freedom of meeting of 1881. The law of associations of 1884 which gave a liberal statute to trade unions (to which some members of the Right were in part favourable) marked a significant advance in social legislation and towards the Republican ideal of 'equality'. The Ferry programme for the introduction of free, compulsory and secular primary education, bitterly opposed by the Right on religious grounds, was completed in 1886. The Republican slogans, programme and legislation found considerable support in the country and contributed to the mobilisation of the *nouvelles couches sociales* (Gambetta's felicitous phrase for the lower middle classes) behind Opportunist and Radical politicians. The Right had no effective counter-weapons and found no substantial counter-arguments. The timid attempt at a French version of Tory democracy, of an alliance between the old aristocratic elite and the new industrial working class against the bourgeoisie failed as a consequence of the apathy and hostility of the majority of conservative notables, some of whom affected to regard the main promoter of this movement, Count Albert de Mun, as a dangerous revolutionary. The alliance was also hindered by the opposition of the Papacy to de Mun's attempt to establish a Catholic party in 1885.[1] The ventures of de Mun and Count René de La Tour du Pin in establishing *cercles ouvriers*, under the guise of social good works, were the only attempts by members of the monarchist Right to recruit new social groups for the conservative cause. Prompted by the highest motives and an altruistic idealism, theirs was the reaction of men shocked by the Paris Commune and the condition of the working class.[2] But the

[1] H. Rollet, *Albert de Mun et le parti catholique*, 1947.

[2] See H. Rollet, *L'Action sociale des catholiques en France, 1871–1914*, 2 vols, 1948–58. C. Baussan, *La Tour du Pin*, 1931. Bossan de Guragnol, *Le Colonel de la*

cercles ouvriers and de Mun's social Catholicism attracted only a small band of devotees. Although many tributes were paid to their broad and lasting educational influence on Catholic attitudes, by the turn of the twentieth century even admirers of de Mun regarded them as more or less moribund.

The fourth factor weakening the Right, and it was the most important, was the nature of their opponents. Men such as Gambetta and Ferry, although not 'moderately Republican', were moderate enough in general policy. Their aspirations in social and political reform were satisfied by the middle of the 1880s. They became conservatives and associated only reluctantly with groups which proposed or threatened further social change. Electoral considerations made co-operation with 'clericals' difficult but the support attracted from the Right by the Rouvier administration in 1887 was the first example of a preference by some moderate Republicans for an alliance with the Right rather than the Radicals.[1]

Boulanger, the Ralliement, the Dreyfus affair, 1886–1902

Despite the involvement in the Boulangist adventure of 1887–8 of leading members of the Right, such as Baron Mackau and Count Albert de Mun,[2] the Opportunists (moderate Republicans) did not renounce for long their quest for at least a tacit understanding with sections of the Right. Although many moderate Republicans remained anti-clerical, they were quite as firmly opposed as the Right to fiscal and social reform which would change the social status quo. The Opportunists therefore wanted an alliance with the Right in parliament, to block social and economic legislation, but an electoral alliance with the Radicals 'in defence of the Republic' in order to be on the winning side. Electorally, the Right was in considerable difficulty because, wedded to the concept of order, it appeared to undermine it by its attacks on the regime. After important members of the Right had shown a taste for political adventure in the Boulanger affair, the Opportunists could imply that they were the only effective defenders of the social order. Some were quite open about their new conservatism. The much quoted speech in 1892 of Constans, who, as Minister of the Interior, played a major role in out-manoeuvring Boulanger, is an example:

Tour du Pin d'après lui-même, 1936. R. Garric, *Albert de Mun*, 1935. H. Fontanille, *L'Oeuvre sociale d'Albert de Mun*, 1926. V. Guiraud, *Un Grand français. A. de Mun*, 1920. A. de Mun, *Ma vocation sociale*, 1908. J. Piou, *Le Comte Albert de Mun*, n.d.

[1] Mermeix, *Les Coulisses du boulangisme*, 1890, pp. 83–4.

[2] A. Dansette, *Le Boulangisme, 1886–1890*, 1947, pp. 156–88, *passim*. See also F. H. Seager, *The Boulanger Affair*, 1969.

'I have been a Republican for forty years. Since I have reached the age of sixty I have turned conservative – but a Republican conservative [laughter and applause]. At one time only very respectable people ["*les gens très bien*"] were conservative [laughter and applause]. Our turn has come to be very respectable people. [Renewed laughter and applause.]'[1]

The evolution of the Opportunists had several important consequences. In the first place, it allowed moderate Republicans to recruit electoral support from milieux which had formerly voted for Orleanist, Bonapartist and even Legitimist candidates. This was apparent on a national scale in the election of 1889. In some areas the evolution was slow, as in Orleanist Normandy where moderate Republicans succeeded to the monarchist positions only on the death or retirement of incumbent Deputies.[2] Secondly, it resulted in a clear split between those who wanted to complete the Belleville programme, the Radicals and Radical Socialists, and those who considered that the reforms of the 1880s were sufficient. This split was manifest in the first ballot of the election of 1885. Discord between Radicals and Opportunists was partly responsible for the Right (the *Union Conservatrice*) going into the election with ninety seats and coming away with two hundred. There were, of course, other reasons. The educational and social reforms of the first five years of the decade had generated considerable opposition in the rural areas and amongst the *bien pensante* bourgeoisie. The civil servants dismissed in the purge provided bitter and sometimes able candidates for the conservative cause. Disillusion and doubt about the fitness of the moderate Republicans to govern were spread by the crash of the Union Générale bank in 1881,[3] which particularly affected the clientele of the conservatives, and the *affairisme* and corruption exposed in the second half of the decade in the Wilson and Panama scandals.[4] Thirdly, as a consequence of the Dreyfus affair, half the moderate Republicans were thrown, with the *ralliés* and the remnants of the monarchist Right, into permanent opposition until the First World War.

Two developments almost contemporaneous with the Dreyfus affair also modified the structure of parliamentary politics – the *Ralliement* was essentially a salvage operation sponsored by Pope Leo XIII who, in 1890, encouraged Cardinal Lavigerie to give, at a

[1] A. Dansette, *Histoire religieuse de la France contemporaine*, 1965, p. 485.
[2] A. Siegfried, *Tableau politique de la France de l'ouest*, 1913, pp. 349–51, *passim*.
[3] See J. Bouvier, *Le Krach de l'Union générale, 1878–1885*, 1960.
[4] A. Dansette, *L'Affaire Wilson et la chute du Président Grévy*, 1936.

dinner for the officers of the French Mediterranean fleet, the famous toast of loyalty to established institutions.[1] The Pope confirmed this directive in the encyclical *Au milieu des sollicitudes* (1892) and it was taken up by three leading politicians of the Right, Jacques Piou, Albert de Mun and Prince d'Arenberg. The Pope considered that the interests of the Church were being damaged by her association with the monarchist Right at a time when there was no hope of a restoration. Jacques Piou and his associates rallied to the Republic out of deference to the Pope and because they agreed with the reasoning behind his policy. They hoped to increase the conservative vote and, eventually, participate in government.

The *Ralliement* came at an auspicious time when it seemed that the Right might profitably change its tactics. The involvement in the Boulanger affair of some of the responsible personalities of the Right, such as de Mun and Mackau, showed how near to despair of ever regaining power the Right had come. To join forces with a general and ex-Minister of War whose recent past was Radical, whose appeal was jingoistic, and whose intentions were, to say the least, uncertain, illustrated a state of mind which Ranc wittily referred to as *n'import-quinisme* – 'no matter who, but not the Republic'.[2] But Boulanger had not the capacity to match his ambitions. He was good at self-advertisement, demonstrating this talent whilst Minister of War in 1886 when, in less than a year, he emerged from obscurity to become the symbol of *revanche*. On the other hand, he lacked political acumen as well as physical and moral courage. Power was probably his for the taking when he had won a series of by-elections culminating in the by-election in Paris in 1888. Urged by his followers to march on the Elysée, his nerve failed and he fled the country.

The Right was compromised by this political suicide and lost more seats at the election of 1889 that it had won in 1885. Political adventure, especially unsuccessful political adventure, was not to the taste of the conservative electorate. This affected the behaviour even of the most notorious Bonapartists and monarchists who ostentatiously refused to rally to the Republic. Cuneo d'Ornano, who was to remain active in the Bonapartist cause until the end of his political career, remarked mildly in his election manifesto of 1893, 'The Republic exists, I seek to purify it . . . the constitution of 1875 can be revised.' In 1897, La Rochefoucauld, Duke de Doudeauville, the President of the monarchist *Groupes des Droites* in the Chamber,

---

[1] For the *Ralliement* see A. Sedgwick, *The 'Ralliement' in French Politics*, 1965. D. Shapiro, 'The Ralliement in the Politics of the 1890s', in St Antony's Papers, No. 13, 1962, pp. 13–48. J. Piou, *Lé Ralliement*, 1928.

[2] *L'Autorité*, 16 September 1894.

was at pains to point out that '. . . for twenty years I have never made a profession of faith, in the monarchy or in anything; I am therefore completely free in this respect'.[1] Although men like the Marquis of Baudry d'Asson, Deputy for Vendée, secure in their electoral fiefs continued to proclaim their monarchist faith, the leaders of monarchism and Bonapartism were aware that attempts to subvert the Republic had, after Boulanger, become unpopular in the country. The Boulanger episode also began a process, consummated during the Dreyfus affair, by which *cocardier* nationalist sentiment ceased to be expressed by the Left and became a weapon in the hands of the Right.[2] Déroulède and his companions who in 1882, founded the *Ligue des Patriotes* were originally Jacobin Republicans but through association with Boulanger became committed to overturning the Republic by force. Henri Rochefort, the old *communard*, and some disciples of Blanqui, previously regarded as revolutionaries of the Left, joined the nationalist side during the Dreyfus affair and were thereafter identified with the Right. Mauric Barrès, as a young Boulangist Deputy for Nancy in 1889, claimed to belong to the extreme Left, and became one of the most distinguished promoters of the nationalist cause in the two decades which followed: after the stormy days of the Dreyfus affair, as one of the early members of the *Ligue de la Patrie Française*, he was recognised as a leading member of the Right. This new radical Right was largely urban in character, lower middle class and usually anti-semitic. Men such as Edouard Drumont, author of *La France juive* (1886), and Jules Guérin, leader of the *Ligue Antisémitique*, introduced an extreme and rabid strain of anti-Semitism which had revolutionary implications and little appeal to the socially secure. Except for a few Bonapartists, the established Right-wing politicians, by temperament and by calculation, were not immediately sympathetic to these new allies.

The *Ralliement* was supported by three factors: the loss of confidence of the anti-Republicans, the emergence of a nationalism of the Right without dynastic associations, and the willingness of some of the moderate Republicans to seek the support on the Right of the Chamber. The *Ralliement* was, however, a political failure because the *ralliés* were unsuccessful in their attempt to gain access to power. The first reason for this was lack of electoral success. After the monarchists had unsuccessfully petitioned in Rome for a

[1] D. Shapiro, op. cit., pp. 22–4.

[2] For a general discussion of this movement of opinion, see R. Girardet, 'Pour une introduction à l'histoire du nationalisme français', *Revue française de science politique*, vol. 8, 1958, pp. 505–28. R. Girardet, *Le Nationalisme français, 1871–1914*, 1966. E. Weber, *The Nationalist Revival in France*, 1959.

modification of the *Ralliement* policy, they mounted a successful rearguard action in the country during the election campaign of 1893. The monarchists refused to retire gracefully and fought to retain their electoral fiefs. The *ralliés* were treated as interlopers in strongly Catholic areas of the country. In other areas Catholics voted for the better placed moderate Republicans rather than *rallié* candidates. According to the best estimate, the *ralliés* emerged from the election with thirty-seven Deputies as against sixty-four monarchists: the leaders of the *Ralliement*, Piou and de Mun, were defeated.

The influence of the *Ralliement* was, at first, greater than the number of *rallié* Deputies seemed to warrant. The government formed by Casimir-Périer, composed entirely of moderate Republicans, made an immediate bid for their support. The Minister of Religious Affairs, Spuller, a close collaborator of Gambetta, replying to a parliamentary question, called for an *esprit nouveau* and an end to petty persecution of religion. The genuine liberalism of Spuller and some of his colleagues in religious matters was reinforced by a desire to secure one flank of a 'Centrist' governmental bloc. Securing a majority for a ministry in this way involved the avoidance of such sensitive issues as religious policy, constitutional revision and income tax. The Radicals reacted to the increasing understanding between the *ralliés* and the moderate Republicans by persistently raising religious questions, particularly in the first two years of the 1893–8 parliament. They colluded with the extreme Right when Gauthier de Clagny proposed a constitutional reform in January 1895, and they sought to foster divisions among the moderates by helping to vote the principle of income-tax in the spring of 1896 – although income-tax was not actually levied in France until the First World War. Despite these quite serious disturbances the *Ralliement* made possible the longest lived ministry, the Méline government from 1896 to 1898, since the voting of the constitution in 1875. The benefits which the *ralliés* derived from voting consistently for Méline were scanty; the concessions made by the *Président du Conseil* to the Right were verbal or touched on matters of administrative detail.[1] But at least Méline barred the Radicals from power. This even influenced the behaviour of the monarchists: in 1898, at the beginning of the new parliament, only two monarchists, Baudry d'Asson and Largentaye, voted against a motion expressing confidence in Méline.

Electoral defeat wrecked Méline's majority. The Right had some share in the responsibility for this defeat. The Vatican exerted

[1] G. Lachapelle, *Le Ministère Méline*, 1928.

influence to establish Etienne Lamy, a Catholic *littérateur*, as the key figure in the preparations for the elections of 1898. Although he had impeccable Republican credentials, having voted with the Republican majority against Marshal MacMahon in 1877, he was not a particularly subtle or resourceful negotiator. As the President of a co-ordinating committee, the *Comité des Intérêts moraux*, he went to see Méline and requested that all those candidates who expected Catholic votes should promise a revision of the *lois scolaires*. Méline would only offer a discreet silence on this legislation, which Lamy rejected as unsatisfactory. The *ralliés* and the moderate Republicans went to the first ballot without an agreed programme and without an agreed list of candidates; the Left made notable gains. Jacques Piou managed to salvage what he could by making an agreement with Méline between the ballots on tactics for the second ballot but the fate of the Méline coalition was already sealed.[1] Even without Lamy's inept tactics the prospects for the coalition were not good: the relative success of the *Ralliement* in parliamentary politics was not always understood and appreciated in the country. Indeed, in many cases, it seemed scarcely relevant at the constituency level where the division between secular and clerical remained all important. Catholic groups launched as fierce attacks on moderate Republicans who defended the *lois laïques* as they did on Radicals and Socialists. The reflex of the 'lay' voters was to vote for the anti-clerical candidate at the second ballot rather than a 'clerical' with whom they might agree on other policy issues. Since the monarchists tended to play down their dynastic allegiance it was often difficult for the electorate to distinguish between the *ralliés* and the so-called 'intransigents'. In electoral terms the *Ralliement* was successful only where the *rallié* candidate enjoyed an impregnable social position, as for example Baron René Reille in the Tarn; or where the clergy were particularly strong, as in Lozère where Piou was elected and in Finistère which sent de Mun and the abbé Gayraud to the Palais Bourbon. Gayraud's election was secured after a particularly bitter fight between the clergy and the monarchist notables whose candidate was Count de Blois.[2]

The parliamentary situation which followed the confused electoral battle of 1898 was transformed by the explosion of the Dreyfus affair.[3] The affair had been simmering since the condemnation for

[1] For accounts of the pre-election manoeuvring see G. Lachapelle, op. cit., pp. 173–81. J. Piou, *Le Ralliement*, pp. 73–8. R. Cornilleau, *Le Ralliement a-t-elle échoué?* 1927, pp. 37–9.

[2] A. Siegfried, op. cit., pp. 182–6.

[3] There are many accounts and interpretations of the 'Affair'. Amongst the

espionage on behalf of Germany in 1894 of the Jewish captain Alfred Dreyfus by a court-martial which did not reveal to the defence the evidence on which the accused was condemned. For almost four years the fight for the revision of the trial was a matter which mainly concerned a small group composed of the family of the condemned man, notably Mathieu Dreyfus the brother of the ex-captain, and a few isolated journalists and politicians. The article by Emile Zola, 'J'accuse' published in January 1898, brought great publicity to the case but revision did not play much part in the electoral campaign of 1898. As the *Dépêche de Toulouse* remarked, it was intellectuals and not the 'crowd' who supported revision. But the intellectuals and events forced the government and parliament to take notice. The suicide of Colonel Henry, an intelligence officer in the Ministry of War, after enquiries revealed that he had forged a document to strengthen the evidence against Dreyfus, exacerbated the situation. The political press was unanimous in commenting that the atmosphere recalled that of the Boulanger affair. Most men of the Right joined the anti-Dreyfusard camp because the revisionist campaign took on the appearance of an attack on the army; the extreme Right were soon trying to use the case to overturn the Republic. Government became unstable: the Brisson cabinet fell to be replaced by one of 'Republican concentration' (which excluded support from the *ralliés*) headed by the Opportunist Charles Dupuy. Dupuy fell in his turn on an interpellation concerning public order after a nationalist aristocrat knocked off the hat of Loubet, the President of the Republic, when he was attending the races at Auteuil; Dupuy's place was taken by a moderate Republican, Waldeck-Rousseau, who was both more astute and more determined and remained in office from 1899 to 1902.[1]

Two important developments took place at this time, the first an initiative of Poincaré, the second the emergence of the leagues. The initiative by Poincaré had more immediate and important parliamentary effects. In February 1899, he sent his resignation from the Progressist group (as the major group of the *Républicains de Gouvernement* was rather inappropriately called) to Jules Méline and founded a group of *Républicains de Gauche*. Méline urged him to think again, saying that the Dreyfus affair would pass but the great interests of the 'Republican party' would remain, adding that

most useful are L. Capéran, *L'Anticléricalisme et l'affaire Dreyfus*, 1948. G. Chapman, *The Dreyfus Case*, 1955. *The Dreyfus Trials*, 1972. D. Johnson, *France and the Dreyfus Affair*, 1966. P. Miquel, *L'Affaire Dreyfus*, 1961. M Thomas, *L'Affaire sans Dreyfus*, 1961.

[1] See the excellent biography, P. Sorlin, *Waldeck-Rousseau*, 1966.

union against the revolutionary forces of the Left would probably
be soon necessary again. Poincaré replied:

'For several months many of my friends have urged me to establish
a group composed of firm Republicans who undertake to defend
the secular laws. . . . I cannot accept the idea that a party should
exist without common principles and without a programme other
than the eternal refrain of resistance to Socialism. You are surrounded by men who, instead of allowing you to be the leader of
a Republican party of government, are intent on making you the
prisoner of a reactionary coalition.'

After blaming Méline for the role of his government early in the
Dreyfus affair, he continued:

'You say that the affair will come to an end, and I hope so . . . but
when it does so, there will be general conclusions to be drawn from
it: the army must be made to realise that it has an interest in
repudiating compromising association; the command structure
must be reorganised. . . . The army must be defended against
clerical intrigue and against attacks of anti-militarists. To achieve
this a Republican party must be reconstituted at an equal distance
from the extremes. . . . I would be happy to collaborate with you
but you only wish to see the danger of revolution at a moment
when the reactionary peril is more menacing than ever.'[1]

This action was the death knell of the *Ralliement* as an important
element in parliamentary politics. The Méline Progressists were no
longer *républicains de gouvernement* and the *ralliés* had no alternative
but to move into opposition with them. Poincaré and his associates
did not relish going along with the Radical tide in 1899, but to do
otherwise would have risked permanent exclusion from power –
precisely the fate of Méline and his associates. Alexandre Ribot was
the only member of parliament who remained loyal to Méline ever
again to hold ministerial office, and he did not do so until the First
World War. In 1899, therefore, a new element was added to the
parliamentary Right – a half of the former *républicains de gouvernement*, called the Progressists. Throughout the aftermath of the Dreyfus affair, the Progressists mingled their votes and their protests with
the *rallié*, monarchist and nationalist Right against the Waldeck-
Rousseau (1899–1902) and the more resolutely anti-clerical Combes
(1902–5) administrations, against the Law of Associations of 1901,
and against the Separation of the Church and the State in 1905.
The Progressists and other components of the Right differed in their

[1] P. Miquel, *Poincaré*, 1961, p. 171.

respective styles but on the great issues of the day they were in accord.

As Poincaré remarked to Méline, there were conclusions to be drawn from the affair. Péguy's famous aphorism, *Tout commence en mystique et tout finit en politique*, applied particularly to the affair: it moved from the disinterested struggle for justice to the settling of accounts. It was not a time for moderate men. Poincaré did not join a government from 1899 until after the passing of the Law of Separation. Waldeck-Rousseau withdrew from power after passing the mildly anti-clerical Law of Association of 1901, ineffectually protesting when his successor Emile Combes gave it repressive interpretation. Combes, backed by the Leftist majority which emerged from the 1902 elections, was determined on the harassment of his political opponents.[1] He was able to stay in office and pursue anti-clerical policies for nearly three years because of the fears and distaste aroused by the self-appointed defenders of the Church and army. The attempt to disengage the Church from the anti-Republican Right through the *Ralliement* was wrecked for a generation by the association of the vocal and politically active section of the clergy, particularly the Assumptionist Order and its newspaper *la Croix*, with nationalism during the Dreyfus affair.[2] The officer corps was engaged in a political issue in a way which it had not been throughout the nineteenth century.[3] In the provincial garrisons the army officer who doubted the guilt of Dreyfus either kept his opinions to himself or was ostracised. The role played by senior officers was serious and damaging to the prestige of the General Staff. It became clear after the Zola case that many senior officers had been actively involved in trying to hush up the affair. Some, like General Mercier, after leaving the army, entered politics to defend their record and opinions on a public platform.

The politicians and propagandists such as Faguet, Lemaître and Maurras, who formulated the doctrine that the army was the conscience of the nation, the incarnation of *la patrie*, provoked attacks on the army.[4] Anti-militarist propagandists such as Urbain Gohier and Gustave Hervé would not have been taken as seriously had not the army been so clumsily defended by the nationalists. Since neither the nationalists nor the extreme anti-militarists gained

[1] Although he attempts to give an impression of liberalism in his memoirs, E. Combes, *Mon Ministère, 1902–1905*, 1956.

[2] P. Sorlin, '*La Croix' et les juifs, 1880–1899*, 1967.

[3] R. Girardet, *La Société militaire, 1815–1940*, 1953

[4] E Faguet, *Problèmes politiques du temps présent*, 1900. J. Lemaître, *Opinions à répandre*, 1901. C. Maurras, 'L'Armée', *Dictionnaire politique et critique*, 5 vols, 1932–4.

power their influence on actual policy was indirect. The conflict between the army and the Republicans did not lead to drastic action by either side. The army was not at this, or any other time during the Third Republic, bent on a *pronunciamento*. Many members of the officer corps were royalist and Catholic in sentiment but the tradition of obedience to constitutional authority was strong and so was the condition on which the partial autonomy of the army as an institution rested. On the other side the Radicals in government had no interest in weakening the military efficiency of the army. The harassment of the officer corps remained, therefore, within tolerable limits.

The first measure against the officer corps, passed in 1899 during the Waldeck-Rousseau administration at the instigation of the Minister of War, General Gallifet, was probably the most important. This was the suppression of the *Commission de classement*, which broke the control of the army over promotions; nominations for jobs and promotions henceforth were dealt with directly by the Minister of War. The full significance of this measure was not clear until the tenure as Minister of War from 1900 to 1904 of General André, the only *général de division* who had the reputation of being a Republican. André used the masonic lodges as an intelligence network to discover the religious and political sympathies of officers and, on the basis of this information, he discriminated against Catholics and royalists. Even members of the government majority found this scandalous and the revelation of the practice, by the nationalist Deputy Guyot de Villeneuve, led to André's resignation.[1] There were other measures: some senior officers were prematurely retired for their part in the affair and the civil power was given clear precedence on ceremonial occasions – the prefect preceding the general, the sub-prefect, the colonel. André's policies raised bitter protests from the parliamentary Right but they did not substantially alter civil-military relations.

Anti-clericalism and the social question

The other great acts of policy during the 'Dreyfusian revolution' were sanctions against the Church, made easier by the long tradition of anti-clericalism in France. Anti-clericalism predated the great revolution and had a lively history during the first three decades of the Third Republic.[2] The clericalism of MacMahon's *ordre moral* in

[1] F. Médine, *L'Armée qui souffre*, 1908. J. Mollin, *La Vérité sur l'affaire des fiches*, 1905. R. Nanteuil, *Le Dossier de M. Guyot de Villeneuve*, 1906.

[2] In the considerable literature on this subject, works of especial value are M. J. M. Larkin, 'The Church and the French Concordat, 1891–1902', *English Historical Review*, vol. 81, 1966, pp. 717–39. E. Lecanuet, *L'Église de France sous la Troisième République, 1870–1910*, 4 vols, 1910–30. J. MacManners,

the 1870s provoked the first great wave of anti-clericalism resulting in the dispersion of the Jesuit order and the *lois laïques* of the 1880s. The spirit of anti-clericalism was kept alive even amongst moderate Republicans by incidents such as the sermon preached by Father Ollivier at a memorial service for the 117 people, many of them society ladies, who had lost their lives in the fire at the Bazar de la Charité in 1897: the President of the Republic was compelled to listen to the thesis that this disaster was a divine punishment for the impiety of France. The anti-Dreyfusard position adopted by the great majority of the Catholic laity and the clergy provoked the most important series of anti-clerical measures. The Assumptionist Order was suppressed in 1900 and six bishops had their stipend withheld for expressing sympathy with the Order.[1] The Law of Associations, passed in 1901, required religious congregations to have State authorisation: if this authorisation was withheld they could be dispersed; members of unauthorised congregations were forbidden to teach. Emile Combes turned this law into an instrument of war, first against the Catholic school system and then against the Orders themselves. An indication of the intensity of anti-clerical feeling was the proposal passed by the Chamber of Deputies in 1903 (although later rejected by the Senate) to forbid even ex-members of congregations to teach. In July 1904 all members of religious Orders were forbidden to teach whether or not their Order was legally recognised. These measures resulted in tension between the Holy See and the French government and after the President of the Republic had paid a State visit to Rome, without paying his respects to the Pope the concordat of 1801 was denounced.[2] The crowning act of the anti-clerical offensive was the Law of Separation of the Church and the State voted in December 1905.

The attack on the Church produced the most rigid distinction in parliamentary politics between Right and Left that the Third Republic experienced before or afterwards. The Left governed between 1902 and 1906 with a firmly disciplined majority, through the apparatus of the *délégation des gauches*, whose moving spirit was the Socialist leader, Jean Jaurès. Although attempts were made to organise the opposition, the Right was not as successful as the Left in co-ordinating tactics either in the Chamber or in the country. The right was firmly isolated by its opponents and forced to fight

Church and State in France, 1870–1914, 1972. L. V. Méjan, *La Şéparation des églises et l'état*, 1959.

[1] P. Sorlin, op. cit., pp. 197–202.

[2] M. J. M. Larkin, 'President Loubet's Visit to Rome', *The Historical Journal*, vol. 4, 1961, pp. 97–103.

the elections of 1902 and 1906 in simple terms of clericalism versus anti-clericalism. The defeat of the Right in 1902 was followed by the even greater electoral debacle of 1906. Anti-clericalism was shown to be popular with the electorate but allegations by the Radicals and Socialists that the Right was the clerical party were a gross over-simplification. The nationalist Georges Berry denied that any member of the Right was a clerical if the term was given a strict interpretation[1] – and it is true that no member of the parliamentary Right argued in favour of clerical supremacy, or even a large measure of clerical influence, in secular matters. The charge of clericalism was, indeed, ridiculous when applied to a Progressist like Alexandre Ribot who, when *Président du Conseil*, had proposed an anti-clerical measure. Most of the Progressists were not Catholics but liberal free-thinkers who defended the Church on the grounds that the liberties of Catholics were being infringed. They considered that excessive importance was being attached to religious policy.[2] They did not oppose the Separation of the Church and State in principle but used the typical conservative argument that it was being carried out by the wrong men at the wrong time. After the papal condemnation of the Law of Separation a split appeared within the Progressist group, between those who held that the Pope was being unreasonable and those who argued that the Pope was within his rights and the only way out of the difficulty was direct negotiations with the Vatican.

There was a minor split within the nationalist group. A handful of Parisian nationalist Deputies, Failliot, Tournade, Roche remained true to their original anti-clericalism and voted for the Law of Separation. But, in 1905, twenty-six out of fifty-five members of the nationalist group in the Chamber were also members of *Action Libérale* and the elections of 1906 increased the conservative and Catholic dominance of the group.[3] The remainder of the parliamentary Right was overtly Catholic. It can be divided roughly into two categories: the *catholiques avant tout* who believed with de Mun that 'all politics are reduced to the inexorable dilemma; reconvert France to Christianity or consent to her destruction',[4] and the others for whom the clerical question was important only because

[1] *La Patrie*, 17 November 1907. Also G. Berry, *Un Page d'histoire. La séparation des églises et de l'état à la Chambre des Députés*, 1905.

[2] See Ribot's preface to G. Noblemaire, *Concordat ou séparation*, 1905, and his speech on article 19 of the Separation Bill, *Débats – Chambre des Députés*, 15 June 1905, especially p. 2253.

[3] *Annuaire du parlement*, 1905, 1906.

[4] Action Libérale Populaire. *Compte-rendu du congrès général de 1907*, 1907, p. 84.

of the peculiar circumstances of the time. Most of the Catholics *avant tout* together with the nationalists believed that the anti-clerical offensive was the product of a deep laid plot which had been nurtured for years in the masonic lodges and had little or nothing to do with the behaviour of members of the Church.

Combiste anti-clericalism was brought to an end by the decision of Clemenceau, Minister of the Interior in 1906, to suspend the inventories of Church property which had provoked violent Catholic resistance of the faithful in some parts of the country. In Clemenceau's view, counting chandeliers was not worth the spilling of blood, whereas Combes had not been deterred by bloodshed from dispersing the religious orders. Parliament finished its discussion of the legislative business arising out of the Separation of the Church and the State in April 1908, but an anomalous situation had been created. The Church had neither legal recognition nor legal representatives. This situation was not rectified until diplomatic relations were re-established between France and the Vatican in 1920 and diocesan associations formed to hold Church property.

The clerical question smouldered on after 1908. In 1909, on the prompting of the Pope, the French bishops issued a letter sternly denouncing secular education. The anti-clericals responded by preparing a bill for its protection which was eventually passed in 1914. There were other incidents such as those provoked by anti-clerical local authorities who wished to demolish Churches and sell their contents. But the wish expressed by the monarchist Denys Cochin in 1910 that the 'interminable clerical puestion' should take up fewer sittings of the Chamber was realised in the parliament elected in 1910.[1] The Right showed that it could overlook the anti-clericalism of a government to help pass in 1913 the law extending military service from two to three years. Maurice Barrès noticed after 1910 the decline of the *pur et dur* anti-clericalism of the Radical Socialists.[2] At the beginning of the First World War Catholic political leaders sought an end to the clerical question in the *union sacrée*, national solidarity in face of the enemy. De Mun gave an example to Catholics by shaking hands with the anti-clerical Socialist Vaillant in the Chamber on 4 August 1914. De Mun wrote in September 1914: 'In our country Catholics have suffered cruel persecutions. No one has felt these more keenly than I. But I do not wish to excite public resentment against the persecutors. . . . If some of my fellow Catholics succumb to bitterness I will not hesitate to denounce them.'[3]

[1] *La Revue de Paris*, 15 April 1910, p. 776.
[2] M. Barrès, *La Grande pitié des églises de France*, 1914, p. 168.
[3] *L'Écho de Paris*, 25 September 1914.

The victory of the Left was clear-cut in the case of the clerical issue, and important points of principle were won by the Left in other areas of policy. Nationalisation of the Western Railway, introduction of old age pensions and income-tax represented the achievement of a considerable social programme, although these measures did not significantly alter, in the short term, the distribution of wealth and power in the community.[1] The nationalisation of the Western Railway was a measure which had been discussed for many years because the Western Railway had needed government subsidies to meet its operating costs in every single financial year since its establishment. The Right, searching for an issue in 1906, tried to represent it as an ideological measure – an aperitif, leading to further nationalisation. The government's case was that there was no genuine alternative to the course which it proposed to take. The nationalisation was not an important measure either in intent or in effect; it did not last long as a major national issue. The minority which opposed nationalisation of the Western Railway was practically the same as that which opposed the Separation of the Church and the State. Perhaps the most powerful motive of the Right was the fear that the measure would lead to a decline in the influence of the conservative notables of the west and an increase in the influence of the administration in that area of conservative electoral dominance.

The delaying action fought by the opponents of a national system of pensions was impressive. The Chamber debated this subject in every year of the decade 1891–1901. It was not until 1906 that the Chamber passed a bill but, as a result of Senate obstruction, a pension scheme was not in effective operation before the First World War. Until 1906, the Right, from the Progressists to the monarchists, was unanimously opposed to a compulsory pension scheme. In attempting to weaken the principle of obligatory participation, the Right found support in other parts of the Chamber. When Groussau (*Action Libérale*) proposed an amendment designed to gain privileges for privately endowed pension schemes in February 1906 it was rejected by only a narrow majority (278 votes to 257). The socially conservative majority in the Senate watered down the bill and the pensions envisaged were derisory, as the Socialists were quick to point out. The most that can be said for the measure is that an important principle had been slowly and reluctantly admitted; it was the first bill passed in France which brought about a small but general redistribution of income.

[1] For a fuller discussion of these issues see M. Anderson, 'The Right and the Social Question in Parliament, 1905–1919', in D. Shapiro (ed.), *The Right in France 1890–1919*, St Antony's Papers, No. 13, 1962, pp. 85–134.

The delaying action fought against income-tax was even more successful. The first committee report on an income-tax bill was presented to the Chamber in 1888. In 1896 the Chamber accepted the principle of income-tax but it was not until 1908 that a bill was passed. The Senate prevented the bill becoming law for another nine years, although income-tax was levied from the end of 1915. The passions raised by the income-tax bill were out of all proportion to the size of the tax envisaged (the standard rate was in the region of 2 per cent). The Right was hostile to the 'vexation and inquisitorial' nature of progressive income-tax. Among Catholics only the *abbé démocrate*, Jules Lemire, welcomed it in principle. *Action Libérale*, as a group, was hesitant in its opposition and its representatives made equivocal statements about the necessity of some kind of reform of the system of direct taxation. The Progressists provided the core of the hard line opposition to the tax and only they presented consistent and reasoned arguments against it. The basic fears of the Right were that there would be political discrimination in the assessment of the tax, that it would lead to greater friction between the administration and the citizen, that, given the individualism of Frenchmen, it would be impossible to collect, and the additional revenue would be unwisely spent. The real reason for the delay of the measure was not, however, the outright opposition of the Right but the hesitations among government supporters who, in the well-worn phrase, had 'their hearts on the Left but their wallets on the Right'. Because of these doubts, the only amendment to a major measure proposed by the extreme Right which came near to success during the period 1888–1914 was the proposal of the monarchist Viscount Villebois-Mareuil, that agricultural profits would not be taxed. It was defeated by 271 votes to 240 on 9 March 1909.

Although the practical effects of the old age pensions, nationalisation of the Western Railway and income-tax were small, the principles on which they were based were important – the redistribution of wealth, the right of the State to take over sections of the economy, and progressive taxation. In 1906 the moderate Republicans, including Poincaré's group *Gauche Républicaine*, accepted the application of these principles with various degrees of reluctance; the Right opposed them with varying degrees of intransigence. The opposition of many of the Catholics and extreme Right was based on political rather than ideological or economic grounds. With the exception of some Progressists, the Right was not particularly attached to *laissez-faire* principles. The dividing line between the Right and some of its opponents was more blurred on these economic issues than on matters touching religion, and there was broad agreement between Right and moderate government supporters on issues related to the preservation of public order and the regulation of strikes.

During successive postmen's strikes from 1899 to 1909, the great majority of the Right opposed the right of civil servants to strike and to organise into trade unions. Members of the Right sometimes criticised the policy of allowing the *de facto* existence of civil servants' unions but a handful of the extreme Right supported the postmen. A strike of the railwaymen in 1910 raised similar issues about the interruption of 'essential' public services and all but three extremist members of the Right supported Briand when he broke the strike by mobilising the workers. Amnesty of workers imprisoned for disturbing public order during strikes always found a limited amount of support on the extreme Right as, for example, proposals to amnesty postmen in July 1906 and workers after the serious disorders at Draveil-Vigneux (Seine-et-Oise) in 1908. A common argument was that the real culprits – the *Confédération Générale du Travail* and the syndicalist leaders – were never punished. However, the *politique du pire*, never practised by more than a small minority of the Right over social questions, disappeared entirely before 1914.

It was clear that social questions had modified the Right's opposition to governments in the years preceding 1914. Clemenceau, as *Président du Conseil*, from 1906 to 1909, could always rely on Rightist votes when strikes were under discussion. His successor, Briand, was non-committal on income-tax and said, on the occasion of the railway strike of 1910, that he was prepared to resort even to illegal methods to defend public order. As a consequence, he had even monarchist and nationalist admirers. In his most famous statement of *détente à droite*, the Périgueux speech in 1909, Briand was evasive on income-tax, made a rousing appeal to patriotic sentiment, called for an end to political tension, and to divisive controversy in the country, and a Republic 'open to all'. Briand, however, was careful to avoid relying on Right-wing votes in the Chamber and withdrew from office when this was becoming necessary.

Briand's policy of *apaisement*, continued by his successors Poincaré and Barthou, and the increase in international tension produced a situation in which the Right showed increasing eagerness to escape from the role of permanent opposition and give occasional support to governments. Moderate Republicans were very cautiously coming once again to accept support from the Right. In January 1913 Rightist votes helped to elect Poincaré to the Presidency of the

Republic.[1] An ex-Progressist, Joseph Thierry, who previously thought that he would never hold office because he was too far to the Right, joined the Barthou government in 1913. The Right, in order to achieve the extension of military service from two to three years, gave general support to the Barthou administration despite its anti-clerical tendencies.[2] The Right showed that it was ready to vote consistently for a moderate government of the Centre if the government was prepared to accept its support.

From the union sacrée to the Bloc National

The Right was displeased by the formation of the Viviani cabinet, judged to be too far to the Left, after the elections of 1914, although Viviani promised to defend the Three Years Law. But, as soon as war was declared, Poincaré's call for a *union sacrée* was enthusiatically received by the Right both in and outside parliament. The Right renounced opposition and even criticism of government policies. In the past, defeat in war had caused a change in regime but the idea of restoration following defeat appealed neither to the parliamentary monarchists nor, apparently, to *Action Française*. No member of the Right in parliament showed the slightest hesitation in supporting the war. Outside parliament, the Anglophobe editor of *L'Eclair*, Ernest Judet, was equivocal and, later in the war, fled to Switzerland after being accused of contact with the enemy.[3] The leading journalists of the parliamentary Right – De Mun, Barrès, Delayaye – quickly turned their talents to war propaganda. The manifestations of loyalty and patriotism of the Right produced some, but not many, concessions from the government. In August 1914, Viviani balked at Poincaré's suggestion that he should include Denys Cochin and Albert de Mun in his government but he chose the Progressist Ribot as Minister of Finance. Throughout the war only two others from the Right of the Chamber – Denys Cochin and Joseph Thierry – held office as compared with three SFIO Socialists (who had previously refused to hold office in 'bourgeois' governments).

It was difficult to organise parliamentary opposition to the govern-

---

[1] F. Payen, *Raymond Poincaré*, 1936, pp. 389–92. G. Wright, *Raymond Poincaré and the French Presidency*, 1942. G. Bonnefous, *Histoire de la Troisième République*, vol. 1, 1956, pp. 316–21.

[2] J. C. Cairns, 'Politics and Foreign Policy, 1911–1914', *Canadian Historical Journal*, September 1953, p. 245. G. Michon, *La Préparation à la guerre, 1910–1914*, 1935.

[3] See E. Judet, *Ma Politique, 1905–1917*, 1923.

ment during the war.[1] When the chambers reassembled in December
1914, it was impossible, for security reasons, to interpellate the
government on the conduct of the war. Eventually, secret sessions
of the chambers were requested; Senators and Deputies could then
demand information from the government in the normal way.[2] But
the request for a secret committee was regarded as a lack of confidence in a government as well as a desire to supervise the executive.
A majority of the Right voted against a government only once
during the war (Painlevé in November 1917) and it was unwilling
to oppose or harass governments in secret session. Members of the
Right intervened rarely in these secret debates. Often they did so
merely to voice patriotic sentiments or make extravagant suggestions
such as that of the monarchist Espivent de la Villesboisnet to use the
rails of railway lines to make cannon. Charles Benoist (*Fédération
Républicaine*) was the most frequent speaker but only once asked
potentially awkward questions. When members of the Right voiced
criticisms it was almost always on particular and technical matters.
Ybarnégaray came near to launching a general attack on the government over the spring offensive of 1917 but all his attack finally
amounted to was the claim that the government had done the right
thing (in appointing Pétain Commander-in-Chief), but rather too late.

Two factors account for the Right's self-abnegating role of
supporting successive governments by word and vote throughout
the war. Firstly, the ideology of nationalism, which influenced all
sections of the Right, made a fetish of national unity; in wartime
this implied standing firmly behind the government. Political opponents who criticised governments were described as bad Frenchmen and, in the cases of the Radical leaders Malvy and Caillaux
in 1917, as traitors. Secondly, the Right, before the war, was agreed
in condemning 'government by Deputies'. This attitude was carried
over into the war; the general feeling was that the government should
direct the war with the help of but with the minimum of interference
from parliament. When, in July 1917, the Chamber debated a
proposal to strengthen parliamentary control over the conduct of the
war, Louis Marin (*Fédération Républicaine*) and Jacques Piou
(*Action Libérale*) strongly opposed this and it was eventually passed
only in an attenuated form. On individual items of legislation the

[1] The records of the secret session of the Chamber of Deputies were published
after the First World War in the *Journal officiel* but those of the Senate not until
1968 when a significant part of the manuscript record had become indecipherable.
See also Mermeix, *Au Sein des commissions. Fragments d'histoire*, 1924. P. Allard,
Les Dessous de la grande guerre révélés par les comités secrets, 1932. J. de Launay,
Les Carnets secrets de Louis Loucheur, 1962, pp. 29–47.

[2] P. Renouvin, *The Forms of War Government in France*, 1927.

Right sometimes formed an isolated minority. This happened on two matters which had religious implications, the education of war orphans and the requisition of cemeteries. Also on several occasions during the discussion of bills on rents, excess profits, extension of accident insurance to agriculture and utilisation of abandoned lands, the Right was isolated, being somewhat more extreme than others in defence of the rights of private, and particularly rural, property.

During the war and until the elections of 1919, the Right behaved very much as regular supporters of the government had done before the war. Their remarks about the men in power were generally discreet and they showed their disapproval by withholding praise rather than by any positive act. They voted like the pre-war ministerial Deputies, indiscriminately for successive governments. When their sectional interests were involved they were prepared to oppose particular pieces of legislation without attacking the government. Finally, when further support of a government seemed likely to have disastrous consequences they promptly and even dramatically withdrew their support.

There was, therefore, a change of role by the Right in parliament (and also of the extra-parliamentary leagues during the war). From 1899 to 1914 members of the Right occasionally acted as an opposition which had temporarily ceased to oppose. Though their support was sometimes necessary it was not considered desirable by the governments of these years – members of the Right were constantly reminded of their anti-Republican character. But only once during the war did a resolution of the Chamber stigmatise part of the Right with anti-Republicanism.[1] Governments desired and required the support of all sections of opinion and those who supported governments consistently were naturally looked on with favour. Members of the Right were thus rehabilitated and once again treated as men with whom it was possible to co-operate. This had its effect after the war.

The elections of 16 November 1919 are an important date in the history of the parliamentary Right for two reasons: they marked the passing of a generation of parliamentarians and they brought together the two wings of the moderate Republicans, divided since 1899, in a combination which was to be influential during the whole of the inter-war period. Nearly all the men who had played an important role on the Right between the time of Boulanger and the

[1] On 18 January the government was interpellated about a publication sponsored by *Action Française* which mentioned the royalist sympathies of some serving officers. Although the Right opposed it vigorously, a motion was passed condemning royalist and other plots against the Republic.

First World War were passing out of politics around 1919. Almost all the pre-war Progressists leadership was in process of disappearing. Jules Méline, Joseph Thierry and Edouard Aynard were dead; Alexandre Ribot was very old; Jules Roche, Charles Benoist and Paul Beauregard were on the point of retiring. Only Louis Marin (first elected in 1905) had a long political career in front of him, but by voting against the treaty of Versailles he had isolated himself. The Liberal leadership was melting away. De Mun died in 1914; Piou was about to retire; Gailhard-Bancel was ageing and l'Estour-beillon was deeply involved in Breton regionalism. On the extreme Right Millevoye, Berry and Delafosse were dead; Denys Cochin retired and died shortly afterwards. There were no younger men in the existing organisations of sufficient stature to replace them. This situation encouraged the Right to look outside its own ranks for leaders. Many members of the Right would willingly have followed Clemenceau in peacetime if he had given them any encouragement. The absence of a leader of his stature resulted in men with insufficient talents as tacticians and organisers, like Maurice Barrès (who died in 1922) and Marcel Habert, assuming leading roles.

The disappearance of many of the old leaders, the inadequacy of the existing party organisations, the atmosphere of euphoria following victory and the social dislocation produced by the war created a situation favourable to new initiatives. But the new parties of 1919 had little success and the prestige of the leaders who had been at the head of affairs during a victorious war remained great. However, the idea of a broad coalition for the elections of 1919, embracing all 'national' candidates, was first voiced by a new party – *Union Nationale Républicaine* – whose leaders were the old nationalist agitators, Marcel Habert and Emile Massard. This coalition, the *Bloc National* was eventually organised by Adolphe Carnot, an experienced parliamentarian of the second rank, one of the founders of the *Alliance Démocratique* in 1901. The ex-Socialist Alexandre Millerand become its most prestigious leader after neither Poincaré nor Clemenceau had shown the slightest inclination to take on this role. Carnot, at first, showed a greater keenness to gain the support of the Radicals than of the Right.[1] Only after most of the Radicals refused to join him was he ready to make concessions to the Right. After delicate negotiations it was agreed that the Bloc should recognise the secularised State, the need to respect the beliefs of all citizens and the necessity for religious peace. Barrès managed to extract slightly more precise commitments when drawing up, with Millerand, the list of candidates for the first constituency of Paris

[1] See his letter to Edouard Herriot published in *le Temps*, 28 September 1919.

and the formulae agreed there were widely copied.[1] Other sections of the programme of the Bloc were vague and conservative. The Bloc stated that its aims were to prolong the unity of the country ('*si heureusement réalisée dans la guerre*') into peacetime in order to rebuild France, to ensure the strict enforcement of the treaty of Versailles and to defend civilisation against Bolshevism. In social policy, proposals were made for arbitration tribunals to settle industrial disputes and for measures to combat bad housing, tuberculosis and 'demoralisation'. The main plank of financial policy was a balanced budget: no mention was made of income-tax. On administrative and constitutional reform the Bloc followed ideas which had been current in Progressist circles before the war: the effective separation of powers, a declaration of Rights in the constitution, a policy of administrative decentralisation and the abolition of some civil service posts.

The elections were a triumph for the 'national' lists and for the Right: 435 Deputies had been elected on these lists.[2] An assessment of the respective gains of the tendencies within the Right must be somewhat arbitrary, but the Progressists certainly gained over 90 seats bringing their total to over 130, the Liberals gained between 35 and 40 (making a total of about 70) and the extreme Right gained 4. The Poincarist *Républicains de Gauche* gained 50 seats, so that the losses were all on the Left. The Socialists increased their total votes by over 300,000 but they lost 33 seats. The Radicals lost even more heavily because, although some participated in *Bloc National* lists, the official policy was to ally only with Left-wing candidates. All sections of the Right applauded the results. Even *Action Française* was elated by them, claiming that 20 'friends' had been elected:[3] Léon Daudet was the only Deputy who had officially stood as a candidate of the League. Maurice Barrès wrote: 'After the military mobilisation of August 1914, we have had the civic mobilisation of 1919. Here is an excellent Chamber, much the best I have known. . . .'[4] But the victory was to prove illusory, although a large new parliamentary group of the Right, the *Entente Républicaine Démocratique*, was formed with a membership of 186 deputies. The *Chambre bleu horizon* as the parliament of 1919–24 was called, accepted as *Présidents du Conseil* and leaders, moderates who had already had long

[1] M. Barrès, *Mes Cahiers*, vol. 12, 1949, pp. 321–36. J. Delahaye, *La Reprise de relations avec le Vatican*, 1921, especially p. 21.

[2] For the composition of these lists see M. Anderson, 'The Right and the Social Question in Parliament, 1905–1919' in D. Shapiro (ed.), *The Right in France, 1890–1919*, St, Antony's Papers, No. 13, 1962, pp. 133–134.

[3] *La Presse de Paris*, 19 November 1919.

[4] M. Barrès, *Chroniques de la grande guerre*, vol. 14, 1937, pp. 181–7.

ministerial careers. Millerand, Leygues, Briand and Poincaré were not new men with new tactics. They governed, in their accustomed manner, by relying on a shifting coalition of the centre. These experienced leaders were not seriously challenged. Their most intelligent and determined critics on the Right, Georges Mandel and André Tardieu, were political mavericks and were not accepted by the Right as its leaders. The former Progressist, Laurent Bonnevay (Minister of Justice in the Briand administration, 1921–2) was mentioned as a potential *Président du Conseil* but he had not the necessary stature. None of the eight other members of the *Entente Républicaine Démocratique* who held ministerial office emerged as a dominating personality.

The failure of imagination and nerve, 1919–1934
With a total of only nine ministers, the proportionate representation of the *Entente Républicaine Démocratique* in the ministries of the period 1919–24 was very small and its ministers were drawn from the moderate wing (roughly equivalent to the old *Union Républicaine*). Despite this, the Right, with the exception of a few extremists urged on by Léon Daudet, did not move into opposition. Part of the reason was that, to a considerable extent, Poincaré satisfied the aspirations of the Right during the years 1922 to 1924. His appointment of Charles de Lasteyrie (*Entente Républicaine Démocratique*) to the Ministry of Finance was well received by Deputies of the Right and they supported the invasion of the Ruhr following Germany's default on reparations payments in 1923. But they were quiescent mainly because of lack of leadership.[1] The amateurish quality of Deputies of the Right was more obvious than usual in the *Chambre bleu horizon*. The Right tended to respect men such as General de Castelnau, ex-chief of staff to Foch, whose virtues were manifestly not political;[2] intelligent politicians such as Mandel and Tardieu were not usually followed. The political thinking of the majority of the Right did not progress much beyond the slogans of the programme of the *Bloc National*. The vacuity of Right-wing analyses of basic questions of political and social organisation seemed to reach a climax in this parliament. Even Millerand's attempt, whilst President of the Republic from 1922 to 1924, to strengthen the Presidency did not receive a coherent response from the Right. The consequences of having neither doctrine nor power were fatal for the *Entente Républicaine Démocratique*. It was for this reason that

[1] R. Cornilleau, *Du Bloc national au front populaire*, 1939, ch. 1. E. Fournol *Le Plutarque moderne*, 1923, p. 146.

[2] V. Guiraud, *Le Général de Castelnau*, 1928. X. Vallat, 'Souvenirs sur le général de Castelnau', *Revue de Rouergue*, 1954, pp. 405–12.

the men participating in the *Bloc National* entered the electoral campaign of 1924 demoralised and without enthusiasm. Even the unimpressive achievements in national organisation of the 1919 campaign were not equalled in 1924.

The 1924 election was the last election of the Third Republic with the multi-member constituency system. As in the previous two elections held under this system (1885 and 1919), victory went to the best organised – in this case the Radicals and Socialists organised in the *Cartel des Gauches*. Fear of revolution, a potent factor in 1919, had much diminished because the Russian Revolution had not been followed by others. The Right was, therefore, without its most power-ful electoral argument. An indication of the size of the Right-wing defeat was the decline of the *Entente Républicaine Démocratique* from a total of 186 Deputies after the election of 1919 to 104 after the elections of 1924. The other elements of the Right fared scarcely any better. But the Left did not enjoy the fruits of its victory. Hampered by the Socialist policy of non-participation in govern-ment, stumbling from one ministerial crisis to the next and unable to contain inflation, the leaders of the *Cartel des Gauches* ceded power to Poincaré in 1926.

The record of the breakdown of the Cartel is complex in detail but the main outlines are straightforward.[1] The President of the Republic, Millerand, was forced to resign, after a boisterous cam-paign in the press and in parliament, because he had openly supported the *Bloc National* in the 1924 elections. This incident revealed the first of the Cartel's difficulties – the vigilant opposition of the Senate, whose centre of gravity was much more to the Right than that of the Chamber. In the elections to the Presidency the Cartel did not succeed in obtaining the election of its candidate, Painlevé, and was compelled to accept the moderate Radical, Gaston Doumergue. The Right, which gained in assurance as soon as it had been excluded from power, reacted immediately. Louis Marin and the *Fédération Républicaine*, Paul Reynaud and the *Parti Républicain Démocratique*, and Millerand, who with Emmanuel Brousse founded the *Ligue Républicaine Nationale*, mounted an anti-cartellist campaign in the country.[2] The two themes of the attack were foreign policy and financial policy, the two often combined in the thorny problem of German reparations payments (or lack of them). Herriot's acceptance of the Dawes plan and his commitment to evacuate the Ruhr was followed by Baldwin's refusal to honour the agreement made between

[1] D. B. Goldey, *The Distintegration of the Cartel des gauches and the Politics of French Government Finance, 1924–1928*, unpublished thesis, 1962.
[2] G. Bonnefous, *Histoire de la Troisième République*, vol. 4, pp. 56–7.

Herriot and MacDonald on collective security and disarmament. The concessions made by France seemed, therefore, unilateral and were condemned by the Right as a sell-out. Herriot's religious policy also aroused the wrath of the Right and led to the rapid growth of the *Union Nationale Catholique*, founded in 1924 and presided over by General de Castelnau.[1] Herriot broke diplomatic relations with the Vatican, attempted to secularise the regained territories of Alsace and Lorraine, and adopted an aggressive posture on the schools' issue. The spokesmen of the Right claimed, as usual, to be upholders of national unity, and condemned Herriot's policies as partisan.

Financial policy was the real Achilles' heel of the Cartel. Banking circles were probably not opposed, *a priori*, to the Cartel as the Left subsequently alleged; they were opportunist in politics and willing to accommodate to almost any government. But the great mass of small businessmen (who made up 98 per cent of the French employers at this time) and the *rentier* class, with more justification, seemed terrified by the Cartel. These groups, encouraged by the propaganda of the Right, believed that the Cartel was intent on increased taxes, deficit financing and inflationary policies in general. But the main failing of the Cartel was that it had no coherent financial policy at all. Herriot seemed to underestimate the seriousness of the situation and did not press for new taxes proposed by Poincaré at the end of the previous parliament. His moves to control the market in gilt-edged stock and to convert short-term loans into medium and long-term loans served only to increase the distrust of investors.

The banks intervened from motives which were probably more technical than political. During the previous parliament successive governments had started to borrow more from the Bank of France than the law allowed and to refund these loans the day before the Bank published its accounts: private banks made twenty-four hour loans to tide the government over. In April 1925 the private banks, probably with the collusion of the Bank of France, refused to carry out the usual manoeuvre. The revelation that the government was borrowing more than it was entitled, caused considerable scandal. Following an attack by Poincaré, the Herriot government fell. Painlevé and Briand led short-lived governments, and then Herriot returned, with the rehabilitated Caillaux as his Finance Minister. The value of the franc continued to fall: it was 225 to the pound in August 1926, compared with 41 at the end of 1919. There was a run

[1] E. Pezet, 'La Fédération nationale catholique', *la Vie catholique*, 22 February 1925. X. Vallat, 'La Fédération nationale catholique', *Écrits de Paris*, November 1954, pp. 65–74.

on the banks. People sold securities in order to buy durable goods. Demonstrations took place outside the Chamber of Deputies and the anti-parliamentary Leagues such as the *Jeunesses Patriotes* demonstrated in the streets. There was an atmosphere of near panic. Poincaré seemed to be excluded from power by the results of the 1924 elections but he was recalled to form a government of 'national union' to deal with the crisis. His government included six ex-*Présidents du Conseil* including Herriot at the Ministry of Education, and two representatives of the Right, Louis Marin at the Ministry of Pensions and André Tardieu at the Ministry of Public Works. Before Poincaré had time to announce the details of his policy the value of the franc rose by 15 per cent against the pound. His policy was very conventional – an increase in taxes, an advance from the Bank of France, a rise in the bank rate and operations on the international money market to defend the franc. When the effects of his deflationary policy began to show, he launched a successful 3 per cent loan. The speed and success of Poincaré's policy (the value of the franc rose to 122 to the pound) showed that to a considerable extent the crisis had been one of loss of confidence. This caused the Left to suspect a plot by the bankers and the Right: the legends of the *mur d'argent* and the two hundred families have their origins in the disintegration of the Cartel.[1]

The fall in the value of the franc and the speculation which accompanied it provoked an anger which no non-Socialist party could ignore.[2] The small investors were very numerous: the victory loan of 1919 had been taken up by seven million investors and, in the 1920s, there were between four and five hundred thousand accounts with the *Caisse d'Epargne* (post-office savings bank). These investors were, therefore, electorally important, and their numbers were reinforced by artisans and small employers who were very close to them in outlook. The readiness with which the defeated Herriot agreed to co-operate with Poincaré in 1926 is an illustration of the strength of this electoral pressure. The fall in the value of the franc was not, however, catastrophic and did not produce the 'revolution of *déclassés*' and Fascism, because the lower middle classes were not completely ruined. It produced an atmosphere which favoured pre-Fascist movements such as the *Jeunesses Patriotes* and the *Croix de Feu*. These were not movements of genuine *déclassés* but only of those who were afraid of becoming so. The vigorous and successful

[1] M. Anderson, 'The Myth of the Two Hundred Families', *Political Studies*, vol. 13, 1965, pp. 163–78.

[2] A. Sauvy, *L'Histoire économique de la France entre les deux guerres*, 2 vols, 1965–7.

fight against devaluation gave to the defence of the parity of the franc an almost sacred fervour: after 1932, when French prices were above world levels, it was a contributory cause of economic stagnation until the Second World War.

The *petites gens*, the *rentiers* and small businessmen, were enthusiastically behind Poincaré's restoration of the franc. Their satisfaction can be gauged by the unwillingness of the Radicals to overthrow Poincaré in the two years from 1926 to 1928 and by the Poincarist majority which emerged from the elections of 1928. But the climate changed when Tardieu came to power a year later. Although Tardieu was certainly in favour of monetary stability, he represented a conservatism more modernising and dynamic than that of Poincaré.[1] He therefore aroused more hostility from the Radicals and more suspicion from the lower middle classes. Tardieu frequently said that he wanted the support of the Radicals and there was nothing in his programme which they specifically rejected, but they remained consistently hostile to him. He carried out a highly, although only temporarily, successful rescue operation on the market for agricultural products, in danger of collapsing early in 1930: the agricultural milieu, however, continued to distrust him. Even the Right which faithfully supported him by its votes did not defend him vigorously and after his fall showed no great desire for his return. The failure of Tardieu was particularly important as it demonstrated the impossibility of imposing a new style of leadership within the existing political institutions. There were a number of reasons, personal, economic and political for this failure.

In parliament, Tardieu's personality was a very large liability. Although deputy for the territory of Belfort he was a Parisian and, as M. Debû-Bridel remarks, 'acted like a Parisian'. There was a wickedly humorous and cultivated cynicism about him, which was bound to offend the susceptibilities of the provincials who dominated the Chamber of Deputies. He lived openly with an actress, was capable, even as *Président du Conseil*, of playing practical jokes and liked showing his intellectual superiority over his opponents. The provincial reflex of hostility and inferiority towards the Parisian operated fully in Tardieu's case; it tended to emphasise the other accusations made against him. The charges of unscrupulousness, of

[1] On Tardieu see R. Binion, *Defeated Leaders. The Political Fate of Caillaux, Jouvenel and Tardieu*, 1960. J. Debû-Bridel, *L'Agonie de la Troisième République*, 1948. P. E. Flandin, *Politique française, 1919–1940*, 1947. R. Kovar, *Les Idées politiques d'André Tardieu*, unpublished *mémoire*, 1959. H. Torres, *De Clemenceau à de Gaulle*, 1958, pp. 87–9. And Tardieu's own writings, especially *La Révolution à refaire*, 2 vols, 1936–7.

affairisme, of mixing business with politics, had some substance but none had, in themselves, enough weight to do irreparable damage to his reputation. His authoritarian temper brought forth the traditional Radical reflex against the 'strong man'; this reflex was usually dulled in times of crisis but the Radicals, like most other politicians at the time, did not realise the full significance of the collapse of the New York stock exchange in 1929. The hostility to Tardieu on the Right is more difficult to explain. He shared with Georges Mandel the characteristic of raising the temperature of political debate. The moderate Right did not like this as they constantly tried to keep passion out of politics in the name of *apaisement* and national unity. Tardieu and Mandel seemed to provoke the Left and the moderates feared reprisals. The *ministrable* Moderates did not want to be on bad terms with any possible governmental combination. The Catholic Right was unenthusiastic about Tardieu and Mandel because of their lack of enthusiasm in the defence of religious interests. The Catholics were also divided in foreign policy between the Briandists and the nationalists:[1] Tardieu and Mandel, having been intimately associated with Clemenceau and the defence of the treaty of Versailles were not entirely acceptable to either wing. However, this split over foreign policy was not to assume really serious proportions in the Right until after 1936.

It was above all the Radicals, helped by the lethargy of the Right, who finally defeated Tardieu and made impossible the kind of leadership he was trying to give. Complaining that the majority on which he based his government included the whole of the Right, the Radicals conducted subversive opposition to it. They did not so much vote against Tardieu as speak against him and prolong interminably the discussion of the measures which he proposed. This rejection of Tardieu by the Radicals was fatal to his ambition to be a 'national' leader. Only an electoral victory of the Right could have brought him back to power. The elections of 1932, held under the shadow of the worsening economic situation, produced a Chamber with a centre of gravity more to the Left than the previous one. It was hailed as a victory of the *Cartel des Gauches* but there was hardly any unity of action by the parties of the Left. The great mass of the Radical party was, and had been since 1919, unwilling to commit itself to alliance either with the Socialists or the Right, except under pressure, and then only for short periods. Having completed their social and religious programme, the Radicals had become conservative opportunists in a situation requiring positive

[1] J. Folliet, *Pacifisme de droite? Bellicisme de gauche?* 1938. R. Rémond, A. Coutrot, *Les Catholiques, le communisme et les crises, 1924–1939*, 1960.

government. Tardieu made no secret of his distaste for the manner in which government was conducted and for *gouvernement d'Assemblée*. After his first ministry he remarked that no matter how much purpose was given to an administration, the final and humiliating achievement was survival.[1] His disgust with the existing operation of institutions was to take a sharper turn after 1932.

He played on the passions raised by the Stavisky affair with the aim of preventing the co-operation of moderate Republicans with Radical cabinets. Although much was subsequently implied about his contacts with the anti-parliamentary leagues, in order to discredit him, his connection with them was tenuous and his sympathy for them slight – he warned his young collaborator Jacques Debû-Bridel against 'these narrow schools of intellectual politicians'. As a politician in the 1930s he was limited by his view, traditional among Republican notables, of the nature of political activity. He did not wish to be a man of a party, but a national statesman who could be supported by several parties, and he considered neither organising a political movement nor taking over an existing party. His view of the political order was that an elite debated the great national issues whilst a network of committees throughout the country followed sections of this elite, organised elections and brought out a largely passive people to vote. Mass participation in politics and the mass movements of Right or Left with their socially and intellectually inferior leaders did not belong to his rather mandarin world.

Tardieu, however, was the first leader to emerge from the Right of the Chamber during the Third Republic to be whole-heartedly and openly in favour of economic expansion, efficiency and modernisation. He regarded these as constituting a major policy area, possibly more important than any other. His declaration of policy as *Président du Conseil* in 1929 contained a proposal for a national investment plan to renovate the infrastructure of the French economy.[2] Although relatively modest, it was the first serious planning proposal by a peacetime government: the Chamber greeted it with a kind of shocked amazement, as a piece of demagogy and a manoeuvre for votes. Mainly because of Radical opposition, it was never taken seriously, discussed or voted on. But Tardieu was in earnest and this partly explains the sympathy between Tardieu and some large economic interests. The coalmine owners and the steelmasters (François de Wendel broke with Tardieu but this was for political reasons) could see the point of the *plan d'outillage national*,

[1] A. Tardieu, *L'Épreuve du pouvoir*, 1931, p. xiv.
[2] ibid., for details of the *Plan d'outillage national*.

particularly in terms of improved transport facilities. On the other hand, it alarmed the small businessman and peasant and Tardieu was not always the best advocate for his own plan: he tended to lecture the business community on its attitudes and organisation. At the *Congrès de l'Union des Intérêts Economiques* in 1930, he presented a formidable list of charges against this body which gave financial support to moderate Republican organisations. On many occasions he referred to *laissez-faire* liberal principles as *doctrines d'hier* quite as irrelevant as Marxism to contemporary problems of economic and social organisation. These views were well received by some large industrialists who were aware of the importance of the role of the State in the management of the economy, by 'technocratic' civil servants who have never during modern French history been wholly absent from public administration and by a small, young intellectual elite searching for new ideas for reform of the stagnating economic and social structures of the country. But they were anathema to the small businessman, the peasant and the economic conservative, with some reason. The general tenor of Tardieu's position conveyed attitudes which, after the Second World War, were to condemn the backward sectors of the economy to extinction. A whole range of schemes were produced in the inter-war period for renovation of the economy, ranging from the corporatism of Georges Valois to socialist *dirigisme*, but the ideas which Tardieu was generating, because they could gather a certain kind of influential support, were dangerous to the 'small man'.

From disorder to defeat, 1934–1940

In the immediate post-First World War period, the Right seemed to have unequivocally accepted Republican institutions. In the 1930s it became once again apparent that many members of the Right could not be counted on to defend these institutions. The deepening economic crisis, the deteriorating international situation and the activities of the anti-parliamentary leagues combined to create an atmosphere of growing lack of confidence in the existing political order. The effect of the depression were felt only slowly in France.[1] The greatest drop in industrial production came in 1934 when, with 1928 as par, production for the four quarters of the year was 86, 83, 80 and 79. Prices collapsed and agricultural prices generally fell more sharply than those of industrial products. On the basis of 1929 prices, in 1935 wheat stood at 55, wine at 49 and

[1] G. Dupeux, *Le Front populaire et les élections de 1936*, 1959, ch. 1. A. Sauvy, op. cit., and *Mouvement économique de 1929 à 1939*, Service national de statistique, 1941. R. Wolff, *Economie et finances de la France*, 1943.

meat at 45. Among manufacturers, textiles were badly hit, the price level in 1935 being 42 against 100 in 1929. Only in industries where conditions of near monopoly existed, such as cement (81 in 1935), were prices maintained at a profitable level. Wages were not substantially reduced but unemployment in the industrial centres rose dangerously. The main burden of the crisis fell on the unemployed and the underemployed, the agricultural sector, and traders and manufacturers in those sectors of the economy exposed to international competition. The revenue produced by direct and indirect taxation dropped from 100 in 1929 to 67 in 1935. Small savings were dissipated: the balance of deposits over withdrawals at the post-office savings bank in 1931 was 885,000 million francs; this was converted into a deficit of 18,000 million in 1933 and 526,000 million in the first six months of 1936. This economic situation encouraged the movement towards political extremism.

The situation was exacerbated by the absence of a stable majority in the parliament elected in 1932. The Radical ministries of Herriot and Chautemps were forced to govern with *majorités de rechange*, sometimes being supported by Socialists and sometimes by the Right. They had no positive plan for overcoming the economic crisis. Léon Blum addressed Herriot in the Chamber in January 1933: 'You must surely believe that there can be no more serious admission [of defeat] than that we are incapable of recommencing what we attempted in 1925 and that we cannot overcome the difficulties of this country by a democratic financial plan?' But the Radicals and the Socialists were, in effect, incapable of agreeing on a positive programme. The Radicals pursued a deflationary policy in the 1932–6 parliament without going as far as they wished in order to avoid completely losing the sympathy of the Socialists. The frustrations of this situation were brought to a head by the collapse of the paper empire of a crooked financier, Stavisky, who was alleged to have powerful political protectors.

The Stavisky affair triggered off the riots of February 1934, started by the nationalist leagues and the Communists, both demonstrating against corruption in the Chamber. The Communists drew back when it became apparent that the leagues could possibly carry a reactionary government to power. Although the course of events on 6 February 1934 presents some difficulties, it is almost certain that there was no concerted plan of the major leagues (*Action Française, Jeunesses Patriotes, Solidarité Française, Croix de Feu* and the *Francistes*) to overturn the Republic.[1] A conventional,

[1] On 6 February see B. C. F. Bankowitz, 'Paris on 6 February 1934', in B. D. Gooch (ed.), *Interpreting European History*, 1967. M. Beloff, 'The Sixth of

though large, street demonstration which turned into a dangerous riot, resulting in numerous casualties, took place. The immediate consequence of the riot was the resignation of the government led by the Radical Daladier and the formation of a government of 'national union' under the aged ex-President of the Republic and moderate Radical, Gaston Doumergue. Tardieu (his last post in government), Louis Marin and Laval (elected as a Socialist in 1914 but drifted towards the moderate Right) were given office and the balance of the Doumergue government was clearly more to the Right than that of previous administrations. Other governments led by Flandin, Buisson, Laval and Sarraut maintained this balance until the end of the 1932–6 parliament. The Socialists went into opposition – the neo-Socialists led by Déat and Marquet split from the sett, moved to the Right, and supported these governments.

On the Left, 6 February 1934 was important in bringing about wide acceptance of the necessity for a Popular Front. For the Right it was the date from which began to develop the positions finally adopted in face of the catastrophe of 1940. Threatening developments abroad started to have a crucial influence over internal French politics, although foreign policy issues did not dominate parliamentary politics until the Munich crisis. The successes of Mussolini and Hitler contributed to a general atmosphere of insecurity and gave encouragement to the activists of the extreme Right. Some financial support was given by the dictators to sympathetic movements and individuals but it was not lavish, and not enough in itself to explain the process which led men to collaborate with the Germans during the Second World War. The nationalism of the leagues of 1934, like that of the leagues of 1900, was directed at an internal enemy rather than at an external threat. These were not, in origin, movements of traitors paid by foreign powers to subvert the Republic.

The allegation that the slogan 'rather Hitler than Blum' represented the general sentiment of the French Right after 1936 is untrue, although the behaviour and attitudes of certain sections of the Right provided some basis for it.[1] The extreme Right openly sympathised

February', St Antony's Papers, No. 5, 1956, pp. 9–35. L. Bonnevay, *Les Journées sanglantes de février 1934*, 1935. J. P. Maxence, *Histoire de dix ans, 1927–1937*, 1939. R. Rémond, 'Explications du 6 février', *Politique*, July–September, 1959, pp. 218–30. *Rapport de la Chambre des Députés sur les évènements du 6 février 1934 et les jours suivants*, 2 vols, 1934. G. Suarez, *La Grande peur du 6 février au Palais Bourbon*, 1934.

[1] See particularly J. P. Chevènement, *La Droite nationaliste devant l'Allemagne*, unpublished *mémoire*, 1960. Dazelle, *De l'Union nationale à la révolution nationale*, unpublished *mémoire*, 1958. W. D. Irving, *The Republican Federation of France*

with the dictators. Mussolini and above all Franco were admired by those influenced by *Action Française*. Sanctions against Italy during the Ethiopian War were opposed by a majority of the parliamentary Right, in part at least, because Ethiopia was not considered important enough to warrant alienating Italy from the Stresa front. There was a tendency on the Right to take Mussolini at his own evaluation and overestimate Italy's military usefulness in a Franco-German war. The sympathy of the majority of Catholics – not shared by the progressive Catholics grouped around the *Esprit* and *Sept* – went to Franco: the anti-religious sentiments of most Spanish Republicans and the atrocities committed against clergy, monks and nuns were execrated. But sympathy for Hitler was much less marked on the Right. Amongst the extremists, particularly the ex-Communists in Doriot's *Parti Populaire Français*, it certainly existed. But Hitler was too much of a revolutionary to be admired by the mass of conservatives. He was less feared than Stalin, as shown by the opposition of 164 deputies to the ratification of the Franco-Soviet pact of 2 May 1935. This alliance with 'communism' was regarded as provocative by much of the Right, and Hitler was undoubtedly regarded by many as a barrier to communism. Sympathy or antipathy towards the regimes of foreign countries had always influenced judgements about foreign policy but, with the possible exception of the period of the Holy Alliance after 1815, these feelings dominated foreign policy debates during the late 1930s more than ever before. Although the international situation was obviously dangerous and threatening, this change, contemporaneous with the formation of the Popular Front, had its roots in French domestic politics.

The first step towards the establishment of the Popular Front was taken on 27 July 1934 with the encouragement of Moscow, when the Socialist and Communist parties agreed on very general objectives. This pact was sealed during the course of 1935. The parties of the Left – including even the Radicals – went united into the 1936 election campaign and emerged the victors. The Right had actually gained votes but moderate conservative seats were lost and the Popular Front had a substantial majority in parliament. Although the Communists refused to participate in government after this victory, they had, for the first time, an important influence on government policy. The Communists held that foreign policy must be conducted in the interests of 'the Revolution' and the working class. The

during the 1930s, unpublished thesis, 1972, ch. 6. C. Micaud, *The French Right and Nazi Germany, 1933–1939*, 1943. Y. Simon, *La Campagne d'Ethopie et la pensée politique française*, 1936. G. Warner, *Pierre Laval and the Eclipse of France*, 1968.

Socialists still claiming to be Marxists, were susceptible to arguments based on this way of thinking. There had always been ideological strands in the thinking of members of the Right on foreign policy matters. In 1936 they were more than ever concerned to oppose the ideologies of the extreme Left, and, in doing so, adopted similar but opposite criteria. The victory of the Popular Front in the elections of 1936 convinced large sections of the Right that France should not do anything to provoke Germany because she was not in a fit state to defend herself. It was a very troubled period and individual politicians frequently changed their views. There was no cohesion amongst the parties and the groups which opposed the Popular Front. The activist extra-parliamentary leagues – La Rocque's *Parti Social Français*, Doriot's *Parti Populaire Français*, Taittinger's *Parti Républicain National et Social*, Bucard's *Francistes* and the *Union Nationale des Combattants* could not agree on a common programme, despite efforts at the end of 1936 and the beginning of 1937 to establish a *Front National*. In parliament the Right was disunited in its attitudes to the regime and the Popular Front, and on social and foreign policy.

There was, during the Popular Front period, much discontent and frustration amongst the clienteles of the Right and there were inflammatory issues on which campaigns could be based.[1] Immediately after the 1936 elections, industrial workers, to ensure that private employers submitted to their demands, occupied many factories. This was a considerable psychological shock for the employers, particularly the small employers. The Matignon agreements between the trade unions and the employers' representatives, arbitrated by the *Président du Conseil* Léon Blum, were regarded by many small employers as a capitulation and a betrayal. Feelings of helplessness and humiliation were prevalent amongst the bourgeoisie. 'As for the young bourgeois', wrote Simone Weil, 'no one had done them any harm, but they had been frightened, and, an unpardonable crime in their eyes, they had been humiliated by those whom they regarded as their social inferiors'.[2] Class tension appeared to become greater; the conviction grew stronger that the industrial working class was completely identified with the Communist Party. France, according to this belief, could be rendered completely defenceless, on an order from Moscow, by strikes in the factories and by mutinies

[1] S. M. Osgood, 'The Front Populaire: Views from the Right', *International Review of Social History*, vol. 9, 1964, pp. 189–201. R. Rémond, J. Bourdin, 'Les Forces adverses' in *Léon Blum, chef de gouvernement*, Fondation Nationale des Sciences Politiques, 1967.

[2] S. Weil, *L'Enracinement*, 1949, p. 113.

in the army. A belief also spread that the middle class was incapable of organising its own defence. Moderate parliamentarians from the Radicals (in increasingly uneasy partnership with the Socialists) to the Right gave the impression of being hither and thither by events, never dominating them. They made concessions when compelled but they had nothing positive to offer. The Radicals joined the Popular Front to avoid electoral defeat; the *patronat* and their allies on the moderate Right conceded social reforms only when intimidated by occupation of the factories.

The more subtle leaders of the Right tried from the beginning of the 1936 parliament to seduce the Radicals from the Popular Front combination. When Blum presented his government to the Chamber in June 1936, Reynaud, Fernand-Laurent, Montigny, Baréty and others promised a loyal and non-obstructive opposition.[1] Even in the heyday of the Popular Front Pierre-Etienne Flandin said that the opposition did not wish to complicate the task of the government by interminable debates. Alarm at social unrest is only a partial explanation of these attitudes. Breakdown of the Popular Front coalition seemed probable: the Communists would not join the government and were opposed to the coalition parties on foreign policy, particularly over the Spanish Civil War; the Socialists, under Blum, were determined on an expansionary economic policy in direct contrast to the deflationary policies pursued by Radical governments over the previous four years. Some leaders of the Right realised that outright hostility to all the men and the measures of the Popular Front would have the effect of strengthening its unity. Also, as the effects of the world depression had spread in France, some protection of the working class from its effects was regarded as legitimate: this sympathy did not extend to measures such as the forty-hour week and paid holidays which were generally thought to be too expensive. In addition, the international situation divided men into 'appeasers' and 'resisters' along lines which did not coincide with the division between the opposition of the Right and the Popular Front.

The representatives of the extreme Right in parliament, particularly those associated with the nationalist leagues such as Vallat, Ybarnégaray and Henriot, openly expressed their preference for an authoritarian regime. Growing disenchantment with the 'weakness' of the regime was voiced on the moderate Right, for example, by Tardieu, and even on the Left, by the 'neo-Socialists' Marquet and Déat. Most parliamentarians on the moderate and extreme Right seemed prepared to compromise with any potentially successful

[1] R. Rémond, J. Bourdin, op. cit., pp. 140–1.

authoritarian movement. The *Croix de Feu*, which became the *Parti Social Français* after the dissolution of the leagues in 1936, might have been such a movement had the war not intervened. There is, however, little evidence that the 'appeasing' Right desired defeat in war, as most elements of the Resistance alleged, so that the recalcitrant working class could be disciplined by the Nazis. This desire was, wrongly, inferred from the masochistic acceptance of defeat, the '*mea culpa* on the bosom of others' as one commentator put it, apparent in Vichy after the debacle of 1940. The policy of appeasement was supported by most of the Right because they were convinced, not without reason, that France was in no condition to defend herself and that she had no certain allies.

Some of the most determined and influential opponents of appease-ment – Paul Reynaud, Georges Mandel, Henri de Kérillis – were men of the Right. They belonged to a tradition of Jacobin nation-alism and refused to be intimidated either by a threatening situation or by the apparent weakness of France. The opposition of Reynaud and Pierre-Etienne Flandin was typical of the split caused by appeasement. Both were firmly rooted in the tradition of 'liberal' parliamentary conservatism and little divided them on the basic principles of domestic policy. Neither was tempted by an authoritar-ian solution to the problems of France although Flandin took office in the first phase of Vichy. Typical of his political and social milieu, Flandin was profoundly pacific, always seeking compromise solutions in conflict situations. As an Anglophile he took notice of, and was influenced by, the evolution of British opinion. Reynaud was also Anglophile but looked in the direction of Churchill, Eden and Duff Cooper rather than towards Chamberlain and *The Times*. His position was to some extent a function of his personality and tem-perament. He enjoyed being a maverick, constantly criticising the conventional conservative wisdom, and he aroused therefore strong antipathies amongst conservatives. His fondness for making a great number of pronouncements and subsequently pointing out that he was right before anyone else also made him unpopular. It was an unusual example of a *grand bourgeois* with a taste for political risk who was unafraid of the prospect of war; he had, however, the great misfortune to be *Président du Conseil* at the very moment of defeat.

Mandel was a member of Reynaud's government in 1940. Deputy for Gironde since 1919 he was perhaps the most disliked major figure in politics in the inter-war period. General Spears remarked that if he could like a fish he would have liked Mandel.[1] Cold,

[1] General Spears, *Assignment to Catastrophe*, vol. 2, 1954, p. 114. In general,

authoritarian, and highly intelligent, Mandel remained faithful to the Jacobin nationalism of his patron, Georges Clemenceau, and like him would not tolerate 'defeatism' in any form. One of the very few Jews in France to make a reputation as a man of the Right, his Jewishness may have caused him to refrain both from attempting a coup against the defeatists in the war cabinet and from going into exile to carry on resistance to the German invader. This uncharacteristic quiescence led to his arrest by the Vichy authorities and his assassination by the *Milice* in 1944. Kérillis was a less important political figure but published a constant stream of anti-appeasement articles throughout the period 1937–40. This made him the target of many attacks from the extreme Right accusing him of collusion with the Communists. Choosing exile in New York during the war rather than accept the armistice, he failed to rally to General de Gaulle and, thereafter, exercised no political influence. The common characteristic of Reynaud, Mandel and Kérillis was that they were unimpressed by the Communist menace and the threat of revolution. They were anti-Communist but considered that, in the last resort, national sentiment would always be stronger than class sentiment.

The French Right, therefore, was not entirely made up of appeasers and was not, subsequently, completely identified with the Vichy regime and collaboration. But men of the Right, particularly the journalist politicians such as Maurras and Brasillach, the leaders of the leagues, Doriot, Déat, La Rocque, Bucard and their parliamentary admirers, helped to convince a large number of Frenchmen that the system under which they were governed was corrupt and rotten. However, the propaganda of the Left had similar corrosive effects: from the point of view of national unity and respect for established institutions the myth of the two hundred families was as damaging as the myth of the *métèques*. The period 1936–40 brought into the open the sometimes unsavoury sources of conservative opposition in France in a manner apparent only in times of extreme political and social tension. This opposition had a complex, swiftly evolving character and occasionally seemed to threaten Republican institutions. Although no prominent leader envisaged a *coup d'état*, manifestations of sympathy with the Nationalist side in the Spanish Civil War could be interpreted as a warning that the same thing could happen in France. This limited the freedom of action of the Popular Front government by implying a risk of civil war. The climate of political violence, created by the extreme Left as well as

Spears had a high opinion of Mandel's intelligence and courage. For an assessment of Mandel in this period see J. Sherwood, St Antony's Papers, No. 5, 1959, pp. 86–125 and by the same author *Georges Mandel and the Third Republic*, 1971.

the extreme Right, weakened the prestige of the government and the stability of the regime. The moderate aim of the leaders of the parliamentary Right – to split the Radicals from their alliance with the Socialists and Communists – contrasted strangely with the terrifying accusations of treason and corruption in *Gringoire, Candide, Je suis partout, Choc, Action française* and other reviews, which encouraged the disposition of sections of the Right towards apocalyptic pessimism.

During the 'phoney war', which lasted from September 1939 to May 1940, there was a closing of ranks behind the government. Even Lucien Rebatet and his Germanophile colleagues of *Je suis partout* responded to the call of national unity. The disgrace and the outlawing of the Communist Party after the Nazi-Soviet pact satisfied the majority of the Right. But despite the patriotic unanimity of the Right-wing press, defeatist sentiments were rampant even in the army and in parliament. With the German breakthrough in the middle of 1940, defeatism came out into the open, and soon after the government moved to Bordeaux the *Président du Conseil* Paul Reynaud, rapidly lost support, both in the government and amongst the army chiefs, for further resistance to the Germans.

Pétain, Minister of State and *Vice-Président du Conseil*, urged political as well as military reasons for the armistice: he argued that social disorder and possibly revolution would be difficult to avoid unless hostilities ceased. The desire of moderates and pacifically-minded men to seek peace when the military situation in metropolitan France became desperate would have been entirely reasonable in the previous war. The agreement with the United Kingdom not to make a separate peace had to be broken, but the British, when consulted, were prepared to accept this. The error of Pétain and his associates was to mistake the nature of the war and the character of their adversaries. As de Gaulle pointed out in his 18 June 1940 broadcast, total war, global in scope, and a totalitarian opponent, undermined the basic assumptions on which they sought the armistice of 1940. National independence was impossible until the invader was defeated. The attempted reform of the political system by the Vichy government was impractical because the military occupation of the greater part of metropolitan France placed it effectively under German tutelage. When the Germans invaded the Free Zone in 1942 and reimposed Laval at the head of affairs even the appearance of independence was removed.

Vichy and Collaboration, 1940–1944
Reactions to defeat were very varied, although most members

of the Right seem to have accepted the armistice and rallied to the Vichy government. Very few Deputies and Senators of the Right were among the eighty who opposed granting full powers to Pétain on 10 July 1940. There were, however, notable minority reactions. Prominent politicians of the Right such as the ex-Ministers, Reynaud and Mandel, were imprisoned and put on trial as war-mongers by the Vichy regime. Others such as the writers Drieu La Rochelle and Robert Brasillach, were convinced from the moment of defeat that Germany would be victorious in the war. They became enthusiastic Collaborators with the Germans and were hostile to the Vichy regime. A majority waited patiently to see which side was going to win. The significance of this *attentisme* is almost impossible to assess.[1] Was, for example, the attitude of Senator Joseph Caillaux, the former Radical *Président du Conseil* who had become very conservative in the 1930s, due more to old age and lethargy than to calculation? The demoralising experience of appeasement and defeat produced a general feeling of lassitude in the population and politicians were not immune from it. The temptation to be carried along by events was, in innumerable cases, overwhelming: the penalties for choosing the wrong side were going to be severe.

Gaullist and Resistance propaganda indiscriminately identified the Vichy regime with collaboration with the Germans. Despite Pétain's famous appeal for collaboration after his meeting with Hitler at Montoire in Autumn 1940, this was a gross over-simplification, even after Laval returned to power in November 1942. There was an important difference between Pétainists and Collaborators as well as deep divisions within these two camps. The Vichy episode, although brief, was of great complexity and revealed many of the aspirations and characteristics of the Right which lay dormant or were obscured in peacetime.[2]

André Siegfried pointed out four main periods of Vichy and in

[1] One of the few examples of an explicit defence of *attentisme* is P. Brisson, *Vingt ans du Figaro, 1938–1958*, n.d., p. 31.

[2] In the voluminous bibliography of the Vichy regime, the most useful works for setting the episode in the context of the history of the Right are R. Aron, *L'Histoire de Vichy*, 2 vols, 1954, English edition 1958. S. Hoffman, 'Quelques aspects du régime de Vichy', *Revue française de science politique*, vol. 6, 1956, pp. 46–69. R. O. Paxton, *Politics and Parades at Vichy*, 1966. J. Plumyène, *Pétain*, 1964. R. Rémond, *Le Gouvernement de Vichy, 1940–1942*, 1972. A. Siegfried, 'Le Vichy de Pétain, le Vichy de Laval', *Revue française de science politique*, vol. 6, 1956, pp. 737–49; *De la Troisième a la Quatrième République*, 1956. A useful summary of documents is contained in J. de Launay, *Le Dossier de Vichy*, 1967. The most illuminating memoirs written by participants are H. du Moulin de Labarthète, *Les Temps des illusions*, 1946. General M. Weygand, *Mémoires*, vol. 3, *Rappelé au service*, 1950.

each period the nature of the regime was different.[1] The first period was from the granting of full powers to Pétain by the French parliament on 10 July 1940 to the ousting of Laval on 13 December 1940. Laval, with considerable tactical dexterity and some callous bullying, had created the conditions for the birth of the regime and he wanted to control the crucial area of relations with Germany, leaving Pétain and his entourage very small effective powers. But the Marshal was an obstacle to their aim and Laval was, therefore, eliminated. The second period was from December 1940 to April 1942 – the period of the National Revolution 'in complete reaction, not only against the Third Republic, but all that had been done for more than a century in the name of the principles of 1789'. The Prime Minister for the first half of this period was Pierre-Etienne Flandin, in an uncharacteristic role, and the second half was dominated by Admiral Darlan who, in terms of personal style and political ideas, was more suitable. The third period was from April 1942 to the eve of the Liberation during which Laval, imposed by the Germans, was in control with Pétain reduced to the role of honorary President. Towards the end of this period, the two leaders were trying to find some 'landing ground' – Pétain with the Gaullists and the Resistance, Laval with the parliamentarians of the Third Republic. This period ended with the entry of the allies into Paris in August 1944. The last period 'dominated by the opportunism of adventurers, does not represent anything profound in French political history'.

The principles, the attitudes and the rancours of the National Revolution were deeply embedded in the French Right. Like the Right itself, the National Revolution was not a coherent unity. The *État Français* was formally a dictatorship, but it was very much a pluralist system. Diametrically opposed tendencies often shared the same administration: the secretariats of youth, information and veterans were examples of administrations which contained the most diverse elements. Different ministries sometimes pursued opposed policies: for example, whilst the Secretariat of State for Labour was attempting to make the unions the basis of social organisation, a section of Pétain's personal staff was trying to reduce the *syndicats* to powerlessness and even to abolish them.[2] Those responsible for the Peasant Corporation argued that the agricultural sector should be the basic element of the French economy but the *Comités d'Organisation* of commerce and industry resulted in a considerable increase in the political power of large industrial interests. On the other hand, the most successful mass movement of Vichy, the *Légion*

---

[1] A. Siegfried, *De La Troisième à la Quatrième République*, p. 77.
[2] These examples are drawn from S. Hoffman, op. cit.

des Combattants, was committed to the defence of small business and vigorously denounced the 'trusts'. The regime constantly sought the support of the Church whilst it pursued policies such as the creation of *jeunesse unique* to which the hierarchy was hostile, and it persecuted Catholic clergy and laymen who opposed the regime.

This confusion of policies and aspirations represented the access to power of minorities, of the conservative forces virtually excluded from the parliamentary regime of the Third Republic. These forces were based to a large extent on the non-wage-earning social groups – peasants and farmers, the liberal professions, artisans, small business-men, and clerical, supervisory and junior administrative staff. Many members of these groups were alarmed by the militancy of the industrial proletariat and alienated from the Republic by financial crises and scandals. The Vichy regime seemed, at first, to favour these middle and lower middle-class groups at the expense of the better organised – the large capitalists and the organised working class. Access to political power for the lower middle-class groups had always been a major and persistent difficulty. They had no strongly organised professional associations. Sections of the peasantry were in some respects well organised but anarchic individualism remained a characteristic of the countryside. Attempts to organise small traders and manufacturers had met with little success. The Vichy regime was attractive to these groups because it fulfilled their desire for an authoritarian structure which diminished the power of their more highly organised rivals and, at the same time, seemed responsive to their demands. This reactionary, authoritarian outlook had little in common with the revolutionary totalitarianism of the Nazis.

On the Paris Fascists, such as Doriot, Déat, Rebatet, Bucard, Constantini, Chack and Chateaubriant leaned towards a genuine totalitarian glorification of the State: they wanted the mobilisation of the masses in a single party.[1] The leaders of Vichy opposed the *parti unique*, although the *Légion des Combattants* under Darnand came to have some of the characteristics of a para-military Fascist party.[2] Many Vichyites feared the revolutionary potential of a mass political movement in much the same way as they mistrusted the dynamism of a powerful and centralised State bureaucracy. One of the more curious convictions held by Pétainists in Vichy was that the old conservative distinction between *pays réel* (the national

[1] M. Cotta, *Les Idéologies de la collaboration à travers de la presse*, unpublished thesis; abridged version, *La Collaboration*, 1964, especially pp. 260–9. For different perspectives on the *parti unique* by Collaborators see M. Déat, *Le Parti unique*, 1942. Saint-Paulien (pseudonym of M. I. Sicard), *Histoire de la Collaboration*, 1964.

[2] J. Delperrie de Bayac, *Histoire de la milice*, 1969, ch. 4.

community) and the *pays légal* (the regime) had been suppressed:[1] the mobilisation of positive support was, therefore, considered superfluous. Legislation, it was thought, would be obeyed without opposition.

Not all the men associated with the Vichy regime were authoritarians, hostile to democratic, representative institutions. The most important parliamentarians, Pierre-Etienne Flandin and the *Président du Conseil* Paul-Boncour, during their relatively brief association with Vichy, thought of it as a Roman dictatorship which would disappear after peace had been restored. But the influence of these parliamentarians was not great because there was a conscious effort to suppress the mores of parliamentary politics. Army and Naval officers were regarded as more suitable office-holders in a State which banished 'partisan quarrels' and political parties. Corporatism was the great principle of Vichyite political theory: the State was restricted to the roles of law-maker and of arbitrator between professional interests organised into corporations.

The main problem of the regime was the contradiction between the actual condition of French society and the rulers' conceptions of it. By raising military men and higher civil servants to positions of national leadership, by granting local leadership in the *commune* and *département* to notables rejected by universal suffrage, and by making the Church and family the basic institutions on which society rested, the government of Vichy was creating a structure even further removed from the *pays réel* than the institutions of the Third Republic. To make reality conform to the image, the control of the State inevitably expanded in many spheres. The direct exercise of power by specialised family, local, and economic communities proved impossible partly because of the occupation of the country by the Germans, but also because these communities were not capable of filling the role assigned to them. The groups originally attracted to the regime as a result became frustrated and hostile. Although the National Revolution might represent their ideal, the parliamentary Republic was a less hostile political system than the totalitarian regime towards which Vichy tended after 1942. There was, therefore, a new *Ralliement* to the Republic at the Liberation. The distinction between society and the State, so deplored in the kind of conservative political theory justifying the Vichy experiment, was seen to have practical advantages.

There was a sharp contrast between the style, atmosphere and attitudes of Vichy and the Collaborationist policies of the Paris

[1] *La Doctrine du Maréchal, classé par thèmes,* 5th edition, 1943, pp. 16, 52, 61.

Fascists.[1] The process of analysing the *agonie de la Troisième République* was carried to greater lengths by the Collaborators than by the men of Vichy because the Collaborators, for the most part, were revolutionary ideologists. Their revolution consisted of integrating France into a new Fascist European order under German leadership. Because the Collaborators believed that this revolution was historically inevitable, ideological purity and the correct policy line pursued over the course of years was as important to them as it was to Marxist sectarians. Like Communists, they were committed to the creation of a one-party state but personal and ideological quarrels were so bitter that the attempt to create a single party of Collaboration collapsed in disorder. Enjoying no real power, the Collaborators were playing politics in a vacuum: they denounced political opponents to the Germans and ran publicity campaigns for causes such as recruitment for the *Légion des Volontaires Français contre le Bolshévisme* to fight on the Russian Front. They were preparing for the situation which a final German victory would have created.

Amongst the Collaborators there were some of the most factious men ever to engage in politics in France. Sectarian warfare, conducted through the columns of their newspapers, finally degenerated into attempted assassinations. The doctrinal differences between the factions mainly concerned the timing and motives for conversion to the cause of 'collaboration'. The greatest claims to ideological purity were made by the editorial team of the newspaper *Je suis partout* headed by Lucien Rebatet and Robert Brasillach, who had commenced their political careers as disciples of Maurras. Brasillach and Fernand de Brinon (Vichy's representative in Paris during the occupation) had been associated in the 1930s with the Franco-German friendship committee run by the wartime German ambassador to France, Otto Abetz. After Hitler's accession to power, Rebatet and his friends predicted that the future of Europe was Fascist and the forces opposing it would inevitably be defeated: the rise of Mussolini, Hitler, Salazar, Franco and the petty dictators of Eastern Europe was part of an historical process leading to the complete dominance of Fascism in Europe. Others shared this vision such as Marcel Bucard, leader of the *Parti Franciste* and Alphonse de Chateaubriant, winner of the Prix Goncourt in 1911, who was converted to Nazism after a visit to Germany in 1935.

Less 'pure' ideologically were those who had evolved from non-Fascist Right-wing positions to eventual Collaboration. Philippe

[1] S. Hoffman, 'Collaboration in France during World War II', *Journal of Modern History*, vol. 40, 1968, pp. 375–95.

Henriot, Deputy for Bordeaux from 1932 to 1944, was a Catholic of the extreme Right, who became a partisan of Collaboration and eventually secretary of Information and Propaganda during the last phase of Vichy. Georges Suarez, biographer of Briand and Clemenceau, political essayist and associate of Tardieu, collaborated probably because of a paranoid hostility to the Left which developed after the victory of the Popular Front. The best known Collaborators had at one time been prominent men of the Left. Marcel Déat was an ex-Socialist and Jacques Doriot an ex-Communist; both had, at one time, been considered potential leaders of their parties. Adrien Marquet, Socialist Deputy and mayor of Bordeaux during the inter-war period, left the Socialist Party with Déat and became Vichy Minister of the Interior. Pierre Laval had started as an Independent Socialist and moved steadily to the Right. Although co-operation between Déat, Doriot and Laval proved very difficult, all three were more at home in their dealings with the Nazis because of their revolutionary and plebeian origins than the men of the traditional Right.

There were many reasons, both personal and political for Collaboration and the Collaborators were not simply opportunists who tried to pick the winning side and made a mistake. There were blatant instances of opportunism – Laval, despite his defenders, is one example; the journalist, Jean Luchaire, another. Personal frustration and disappointment, the desire for revenge on the parties (and even on the country) which had refused to follow them, partly explain the behaviour of, for example, Déat and Doriot. The subversive activities of the Nazis before the war, encouraged Collaboration during it: the Nazis had recruited a sizeable Fifth column in France and the members of Abetz's Franco-German friendship committee can be regarded as a part of it. There were adventurers with a taste for violence and conspiracy, such as the *Cagoulard* Eugène Deloncle, who was eventually killed in a gun fight with the Gestapo. But underlying all the personal reasons for adopting the course of Collaboration was an alienation from the national community, very similar to that felt by many Communist militants. The Collaborators believed that the political, economic and social elites of France were corrupt beyond redemption. In the minds of these men, the only way to salvation was through close alliance with revolutionary forces which transcended national frontiers.

The intellectuals of the extreme Right like Brasillach and Drieu La Rochelle, wartime editor of the *Nouvelle Revue Française*, chose Fascism as others of their generation chose Communism. Drieu eventually admitted that, in the last resort, it was only a kind of snobbery which determined his choice and, after the defeat of the Axis powers, he was convinced that the future lay with the Communists.[1] Patriotism in the conventional meaning of the word no longer had much significance for the Collaborators. The Socialist Minister of the Fourth Republic, Christian Pineau, wrote of the Left-wing journalist Francis Delaïsi who collaborated: 'It is impossible to doubt the sincerity and intellectual honesty of Francis Delaïsi, he did not choose by cowardice, but because his way of reasoning escaped the passion which moved us.'[2] The Collaborators had narrow and peculiar sympathies. Their loyalties were not, as for a nationalist like Barrès, to a political community composed of a multiplicity of spiritual families, but a restricted group of 'uncorrupted' men.

The Right was represented in the Resistance from the very beginning. The first Deputy to rally to de Gaulle was the Peasant Party leader, Paul Antier. The moderate Republican Deputy for Calvados from 1932 and future *Président du Conseil*, Joseph Laniel, and Max Brusset and Jacques Debû-Bridel, the young collaborators of Mandel and Tardieu, soon followed. The most widely respected figure of the nationalist Right in parliament, Louis Marin, rallied to de Gaulle after a sojourn at Vichy. Moreover, the Free French enterprise in London during the first eighteen months of its existence gave the impression of being a movement of the Right, because of the authoritarian personality of its leader and the exalted patriotism of its propaganda. The appeals to Joan of Arc, Deroulède and Foch were not attractive to the Left and the 'sacred egoism' of de Gaulle which placed the interests of France before the success of the allies was alien to leftist internationalism. Anti-parliamentary remarks and scrupulous avoidance of the word Republic also helped to give a Right-wing impression. When it became apparent that many more men and organisations of the Left than of the Right were resisting the German occupation, and that the Vichy regime drew much of its support from the Right there was a change in the complexion of the movement and in de Gaulle's outlook.

'The treason of the *classes dirigeantes*, the patriotism of the workers and the encouragement of his Communist and Socialist associates, led him, little by little, not to elaborate a politico-economic system, but to adopt a certain number of ideas; abolition of the trusts, a more equitable distribution of wealth, improvement of the con-

[1] For his political evolution see P. Drieu La Rochelle, *Chronique politique, 1934–1942* 1943. F. Grover, *Drieu La Rochelle*, 1962.
[2] C. Pineau, *La Simple vérité, 1940–1945*, 1961, p. 72.

dition of the working class, participation of trade unionists in management, nationalisation and a planned economy. This was very close to the programme of the Socialist Party. . . .'[1]

Although de Gaulle continued to distrust the political parties and their constitutional ideas, the parties of the Left played an ever increasing role in Free France. In the internal Resistance, this role was even greater, to a point where it seemed that progressive Catholics, Socialists and Communists were alone in the struggle against the invader. Members of the Right were present in the *Conseil National de la Résistance*, in the consultative Assembly created by de Gaulle in Algiers in 1943 and amongst the advisers of de Gaulle, but their voices were muted and their influence small amidst the reformists and revolutionaries who dominated the Resistance. Some, such as Louis Marin and Jacques Debû-Bridel, worked closely with the Communists and were exposed to the charge that they allowed themselves to be used as Communist tools. Participation in the Resistance, therefore, did not rescue the Right from comprehensive charges of responsibility for appeasement, defeatism, collusion with Vichy and Collaboration. Although thoroughgoing Collaboration was a course chosen by a restricted and comparatively unimportant section of the Right, these charges had enough basis to make them very damaging.

The defeat, the armistice, the establishment of a new regime at Vichy, the occupation of half, then the whole of France, was a traumatic experience for the French population. 'The war changed everything', wrote Simone de Beauvoir in *La Force de l'Age:*

'After June 1940, I no longer recognised things, located places, remembered either times or even my own identity. Time which had calmly passed for ten years, suddenly jolted and I was carried away; without leaving the streets of Paris, I was more of a foreigner than I had previously felt across the seas. The world revealed another of its faces: violence was unleashed and with it, injustice, scandal stupidity and horror.'[2]

The material life of the nation was completely disrupted. There was widespread destruction of property, reduction of road and rail traffic, decline of trade, closing of factories and a drastic fall in industrial production. Material problems of heating, clothing and moving about oppressed the great majority of the nation from the defeat until the reconstruction after the war was well advanced.

[1] H. Michel, *Les Courants de la pensée de la Résistance*, 1962, p. 107.
[2] S. de Beauvoir, *La Force de l'age*, 1960, p. 613.

This made many people apathetic about public issues and political problems which were unrelated to these basic material issues. About a half of the population had taken flight on the approach of the Germans; almost the whole of the French army was taken prisoner; young men were drafted for labour service in Germany and those who wished to escape this fate took to the *maquis*. The number of combatants killed in the First World War was far greater but the displacement of population was much more serious in the Second. The demoralising effect of occupation, the black market and the crisis of loyalty, deeply felt by all serving officers and administrators, had a corrosive effect on group loyalties and social relationships.

The revival of the droite classique, 1945–1953

The circumstances of the Liberation period encouraged radical, even revolutionary, social change. They were uncongenial and very confusing for conservatives. But the historical experience of previous revolutions and invasions, the ordeal of the occupation which had encouraged retreat into private life and dissimulation in face of authority, helped conservative groups to survive and preserve ways of life during a period when they were almost completely impotent politically. The years from 1944 to 1947, the period of the purge of Collaborators, the provisional government of de Gaulle and of tripartism, the elections and referenda which established the Fourth Republic, the beginnings of the Cold War, the isolation of the Communist Party and colonial wars, were little marked by men belonging to *la droite classique*, by those readily identified with the Right. De Gaulle's achievement in the period 1944 to 1946 in re-establishing the authority of the State machinery, removing military power from the hands of the Communist Party and other Resistance formations, and unwittingly assisting the emergence of the *Mouvement Républicain Populaire* as a mass political party was based to some extent on the existence of the large, disorganised and inarticulate conservative mass in the country.

Very few men of the Right who had been active in politics in 1940 emerged from the war with unsullied reputations. The press of the Right, with the exception of *le Figaro*, was confiscated at the Liberation because it had been published under the Occupation. An arbitrary and summary justice was meted out to Right-wing men by Resistance groups during the Liberation of France. Many suffered for their opinions as much as for their acts.[1] Those fortunate enough to survive this rough justice were given a fuller hearing in the duly constituted courts of law but the final result was often the

[1] R. Aron, *L'Histoire de l'épuration*, 2 vols, 1967–9.

same: Darnand, Brinon, Brasillach, Laval and many others, faced the firing squad at Fresnes. Pétain, reprieved by de Gaulle after being sentenced to death, was imprisoned along with other high officials of the Vichy regime. The official purge was based on a mixture of ideological bias, *raison d'état* and genuine judicial process. This mixture had been apparent as early as 1943 when Pierre Pucheu, after rallying to the Algiers government of General de Gaulle, was tried and executed ostensibly for his record as Vichy Minister of the Interior when he surrendered hostages and Jews to the Germans.[1] The confusion of the Liberation period is epitomised by the cases of Right-wing men who were imprisoned first by the Germans and subsequently by the provisional government. Colonel de La Rocque had been put in Ravensbrück concentration camp by the Germans for Resistance activities and then incarcerated at the Liberation, without charges being made against him: he was released only to die. Alfred Fabre-Luce suffered a similar fate, sharing his prison experiences at the Liberation in the distinguished company of the actor Sacha Guitry, the academician Abel Hermant and the lawyer, Bâtonnier Ripert: he was one of the few to make a vigorous public protest in a short book *Au nom des silencieux* (1946).

Some of the lawyers who defended the Vichyites and Collaborators, notably Jacques Isorni, made their clients' cause their own and continued over the years to press for total amnesty. Their activity helped to create a feeling of misgiving about the purge and was a factor in undermining the political ghetto into which everyone connected with Vichy was temporarily cast. They were supported by some conservatives with impeccable Resistance records such as Joseph Laniel, who openly doubted the prudence and legitimacy of the purge. Antoine Pinay and others had voted full powers to Pétain and had been involved with the Vichy regime in the early days, only to rehabilitate themselves through Resistance activities later: they understood the reasons why so many had chosen to support Vichy and, therefore, did not accept that Vichyites should suffer political ostracism for a prolonged period of time.

Despite the hostile environment, conservatives achieved creditable performances in the first three elections held after the war, in 1945 and 1946. Paul Reynaud, Joseph Laniel and André Mutter assembled a heterogeneous electoral alliance called the *Entente Républicaine pour la Liberté et le Progrès Social*, composed partly of old parties of the Third Republic and partly from new groups emanating from the Resistance: *Fédération Républicaine*, *Alliance Démocratique*, *Radicaux Indépendants*, *Union Patriotique Républicaine*, *Français*

[1] P. Buttin, *Le Procès Pucheu*, 1947.

Libres, Parti de la Rénovation Républicaine. In the first two elections, in October 1945 and June 1946, conservatives belonging to this coalition and to other groups polled over two and a half million votes: in the third, held in the autumn of 1946, they reached over three million votes and increased their representation from 64 to 71 Deputies. There was a notable absence of confident and effective leadership in this period, caused partly by the general discredit of the Right and partly because there were no common positive ideas: conservatives were divided on the constitutional question – almost all the old parliamentarians, like their Radical colleagues wanted a return to the constitution of the Third Republic. In parliament they were split into six groups – *Parti Républicain de la Liberté, Républicains Indépendants, Union Démocratique des Indépendants, Action Paysanne, Action Démocratique et Sociale, Républicains Populaires Indépendants* – each with its own leader. The largest, the *Parti Républicain de la Liberté*, was led by an ageing and ineffective chairman, Michel Clemenceau, chosen more for his illustrious name rather than for his political talents. The Peasants such as Camille Laurens, declared ineligible by the Constituent Assembly because of his association with Vichy's peasant corporation but subsequently re-elected, were sometimes shrewd but always narrow men, possible components of a conservative coalition but never leaders of one. The third significant group, the Independents had considerable and loyal local followings but little to bind them together in national politics. The three best known members of the parliamentary Right all had some of the characteristics of national leaders but they were ill-equiped to federate the dispersed groups, let alone broaden the basis of conservative electoral support in the immediate post-war period. Paul Reynaud had been *Président du Conseil* in 1940: although few held him mainly responsible for the collapse of France he certainly shared in the responsibility and this tarnished his reputation. Joseph Laniel had a distinguished record and had been a member of the *Conseil National de la Résistance* but he lacked both force of character and positive ideas to qualify him as the leader of a political movement. Louis Marin, Deputy for Meurthe et Moselle since 1905 and Secretary General of the *Fédération Républicaine*, had much experience of parliamentary and electoral politics but he was a voice from the past: he was too old and too far to the Right to do more than represent the Barresian nationalist tradition.

As on previous occasions when the electorate had made a definite movement to the Left, the parliamentary Right seemed to be left stranded.[1] They were incapable of offering more than a token resis-

[1] For the parties and politics of the early Fourth Republic, see particularly

tance to any determined attack on their interests and they were largely ignored by the more powerful political forces. Their only hope lay in the division of their enemies; the divisions eventually emerged to transform their weak and vulnerable situation into one of considerable influence. The three main parties, the Socialists, Communists and Popular Republicans, succeeded in co-operating in the provisional government and in the first governments of the Fourth Republic, for nearly three years after the liberation of Paris, because they had shared the enthusiasm and the experience of the Resistance. The *esprit de la Résistance* gave a sense of common identity to men who differed radically in political principles, policies and interests. This psychological bond, although it was occasionally apparent in subsequent years, was certainly gravely weakened by the beginning of 1947 as a result of the strains of reaching major policy decisions in the system of 'tripartism'. It was virtually destroyed by the formation of the Gaullist *Rassemblement du Peuple Français*, in April 1947, and the dismissal of the Communist Ministers from government by the Socialist *Président du Conseil* Paul Ramadier in May 1947.

The international environment of the Cold War, the intent of the Communist Party in 1947 and 1948 to disrupt government and parliament, the Gaullist attack on the institutions of the Republic and the poor economic state of the country resulted in the most surprising *majorité de reflux* that a French parliament had witnessed. Confronted by Communist opposition on the Left and Gaullist opposition on the Right, the Socialists and the MRP needed the support of the Radicals and a section of the Right in order to keep the Republic in being. The most Left-wing Assembly ever elected by universal suffrage in France turned to the moderate men and parties which had survived from the previous Republic; first the Radicals were taken into the Schuman government of November 1947 and then the National Assembly invested the Radical André Marie, Deputy since 1928, as *Président du Conseil* with the Independent Paul Reynaud, Deputy since 1919, as his Minister of Finance. They were followed by the second longest surviving government of the Fourth Republic, led by the Radical Henri Queuille, Deputy since

G. Elgey, *La République des illusions, 1945–1951*, 1965. J. Fauvet, *Les Partis politiques dans la France actuelle*, 1947. P. Marabuto, *Les Partis politiques et les mouvements sociaux sous la IVᵉ République*, 1948. D. Pickles, *French Politics: the First Years of the Fourth Republic*, 1953. R. Priouret, *La République des partis*, 1947. For the whole period of the Republic see J. Fauvet, *La Quatrième République*, 1959. D. Macrae, *Parliament, Parties and Society in France, 1946–1958*, 1967. P. M. Williams, *Crisis and Compromise: the politics of the Fourth French Republic*, 1964 (this contains a comprehensive bibliography).

1914. Helped by the Socialist 'strong man' Jules Moch as Minister of the Interior, these governments bore the brunt of the attacks on the Republic, repressed violent strike action and brought some order into the finances of the State.

The electoral consequences of resisting Gaullism in the late 1940s seemed formidable. The apparently anti-parliamentary bias of Gaullism both tempted and alarmed the parliamentary Right and its supporters. The Gaullist platform of a strong State and stable government had much appeal to them but the experience of Vichy had bred a certain caution. Also accommodation with de Gaulle was made difficult by his uncompromising condemnation of Vichy and his intransigent refusal to work with Vichyites. Nevertheless, pressure to go with the Gaullist tide was considerable: Gaullist candidates received six million votes (over 40 per cent of the poll) at the local elections of October 1947. Partly because of the opportunist behaviour of Radicals and Conservatives, who accepted the Gaullist label in order to get elected, this success was not translated into a majority in the upper chamber, the *Conseil de la République*, in the elections (by indirect suffrage) in November 1948. The RPF could muster only 130 out of 320 members of the *Conseil de la République* and a maximum of about 80 for its inter-group in the National Assembly. From this point, the RPF declined and dissension broke out within its ranks – the menace of a Communist takeover seemed to recede and inflation was temporarily halted, thus removing the most powerful incentives for joining and voting for the RPF.

In the apparently unpromising circumstances of 1948, Roger Duchet launched the highly successful electoral co-ordinating body, the *Centre National des Indépendants*, which the Peasant Party subsequently joined. De Gaulle indirectly helped the CNIP by his exclusive attitude towards candidatures: after the setback of the *Conseil de la République* elections of 1948 he determined that all those who were elected in his name would be disciplined and therefore he refused all alliances with other parties. The conservatives were, as a consequence, very deeply impressed by the necessity, in order to survive, of co-operating amongst themselves and of avoiding disputes over candidatures. Taking skilful advantage of the 1951 electoral law, allowing alliances between lists of candidates, the CNIP managed to increase the number of conservative Deputies from 71 to 98 despite a drop in the vote from just over three million to just over two and a quarter million; the Radicals jumped from 43 to 76 Deputies whilst losing over 150,000 votes. The Gaullists, by comparison, with four and a quarter million votes had only 121 Deputies. The elections of 1951, even discounting the Gaullists, produced a National Assembly with a centre of gravity which was clearly much further to the Right than the previous one. The consequences were soon apparent.

At the beginning of the 1951 parliament, the Gaullists attempted to make government impossible by exploiting the clerical question. By pressing for State aid to Catholic schools, albeit indirectly, the Gaullists hoped to destroy the possibility of co-operation between the Catholic MRP and the anti-clerical Socialists, thus undermining the basis of stable government. The passage of the *loi Barangé*, giving financial assistance to families with children at the *école libre*, confirmed the Socialists in their view that a period in opposition would be good for the party. They did not participate in governments for the rest of the parliament. The true balance of the legislature was revealed when, after the short-lived Pleven and Faure governments, twenty-seven members of the Gaullist group broke discipline, ignored the General's instructions and helped to invest as *Président du Conseil* an ex-member of Vichy's National Council, Antoine Pinay, on 8 March 1952.

Prior to this investiture the Right had been instrumental in bringing down the Faure government, rebelling over concessions to nationalist sentiment in the North African protectorates and over higher taxation. Pinay was nominated by the President of the Republic ostensibly to illustrate that a government led by a man more to the Right than a member of the Radical Party was an impossibility. The opportunity to support both a tough line in the colonies and a balanced budget at home was too great a temptation for the conservative Gaullists led by Edmond Barrachin. The simple financial and economic policy which Pinay presented to the Assembly in 1952, coupled with his appearance and manner as the *Français moyen*, made him one of the two most popular *Présidents du Conseil* in the Fourth Republic. Pinay's programme can be summarised as combating inflation, stabilising prices, holding down public expenditure and defending the franc; this was identical in broad outline to Poincaré's programme in 1926. In a sense, the programme 'worked': prices stopped rising, the exchange rate of the franc against the dollar rose approximately 20 per cent, the balance of trade on current account improved dramatically, the government successfully floated a low interest loan, did not raise taxes and there was no significant increase in the number of unemployed. This formidable list of successes was made possible by an unusually favourable set of circumstances. The steady rise of industrial production since 1948, the slowing down of wage inflation, the drop in the index of raw material prices which commenced just before Pinay came to power, the ending of the inflationary boom of the Korean War, all helped to sustain the 'miracle'.

At the time critics were astonished by the success of a policy which consisted mainly in economising on public expenditure, an amnesty for tax defaulters, refusing to raise new tax revenue and repeatedly asking for a voluntary limitation on prices. His predecessor, Edgar Faure, wrote an article anonymously in *Combat* entitled 'The Politics of Magic': 'It is a fact, and a very remarkable fact, that the government, despite its inaction has obtained results. This is one of the rare cases in history when results do not correspond to any positive effort and are produced more or less in a vacuum.'[1] But the magic did not last: the MRP and the Radicals turned against him in December 1952 and he was forced to resign. He left a record budgetary deficit for his successor and his economic policy was probably ill-founded and doomed to failure in the long term, as many professional economists claimed. In other areas of policy, his government had no notable successes. The ill-fated European Defence Community treaty was signed but not brought to parliament for ratification. The situation in Morocco and Tunisia got further out of control. But impressions were more important than achievements and the impact which Pinay made on public opinion was considerable. Mendès-France was the only other *Président du Conseil* to win widespread and genuine respect, and the favour which he enjoyed with public opinion was more temporary. Pinay's reputation persisted: he was recalled by General de Gaulle in 1958 to carry through devaluation and currency reform and there was even an attempt to get him to lend his prestige to the second devaluation of the Fifth Republic in 1969.

The Republic in decay, 1954–1958

Although the Pinay government was largely a personal triumph, his party gained from it. The moderate Right had not governed with such success since the Poincaré administrations from 1926 to 1929. The Pinay government was the first real revival of the Vichyites and the damage caused to the 'Moderates' by the Vichy episode was largely repaired. The Independents and many of the Peasants began to look like a serious, tolerably united and confident party of government. Some of these gains were undermined when another Independent, Joseph Laniel, presided over the nadir of France's post-war military and diplomatic fortunes in 1954: he was snubbed by Eisenhower and Churchill at the Bermuda conference, and the

[1] Quoted J. Fauvet, op. cit., p. 199.

army in Indo-China suffered the catastrophic defeat at Dien Bien Phu, the prelude to French withdrawal from the country. But even at the time of governmental success and popularity in the country, the seeds of disaster for this particular generation of the parliamentary Right were present. In the previous parliament governmental crises had become regularised, in the 1951–5 parliament they became institutionalised, a process with recognised rules for getting round serious difficulties and policy decisions.[1] The prominent members of the parliamentary Right – Reynaud, Laurens, Pinay, Temple, Duchet, Mutter and Jacquinot – were all deeply involved in the making and unmaking of governments. Although they criticised the working of the institutions of the Fourth Republic, and these criticisms became severe and sanctimonious after 1956, this involvement in the 'poisons and delights' of the system was to their discredit and weakened their effectiveness in the long term. Government responsibilities in 1952 to 1954 were therefore a mixed blessing.

During the 1951–5 parliament, the Right's obsessions were also fully exposed. They divided it, occasionally made it virulently hostile to political opponents, and sometimes produced erratic behaviour by its individual members. These obsessions were 'irrational' fiscal demands, defence of the army and the preservation of French Algeria. The CNIP also had the misfortune of seeing the electoral threat of Gaullism disappear in 1953, after General de Gaulle officially disbanded the RPF, to be replaced by another more corrupting rival. The Poujadist movement drove some members of the CNIP both to more ignominious compromises and to a more extreme demagogy than had the threat of Gaullism. The defence of peasant, artisan and small trader interests was the most important single function of CNIP and allied Deputies. When a more aggressive movement organised tax strikes, chamber of commerce elections, resignations of local councils, demonstration in CNIP constituencies and mass meetings in the largest meeting places of Paris such as the Vélodrome d'Hiver, Independent and Peasant Deputies were intimidated. By the degree to which they were prepared to humiliate themselves to avoid losing popularity and votes, they brought discredit on themselves, on parliament and on the regime. At the sitting of 18 March 1955, Pierre Poujade was observed in the public gallery of the Assembly openly directing the tactics of a group of Independent and Peasant Deputies by word and gesture.[2] After the craven concessions of the Assembly to interest groups such as the

[1] See P. M. Williams, op. cit., ch. 29, 'Parties and Coalitions: Crisis as an Institution'.
[2] Le Monde, 19, 20 March 1955.

sugar beet lobby, on the privileges of the private distillers (the *bouilleurs de cru*), and on ex-servicemen's pensions, this was taken by many observers as final proof that the regime was incapable of taking unpopular measures. At the 1956 elections the CNIP and allies just maintained their parliamentary representation, with 97 deputies compared with 98 in 1951, although the Gaullists lost close to one hundred seats. The Poujadists had fifty-two candidates elected, although ten of these were disqualified for electoral irregularities. The CNIP had thus succeeded in maintaining its position at the cost of some of its members adopting the style and the demands of the Poujadists.

The foreign and colonial policy problems, which became intimately connected with the issue of loyalty to the regime, were crystallised during the ministry of Pierre Mendès-France from June 1954 to February 1955.[1] Mendès, a harsh critic of successive governments, had not taken office since he resigned from the provisional government at the Liberation. He brought a new style to government, promising to take unpopular decisions and to take them quickly. He was invested with a mandate to negotiate peace in Indo-China within a month and he succeeded. This decisiveness and the willingness of the *Président du Conseil* to appeal over the heads of the Deputies to the country attracted the Gaullists and a section of the Independents but it scandalised the men of the system – many Radicals and Popular Republicans and some Independents. Certain policy directions which he intended to impose were anathema to the MRP. Allowing parliament to kill the European Defence Community and admitting the rearmament of Germany through the London agreements earned him the lasting hostility of the opponents of German rearmament in all parts of the political spectrum; but some MRP leaders were particularly bitter because, since the ratification of the Schuman plan in 1950, they had adopted European integration as their only major positive aim.[2] Also, like the Gaullists and the Independents, the MRP was prepared to accept the cutting of losses in South-East Asia, and therefore welcomed the Geneva agreements. But a section of the party was intransigently opposed to the moves towards independence for Tunisia and Morocco. Hostility to Mendès, and separation from their Socialist allies in government, shifted the MRP towards the Right so that a tendency within the movement became almost indistinguishable from the 'liberal Europeans' amongst the Independents. Another tendency around Georges Bidault was gradually identified with the hardline nationalists among the Independents. Hostility to Mendès amongst the

[1] P. Rouanet, *Mendès-France au pouvoir*, 1965.
[2] R. E. M. Irving, *Christian Democracy in France*, 1972, pp. 159–98.

Radicals and the Independents was not confined to his authoritarian style and his foreign and colonial policy. He antagonised the alcohol lobby by his campaign against alcoholism and his 'economic brains trust' threatened an attack on established interests in the name of economic modernisation. As spokesmen of a range of interest groups and representatives of some of the most backward sectors of the French economy, the Independents and some fellow members of the Radical Party became violent opponents of Mendès, intent on the destruction of his reputation.

The Algerian War, whose first shots were fired during the Mendès-France period in office, was a quagmire which swallowed up virtually the whole of that section of the French Right which refused to follow de Gaulle towards a negotiated solution. Indo-China had been economically very important to France and some politicians had been very committed to keeping it within the French Union.[1] But Indo-China was a long way away and did not have the same impact on domestic French politics as Algeria. The Algerian war created new divisions, exacerbated divisions which already existed, and caused difficulties in every major party and political formation in the country. For many supporters of the war it came to have great symbolic significance, representing such things as energy, youth, struggle and suffering. Violent passions were raised and identification with the French Algeria lobby eventually drove some Moderates and a few men of the Left temporarily into the arms of the extreme Right.[2] Repression of dissident opinion, unsavoury police methods, torture of suspects by soldiers, disaffection within the army, agitation in the streets by ex-servicemen, the establishment of subversive networks, the vacillation and uncertainty of governments all created an atmosphere of alarm and insecurity, reminiscent of the 1930s. The elections of 1956 which shifted the parliamentary majority to the Left and allowed the investiture of a Socialist *Président du Conseil*, Guy Mollet, had presented the opportunity for a negotiated solution but the opportunity passed with Mollet's visit to Algeria in February 1956. Badly protected by the police, Mollet was bombarded with tomatoes by the protesting populace, withdrew the nomination of Governor General Catroux and replaced him by a Socialist partisan of French Algeria, Robert Lacoste. The parliamentary Right, thereafter gave support to Mollet's repressive policy in Algeria, but was constantly wary of the long-term intentions of the

[1] R. E. M. Irving, *The MRP and French Policy in Indo-China*, unpublished thesis 1968, p. 403.
[2] I. R. Campbell, *Political Attitudes in France to the Algerian Question, 1954–1962*, unpublished thesis, 1972, gives a full account of the divisions within parties.

government. Increasingly irritated by the social and economic policies of the government, over half the Independent Deputies joined a heterogeneous coalition of malcontents to turn Mollet out of office in May 1957 on the issue of increased taxation. The Independents and the French Algeria faction in the other parties then played a critical part in weakening the regime by first supporting the governments of the Radicals Bourgès-Maunoury and Gaillard, and then withdrawing their support because of these governments' timid proposals for reform in Algeria. The unauthorised bombing by the French army of the Tunisian village of Sakiet-Sidi-Yousef in February 1958 and the subsequent imposition of the Anglo-American good offices mission showed that the Algerian situation was virtually slipping out of the control of the French government and that the army in Algeria was only nominally under its orders.

There was not, however, a 'French Algeria' majority in the Assembly. Even in the tense days of the ministerial crisis of April 1958, the most distinguished leader of the lobby, M. Georges Bidault, failed to gain investiture as *Président du Conseil*. Maurice Duverger remarked: 'M. Bidault has rendered a considerable service to the country. His attempt has shown that the policy of the Right does not command a majority in the parliament. The cantonal elections have shown the stability of the opinions of the electorate and the majority in parliament is clearly identical with the majority of the nation.'[1] Despite this demonstration, the French Algeria minority continued to believe that a government of its persuasion could be imposed on the country. With the storming of the government headquarters in Algiers on 13 May 1958, they thought that their moment had come. On 14 July the Christian Democrat, Georges Bidault, the Independent Roger Duchet, the Radical André Morice and the Gaullist Jacques Soustelle issued a proclamation:

'In the name of the common endeavour on which we have embarked to establish a government to protect French Algeria, we the undersigned, certain of expressing the passionate conviction of innumerable Frenchmen, proclaim:
1. Algeria is and will remain French;
2. No 'cease-fire' is admissible which keeps arms in the hands of those who use them for slaughter;
3. The army of Algeria is the shield and the honour of the nation; it is wedded to Republican liberties; it is defending them, together with the integrity of its territory, at the cost of its blood.'

The statement went on to say that the formation of a government

[1] *Le Monde*, 29th April 1958.

of Union and National Safety should be formed without delay. But the holders of the key to a parliamentary majority, Pinay, Mollet and Pflimlin were convinced or soon became convinced that the return of General de Gaulle was preferable to government by the *Algérie Française* parliamentarians backed by the army. The Gaullist, Jacques Soustelle, with his escape to Algiers, played some part in rallying the army and the French Algeria lobby to a Gaullist solution, but his subsequent behaviour demonstrated that his first concern was to keep Algeria French rather than bring de Gaulle to power.

The same general question which was asked on the demise of the Third Republic in 1940, was posed again in 1958. Was the Republic assassinated or did it commit suicide?[1] The thesis of assassination and that of suicide do not necessarily conflict: they represent different emphases. There was an enormous political vacuum around the government in May 1958 and there were also various attempts to destroy the Republic. Depending on the emphasis given, the moderate and extreme Right had the greater or the lesser responsibility in the change of regime. Like one of the most influential figures of the regime, Robert Schuman, who, in 1953, complained about the impotence of a Minister faced by *faits accomplis* of colonial officials, the parliamentary Right denounced the workings of the institutions without being able to co-operate effectively with others to reform the major deficiencies of the system. Some useful procedural reforms were passed by the Fourth Republic but the regime was incapable of tackling the crucial questions of governmental authority and stability. The existence of a pool of 100 to 175 Radical and Independent Deputies, alongside the more highly organised parties, the PCF, SFIO and MRP, was a permanent encouragement to ministerial crises. The Radicals and the Independents, despite attempts to turn them into disciplined political parties with coherent programmes, remained loose collections of political clans with vague memberships and vague policy positions. The number of possible governmental coalitions multiplied dangerously without any clear policy differences existing between them. Although the most vehement critics of a system which promoted ministerial instability were members of the parliamentary Right, they were also heavily involved in it. The Deputies of the Right were also excessively sensitive to movements of public opinion, particularly in the xenophobic period from 1955 to 1958. This led them both towards demagogy and hasty withdrawal of support from governments. They usually owed their elections more

---

[1] For an extended discussion of this question see P. M. Williams, 'The Fourth Republic: murder or suicide?' in *Wars, Plots and Scandals in Post-War France*, 1970, pp. 129–166.

to their personal status in their constituency than to membership of the CNIP or any other national political group, but in their anxiety not to lose votes they voiced, sometimes crudely, the transient passions of their most vocal constituents. The notables of the CNIP often became brokers and not leaders of opinion to the detriment of their prestige and that of parliament: they undermined the system of which they were the sovereign representatives.

The extreme Right and the French Algeria lobby were involved in subversive activities, at least from the time when the first military plot (by General Faure who was sentenced to thirty days house arrest) was revealed in 1956. Immediately before the events of May 1958, the government telephone tapping service became aware of a network involving the army generals, the veterans of Indo-China and their Algerian associates, together with various picturesque conspirators of the extreme Right. This network had its parliamentary sympathisers and even associates. These conspiracies and their ramifications were mainly based on Algerian soil, amongst the European settlers and dissident army officers, but they were assisted in metropolitan France by neo-Fascists, Right-wing extremists, ex-servicemen and people carried away by the troubled and sometimes sinister atmosphere of the times. Most of the Brombergers' 'Thirteen Plots of the Thirteenth of May' came under this general counter-revolutionary heading.[1] The other main category of plots were those of the Gaullists: Debré, Soustelle, Frey, Blocq-Mascart and others, observing the accelerating decline of the institutions of the Fourth Republic brought about by the Algerian War, regarded it as the long awaited opportunity to get de Gaulle back into power. This second kind of 'plot' was based mainly in metropolitan France, but Chaban-Delmas, as Minister of Defence, had placed an agent, Léon Delbecque, in Algiers, probably to divert Fascist conspiracies. Although Gaullist representation in parliament had been drastically reduced by defections and by the elections of 1956 (in which Gaullists obtained only 2.9 per cent of the votes), there were faithful Gaullists in the *Conseil de la République* (Debré, Debû-Bridel), in the National Assembly (Koenig, Clostermann), in the government (Chaban-Delmas, Soustelle), in public service (Couve de Murville) and, to a lesser extent in the security service of the State and in the army. The Gaullists were personally of much higher calibre and had a much greater sense of the realities of power than the extremist counter-revolutionary plotters, although they were less united on the priorities of Algerian policy.

There were three crucial figures in the events surrounding the

[1] M. and S. Bromberger, *Les Treize complots du treize mai*, 1959.

return of General de Gaulle to power in May 1958. Delbecque, by his presence and skilful manoeuvring, had important influence over the army in Algiers; Guy Mollet persuaded the majority of the Socialists to accept de Gaulle and, therefore, ensured both a parliamentary majority and a broad base to de Gaulle's authority; and de Gaulle himself, by skilful diplomacy, won speedy acceptance for his return, antagonising neither the Army and the French Algeria lobby, nor those who desired both the preservation of parliamentary institutions and a negotiated solution in Algeria. The very weakness of the forces involved in May 1958 excludes any suggestion that the demise of the Fourth Republic was a revolution. Except in the city of Algiers, there was no genuine mass involvement. The demonstrators in Paris, led by the brothers Sidos of *Jeune Nation* and Yves Gignac of the *Anciens de l'Indo-Chine*, represented only several thousand hard-core activists. Electorally, the Gaullists, at this time, and the extreme Right represented only a tiny minority of the French people. The Algerian lobby in parliament was sizeable but confused, and its members had very varying degrees of commitment to the cause. The army, which was the instrument of the final breakdown of governmental authority, was not prepared to install a military regime. The Communist Party and the Left would demonstrate in favour of the 'Republic' but were not ready to defend the institutions of the Fourth Republic. There seemed to be only one man available with the intarnished reputation, the stature and the talents necessary to bring some order and authority to the situation. The Right needed an alibi and a rallying point: when both Soustelle and Pinay were appointed by de Gaulle to his government, the whole of the Right with the exception of a few eccentrics such as Pierre Poujade and some unrepentant Vichyites such as Tixier-Vignancour, followed, for several months, the last *Président du Conseil* of the Fourth Republic with, at least, feigned enthusiasm. De Gaulle led them to a great electoral victory in November 1958, but under the new Republic they were to be given the choice of subordination to his will or electoral annihilation.

CHAPTER II

Conservative Societies

All the *sociétés de la nation*[1] have influenced the nature of Right-wing politics in France. The attempt to describe and assess the significance of families, informal networks, social classes, ethnic groups, regional cultures, educational institutions, business enterprises, friendly societies and social clubs is a venerable and difficult exercise. '*La France est variété*,' wrote Lucien Febvre, and it is a variety which has been constantly changing, even between the two World Wars when France was superficially a static 'Malthusian' society. The connections between aspects of the social structure on the one hand, and political action and behaviour on the other, are often tenuous and obscure. For example, a general interpretation of Right-wing politics in terms of social class is difficult and speculative. To assign particular populations to broad social classes, such as the proletariat, the bourgeoisie and the peasantry, and to describe the politicians elected or acting on behalf of these populations as, in some sense, representing their class interests, is highly schematic and arbitrary.

This is neither to deny the reality of classes, which a certain Republican orthodoxy during the Third Republic sought to do, nor to ignore the powerful emotions occasionally raised by class loyalties. At the most general level, classes can be defined and characteristics ascribed them, but the existing socio-economic data, whether provided by survey or census, are not very informative about the composition and functions of social classes. Identification of classes and class interest in terms of 'objective' criteria is probably impossible. But certain perceptions of the class system have been deeply entrenched. Left-wing, particularly Socialist, politicians in the Third

---

[1] The phrase is from E. Martin-Saint-Léon, *Les Sociétés de la nation*, 1930. Two outstanding recent works which analyse relationships between political and social change are G. Dupeux, *La Société française, 1789–1960*, 1964. P. Sorlin, *La Société française, 1840–1968*, 2 vols, 1969, 1971.

and Fourth Republics have regarded classes, if not as monolithic blocs, as having a high degree of cohesion and, consequently, have often referred to them in the singular – *la classe ouvrière, la paysannerie, la bourgeoisie, la noblesse*. On the Right, the use of the plural was more common – *les classes laborieuses, les classes moyennes, les classes aisées* – indicating that classes were rather miscellaneous groupings. The distinction between Right and Left in terms of views on social classes has never been clear cut: perceptive Marxists have observed many and subtle intra-class divisions, whilst some *patrons de combat* have had simple, almost vulgar Marxist, views on social conflicts. Perceptions of class by people in the same social category have varied considerably from one period to another and they have also been affected by the type of community in which people have lived.

The political importance of class resides in the strength of class identification. Class consciousness has been particularly influential in periods when there has been acute awareness that ways of life are being undermined and when there has been an overt threat to the social status quo. From the early nineteenth century the fear of proletarian or popular revolution among middle-class groups has been fairly constant. Although in the twentieth century the possibility of such a revolution has, with the possible exception of the Liberation period, been slight, repeated violent strikes and incidents have kept bourgeois *paniquards* in a constant state of alarm. The reactions to the strikes of *la belle époque*, the long struggle against income-tax and social legislation before the First World War, the politics of 'bourgeois defence' after it, the nature of the opposition to the Popular Front in 1936 and the ostracising of the Communist Party after the Second World War illustrate a wide, persistent and highly developed 'bourgeois' class consciousness. But it has never been uniformly expressed: during all these periods of social tension, spokesmen for the *classes moyennes* – usually defined rather vaguely as 'all those between the proletariat and the capitalists'[1] – have claimed interests different from the large employers of labour and, indeed, to belong to a different social class. The very obvious division within the bourgeoisie has tempted some sociologists, such as Jesse Pitts, to establish a general scheme and divide the bourgeoisie into categories using the labels in common usage, *la haute, la bonne* and *la petite bourgeoisie*.[2] This is an attractive way of bringing some

---

[1] Definition adopted by authors as widely separated as E. Martin-Saint-Léon, *Le Problème des classes moyennes en France*, 1903 and G. Lecordier, *Les classes moyennes en marche*, 1950.

[2] J. R. Pitts, 'Continuity and Change in Bourgeois France' in S. Hoffman (ed.), *France: Change and Tradition*, 1963, pp. 235–304.

order into a highly complex social reality, but classifying groups and occupations into these three categories must be either arbitrary or done on the basis of their general reputation which could be determined by conducting opinion polls. The relationship between the status hierarchy revealed by surveys and the actual behaviour of social groups would pose difficult problems of interpretation, and it is doubtful whether it is a fruitful line of enquiry.

The social bases of conservative politics have a kaleidoscopic quality. The significance and importance of the pieces which make up the pattern change according to the perspective adopted and the moment when they are examined. Particular elements of the social context in which conservative politicians have been operating must be examined over an extended period of time in order to obtain some impression of the way in which these elements interrelate. However difficult it is to define their membership, some bourgeois and peasant groups have been of fundamental importance in moulding conservative political action. Traditions associated with old institutions – the Church, the army and the aristocracy – have exerted a powerful influence over conservative attitudes. But, until the Fifth Republic, the most obvious general characteristics of conservative societies and Right-wing politics was localism. Attachment to locality and the bewildering variety of local social situations resulted in the dominance of local considerations in electoral politics. National political issues were often seen through a distorting prism of local affiliations and conflicts.

Localism: Paris
Parisian political life has a paradoxical nature. Nowhere else in France has the electorate been so sensitive to national moods. Yet conservative politicians have been able to establish strong personal positions based on an intimate knowledge of their constituencies and on the provision of favours and services for individuals and interest groups. Issues of parish pump politics and great national issues have uneasily co-existed, intermeshing in various obscure patterns. On the Right, political agility and willingness to adapt to changed circumstances has often been required for survival, giving politicians like Joseph Denais, Bernard Lafay and Frédéric-Dupont reputations for cynicism rarely rivalled by their provincial colleagues.

The city itself, feared by rulers of the nineteenth century as the arbiter of regimes, acquired the reputation, after the establishment of the Third Republic, of having the most volatile electorate in the country. It was dominated by the Radicals in 1880, but the temporary inroads made by the Boulangists in 1889 were followed by the most overwhelming success the Left was ever to achieve. In 1893, only four out of the thirty-three Deputies elected for the city (the *Ville de Paris*) belonged to the Right. In the municipal elections of 1900 and the general election of 1902, the Nationalists won a third of the votes and were able to swing the municipal council and the majority of the parliamentary seats (twenty-three to seventeen in Seine) to the Right. The collapse of the main Nationalist organisation, the *Ligue de la Patrie Française*, helped the Radicals and Socialists to return to their majority position in the municipal elections of 1904 and the general election of 1906.[1] By 1914, Right and Left were more or less in equilibrium and in the inter-war years the balance oscillated: the Right dominated the elections of 1919, 1928 and 1932, and the Left the elections of 1924 and 1936. The centre of gravity of the Left was moving towards the suburbs, establishing the celebrated 'red belt'. For example, in the 1924 elections the *Bloc National* won nineteen city seats and only five suburban seats, whereas the Left captured fourteen seats in the Ville de Paris and fifteen in the suburbs. After the Second World War, the capital tended to exaggerate national trends. The electorate gave overwhelming support to the parties of *tripartisme* (Communist Party, Socialist Party and MRP) in the elections of 1945–6, showed a marked tendency to go to extremes in 1951 (seventeen RPF and nineteen Communist Deputies in Seine) and in 1956, whilst the Communist Party retained its strength, the Mendèsiste Radicals had considerable success with thirteen Deputies elected; the extreme Right also got a foothold with the election of the Poujadists, Dides and Le Pen.

In the Fifth Republic the Gaullists have dominated, establishing such a strong position in the city itself that the Left has been reduced to an impotent rump. The non-Gaullist conservatives, using national-ist slogans and their great local knowledge, resisted well in 1958 but the Gaullists nonetheless won twenty-four seats out of thirty-three in Seine. They progressed to win forty-one seats, including all the city seats, in 1962. In the 1967 election there was, as in the country as a whole, a decline in their strength: they retained twenty-one out of thirty-one city constituencies but won only fourteen out of thirty in the suburbs. The reaction against the events of 1968, how-ever, brought them all but one of the seats in the city.

The political sociology of Paris has yet to be written but there is little doubt that the capital during the last century has had a floating vote of considerable proportions.[2] Tens of thousands of voters have

[1] D. R. Watson, 'The Nationalist Movement in Paris, 1900–1906', St Antony's Papers, No. 13, 1962, pp. 49–84.

[1] For the political sociology of the capital see L. Giard, *Les Elections à Paris,*

had no stable political loyalties. National moods, fashionable opinion, political clubs and extra-parliamentary leagues have apparently had greater effect in Paris than in provincial France. The approximate size of this volatile mass is difficult to assess over any long period of time because of the very complex and considerable population movements in the capital. The broad brush strokes of historical demography – the pushing of the working class out of the central and western *arrondissements* in the nineteenth century and the penetration of middle-class groups into the horseshoe formed by the northern, eastern and southern *arrondissements*, particularly after the Second World War – give a very general background to voting behaviour.[1] The long Rightward drift of the city can be broadly explained in terms of the changing class composition of the population: the Left-wing vote declined as the proportion of voters in the higher income groups increased. This kind of general observation obscures interesting and important details such as the powerful middle-class Left-wing groups, particularly the intellectuals, and the success of certain Right-wing campaigns – anti-Semitic, monarchist and nationalist – in some working-class milieux. Moreover, it does not provide a starting point for any kind of explanation of the particular forms taken by the Parisian Right. Local, personal, historical factors have been the most important influence over these forms.

From the late nineteenth century, the Right in Paris has had a sedimentary character. Men have been launched in their political careers by particular crises and issues: by skill and good fortune, some have always managed to survive the next wave of politicians, brought to office by a new movement or mood. Thus, in the decade before the First World War, among the Deputies of Paris were a reluctant *rallié*, privately retaining monarchist sentiments, Denys Cochin; the Christian Democratic member of *Action Libérale Populaire*, Jean Lerolle; ex-Boulangists such as Lucien Millevoye and Maurice Barrès; a moderate Republican *Progressiste*, Charles Benoist (later a convert to monarchism); and nationalists such as Tournade, Failliot and Roche. Again, in the late 1950s, the Deputies and municipal councillors grouped in the autonomous *Centre des Indépendants et Républicains Nationaux* (affiliated to the CNIP), contained pre-war survivals, supporters of Vichy, wartime and RPF

1871–1939, unpublished *mémoire*, 2 vols, n.d. F. Goguel, 'Structure sociale et répartition des votes dans les élections du 17 juin 1951', *Revue française de science politique*, vol. 1, 1951, pp. 326–33. *Paris et sa région*, Association française de science politique, 1966.

[1] P. Ariés, *Histoire des populations françaises*, 1971, pp. 135–98.

Gaullists, dissenting Poujadists and activists recruited before and after 13 May 1958. The success of the Gaullists in parliamentary and, to a lesser extent, in municipal elections has transformed this sedimentary character. The diversity of party labels and allegiances had been replaced by 'generations' of Gaullists. Whilst differences of generation have created diversity within the Gaullist Party, they do not have the same significance as they had for the old Right. The independence of outlook and action of the conservatives of the Third and Fourth Republics has been replaced by a less personal style of representation.

Until the 1960s, the careers, role and influence of Parisian Deputies have been intertwined with those of municipal councillors because of the close relationship between national and local government in the capital. With less power but more prestige than in provincial towns, the municipal council has nevertheless been the fulcrum of the organised interests in the city. Deputies of the pre-Gaullist Right often had long careers as municipal councillors and almost always had close relations and a following among the councillors. Both the constitutional position of Paris government and the pressure of interest groups helped to keep the Paris Deputies localist in attitude. As late as the beginning of the Fifth Republic, Deputies of the Right such as Frédéric-Dupont on the Left Bank and Jacques Féron in the 8th *arrondissement* were considered very much as representatives of their *quartiers*. This closely reflected long established social patterns: many of the *quartiers* were urban villages with their own special activities and atmosphere and in which people both lived and worked.[1] These urban villages have, however, been breaking up since the beginning of the economic revival after the Second World War. Their particularity has been undermined by urban redevelopment, by new styles of housing and by the spread of commercial and administrative activities to new areas of the city resulting in the loss of residents in some *quartiers*. Until the Fifth Republic, however, social and political factors encouraged the surprisingly parochial nature of Parisian politics.

Other factors, which have hindered Parisian Deputies in assuming roles of national leadership, relate to the place of the capital in the national social system. The inexorable demographic growth to the point where one sixth of the nation live in the Paris conurbation, the concentration of intellectual, administrative and political activities in the capital and its overwhelming dominance as a financial and commercial centre have long been denounced but have proven very difficult to remedy. Certain attitudes, even complexes, about the

[1] L. Chevallier, *Les Parisiens*, 1967, pp. 135–7.

over-mighty capital are commonly found among provincial Frenchmen:

'... Parisians are usually regarded as pretentious, boastful big talkers; as superficial and convinced that they are intelligent simply because they live in Paris; as frivolous and incapable of taking an interest in anything but futilities. Knowing nothing at any serious level, not even their own city, they are vicarious observers, always agitated and in a hurry, and living like madmen. If their private lives ... are their own concern, their public life, unfortunately, concerns the whole country: in this domain they are taken in by the most crass appearances, rush to extremes, give themselves up to great enthusiasm only to sink subsequently into the depths of indifference. They substitute passion for good sense and transform politics into a kind of game of love and chance.[1]

These kinds of images of Parisians have a long history and politicians of the Right born in and representing the capital have suffered from them.

A provincial background is no handicap to a successful career in the capital. Parisian origins, particularly *bourgeoises* and *haute-bourgeoises* arouse suspicion and hostility in the provinces. The only Right-wing Minister in the twentieth century to flaunt his Parisian origins, André Tardieu, was damaged politically as a consequence.[2] Political movements, as well as individuals, have been affected by close association with Paris. Extra-parliamentary movements of the Right often originated and were based in Paris. This probably limited the impact in the provinces of such movements as *Action Française* (despite the Provençal birth and connections of Maurras), the *Jeunesses Patriotes*, the *Centre de Propagande* of Kérillis, and the groups of the extreme Right in the 1950s.[3] Successful electoral organisations have been firmly rooted in the provinces. Roger Duchet, for example, built the CNIP by first approaching the provincial notables and the Parisian Independents retained a separate organisation. Paris-based national organisations such as the *Bloc National* of 1919 and 1924 were usually superstructures which

[1] ibid., pp. 7–8.

[2] In 1932, on the first occasion that radio was used in an election campaign, Tardieu caused great offence by remarking in a broadcast 'coming from a Parisian family with three hundred years of local heredity ... I talk to you this evening from the house where I was born and in which I have lived for fifty-five years'. He was standing as a candidate for Belfort.

[3] The attempts of the leagues to develop their organisations in the provinces often seemed to strengthen the Left. See, for example, B. Marienne, *Sociologie électorale de la Somme de 1919 à 1939*, unpublished *mémoire*, 1962.

made little real impact in the provinces. Activists and intellectuals of the Right, like many journalists, often held the view that provincial opinion could be moulded and led from Paris. Astute electoral tacticians understood very well the limitations of this view.

Major figures of the parliamentary Right have inevitably had Parisian connections – a family apartment or *pied-à-terre*, professional or business associations. But they have almost always been identified with a province as, for example, the *princes de Lorraine*, Poincaré, Marin, Jacquinot, Mondon, or Bretons like L'Estourbeillon, La Ferronays, Marcellin and Pleven, or men of the North such as the abbé Lemire, Jean Plichon and Bertrand Motte. Amongst the old Right, Paul Reynaud was an exceptional case: born in Basses-Alpes, he was first elected (1919) for that *département*, which he deserted in favour of Paris (1928), and terminated his career as Deputy for Nord (1946–62). Carpetbaggers or *parachutés* were relatively rare on the Right and their experiences generally unhappy until the dearth of suitable local candidates and the relatively large number of 'technocrats' and Parisian professional men among their supporters made the Gaullists put up men without strong local connections. The Gaullists also seem to have made some attempt to break down the tradition of strong local connections. De Gaulle himself, despite his Parisian childhood and youth, always sought to keep his distance from the Parisian establishment and Colombey-les-Deux-Eglises was an important part of the Gaullist imagery. President Pompidou assiduously draws attention to his Auvergnat origins and connections. But the national nature of the Gaullist support makes it feasible to 'parachute' for example, an Alsatian in Brittany without necessarily diminishing the chances of electoral success. Gaullist candidates who do not come from the locality, perhaps uncertain about the importance of this, often find a convenient grandparent or cousin who has local connections. However, the relatively large proportion of non-local candidates in the Gaullist ranks will probably tend to increase the number of Deputies who originate from the capital.

The careers and prestige of members of parliament of the Right have not apparently corresponded to the prestige and demographic importance of the capital. But the impact of Paris on conservative politics in general extends far beyond the influence of its elected representatives. The Right has been connected with a large number of groups and institutions which have been Paris based. Not only the myriad of extra-parliamentary political associations, but also ex-servicemen's leagues, industrial and agricultural pressure groups and Catholic organisations have had their headquarters in Paris and conducted most of their important business there. Also many institutions, including all the important ones, not overtly associated with the Right but which are powerful defenders of the social status quo – such as the *grands corps de l'État*, the senior civil service, the Académie Française, the judiciary and the army high command – have been concentrated in Paris. The city therefore has an important place in the history of the Right and associations with conservative interests of considerable complexity. However, for many provincial conservatives, despite the voting behaviour of the capital in recent years, Paris has not completely lost its reputation for being the source of potentially destructive innovation.

Localism: the examples of Brittany, Alsace and Basses-Pyrénées
The ethnic diversity of France has had little significance for national unity, despite various incidents in the frontier provinces during the Second World War. Some French politicians and administrators, it is true, have shown extraordinary alarm and concern about particularist sentiments, especially in frontier provinces. For example, when the abbé Gantois, leader of the Flemish league in France during the Second World War, had purged his prison sentence for Collaboration, he was forbidden to reside in the four *départements* where the Vlaamsh Verbond had been active (Nord, Pas-de-Calais, Somme, Aisne), the five Breton *départements*, the two Alsatian *départements*, and the frontier *départements* of Moselle, Savoie, Haute-Savoie, Alpes-Maritimes, Pyrénées-Orientales and Basses-Pyrénées.[1] In all these areas autonomists were active, but not on a scale which had any substantial irredentist or separatist implications. The violence of the Breton autonomists in the 1930s and again in the 1960s caused scandal and publicised regional discontents but the direct political impact has been negligible.

A common characteristic of provinces on the periphery of the country is the relative survival of local languages and patois. Since the spread of the railway network in the nineteenth century and the introduction of universal primary education, local languages and patois have generally been in retreat. Their use was very actively discouraged in the school system in the Third Republic. Although there has been some modification of attitudes since the Second World War, the speaking of local languages has usually been associated with the old-fashioned, the uneducated and the reactionary. The persistence of these linguistic practices is indicative of a state of mind and of fidelity to the traditions of the *petit pays*. These traditions are often of a very conservative kind and the contribution of the

[1] P. Sérant, *La France des minorités*, 1965, p. 83.

KEY·

RENNES = Prefecture
ERSTEIN = Sub-Prefecture
Bidache = Administrative centre of Canton

Inhabitants of
administrative
centre of Canton

△ less than 3 000
□ 3.000+
⊙ 5 000+
∅ 10 000+
⊠ 20 000+
● 30 000+
◉ 100 000+

BRITTANY

peripheral provinces to conservative politics has been considerable.[1]

Brittany, the largest of them, has made the most substantial contribution. Until the Fifth Republic, when it was surpassed by Paris, more Deputies of the Right came from Brittany than any other region. It was not a region greatly influenced by the main currents of ideas of the nineteenth century and throughout the Third Republic was considered remote and backward, rural and conservative. In a classic text on the Breton character Le Goffic wrote:

'Brittany is a country of the past. Nowhere else have manners retained such a penetrating perfume of the archaic, of nobility and of old-fashioned charm. On this advanced promontory of the world, shrouded in an eternal dusk, life is permeated with mystery.'[2]

The general political impression in the first half of the Third Republic was, in André Siegfried's words, *'catholique, clérical, conservateur et d'esprit peu républicain'*.[3] Beneath this general impression there was considerable diversity; monarchist, ultra-Catholic, moderate conservative, Boulangist or Nationalist, moderate Republican and Radical populations co-existed in the Breton peninsula. Siegfried, for the period before 1914, emphasised the general contrast between the towns which tended to be Republican and the more conservative countryside. In the countryside, however, there was a marked difference in western Brittany between Republican Cornouaille (Brittany's 'red belt') and the 'clerical democracy' of Léon. The priests of Léon were probably of the very few genuine examples of clericalism in France; drawn from the better off peasants known as *julots* they exercised a dominance over their parishioners which allowed them, in elections of the 1890s, to deliver the vote for the Social Catholics, Albert de Mun and the abbé Gayraud,[4] against the opposition of bishops and nobility. The eastern half of the province tended to be more conservative. In Loire Inférieure – excepting Saint-Nazaire –

---

[1] Only electorally important areas are discussed in this chapter. There are interesting smaller areas such as Maurienne in Savoie. See P. Rambeaud, *Economie et sociologie de la montagne: Albiez-le-vieux en Maurienne*, 1964. S. Hugonnier, 'Tempéraments politiques et géographie électorale des deux grandes vallées des Alpes du nord: Maurienne et Tarantaise', *Revue de géographie alpine*, vol. 42, 1954, pp. 45–80.

[2] C. Le Goffic, *L'Ame bretonne*, 1902, p. 1.

[3] A. Siegfried, *Tableau politique de la France de l'Ouest*, 1913, p. 504.

[4] The elections of de Mun in 1893 and Gayraud in 1897, both for constituencies in Finistère, aroused considerable national interest because of the decisive role of the clergy. See particularly, 'Enquête sur l'élection de M. Gayraud', *Chambre des Députés – Débats. Annexe, 24 mai 1897*, pp. 12881–12890. Abbé Trochu, *Trente-cinq années de politique religieux*, 1936.

Nantes and the Loire valley, a solid majority voted for aristocratic notables who retained monarchist sympathies until the Second World War even though not often expressed openly. Ille-et-Vilaine, excepting the monarchist centre of Vitry and an ultra Catholic fringe in the west, was *ni franc-maçon ni jésuite*, prudent in religious practice and expressing the kind of moderate conservatism in politics usually associated with Normandy.[1] Within these typical temperaments of some of the *pays* of Brittany, there were many variations, and eccentric populations which stood out against the majority attitudes. The persistence of political outlooks at least from early in the Third Republic has been remarkable: in the Fifth Republic they have been obscured at the parliamentary level by the Gaullist dominance but can still be discerned in cantonal and municipal elections.

The demographic evolution of the province, unusual not only in France but in western Europe, and the regional economic development partially explains the political peculiarities of the region. Despite heavy emigration and a high mortality rate in the nineteenth century the maximum population was not reached until 1911: the province maintained an unusually high birth rate whilst that of France and western Europe was falling. In 1911, the urban population (26 per cent) was well below the national level (44 per cent) but the density of the population was about a quarter higher than the national density. Industrialisation was very slow and small artisanal enterprises proliferated. Although 325,000 *établissements industriels* were recorded in the industrial census of 1896, only a quarter of Bretons worked in industrial occupations in 1911. Large-scale industry was restricted to the mouth of the Loire. Commercial and industrial wealth were, therefore, virtually absent from Brittany and, despite technological change, the period from 1880 to 1914 was one of consolidation of social and political structures inherited from the past.[2] The social authority of the priests and the nobility, particularly the resident nobility, was preserved for much longer in Brittany than elsewhere in France with the exception of *départements* bordering on Brittany – Vendée, Maine-et-Loire, Mayenne – and very small areas elsewhere in *départements* such as Lozère, Hérault, Ardèche and Aveyron.

The Right-wing Deputies elected from Brittany before the First World War belonged to all ranks of the aristocracy, for example,

[1] Monseigneur Perrin, 'Un Exemple de géographie religieuse: les vocations sacerdotales en Ille-et-Vilaine', *Economie et humanisme*, 1947, pp. 523–9.

[2] G. Le Guen, 'L'Evolution conservatrice, 1880–1914' in J. Delumeau (ed.), *Histoire de Bretagne*, 1969, pp. 464–88.

Duke de Rohan, Prince de Léon, Marquis de La Ferronays, Marquis de l'Estourbeillon, Baron Ginoux-Defermon, Baron Le Gonidec Traisson, Count de Lanjuinais and Count de Largentaye.[1] The aristocracy occupied an important place in local government: in 1909, 216 mayors out of a total of 1,500, 67 *conseillers généraux* out of 216 were nobles.[2] The aristocracy began to lose its position after the First World War but a dominant figure like the Marquis de la Ferronays not only kept his seat but retained a wide political influence in Loire-Inférieure and even in Morbihan, until the Second World War. Compromise with Vichy weakened the position of the aristocracy still further although some of the prominent members of the Breton nobility, such as the Duke de Rohan, were in Resistance networks. After the war Loire-Inférieure continued to send some aristocrats such as Grandmaisons and Sesmaison to parliament but they were relatively rare in the Breton *départements*.

Left-wing politicians tended to dismiss the noble Deputies of the west *en bloc* as *fin de race* aristocrats. But there were many divergences within the milieu both noticed and resented in the region. There were differences between the *grands seigneurs* such as the Rohan, and *hobereaux* (squires) like the Halgoüet (whose family fortunes were much restored by a marital alliance with the Wendel family of steelmasters), who both supplied more than one Deputy for the Morbihan; between the resident, the intermittently resident and non-resident; between those whose only wealth was in land and those whose interests extended, often by marriage, into industry and finance. These differences were sometimes expressed in different political options. Legitimist fidelities, for example, tended to die harder in the resident nobility whose modest fortunes were almost entirely bound up in land. The tendency towards reactionary extremism persisted among the poorer *hobereaux* of the west down to the 1960s when some were implicated in the Secret Army Organisation, the last ditch defenders of French Algeria. After the *Ralliement* they contrasted with most of the aristocratic Deputies of the region who were undifferentiated conservatives. The Deputies did not publicise their monarchist convictions, if they still retained them, and, despite private reservations about Catholic dogma, always presented themselves in public as defenders of the Catholic Church. There were eccentric personalities among them such as nationalist motor car pioneer, Marquis de Dion, and the regionalist Marquis de l'Estourbeillon, but most preferred to avoid positions and actions

---

[1] For the genealogy of the Breton aristocracy see H. de la Messelière, *Filiations bretonnes*, 1913, reprinted 1965.

[2] G. Le Guen, op. cit., p. 482.

which might alienate potential voters. The luxury of sympathising in public with *Action Française* was usually left to those who played no part in electoral politics or whose ambitions did not extend beyond the local level.

Cracks in the traditional alliance between chateau and presbytery were apparent from the 1890s when Christian Democratic ideas first got a significant foothold among the lower clergy. There were bitter local battles between aristocratic politicians and democratical priests and a long, slow general deterioration of relations. The first signs of Right-wing anti-clericalism appeared after the papal condemnation of *Action Française* in 1926. In the post Second War period a bitter anti-clericalism was apparent in some *hobereaux* families, particularly those with a military tradition. The clergy were very active in the agricultural unions, in encouraging the Catholic trade unions and in supporting the MRP, many of whose leaders had commenced their careers in Catholic Action (and there were few nobles even among the *droitiers* of the MRP). None of these activities appealed to the aristocratic notables and were, on occasion, against their interests. The old alliance eventually degenerated into mistrust as a result of the attitude of the clergy towards decolonisation, particularly towards Algeria.

Although the local prestige of the clergy and its relationship with the aristocracy varied considerably, the support of the clergy was essential for the maintenance of the political position of the aristocratic notables. The great days of opposition to anti-clerical measures, which preserved the relative unity of the Right and maintained the old alliance, were over by the end of the First World War. On a more limited front, the defence of the *école libre* survived as an issue until the beginning of the Fifth Republic. Where there was a socially powerful aristocracy as in Morbihan, Loire-Inférieure and part of Ille-et-Vilaine, the priests continued to seek the support of the *châtelain*. Where its influence was waning the seeds of mutual disillusion and of conflict were present. The clergy seemed consciously trying to create a new kind of notable in Catholic Action and in the agricultural unions, who would replace the *châtelain*. In Brittany the class which usually replaced the nobility in parliamentary elections was neither the agrarian syndicalists nor the Catholic militants but the old bourgeoisie – doctors, *notaires*, *avocats*, officers and *rentiers*. These professional middle-class groups had lived without too much tension with the nobility, tending to be only a little more 'advanced' in general political position. The best known bourgeois Deputies of the Right of the first half of the Third Republic were René Brice and Le Hérissé. They were *progressistes*, liberal, anti-Radical and usually very anti-Socialist. In the Fifth Republic, René Pleven[1] and Raymond Marcellin are, in different ways, in the same tradition as Brice and Le Hérissé. The moderately conservative 'bourgeois' Deputies of Brittany have almost always been marked much more by personal idiosyncracy than by strong ideological commitments.

The changeover from aristocratic Right to bourgeois Right in Brittany was not, however, altogether smooth. In elections following both World Wars there was a surge to the Left. The 1919 elections produced a surprising result, partly because of the complex transition between the two social groups. Against a national trend, the Left had, for the first time, a majority of the Breton Deputies. Of a total of forty-five Deputies, twenty-four were members of the Left-wing coalition, the *Union Républicaine*. The divisions of the Right were not as damaging in 1924 and only Trégor, Haute Cornouaille and the Loire estuary produced Left-wing majorities. In 1936 the Popular Front could only muster between 20 per cent and 35 per cent of the votes in the Breton *départements*. A similar general evolution took place in the post Second World War period. A balance in favour of the Left-wing parties in the 1945–6 elections as a result of the dis-organisation of the Right was converted into a preponderance of CNIP and RPF Deputies in 1951 with the MRP and the *Union Démo-cratique et Sociale de la Résistance* (led in Brittany by René Pleven) maintaining strong positions. The Left retained seats (five Com-munists and four others in 1956) but in the Fifth Republic they were swept away. In 1958, in the newly defined Breton administrative region (which excluded Loire-Atlantique), no Socialist, Radical or Communist was successful whilst six Gaullists, seven CNIP and twelve MRP and Plevenists were elected. There was a slight revival of the Left in 1967 when it won three seats: the Left as a whole maintained its voting strength and the Communists increased theirs, but the electoral system of single-member constituencies worked against them. The MRP and the Plevenists declined in number at each election from twelve in 1958, ten in 1962, eight in 1967 to four in 1968. René Pleven saw the end in sight, rallied to the regime and joined the Chaban-Delmas government in 1969 as Minister of Justice. The Gaullists, including after 1962 the *Giscardien* Inde-pendent Republicans who, led by Raymond Marcellin, dominated Morbihan, went from strength to strength: six in 1958, fourteen in 1962, and twenty-one in 1968 (84 per cent of the representation of the region. The Gaullists did not make much inroad into the 'red belt' of central Brittany and the coastal zones of Trégor and Cor-nouaille, but they gathered most of the Right-wing vote and virtually

[1] Pleven was, however, an ally of the Socialists in the Fourth Republic.

extinguished the notables in elections to the National Assembly, with the exception of those, who, like René Pleven, rallied to them.

An electoral history of Brittany, however, gives a narrow perspective on the political system of the region. It indicates certain broad trends – longstanding political divisions between 'Republicans' and 'Chouans', between Left and Right, the replacement of aristocratic notables by bourgeois notables in the inter-war and post Second World War periods, and a region ripe for Gaullist picking in the Fifth Republic. Examined in detail, the parliamentary election campaigns, of course, show other things – the painful establishment of Christian Democracy in Brittany, occasional popular revolts against the notables, the rise of 'peasant' politics in various forms, the slow decline in the role of the priests – but even with these embellishments the features which give an unusual quality to the regional political system do not stand out.

In Brittany there has been a great proliferation of groups and associations of all kinds – cultural, political, social and economic. These may not have intervened much in elections and not exercised great influence when they did but, nevertheless, they could occasionally exert considerable pressure. Collectively they added an important dimension to Breton politics. The *Association Bretonne*, a society of Breton erudites founded in 1843, which lived some dangerous moments during the Second Empire when it was considered the centre of Legitimist opposition, is a venerable example. The first great flowering of Breton associations took place at the turn of the twentieth century. The *Union Régionaliste Bretonne* was founded in 1898 and in the fifteen years which followed a number of groups were established – *Gorsedd des Bordes*, *Bleu-Brug*, *Fédération Régionaliste Bretonne* and the first modern militant autonomist league, *Breiz Dishuel*. The *Breton mouvement* languished during and immediately after the first World War although the *Action Libérale* Deputy, the Marquis de l'Estourbeillon, President of the *Union Régionaliste Bretonne*, petitioned President Woodrow Wilson at the 1919 Peace Conference, on behalf of the Breton organisations, for recognition of the rights of the Breton people. This caused a small scandal but had no consequences. In the 1920s there was a revival of the autonomist movement with the establishment of the *Parti National Breton* and the clandestine terrorist organisation, *Gwenn Ha Du*. This latter organisation was responsible for, amongst other outrages, blowing up in 1932 the monument in Rennes, symbolising the union of Brittany and France on the fourth centenary of the act of union.[1]

[1] G. Leclerc, *Le mouvement breton de 1914 à nos jours*, 1968, pp. 7–11. Also

During the Second World War the autonomist movement was badly compromised with Collaboration and the more moderate regionalist movement with Vichy. The propaganda of the Vichy regime encouraged the revival of sentimental attachment to the old provinces of France. Brittany was one of the few areas where this had practical results. Yann Fouéré, through the columns of his newspaper, *la Bretagne*, reached a wide audience (much wider than the autonomist and Collaborationist, *l'Heure bretonne*) and rallied regionalist sentiment to the regime. An energetic regional Prefect, Jean Quenette, helped to create a regional assembly, the *Comité Consultatif de Bretagne*.[1] Some encouragement was given to the Breton language and Breton cultural activities. Despite the severe toll of the regionalist movement (especially the autonomist faction) taken by the purge at the Liberation, the old Breton associations, *Bleun-Brug*, *Gorsedd des Bordes*, *Fédération Régionaliste Bretonne* – all re-emerged in the years immediately after the war and there was a noticeable increase in Breton cultural activity around the *Cercles Celtiques*.

After the Second World War, 'Breton consciousness' helped the formation of a relatively efficient lobby to defend regional economic interests.[2] The autonomist movement in the inter-war period stressed an allegedly persistent, and perhaps deliberate, exploitation of Brittany by 'France'. In was not, however, until 1950 that a broadly based and respected organisation, the *Comité d'Etudes et de Liaison des Intérêts Bretons* (CELIB), was formed to defend and promote regional economy. The President of the committee was René Pleven, a wartime Gaullist, Deputy of Côtes-du-Nord, *Président du Conseil* of the Fourth Republic and, eventually, a Minister in the Fifth Republic. The membership of the committee included almost all the Deputies and Senators of the region as well as 'personalities' and representatives of interest groups. Its secretary was an economist, Martray, who like Pleven rallied to Gaullism in the Fifth Republic. The most committed regionalists thought that CELIB did not have a sufficiently 'political' programme – essential, in their view, for the effective defence of Breton interests. Yann Fouéré founded the *Mouvement pour l'Organisation de Bretagne* (MOB) in 1957 and a new journal, *l'Avenir*, to present a more determined form of regionalism. Shortly afterwards the *Union Démocratique de Bretagne* (UDB) was

Parti National Breton, *Notre lutte pour la Bretagne, notre histoire, nos idées, nos buts*, 1941.

[1] Y. Fouéré, *La Bretagne écartelée. Essai pour servir à l'histoire de dix ans, 1938–1948*, 1962. Y. Gicqel, *Le Comité consultatif breton*, 1960.

[2] G. Dargnies, *L'Action régionale et l'opinion en Bretagne*, unpublished thesis, 1966, especially pp. 40–53.

established with a similar intent but with a Left-wing orientation: the most intellectually distinguished of contemporary regionalists, Michel Phlipponneau, joined this group after his disillusionment with CELIB.[1] An activist organisation, the *Front de Libération de Bretagne*, appeared in the late 1950s prepared to engage in bomb outrages and acts of sabotage: the most spectacular was the destruction of the garage of the riot police (CRS) in Saint-Brieuc. When the police began to break up the FLB networks from 1968, the youth and the range of social backgrounds of the participants came as a considerable surprise to the public.[2]

None of these organisations made any electoral impression but they are symptoms of sentiments of exclusion and even discrimination which have been widespread in the region. In 1961, René Pleven, always a very moderate regionalist, wrote:

'... Breton patriotism, co-habiting with French patriotism in every Breton bosom, is neither separatist nor nationalist and it has suddenly reawakened. Bretons have realised that, since 1911, the population of the four *départements* has decreased by 262,000 whilst the population of the whole of France has increased by 1,255,000. ... Bretons feel very strongly that their ways of feeling, of looking at things, of thinking, are not the same as those of other Frenchmen.'[3]

There was, alleged Pleven, a Breton complex, not that of inferiority, being regarded as old fashioned and slightly ridiculous, but of being exploited. He argued that if the province was not given the opportunity to expand and play its role in national development, then 'France would be torn by strife the like of which she has not dreamt'.[4] Events of the 1960s have indeed tended to encourage regionalist sentiment.[5] The so-called 'battle of Brittany' in 1963–4 when the great hopes raised for the development of influential regional institutions were dashed,[6] the closing of the 'Breton steel industry', Forges d'Hennebont, the stagnation of industrial develop-

[1] Author of the most impressive statement of the regionalist position, *Debout la Bretagne!*, 1970.

[2] On Breton autonomism see the books by R. Caerléon, *Complots pour une république bretonne*, 1967; *La Révolution bretonne permanente*, 1969; *Au Village des condamnés au mort*, 1970. H. Le Boeterf, *La Bretagne dans la guerre*, 1969. P. Sérant, *La Bretagne et la France*, 1971.

[3] R. Pleven, *Avenir de Bretagne*, 1961, p. 35.   [4] ibid., p. 37.

[5] See M. Lebesque, *Comment peut-on être breton?*, 1971, for a view by a 'Breton de Paris'.

[6] J. E. S. Hayward, 'From Functional Regionalism to Functional Representation in France: The Battle of Brittany', *Political Studies*, vol. 17, 1969, pp. 48–75.

ALSACE

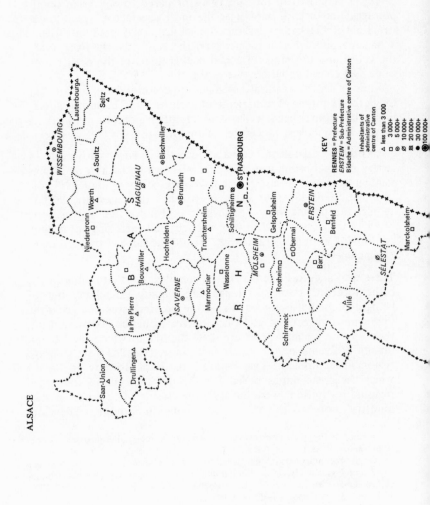

WISSEMBOURG
Lauterbourg△
Seltz △
△Soultz
⊕Bischwiller
Niederbronn Woerth△
HAGUENAU
S
Brumath⊕
Bouxwiller□
B
A
Hochfelden△
Truchtersheim△
Wasselonne□
la Pte Pierre△
SAVERNE
Marmoutier⊕
Drullingen△
Saar-Union△
Schiltigheim⊠
N
⊙STRASBOURG
MOLSHEIM
Rosheim□
□Obernai
Getspolsheim□
⊙ERSTEIN
Benfield
H
R
Schirmeck△
Barr□
SÉLESTAT
Marckolsheim
Villé△

KEY

RENNES = Prefecture
ERSTEIN = Sub-Prefecture
Bidache = Administrative centre of Canton

Inhabitants of
administrative
centre of Canton

△ less than 3 000
□ 3 000+
⌀ 5 000+
⊘ 10 000+
⊠ 20 000+
● 30 000+
⊙ 100 000+

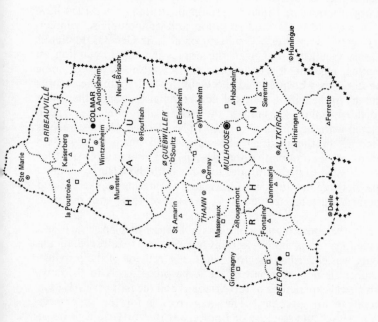

ment in Brittany with the exception of that location in the regional capital, Rennes, and revived rural emigration all contributed to a 'malaise'. The contrast between the vocal expressions of discontent, even expressed personally to de Gaulle, coupled with violent demonstrations of discontent by the peasants, and the electoral success of the government party is extraordinary.

The assertion that de Gaulle appealed to the monarchist and 'clerical' sentiments of the ordinary voter (if not the notables) is too simple an interpretation, although the success of Gaullism in other regions with similar historical traditions gives some support to it. The desire for stability in government, and old monarchist concern, has a new basis when populations realise that government-promoted and long-term structural changes are necessary to extract a region from an invidious economic situation. The activities of CELIB, municipalities, general councils of the *départements*, most agricultural organisations and interest groups in Brittany since 1950 have been directed towards modernisation and adaptation to contemporary economic realities. Gaullism, or at least General de Gaulle and some Gaullists, has given the impression of representing an innovating, efficient, if technocratic, conservatism. Although some of the notables who preceded the Gaullists had creditable records of activity on behalf of the local and regional economy, they were too divided politically among themselves and often too much associated with the forces of the past to be effective. Gaullist success in elections to the National Assembly owed much to the sheer confusion of the conservative notables: divided among three political parties, divided in their attitudes towards both the Algerian conflict and the new regime, they were incapable of offering a coherent and determined resistance to the Gaullist assault on their positions.

Alsace is the most Gaullist region in France in plebiscitary and parliamentary terms: in the elections of 1968 every Gaullist candidate in Alsace was elected at the first ballot. The rallying of the province to Gaullism is not the result of the same processes as in Brittany. The historical experiences of the Alsatians and the nature of Alsatian conservatism are peculiar.[1] The main reason for the differences between Alsace and the rest of France was the forty-eight years of German rule between 1870 and 1918.[2] The annexation deprived

[1] For a fuller treatment, P. Maugé, *Le Particularisme alsacien*, 1972. See also, M. Anderson 'Regional identity and Political Change: the Case of Alsace from the Third to the Fifth Republic', *Political Studies*, vol. 20, 1972, pp. 17–30.

[2] F. L'Huiller, 'L'Alsace dans le Reichsland, 1871–1918' in P. Dollinger (ed.), *Histoire de l'Alsace*, 1970.

Alsace of many of the men who made the *notabilité* in other French regions. The majority of the university and *lycée* teachers and a large proportion of the business and rural notables were among the 13 per cent of the population who preferred to emigrate rather than become German. The departure of so many social leaders left a vacuum, temporarily filled by ecclesiastics: this gave the impression that Alsace was a clerical province, a reputation which it had not previously possessed.

Catholicism and local patriotism became inextricably bound together in the 1870s; annexation by Germany was quickly followed by Bismarck's anti-clerical *Kulturkampf*. When the first elections took place in 1874, eight out of the eleven Deputies to the Reichstag belonged to the Alsatian Catholic Party and they included the Bishop of Strasbourg and five other priests. The Church played an expanding role in social life, in the press, youth movements, and agricultural and industrial unions. The Catholic Party continued to dominate electoral policies and was drawn into modest co-operation with the German *Zentrum*. The Alsatian Protestants were less localist in outlook than their Catholic compatriots. They had confessional sympathies with German Lutherans and were repelled neither by the *Kulturkampf* nor by the anti-clericalism of the French Republic. The Protestants were better educated and tended to hold a very large share of the senior administrative posts in the imperial and local administration. There were strains between the imperial German government and Alsace but rapid economic expansion, prosperity in the textile industry, improvements in the transport system and better social services than existed in France were all a source of satisfaction. There was probably a decline in pro-French sentiment in Alsace from the 1890s and, by 1914, although romantic nostalgia for the French connection continued to exist, Alsace was integrated into the German community. The division between Alsace and France was sealed in blood during the First World War when a quarter of a million Alsatians were mobilised and 30,000 were killed in action.

The reintegration of Alsace into France in 1919 therefore posed serious political and administrative problems. The problems centred on three areas – the administration, the concordat, and the language. The reimposition of the standardised and centralised French administrative system in which local officials had much less prestige was an obvious source of difficulties. The way in which teachers and civil servants were absorbed into the French system caused ill-feeling and special unions were established to protect their interests. Although the first High Commissioner in Strasbourg, Alexandre

Millerand, showed tact and understanding, many officials who came from the interior of France did not.[1] One of the main reasons for this lack of understanding was a misconception about the language problem. When Alsace returned to France 2 per cent of the population spoke French fluently and only a further 8 per cent had a reasonable understanding of the language. Many Frenchmen thought that this situation had been created by an aggressive Germanisation and could be reversed by a similar policy. This ignored the obvious fact that, although in 1870 the social elites spoke French, the mass of the people spoke the Germanic dialects which had been the everyday language of the province throughout recorded history. The assertion of the absolute primacy of French in the school system created much bitterness.

The attempted introduction of French anti-clerical legislation caused Catholic Alsace to rise up in fury. When Herriot, in 1924, announced his government's intention to abrogate the concordat which still regulated Church/State relations in Alsace, the campaign mounted against this was so intense that he was compelled to desist: the Blum government's attempt in 1936 to modify the *statut scolaire* of the province met with equally effective opposition.[2] In the mid-1920s autonomist movements were founded to take advantage of Alsatian grievances. The French government either could not see or could not understand the difference between an autonomist and an irridentist movement and it engaged in rather clumsy repressive measures. Partly because of these, three autonomist Deputies were elected in the elections of 1928. The autonomists did not remain a powerful electoral force for very long but the autonomist crisis of the middle 1920s split all the major parties, even the Communist Party. It particularly affected the party which incarnated Catholic Alsace, the *Union Populaire Républicaine*. Towards the end of 1925 the UPR, feeling pressure from the autonomist groups, hardened its regional programme, calling for administrative decentralisation, a regional elective assembly and a recognition of bi-lingualism. This resulted in an internal crisis in the party and a split in 1928 when those who thought the programme too extreme set up *Action Populaire Nationale d'Alsace*. Despite various attempts at reunification this split lasted until the Second World War.

The Second World War confirmed the Alsatian allegiance to

[1] A very valuable work for the whole inter-war period is F. G. Dreyfus, *La Vie politique en Alsace, 1919–1936*, 1969. See also G. Delahache, *Les Débuts de l'administration française en Alsace et en Lorraine*, 1921. J. Fonlupt, 'Notre administration et la crise alsacienne', *La Revue des Vivants*, October 1928. A. Millerand, *Le Retour de l'Alsace-Lorraine à la France*, 1923.

[2] J. Senger, P. Barret, *Le Problème en Alsace-Lorraine*, 1948.

France. As Frédéric Hoffet remarked, Hitler did more for the cause of the French State in Alsace than all the 'patriots' put together.[1] Grievances against the French State were petty compared with Nazi repression. Collaboration in Alsace was less widespread than might have been expected. Some prominent autonomists confirmed the worst suspicions by announcing that their pre-war activities had been directed towards returning Alsace to Germany. But no party, even among the autonomist groups, officially collaborated with the Germans and there were Collaborators in all parties. Collaboration had a different meaning in Alsace than in the rest of France because Alsace was annexed by Germany, Alsatians treated in every way as German and young men conscripted into the German army. The purge after the war, which took little account of this, created a sentiment of injustice, kept alive in the 1950s by the Oradour massacre trial, in which Alsatians conscripted into the SS were among the accused. A man such as Pierre Pflimlin, never suspected of disloyalty in any way, sympathised with this sentiment.[2]

In the Fourth Republic, Alsace manifested strong regional pecularities. In the immediate post-war elections the Socialist Party, doubling their votes by comparison with the 1936 elections, seemed to be establishing an important position in the region, but in subsequent elections they faded rapidly. The Communist Party was unusually unpopular in Alsace, partly because of the behaviour of men such as Charles Huber, the ex-Communist former mayor of Strasbourg, who became an official orator of the Nazi Party, and partly because so many young Alsatians had unpleasant experiences on the Eastern Front fighting against the Soviet Union. The Radicals and Independents had small followings but the main battle was between the *frères ennemis*, the Gaullists and the MRP. The MRP was a union of the various strands of pre-war Christian Democracy in Alsace – the UPR, the APNA and some of the *Parti Démocrate Populaire*, together with new men such as Pierre Pflimlin who became, with Henri Meck (UPR Deputy for Molsheim from 1928 to 1940), the leading notable of the MRP in Alsace. The MRP was not a 'new' party in Alsace, as it was in most of the rest of France, but a new form of the Alsatian Catholic party whose origins lay in the 1870s. Unlike the movement nationally, it was officially Christian and took up the defence of the special religious and educational status of the region. The MRP was the respository of Alsatian political particularism.[3]

[1] F. Hoffet, *Psychoanalyse d'Alsace*, 1951. See also M. J. Bopp, *L'Alsace sous l'occupation allemande*, 1945. E. Schaeffer, *L'Alsace et Lorraine, 1940–1945*, 1953.
[2] P. Pflimlin, R. Uhrlich, *L'Alsace, destin et volonté*, 1963, p. 141.
[3] M. Nicolas, *Le MRP en Alsace de 1947 à 1956*, unpublished *mémoire*, 1969.

Some members, using the language question, seemed to be working towards dividing the MRP and re-establishment of a regional party. The older generation of clergy, who supported figures in the MRP such as Senator Wach, were genuinely clerical and wanted a party which would defend the *Muttersprache* and minimise the contagion of irreligious and immoral ideas from the interior of France: they were generally the communicators of the old autonomist tradition. The MRP had other dimensions, such as the strong trade union connection through Meck and later through Théo Braun, but the legacy of the past was strong.

The replacement of entire generations of politicians at the end of the Second World War and at the beginning of the Fifth Republic took place in other French regions, but it was particularly complete in Alsace and marked something more than the defeat of parties which had become identified with lost causes. The changeover reflected important social changes, especially within elite groups. The status of the clergy was one of the more obvious changes. Catholic priests were crucially important in the life of the inter-war regional parties, the UPR and APNA, both as elected representatives and as electoral agents. In the Fourth Republic, a time of declining religious zeal and a decreasing number of clerical vocations, they were influential sympathisers rather than militants. In the UNR and UDR they played a very minor role and mention of religion faded almost entirely from the manifestos of Gaullists. During the MRP period the trade union network replaced the clerical network as the support for the dominant party. The decline of the MRP coincided with division and disorder within the 'Christian' trade union movement, which culminated in the split between the CFTC and CFTD in 1964. The Gaullists in the Fifth Republic were not supported by a social institution analogous to the Church or the trade union movement.

Gaullism in Alsace was a new phenomenon which owed its success in the 1940s partly to circumstances. The personal prestige of de Gaulle in the region was very high because his intervention had saved Strasbourg from reoccupation by the Germans in the closing stages of the Second World War. The founder of the first Gaullist Party, the *Union Gaulliste*, was René Capitant, a former Professor of Law at Strasbourg who understood the problems of the region. He managed to get a good turnout for his party in Alsace and Moselle in the elections of autumn 1946, although it was a failure elsewhere in France. General Koenig, an Alsatian war hero with great prestige in the region, greatly helped the cause of the RPF and was elected Deputy for Bas-Rhin. Most important of all, however, the Gaullists had the double advantage of being moderate defenders of the religious, educational and linguistic character of the region and, at the same time, being French nationalists. The Gaullists solved the problem of national identity for the Alsatians much more effectively than the MRP, so obviously the heir of the *Zentrum*. A Gaullist voter could not be regarded as anything but a good Frenchman whereas an MRP voter might be a scarcely disguised autonomist who had associated with men whose allegiance to France was suspect.

Although the MRP completely routed the *Républicains Sociaux* in 1956, the electoral conquest of Alsace by the Gaullists in the Fifth Republic was rapid and complete. Over 90 per cent of the Alsatian electorate voted in favour of the constitution in the referendum of September 1958. In the general election of November 1958 the MRP lost eight of its twelve seats and the UNR won six. From that starting point, after Meck's death in 1966 and Pflimlin's retirement from the National Assembly in 1967, they won all the seats in the region. Their electoral success has a somewhat different significance from that of the MRP. It marked an important stage in the decline of traditional regionalism or particularism, and the integration of Alsace into the national political community. Whereas the old MRP men such as Meck, Sigrist and Schmitt had the aura of local men, close in all respects to the people they represented, General Koenig in the Fourth Republic and André Bord in the Fifth seemed to belong to a national rather than a local elite. Bord, Deputy for Strasbourg, has been outstandingly successful at the local level – President of the Regional Economic Development Council and President of the *Conseil Général* of Bas-Rhin.[1] But the Gaullists have not yet been able to wrest many of the prominent local positions from the MRP notables. They have yet to come to terms with the new form of regional consciousness, which has been emerging since the 1950s, based on an awareness of the precarious position of the regional economy. The regional elite which thinks very much in terms of regional prospects and economic development is divided about the situation of Alsace and is not particularly Gaullist. Attempts, similar to those in Brittany and the north, have been made to stimulate economic activity and initiative. A belief in the 'European' vocation of the region and the importance of breaking down the importance of the Rhine frontier is fairly widespread. This is not an idea which appeals to Gaullists either locally or nationally.[2]

[1] L. Rudloff, *La Carrière politique d'un homme politique local: André Bord*, unpublished *mémoire*, 1969.

[2] M. Anderson, op. cit., pp. 26–7.

The regional elite has been composed, since the decline of the family textile firm in the inter-war period and the loss of influence of the clergy, of professional men – doctors, teachers, lawyers, engineers, trade union leaders. The heavy toll taken by the passage from one national economy to another on three occasions, more minor incidents, such as the reattachment of the Saar to Germany on two occasions, and long-term trends such as the decline of the textiles and the fragmentation of landholdings, have meant that prominent industrialists and landowners are a rarity.[1] Foreign capital, particularly German but also Swiss and American, is very important in the economy of the region.[2] The perspectives of the Alsatian elite have, therefore, been unusual in the French context and have greatly changed over time. For historical reasons there has been a much stronger sense of regional identity than that which is found in other French regions – even in Brittany.

The mentality of the Right-wing voters has also been unusual: Alsatian conservatism is a 'popular' conservatism emanating from the notables. The notables themselves have seemed to owe their position less to their qualities, qualifications and social status than to popular goodwill. It is a conservatism closer to the *Landespartei* than to the CNIP and has therefore allowed the development of better organised and disciplined political parties. 'Popular' conservatism elsewhere in France has usually been 'populist' in the manner of Dorgères. This has not been entirely absent from Alsace and can be found in the autonomist groups and in organisations such as the *Union Paysanne d'Alsace*, led by Joseph Bilger in the inter-war period. But the relative moderation and undemonstrative nature of the political habits of the region have generally encouraged more regular styles of political action. The regional parties before 1940, the MRP and briefly the RPF during the Fourth Republic, and UNR/UDR have attracted the votes of this moderate conservative electorate during the last half century of great upheavals and rapid change.

The *département* of Basses-Pyrénées (Pyrénées-Atlantiques since 1967) contains two *petits pays* – the Béarn and the Pays Basque – which, in different styles, have been predominantly conservative

---

[1] For the economic problems of Alsace see J. M. Guegan, *Un Exemple d'expansion économique régionale: L'Alsace de 1944 à 1961*, 1961. E. Juillard, *Problèmes alsaciens vus par un géographe*, 1958. A. Mutter, *L'Alsace à l'heure de l'Europe*, 1968. P. Pflimlin, R. Uhrlich, op. cit.

[2] J. P. Sicre, 'Les Allemands à la conquête de l'Alsace', *Revue politique et parlementaire*, vol. 71, 1969, pp. 38–55.

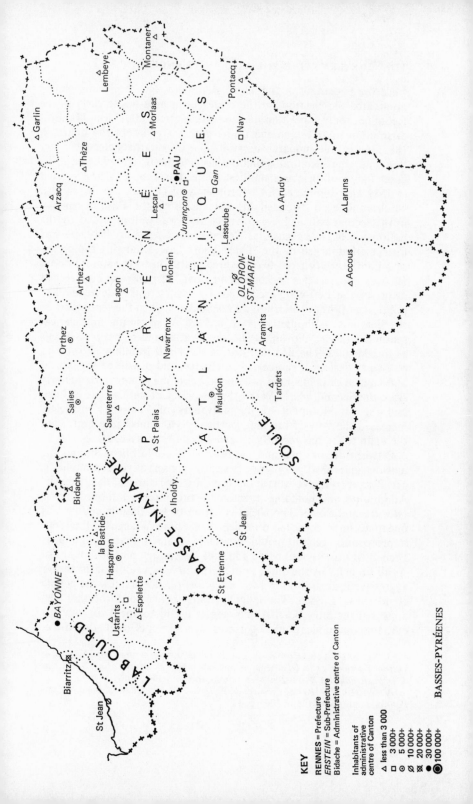

KEY

RENNES = Prefecture
ERSTEIN = Sub-Prefecture
Bidache = Administrative centre of Canton

Inhabitants of
administrative
centre of Canton

△ less than 3 000
□ 3 000+
⊙ 5 000+
∅ 10 000+
⊠ 20 000+
◉ 30 000+
● 100 000+

BASSES-PYRÉENES

since the beginning of the Third Republic.[1] The Right completely dominated the elections in the *département* as a whole early in the Republic: only one Republican was elected after MacMahon's dissolution in 1877 and the *Union des Droites* swept the board in 1885, with three monarchists and three Bonapartists elected. After that date the electoral situation became more complicated. The great figure of Béarnais politics, Louis Barthou, was first elected in 1889 and dominated his constituency of Oloron, the Béarn as a whole, and even extended his influence into the Basque country in the second half of his career. Barthou was well regarded by the nationalist Right because, as *Président du Conseil* in 1913, he was instrumental in getting the 'Three Years Law' (changing the period of military service from two to three years) on to the statute book. He was conservative in social and financial policy but succeeded in preserving Left-wing credentials by anti-clerical statements. The political position of Barthou corresponded well to the sentiments of the Béarnais. Although he was accused of spreading anti-clerical sentiment in the Oloron valley, the Béarnais were never as pious as the Basques. The Béarnais during the Third Republic showed no particular desire for radical social change, and preserved the typical nationalism of the frontier provinces. Economic change, particularly since the Second World War – the discovery of natural gas at Lacq and the establishment of the university of Pau – has indirectly increased the vote of the Left, particularly the moderate Left. Pau, the main town, has recently elected a Socialist mayor.

Between the Basques and the Béarnais there has been an amiable tension and rivalry of two basically conservative communities. The Basque country covers about one third of the area of the Pyrénées-Atlantiques and contains three small 'provinces' – Labourd, Basse Navarre and Soule. The social isolation of the Basque country, at one time almost total, has diminished over time. Whereas in the 1860s a prosecutor general could complain that in many communes French was totally unknown and half the Basque mayors could not speak French,[2] by the mid-twentieth century, as a result of the rather aggressive Francisation by the *école primaire*, all but a few old people could speak French. The language barrier has not altogether disappeared (country doctors still find it useful to speak Basque for efficient communication) but it no longer presents great administra-

[1] J. Micheu-Puyou, *Histoire électorale du département des Basses-Pyrenées sous la Troisième et la Quatrième République*, 1965. P. Brunot, *La Droite traditionaliste dans les Basses-Pyrénées*, unpublished *mémoire*, 1969.

[2] V. Wright, *The Basses-Pyrénées from 1848–1870 – a Study in Departmental Politics*, unpublished thesis, 1965, p. 3.

tive and social difficulties. Emigration of Basques to many parts of the world is an old phenomenon but serious depopulation is relatively recent. A strong sense of community conserved a traditional society into the post Second World War period. An historian of the politics of Basses-Pyrénées in the twentieth century wrote in the 1950s:

'... there [in the Basque country] there is a country, a language, a race which are perfectly distinctive. Customs are quasi-national traditions. Assimilation with the rest of France has been accomplished in the hearts of the Basques but it has not affected the spiritual bond (*spirituel commun*) which has made their country impervious to outside social and political pleas.'[1]

The 'mystery' of the Basque race might have been exaggerated by romantics and its ethnic singularity is unproven,[2] but the Basque language is unrelated to any European language. This, like the very popular and typically Basque sports such as Pelote, is a source of pride and assurance, unusual in French peasant communities.

Despite this strong sense of identity, the Basque constituencies Bayonne II and Mauléon, were for many years represented by non-Basque politicians. For example, in the first years of the twentieth century, Bayonne II was represented first by the Catholic Republican Harriague Saint-Martin, then by Léon Guichenné (*Action Libérale*), and Mauléon by the Catholic Republican Pradet-Balade. The men who represented the most Rightward leaning Béarnais constituencies such as Jean de Gontaut-Biron of Pau II were not very different in outlook. This situation changes when Jean Ybarnégaray was elected youngest Deputy of the Third Republic in 1914 for Mauléon. During his long tenure, which lasted until his disqualification at the Liberation because of his role as a Vichy minister, 'Ybar' became a folk hero among the Basques. He helped to revive Pelote and was an effective patron of many Basque activities.[3] Like his colleagues, Lissar and Coral, who occupied the other seat of Bayonne II, he regarded himself as *Basque et Français*, adopting typically French nationalist positions. He was involved, like Lissar, first in Taittinger's *Jeunesses Patriotes* and then in La Rocque's *Croix de Feu*. Béarnais figures were also associated with the extreme Right in the inter-war period. The greatest notable of Béarnais politics after Barthou, Léon Bérard, first elected for Orthez in 1910, Minister of Education immediately after the First World War in

[1] H. Descamps de Bragelonge, *La Vie politique des Basses-Pyrenées*, 1958, p. 7.
[2] P. Marquer, *Contribution à l'étude anthropologique du peuple basque*, 1963.
[3] L. Boussard, *L'Irrentzia ou le destin des basques*, 1969.

the Clemenceau, Briand and Poincaré cabinets and again during Vichy, was personally friendly with Charles Maurras and the leaders of *Action Française*. Lamazou-Betbeder and Tixier-Vignancour (first elected as Deputy for Orthez in 1936) had connections with the extreme neo-Fascist Right. Monarchism never revived in any electorally significant way in Basses-Pyrénées after the *Ralliement*, but there was at least five hundred sympathisers of *Action Française* and, before the condemnation of 1926, there were a number of priests among them.[1] The Béarnais were much more receptive to new ideas and movements. Such influence as the leagues acquired in the Basque country was probably due to the sympathies of notables such as Ybarnégaray and Guy Petit rather than genuinely popular feeling.

The *département* seemed to move further to the Right with the approach of the Second World War. The bitterness with which Christian Democracy was opposed even when it was represented by such respectable figures as Auguste Champetier de Ribes (Deputy for Pau I from 1924 to 1935 and then Senator) is an indication of this. In the last election before the war the Popular Front was decisively beaten. The only two Deputies who were considered to be on the Left at the local level, Delomb-Sorbé in Pau II and Mendiondou in Oloron, were regarded as indecisive moderates in the Palais-Bourbon. This apparent Rightward drift of the *département* was a general feature of 'static' France during the inter-war period. It was helped in Basses-Pyrénées by the involvement of Garat, the Radical Socialist Deputy and Mayor of Bayonne, in the Stavisky affair. Which was the more important factor is difficult to say but the caution and conservatism of the members of parliament from the *département* was expressed in the overwhelming vote in favour of full powers to Pétain in 1940. Only Champetier de Ribes in the Senate and Mendiondou in the Chamber voted against them.

The *scrutin de liste* electoral system of the Fourth Republic tended both to submerge the Basque element of the *département* and give a false impression of political instability. Despite the support given by two ineligible notables, Ybarnégaray and Tixier-Vignancour, to the *Parti Républicain de la Liberté* list led by Guy Petit (elected to the second constituent Assembly), the MRP was the great victor in the post-war elections. The MRP was clearly regarded as temporary substitute for the Right-wing notables who were temporarily unavailable because they were in disgrace for Collaboration: the influence of the movement declined rapidly when the Vichyite and Gaullist Right reasserted themselves in the late 1940s. Only Pierre de

[1] R. Moreau, *Histoire de l'âme basque*, 1970, p. 572. P. Brunot, op. cit., pp. 29, 98.

Chevigné of the MRP survived the 1951 elections and two most prominent MRP notables Tinaud and Errecart (after a brief return to the National Assembly in 1955) took refuge in the Senate. At the national level, despite his strong opposition to the Algiers uprising of May 1958, Chevigné was regarded as an MRP *droitier* because of his defence of French colonies, but he was bitterly attacked by the Right in the *département*. The *scrutin de liste* also had the novel effect of allowing the Left a foothold: the leaders of the SFIO and Communist lists were regularly elected. Disunity of the Right excluded the possibility of complete victory. In the 1951 election the heads of three Right-wing lists were elected – Goislard de Monsabert for the RPF, Guy Petit for the CNIP and Loustanau-Lacau (who had been involved in the Cagoule affair in the 1930s) for the extreme Right. There was an increase in the proportion of voters who cast their ballots for Left-wing candidates and the regular election of the leaders of the Socialist and Communist parties was only partly due to the electoral system.

The electoral system of the Fifth Republic certainly worked against the Left and the Communists and Socialists lost their representation.[1] The elections of November 1958, surprisingly in view of the return to single member constituencies but following a national trend, brought the defeat of the best known notables of the *département* – Cassagne, Chevigné, Errecart, Garat, Petit, Tixier-Vignancour. The elections in the Basque constituencies were particularly interesting and gave further support to the spurious reputation of political instability. The Basque constituencies were very much in favour of the new Republic, giving higher than average 'yes' votes in the first three referenda and a 66.2 per cent 'yes' vote in the referendum on the constitutional reform in autumn 1962. They were not, however, loyal to their Deputies. In November 1958, Guy Petit, the pro-French Algeria Mayor of Biarritz first elected Deputy in 1946, was defeated in Bayonne-Biarritz by an even more extreme defender of French Algeria, Colonel Thomazo who stood as a UNR candidate. Eventually excluded from the UNR for his views on Algeria, his behaviour and that of the French Algeria lobby in general was not appreciated in the constituency. As a result, in 1962, an almost apolitical campaign by Dr Grenet, the Mayor of Bayonne, who ran without the official sponsorship of any political party, was successful. This result reflected specific dissatisfaction with those who claimed to be the followers of de Gaulle (Tardrew, the Gaullist who ran against Grenet in 1962, was a weak candidate). Despite Dr Grenet's high reputation

[1] J. Martinez, 'Les Elections législatives de 1958 à 1967 dans la vie politique des Basses Pyrenées' in *Trois études sur le Sud-Ouest*, 1968, pp. 161–261.

as a municipal administrator, he could not repeat his performance in 1967 when he was beaten by a stronger Gaullist challenger, Marie. In the other Basque constituency of Mauléon-Saint Palais events followed an almost parallel course. Dr Camino, the CNIP Deputy, became deeply involved in the French Algeria cause. In 1962 the MRP candidate, Labéguerie, won a crushing victory at the first ballot after Camino had implicitly accused him of treason by plastering the constituency with posters – *Votez basque, votez français, votez anti-séparatiste*. Interpreted as an allusion to Labéguerie's activities in Basque organisations, it was widely resented.

Labéguerie's victory perhaps gave exaggerated hopes of electoral success to the new autonomist organisation *Enbata*, founded with some eclat in 1963, which unsuccessfully put up candidates in 1967 and 1968 in both Basque constituencies.[1] But neither the *basquisant* aspect of Labéguerrie nor his party, the MRP (until 1962 almost certainly the strongest in the *département* in terms of organisation, militants and notables) represented the aspirations of the electorate. The election of 1967 demonstrated that a good Gaullist candidate, preferably with local connections, was bound to win. Michel Inchauspé, a Basque whose father had been President of the General Council and whose family owned a local bank, defeated Labéguerie by over 5,000 votes at the second ballot, at a time of national swing against the Gaullists. Despite his name and local connections, Inchauspé has not managed to acquire anything like the dominance over his constituency which his predecessor in the Third Republic, Ybarnégaray, possessed. After a brief career as a junior minister his *suppléant*, Duboscq, refused to resign to allow him to re-enter parliament and Inchauspé's standing has, with time, diminished rather than increased.

In the first three general elections, therefore, both Basque constituencies changed their Deputies. This apparently fickle behaviour has a simple explanation. The two Gaullist Deputies elected in 1958 revolted against the Algerian policy of de Gaulle, were excluded from the Gaullist Party, and it proved impossible to find sufficiently prestigious Gaullist candidates to replace them in 1962. This allowed the temporary return of the moderate conservative notables. The Béarnais constituencies gave the appearance of greater stability. The son of the mayor of Pau, Pierre Sallenave, was elected for the Pau constituency in 1958 as an Independent and in subsequent elections was endorsed both by the *Centre Démocrate* and the CNIP. He was briefly unseated by Labarrère of the Federation of the Left in the short 1967–8 parliament. Tixier-Vignancour, who had a con-

[1] J. L. Davant, *Histoire du Pays basque*, 1972, pp. 71–2.

siderable following in his old seat of Orthez, stood for the enlarged constituency of Orthez-Oloron but was beaten by a young Radical, Dr Ebrard. Ebrard held the seat until 1968 when he was defeated by Plantier (UDR), who had challenged Sallenave unsuccessfully on three occasions in Pau. The two Béarnais constituencies were, however, much more marginal than the two Basque seats which were always winnable by a good Gaullist candidate.

Pyrénées-Atlantiques is in most respects a microcosm of the highly complex social and political situation which the Gaullists are precariously dominating in France as a whole. The legacy of the past is clearly apparent. There are irreducible Left-wing bastions in the valley of the Oloron, Boucau on the estuary of the Adour and in the scattered industrial centres in the *département*. The traditional notables retained their positions in the *mairies* such as Grenet in Bayonne and Petit in Biarritz, in the *Conseil général* (Pierre de Chevigné remains the President) and in the Senate (Guy Petit, Tinaud and Errecart). The great Gaullist success has been in the elections to the National Assembly: three of the four seats are held by Gaullists and, in 1968, the UDR candidate made a strong challenge in the fourth. The Gaullists have broken through the socio-political framework established in the first half of the Third Republic but the old cleavages and loyalties remain and are expressed in local elections. The Gaullist triumph can appear superficial and fragile. The great social and economic changes which the *département* has been undergoing in the last two decades could produce a fickle electorate. Technologically advanced industry, such as aircraft construction has come to the *département*, but an important element of it, the natural gas at Lacq, is likely to be exhausted in the near future. Traditional industry, such as the *forges de Boucau* (closed in the early 1960s) and the Basque shoemaking and linen industries, is dying without the workforce being absorbed by the new industries. Rural depopulation has accelerated to the level of a flight from the land in some parts of the Basque country where landholdings have always been very small. Together with the repression of Basque nationalism on the other side of the frontier, this has created a malaise and the first signs of genuine radicalism among the French Basques. Mass tourism on the coast and in part of the *Pays Basque intérieur* has created both a desire for a higher standard of living and a wish not to be too dependent on this seasonal industry. The consequence of these changes is that, during the period of the electoral ascendency of Gaullism, the political history of the *département* has been punctuated by protest movements by workers, peasants, fishermen and Basque autonomists. The same general observations can be made about both the *département* and France as a whole. No party has been able to organise these sporadic explosions into a broad movement of opposition. The Gaullists have been in a position to offer hopes of concrete improvements as well as presenting themselves as the guarantors of tradition and order. For the time being, their electoral position is very strong in the Basque country, but much less so in Béarn.

Traditionalisms: Church, army, aristocracy

In the nineteenth and twentieth centuries, the Catholic Church has been deeply involved in conservative milieux and Right-wing politics. From 1791, the year of the Civil Constitution of the clergy, religious belief was inextricably involved with the counter-revolution. Despite repeated attempts by 'liberal', 'democratic' and 'progressive' Catholics in the 150 years after the Great Revolution, it was not until the Algerian War that a substantial break between the Church and conservative political forces can be discerned.[1] But the influence of the Church has never been in one direction and Catholics have usually been divided on political issues. The ecclesiastical nucleus, the Cardinals, Bishops and Priests, have sought political influenec in order to maintain the religious interests of the Church and to safeguard morals. Both of these general purposes could be interpreted in many different ways in particular circumstances. The most authoritative spokesmen of the Church, the cardinals and bishops, have differed on issues such as the *Ralliement*, the Separation of the Church and the State, the Vichy regime and Gaullism. The relatively rare interventions of the Papacy in French political matters have usually been directed at imposing unity on a divided Church.

The organisation of the Church has always made political unity of Catholics difficult to achieve. Occasionally there has been a difference of outlook and some tension between higher and lower clergy. There have frequently been differences of perspective between the regular and the secular clergy. The act of joining a religious order has always represented a radical break from a local community. The secular clergy have usually been locally recruited and locally trained, and have returned from the seminary to foster parishes whose people they know well. Their political views and

[1] The main official declarations which caused offence on the Right were: Assemblée des cardinaux et archevêques, 'Problèmes de l'Afrique du Nord devant la conscience chrétienne', October 1955; 'Au sujet de l'Algérie', 1957; 'Sur l'Algérie', March 1958; 'Les Chrétiens devant la conjoncture actuelle', November 1960; 'Communiqué de l'assemblée plénière de l'espiscopat sur l'Algérie', May 1960; and the declarations of the bishops of Algeria in February 1956 and March 1958.

their assessment of what was politically possible were necessarily influenced by this localism. Joining a religious order has often been of much more specific political significance. For example, in the last years of the nineteenth century, the Assumptionist Order was regarded as clerical, anti-Semitic and militantly anti-Republican. In the very different circumstances of the Fourth Republic, the Jesuits and Dominicans were involved in different forms of social action from which different political attitudes were implied. Since the beginning of the twentieth century, the multitude of organisations dominated by laymen, ranging from the semi-official Catholic Action at one extreme, to the political parties of Catholic inspiration but with no official connection with the Church at the other, have given the impression of a very diversified Catholic community. Also struggles between Catholics, as for example between modernists and *intégristes* (those who sought to conserve the 'integrity' of Catholic doctrine)[1] have been at least as bitter as those between clerical and anti-clerical. These struggles have always involved, to a varying extent, both doctrinal and political considerations. Those seeking liturgical change and experiment have often, although not invariably, been the same people as those who sought to identify the Church with progressive social policies.

Various opinions have been current about the general political influence of the Church since the Second World War. The old Radical anti-clericalism continued and showed its force during the passage of the Debré law on State aid to private (mainly Catholic) schools in 1959. According to this strand of opinion the Church is the supporter of the social status quo and the property-owning classes, a barrier to any kind of social and intellectual progress, and accepts democracy only because it is inevitable. This anti-clericalism of *le Canard enchaîné* and *la Dépêche du Midi*, sections of the Radical Party and the old Socialist Party (SFIO) recognised that there are progressive minorities among the Catholics but regarded these as aberrant and lacking in real influence within the Church. The second view, shared by some army officers, some sections of the extreme Right and some employers, was almost the exact antithesis. According to this view, the positions taken by priests and bishops indicate that the Church supported the political

---

[1] There are interesting connections between *intégrisme* and the extreme Right. See Y. Congar, 'Mentalité de droite et intégrisme', 'Documents sur l'intégrisme', *La Vie intellectuelle*, June 1950, September 1952. M. Garrigou-Lagrange, 'Intégrisme et national-catholicisme', *Esprit*, November 1958. J. Domenach, 'Le Regroupement de droite et l'intégrisme', *Synthèse*, December 1953. J. Madiran, *L'Intégrisme: histoire d'un histoire*, 1964.

interests of the Left. Examples are the pronouncements of bishops against torture by the army during the Algerian War and in favour of Algerian independence, for the grievances of workers during strikes such as the miners' strike of 1963, for peace in general and peace in Vietnam in particular. Some evidence has been cited from voting behaviour such as the million Catholics who voted for Mendésiste candidates in the elections of 1956 and the transference, at the second ballot in the general election of 1967, of 'Catholic' votes from the *Centre Démocrate* to candidates of the Federation of the Left. A third view prevails among many Catholic intellectuals and some members of the hierarchy that the Church has become progressively disengaged from the political spectrum. This, it is argued, is partly due to the evolution of religious practice. Even in the most Catholic areas of France, church attendance has become the practice of a large proportion of the population and not the practice of almost everyone as it had been at the beginning of the century; in some areas, the so-called *pays de mission*, and in some social groups religious practice has become a rarity. In these circumstances, the Church can neither have, nor should aspire to have the status of a separate but equal partner of the State, defending the spiritual and moral interests of all Frenchmen, using political weapons if necessary. According to the exponents of disengagement, the Church has an evangelical task and should bear witness to the faith in all professions and social milieux; to do this effectively, connections with the existing order and with social and political authorities should be as limited as possible.

Each of these views can be supported by a selective view of the evidence. The diversity of the statements and activities of priests and laymen give rise to a variety of interpretations. Pressure from the hierarchy on the government has been relatively rare and this supports the hypothesis of disengagement. However, the correlation between religious practice and voting for Right-wing candidates in elections has not greatly diminished since this was first exhaustively studied by the pioneers of electoral and religious sociology. From the beginning of the Third Republic religious practice, more than any other general factor, has correlated closely with voting for Right-wing candidates in elections. It was the dominant correlation in the 1965 presidential election when de Gaulle confronted Mitterand at the second ballot. This relationship encourages somewhat simple interpretations of the basic importance of religion in influencing the way Right-wing voters cast their ballot. The rapidity with which, for example, Breton emigrants to urban areas have ceased to attend church suggests that there are general social and environmental factors which support both the practice of religion and Right-wing voting in Brittany.[1] This 'sociological' Catholicism can be found in other regions such as Alsace, the Basque country, Lozère and other *départements* on the southern fringe of the Massif Central. In fashionable districts of Paris and in some provincial towns, social conservatism and Right-wing political attitudes have supported church-going rather than vice-versa.[2] This 'Maurrassian' Catholicism has been present in some middle- and upper-class milieux throughout the history of French democracy. The diversity of French Catholicism makes for an intricate relationship between religious practice, voting behaviour and political action.

The only major institution which rivals the Church for its importance in the politics of the Right is the army. Recruitment to the officer corps tended to identify the army with the Right. Studies of recruitment to the officer grades in the Third and Fourth Republics have shown the importance of promotion from the ranks and, partly as a consequence, the humble origins of a sizeable proportion of the officer corps.[3] Also, some famous officers, such as Philippe Pétain, who passed through the prestigious military training schools of Saint-Cyr, Saumur and the Polytechnique came from relatively poor families. But, as in the diplomatic corps, the presence of aristocrats in the army, often from less well off provincial families, set a tone. This tone was more apparent in some sections of the army than in others. Saint-Cyr and Saumur were considered, in the Third Republic, to have a reactionary and aristocratic ambience and this reputation survived into the post Second World War period. The Polytechnique which trained engineers for the army, although many of its graduates opted out of the army as a career, was more meritocratic, bourgeois and 'liberal'. Cavalry regiments were considered more aristocratic than gunner regiments and so on.

The involvement of the army in Right-wing politics has varied over time. After the professionalisation of the army in the revolutionary and Napoleonic period, the integrity of the army was preserved through successive regimes by an apparent corporate political neutrality (*la grande muette*) accompanied by the resignations of individual officers who could not stomach a particular regime or one of its acts: the resignation of Legitimist officers after the overthrow of the Bourbon monarchy in 1830 or that of Catholic officers

[1] L. J. Lebret, *La France en transition*, 1957, especially ch. 4.

[2] G. Lebras, 'Nuances régionales du catholicisme en France', *Revue de psychologie des peuples*, vol. 8, 1953, pp. 12–23.

[3] The main works on recruitment to the army are Capitain d'Arbeux, *L'Officier contemporaine. La Démocratisation de l'armée*, 1911. R. Girardet, *La Société militaire, 1915–1939*, 1954. Same author, *La Crise militaire, 1945–1962*, 1964.

after the expulsion of the Jesuits in 1879 are examples. The use made of the army by 'bourgeois' governments to suppress Left-wing or proletarian movements in Paris in 1848 and 1871, the part played by the army in the *coup d'état* of 1851 and in maintaining order during strikes, as for example during Clemenceau's first ministry from 1906 to 1909, compromised this neutrality in the eyes of the industrial working class. From being, in the 1870s and 1880s, a symbol of *la revanche* and restorer of the national honour after the defeat, the army became identified with nationalism and Right-wing politics during the Dreyfus affair. The nationalist leagues glorified the army and wanted a military coup to replace the Republic by a more authoritarian regime. There remained, however, a fairly wide spectrum of political opinion within the army itself.

Although the arguments of the Right-wing nationalists in the late nineteenth and early twentieth centuries appealed to officers, severely provoked by anti-militarist propaganda from the extreme Left, there is no evidence that important sections of the army ever seriously contemplated a *coup d'état*. However, there were general social, political and ideological reasons why, after the 1890s, the army was increasingly identified with the Right. The army represented values of order, hierarchy and discipline which were execrated by sections of the Left and looked on as a threat to democratic institutions. Colonial campaigns were regarded by the army as true titles to glory and soldiers, such as Marshal Lyautey, were the most prestigious and effective exponents of the imperial idea. Although monarchists and Right-wingers had attacked Ferry's forward policy in Tonkin in the early 1880s, the defence of Empire gradually became a Right-wing theme.[1] It was never exclusively so: in the period immediately preceding the First World War virtually everyone except a few members of the extreme Left accepted the Empire and there always remained individual imperialists on the Left. However, after the First World War, attacks on the repression of colonial uprisings or liberation movements, excepting the occasional conscientious protest, about the methods used, came exclusively from the Left. Inevitably army officers came to regard certain Left-wing politicians and journalists as their enemies whose behaviour, at least from the time of the Communist campaign in favour of the Moroccan rebellion of Abd El Krim in 1925, was on the borders of treason. The imperial question remained a source of discord between the army and the Left until the Evian agreements in 1962 completed French withdrawal from North Africa. The

[1] This movement is well illustrated in R. Girardet, *L'Idée coloniale en France de 1871 à 1962*, Course at Institut des Études Politiques, 1965–6.

Dreyfus affair and the First World War also caused political rifts between sections of the Left and the army. In the Dreyfus case senior army officers seemed to put their own corporate interests before justice for an individual. The nationalists, Catholics and monarchists who rallied to the defence of the army also alienated the Left from the army. The alliance of 'the sabre and the holy water sprinkler' was alleged by anti-militarist propagandists to be the basis of the reactionary, obscurantist and Right-wing forces in the country.

The divisions created by the First World War were less clear-cut. Most officers and ex-officers felt bound to justify the carnage of trench warfare, exalt the virtues of those who died and demand that their sacrifice should not be in vain. Many men of the Left regarded the experience of the First World War as evidence of both military incompetence and the futility of war: they were more than ever convinced of the need for international understanding and the peaceful conciliation of disputes between states. The *esprit combattant*, the comradeship of men who fought in the trenches and who felt separated from the non-combatant population of the rear, was translated into the *esprit ancien combattant* of the inter-war period.[1] The ex-soldiers who became active members of the veterans' leagues felt that the fruits of victory were being dissipated by attempts at international conciliation and by the incompetence of corrupt politicians. Just as the army's reputation was affected by its defenders during the Dreyfus affair the ex-servicemen's leagues, when they took to the streets and demonstrated against the regime, were regarded as expressing the point of view of many serving officers. The degree of identity between serving officers' and ex-officers' views in the inter-war period must be a matter for conjecture but it is the case that *la grande muette* was largely a mythical, although useful, tradition.[2]

Overt and implied political views were scattered through military journals and other publications of soldiers.[3] These were often of a cloudy nature but a distinction was generally made between loyalty to the nation, an absolute necessity, and loyalty to the regime, which was conditional on the regime providing the necessary *conditions*

[1] R. Rémond, 'Les Anciens combattants et la politique', *Revue française de science politique*, vol. 5, 1955, pp. 267–90.

[2] For an extensive discussion see B. C. F. Bankowitz, *Maxime Weygand and Civil Military Relations in France*, 1967. This work contains an excellent bibliography.

[3] These views can be found, for the period of the Third Republic, in the *Revue militaire française*, *Revue militaire générale*, and after 1945 in *Revue de défense nationale*, *Revue militaire d'information*, *Messages des forces armées*.

morales for the army.[1] These can be roughly summarised as according the army respect and providing it with sufficient funds, giving the soldiers just causes to fight, emphasising some parallelism between the values of civil and military society (that is laying some stress on authority, discipline and sacrifice), providing authoritative government and repressing 'anarchy'. Professional soldiers after the fall of France in 1940, whether they chose the Free French or the Vichy regime, showed the limited nature of their loyalty to the regime and, on both sides, emphasised their higher loyalty to the nation. The breakdown of army loyalty and, on some occasions, of military discipline in the years 1957 to 1961 can be attributed to the failure of governments to provide these *conditions morales* rather than a change in the attitude of the army. In the latter half of the 1930s tension between the army and the civil power was by no means as great although, as the 'Corvignolles' incident showed, a breakdown of civil-military relations was possible.[2] But, by and large, for most of the time the Third Republic fulfilled the *conditions morales*. In addition, it allowed the army a degree of autonomy over its own administration and over military policy-making which both satisfied the army's *amour propre* and could bring about something approaching military dictatorship in wartime, as the power of the High Command over general policy in the first two years of the First World War demonstrated. However, the *conditions morales* and the partial autonomy of the army were more likely to be supported by the Right than by most sections of the Left at any time after the 1890s.

The last major intervention of the army in politics in the period between the support given to the rioters in Algiers in May 1958 and the putsch of the four generals in April 1961, was symptomatic of a very serious, although temporary, crisis in civil-military relations.[3] Bitter about defeat in Indo-China, compelled by governments of the Fourth and Fifth Republics to play political, administrative and police roles in Algeria, soldiers came to hold strong views on general policy matters. Some of the most influential members of the officer

[1] These conditions were a nineteenth-century formulation. See P. Chalmin, 'Crises morales de l'armée française au 19ᵉ siècle', *Revue de défense nationale*, vol. 6, 1950, pp. 554–70. F. Bédarida, 'L'Armée et la République', *Revue historique*, vol. 232, 1964, pp. 119–64.   [2] See below, p. 226.

[3] For this crisis see J. S. Ambler, *The French Army in Politics, 1945–1962*, 1966. H. Azeau, *Révolte militaire, Alger 22 avril 1961*, 1961. J. M. Darboise *et al.*, *Officiers en Algérie*, 1960. J. Fauvet, J. Planchais, *La Fronde des généraux*, 1961. R. Girardet, op. cit., and 'Pouvoir civil et pouvoir militaire dans la France contemporaine', *Revue française de science politique*, vol. 10, 1960, pp. 5–38. G. A. Kelly, 'The French Army Re-enters Politics', *American Political Science Review*, vol. 76, 1961, pp. 354–67.

corps rejected the Fourth Republic because of the weak and vacillating leadership it provided and rebelled against the Fifth Republic because it was leading in a direction contrary to the one for which many soldiers had laid down their lives. The result was a series of desertions, the spread of apocalyptic neo-Fascist views among regular soldiers and the involvement of some officers in the Secret Army Organisation led by ex-General Salan. The government responded by setting up special tribunals which passed relatively mild sentences on dissident officers, except in the case of those who had attempted to assassinate the Head of State. Soldiers served out prison terms in the 1960s amid general public indifference, punctuated by eventually successful demands for amnesty from their political friends. The effective repression of military dissidence, the end of Empire and the transformation of the army into a modern fighting force based on nuclear weapons removed the army from the political arena. The prestige of the officer corps seemed, however, to be damaged. 'Preserving the honour of the army' was not a major propaganda theme of the Gaullists, as it had been for the CNIP in the Fourth Republic. At both the symbolic and practical levels the army was, after 1962, less important in conservative politics than ever before.

An author writing in 1970 remarked: 'The evolution of attitudes has not followed juridical transformations. The nobility exists in the public mind, although not in the law.'[1] The mild interest aroused by the exposure of the *fausse noblesse* of Giscard d'Estaing and Couve de Murville showed that the distinctions based on noble titles or the appearance of nobility still have some social importance.[2] Eccentric propagandists continue to write tracts in favour of the restoration of a titled aristocracy:

'We must guard against false elites, and particularly those based on money. Money is the greatest enemy of the elite because it is fleeting, factitious and demoralising. How can the effects of money be avoided? By a return to natural elites based on landed property. . . . The task is enormous but public opinion is versatile. A strong regime is always respected. . . .[3]'

Some take questions of nobility very seriously indeed: this was

[1] *Dictionnaire des vanités*, Documentation sociale contemporaine, Cahier No. 1, 1970, p. 9.
[2] ibid.
[3] P. de Sarcus, *De l'Elite. Essai sur la restauration d'une noblesse nouvelle*, 1966, pp. 13, 166.

illustrated by a bitter libel case in the middle 1960s which opposed Baron Barclay de Lautour, author of *Paradoxe de la noblesse française* (1967) and G. de Sède, author of *Petite encyclopédie des grandes familles* (1962). Aristocrats who wish to preserve the distinction between themselves and commoners are members of the *Société d'Entraide de la Noblesse française* which 'validates' titles, publishes the *Cahiers nobles* and provides services for needy members.

The contemporary manifestations of the aristocracy are, however, of trivial political importance compared with those of the Third Republic when the social influence of the aristocracy had a pervasive, if immeasurable effect on Right-wing politics. The attitudes, prejudices and behaviour of some sections of the nobility in the first half of the Third Republic contributed to the ineffectiveness of the parliamentary Right. They were the product of a specific social and political history. Deprived by the centralising monarchy in the seventeenth century of most of the substance of political and administrative power, and removed from the activities of commoners such as commerce and industry, the aristocracy enjoyed a brief Indian summer under the Bourbon restoration (1815–30). The legal status of noble titles was restored and an aristocratic second chamber of parliament created. Nobles dominated the lower chamber and the administration, received preferment in the Church and were given a large grant as compensation for lands confiscated during the revolution:

'Noble families . . . battened on the budget of the State and sought all the paid jobs, even those which the old aristocracy regarded as inferior to their station. Many aristocrats became officers of the gendarmerie, judges of the peace, tax collectors and even postmasters. For the first and last time in the history of modern France, the prestige of birth and name was intimately connected with political and administrative power.[1]'

After 1830 the political influence of the aristocracy went into rapid decline. It retained important positions in the army and State bureaucracy, and enjoyed a brief Indian summer in parliamentary assemblies in the *République sans républicains* from 1871 to 1876.

The relative and perhaps absolute decline of the wealth of the aristocracy accounts to some extent for its political eclipse. Either through lassitude or lack of confidence the compensation awarded to the aristocracy by the Restoration regime was only partly used by the nobility to reconstitute its patrimony. In the nineteenth century aristocrats were not particularly active in the creation of

[1] Berthier de Sauvigny, *La Restauration*, 2nd edition, 1962, p. 248.

wealth either by sponsoring agricultural improvements or by promoting industrial and commercial enterprises although some had
interests in mining and metals. They were virtually absent from the
new financial institutions of the first half of the century: only one
noble participated in the foundation of the Bank of France and the
great names of Legitimist France were slow to appear on its list of
governors and regents. Frequently, the aristocracy got a foothold
in banking and business as a result of marriage and by the end of the
century marriages with rich heiresses, whether bourgeoises or Jewish
or American, were common. But many noblemen seemed to con-
ceive of participation in business only as an accident or a temporary
necessity.

The disdain of the aristocracy helped minority groups, such as
Jews and Protestants, to dominate important sectors of economic
activity. This exacerbated prejudices and hostility to the new capi-
talist wealth which easily turned to anti-Semitism when a bank, the
Union Générale, in which aristocrats and Catholics had a major
interest, crashed in 1881.[1] There was also an aristocratic disdain for
Republican politicians. Jules Simon, academician, Minister and
Deputy at the beginning of the Third Republic, wrote:

'These people are polite, they receive you, offer you an armchair,
the best armchair; they place you on the right of the mistress of
the house, but something about them always makes you feel that
they are showing you how liberal they are by receiving you in the
salon when you are made for the antechamber.[2]'

Prejudice against the Republic seemed more like a device for maintaining a certain kind of social exclusiveness than a political conviction. Count de Magny wrote in 1890s:

Proclaim ultra-royalist opinions, even though a restored monarch
would calmly relegate you to the antechamber, and society receives
you with open arms, despite the fact that hardly anyone is basically
royalist. Admitting Republican sentiments is generally sufficient to
bar entry; even if one is a Montmorency it creates suspicion.
Believing in neither God nor the Devil, having a whole series of
small crimes on one's conscience is no hindrance to having a
prominent place in society, but disputing the temporal power of the
Papacy prevents you from aspiring to such an honour.[3]

The nobles who moved in some fashionable circles gave the impres-

[1] J. Bouvier, Le Krach de l'Union générale, 1878–1885, 1960.
[2] Quoted in le Crapouillot, March 1937.
[3] Count de Magny, La Société parisienne, 1891.

sion of being emigrés from a country which no longer existed, no more capable of adapting to contemporary circumstances than the emigrés of the revolutionary period were capable of earning their living abroad.

There was, however, no homogeneous aristocratic milieu. The origins of noble titles were very diverse and it is very often difficult to establish whether those who used titles had a just claim to them.[1] There were nobles *d'épée ou de robe* of the *ancien régime*, whose numbers had been decimated by war, revolution and exile, an imperial nobility with titles dating from the First or Second Empire, a Legitimist aristocracy ennobled between 1815 and 1830, an Orleanist aristocracy from the period 1830 to 1848, a papal nobility and a false nobility of people who assumed titles with no hereditary claims on them. There was also an ersatz aristocracy composed of leading Jewish families (although the titles of the Rothschilds were authentic enough) and members of the *haute société protestante* (HSP). There was a great deal of mutual denigration between these groups. Within them, there were great differences in wealth and style of life. 'Society' in the late nineteenth and early twentieth centuries was not a coherent group but a collection of prominent and fashionable coteries. Some of them were tending to become more, rather than less exclusive. It was, for example, probably more difficult, although Rothschilds were members, to obtain membership by wealth alone of the most fashionable Paris club, the Jockey Club, in 1900 than it had been fifty years previously.[2] At the turn of the twentieth century it was the meeting place of the old aristocracy and a few great families dominated the membership. Similarly the old Legitimist social circle, *Faubourg Saint-Germain*, named after the quarter of Paris in which many of its members lived, declining in wealth and self-confidence, became more inward looking.[3]

The literary chroniclers of the first thirty years of the Third Republic drew unflattering portraits of aristocrats as public men, sometimes to the extent of representing them as unfit for any public office. As soldiers they were described as generals of the *ancien régime* in a democratic army and as civil servants, only interested in unusual or distinctive promotions. When they entered politics they tried to prevent the progress of democracy by outmoded forms of opposition and, although pacifically inclined, they followed courses of action which could lead to violence. As Deputies of the Right in

[1] Baron Barclay de Latour, *Paradoxe de la noblesse française*, 1967.
[2] J. A. Roy, *Histoire du Jockey club de Paris*, 1958, p. 101.
[3] 'Les Directeurs', *Annales d'histoire économique et sociale*, vol. 8, 1936, pp. 254–5.

the Chamber of Deputies, they engaged in sterile and theatrical opposition; mulish stupidity made them politically important. Others were portrayed as eccentric, becoming dilettante anarchists and Socialists.

The portraits of the novelists tended towards caricature but a selective view of the statements and behaviour of aristocratic politicians would give a similar impression.[1] Often ill-informed about contemporary society outside their own circle, their statements about issues and trends often gave the impression of superficiality and irresponsibility. In the course of an enquiry into the 'social question in Europe' in the 1890s, Jules Huret interviewed the President of the monarchist group of the Chamber, La Rochefoucauld, and asked him what he thought of socialism:

'Ah! Ah! Socialism. Yes, a burning question. It's very large, very large and damnation it's necessary to think about it. I haven't had time to think about it, except superficially, you understand. There are so many other important questions nowadays. . . . In the first place, they don't know what they want these Socialists. What do they want? How can one talk about it when they don't know themselves? Moreover, I don't believe there are any Socialists in France – or perhaps only a few. There are more in Germany because the Germans are dreamers, a bit up in the clouds. . . . What would society be like if there were no more rich people? No more workers either, perhaps. Firstly it would be impossible and then . . . a return to barbarism.'[2]

The Duke's replies to other questions on income-tax, State intervention in the economy and constitutional reform were almost equally frivolous.

Despite the lack of intellectual energy devoted to the analysis of social and political questions, many representatives of the oldest noble families of France felt it to be their civic duty to participate in public life. In the first forty years of the Third Republic most of those families who claimed that their noble titles predated the fifteenth century had a representative in parliament. The genealogy of the La Rochefoucauld family went back to 1019 and others of similar antiquity who had representatives in parliament were Rochechouart, Maillé, Castellane, Harcourt, Gontaut-Biron, Arenberg, Levis-Mirepoix, Rohan and Broglie. In the last decade before the First World War at least one prince, three dukes, sixteen marquises,

---

[1] M. A. Leblond, *Littérature sociale. La Société française sous la Troisième République*, 1905.

[2] J. Huret, *Enquête sur la question sociale en Europe*, 1897, pp. 107–8.

six viscounts and twenty-three counts sat on the Right of the Chamber of Deputies. Not all representatives of these families were ineffective and ill-adapted to their times. A Duke of Broglie was *Président du Conseil* of the early Third Republic, another was later a Nobel prize winner for physics and a Broglie was a Minister of the Fifth Republic whilst other members of the family had and have distinguished careers in other fields.

Before 1914, many aristocrats firmly believed in the value and importance of the old nobility. Senator Count Emmanuel de Las Cases was an open apologist for it and professed to believe that the lower classes could not order their affairs without help from the *autorités sociales*, the celebrated phrase of the sociologist Le Play which Las Cases perverted to refer to the old titled nobility.[1] In 1911 Count de Puységur organised an *Association de la Noblesse* under the chairmanship of the Duke de Luynes, but it languished.[2] In 1914 Count Sorbiers de la Tourasse issued a stirring manifesto *Projet d'une Reconstitution de la Noblesse* but it had no impact.

The more intelligent aristocratic parliamentarians seemed aware that there was no persuasive case for reasserting the social and political leadership of the nobility. They still hankered after the aristocratic principle and were attracted by elitist theories. Senator Gustave de Lamarzelle, in a book published in 1907,[3] wrote that political leadership was inevitably the prerogative of a fairly restricted class and called for the creation of a new enlightened aristocracy from the representatives of voluntary organisations and interest groups. Lamarzelle argued, rather in the manner of Lord Acton, that only strong voluntary organisations could resist the pretensions of the modern State and also that where such organisations flourished *laissez-faire* and liberal doctrines would wither. The new aristocracy based on these organisations would resist political and administrative centralisation and counter the evils of industrialism. Lamarzelle hoped that many of the old nobility would be members of the new aristocracy. This vision was similar to that of the Deputy Count Albert de Mun, the leading social Catholic of his generation, although he showed less optimism than Lamarzelle that trade union leaders and industrialists could acquire aristocratic virtues. De Mun hoped for the emergence of 'social authorities' whose distinguishing mark would be Christian virtues and amongst whom would be many

---

[1] E. de Las Cases, *Les Autorités sociales dans une démocratie*, 1903.

[2] Count A. de Puységur, *De l'Epée au tango*, 1914.

[3] G. de Lamarzelle, *Démocratie politique, démocratie sociale, démocratie chrétienne*, 1907.

members of his own class.[1] Charles Maurras, when he revived monarchist theory at the beginning of the twentieth century, argued on parallel lines. Under a restored king, according to Maurras, political and social leadership would be exercised by 'the most French' section of the community. Since this section would have been rooted for the longest period on French soil, the old nobility would figure largely in the new elite.

These programmes and doctrines made little impression on the aristocratic milieu as a whole. They probably appealed more to the relatively poor *hobereaux* of the West and the *petite noblesse d'épée de province* than to the rich and modish who during the *belle époque* divided their time between setting the tone of Parisian society, leading a *vie de château* during the summer and taking occasional trips abroad.[2] The political views of these people was influenced much more by sentiment and fashion than doctrine. They behaved as celebrities rather than aristocrats. The social figures, such as Count Boni de Castellane, an active nationalist Deputy, gave the impression of stylish irresponsibility.

The world of ostentation, of luxurious irresponsibility which Marcel Proust described in his series of novels *A la recherche du temps perdu* was shattered by the First World War. The military tradition of the aristocracy resulted in heavy casualties: this tradition probably led to even greater proportionate losses in the Second World War.[3] A tendency towards profligacy exacerbated the effects of both war and economic crises. After the First World War the financial resources of many families were reduced to a level below that required to maintain an active social life in the capital. Some attempted to revive the pre-war atmosphere and way of life of the *belle époque* but they did so with reduced means and in a different climate. The Second World War damaged the social prestige of the nobility even more. As Marquis d'Argenson remarked in 1953: 'Generally speaking, the *haute bourgeoisie* and the nobility gave complete support to the regime which emerged from the defeat and thus abdicated the role of social leadership to which they had always believed themselves destined.'[4]

Aristocratic milieux nonetheless survived, continuing to send their sons into the army or the diplomatic corps rather than the home civil service, being represented in parliament throughout the Third

[1] See especially A. de Mun, *Ma Vocation sociale*, 1908.

[2] J. Chastenet, *La France de M. Fallières*, 1949, pp. 128–46.

[3] Count Georges de Morant, *La Noblesse française au champ de l'honneur*, 1918. J. A. Roy, op. cit., p. 120.

[4] Marquis d'Argenson, *Pétain et pétinisme* [*sic*], 1953.

and Fourth Republics by well-known names such as Le Cour, Baudry d'Asson, Grandmaison, Sesmaisons, Reille-Soult, La Ferronays, Aillières, having the occasional member of the Académie Française, retaining a pale shadow of the *Faubourg Saint-Germain* and maintaining social circles which were difficult to enter for those without aristocratic connections and in which marriage with a commoner was frowned on. Inevitably, there was a coming together of the most active of the aristocratic families and the *haute-bourgeoisie*. This had commenced in the nineteenth century with the marrying of rich heiresses[1] and was consummated after the Second World War when it had become the practice for virtually all male members of aristocratic families to have business or professional careers. Influential *grandes familles* have been based on this amalgamation such as the Giscard d'Estaing with relations in industrial, academic, financial, political and aristocratic circles. This sort of family is not a new phenomenon but the persistent high regard for the aristocratic element is remarkable after the social and political changes which have taken place since the beginning of the Third Republic.

Patrie Française, Action Libérale Populaire, Fédération Républicaine (in the 1930s among Deputies of the *Fédération* were at least one prince, two dukes, two barons, five marquises and eleven counts) and to a lesser extent the *Centre National des Indépendants et Paysans*, all contained aristocrats, readily identified as such, who were attempting to preserve local family fiefs. Their aspiration to parliamentary careers was based on family tradition and the social prestige which they enjoyed as aristocrats in particular areas. Although the nature of their political dominance differed little from strongly entrenched notables of bourgeois origin, they appeared as anachronisms – undemocratic elements in a democratic Republic. Their presence gave the parties of the Right, before the rise of the Gaullist party, a reactionary, backward-looking image which was electorally disadvantageous. Efforts of the leaders of *Action Libérale Populaire* and of men like Tardieu and Lucien Romier in the inter-war period to present the image of a forward looking conservatism, directed towards a renovated society, lacked plausibility because of the connections of the Right with the past. Parties of the Right always had the ambition to be national parties, and made a habit of calling themselves such, but they could not acquire a following which was a cross-section of the community because their leaders and parliamentary candidates so often represented sectional interests and particular social categories.

[1] For a bitter commentary see Count A. de Puységur, *Les Maquéraux légitimes: du coursier des croisades au bidet de Rebecca*, 1938.

There is no evidence that those men who had either titles or the appearance of nobility who entered the MRP after the Second World War such as Reille-Soult or Menthon, or the aristocrats who have sat for the Gaullists in the Fifth Republic such as Argenlieu, Halgoüet, Montalembert and Pontbriand have had the slightest adverse effect on the reputation of those parties or on their electoral achievements. There is possibly an analogy between the Gaullist *compagnonnage* and a notion of aristocracy or, at least, a *chevalerie*, but neither the Gaullist parties nor the MRP have anything to do with the maintenance of an aristocratic principle, position or tradition. De Gaulle, having led a genuine national resistance movement, could broaden the social base of the Right-wing electorate and make it remarkably close to the total population in terms of social composition and professional activities. Clearly, it would be exaggerated to assert that the aristocratic connection was the main reason for the organisational and electoral weaknesses of the Right during the Third and even more the Fourth Republic. It was, however, a factor amongst others which made the establishment of disciplined parties and the winning of elections more difficult.

Peasants[1]

Throughout the course of modern history rural societies in France have been and remain, despite the unifying effect of recent changes, of great variety.[2] Every historian, agricultural economist and sociologist who has approached the problems of the countryside in a scholarly manner has emphasised this difficulty in the way of making generalisations about the inhabitants of predominantly rural areas. Situations and sentiments have varied greatly from commune to commune, between market towns and villages, between villages and isolated settlements. A river, a break in the communications system, bitter, even if half forgotten, religious and political conflicts between communities have helped to create different collective personalities and different communities of interest.[3] The persistence of traditions

[1] The basic works on the agricultural sector are M. Augé-Laribé, *La Politique agricole de la France de 1880 à 1940*, 1950; P. Barral, *Les Agrariens français de Méline à Pisani*, 1958. Some of Barral's themes have been criticised in P. Gratton, *Les Luttes de classes dans les campagnes*, 1971; J. Fauvet, H. Mendras, *Les Paysans et la politique*, 1958. M. Faure, *Les Paysans dans la société française*, 1966. A recent and very important case study of Finistère is S. Berger, *Peasants against Politics*, 1972.

[2] This variety was noticed by Arthur Young in the eighteenth century, by L. de Lavergne, *Economie rurale de la France*, 2nd edition, 1861, and others in recent opinion polls, *Sondages*, 1966, Nos 3–4.

[3] P. Bois, *Les Paysans de l'Ouest*, 1971, especially pp. 354–64.

and mentalities in the countryside is often surprising: developments which seem decisively to modify the political and social environment – political revolutions, the spread of education, great wars, industrial changes – have often had little more effect than a tide on a reef. But the continuities in the twentieth century should not be overestimated: the changing balance between town and country has altered the respective weight of political forces in France and, indeed, Frenchmen's conception of themselves as a nation.

In 1885, Jules Ferry, referring to the rural population, alluded to '. . . this immense strength on which rests the security of our society – this population of small proprietors so numerous that they constitute the majority of the nation'.[1] There was an element of hyperbole in this opinion. The rural population had been in continuous decline since the 1840s and the urban population of France had overtaken the rural population in the 1870s. The evolution continued: by the beginning of the Fifth Republic the agricultural population was about 20 per cent of the nation and the age structure of the peasantry condemned the rural community to an even more drastic decline. Despite this secular trend, the notions of France as an agricultural country and of the peasantry as the 'backbone of the nation' died very hard. It was a commonplace of politicians of all political persuasions who represented rural constituencies in the Third Republic, and it was erected into a semi-official doctrine by Pétain in his speech to the peasants of France delivered at Pau in 1942. It was revived immediately after the war and given one of its most lyrical expressions by Count de Neufbourg in a book published in 1945:

'The peasantry is the source of life, the only inextinguishable element. Only the peasant has truly a past. . . . Only the peasants are indispensable. The social edifice rests on them, with all its weight. The peasantry is the essential mother. Men emerge from it, by decay to become proletarians, by shrewdness merchants, by education civil servants.'[2]

De Gaulle paid tribute in similar terms during the RPF period to the peasantry in a speech at Nevers in 1948:

'Of all the resources of France, the first, the most noble, the most important is the land . . . those who cultivate it have the feeling, deep inside themselves, that they essentially are France because they hold, mould and marry the land. . . . They are right! In the coming national revival it is they to whom will come the premier role and the highest dignity.'[3]

[1] J. Ferry, *Discours et plaidoyers politiques*, vol. 7, p. 42.
[2] Count de Neufbourg, *Les Paysans*, 1945, p. 27.
[3] *Le Rassemblement*, 19 June 1948.

The Peasant Deputies of the Fourth Republic, led by Camille Laurens and Paul Antier, and some specialists in agricultural matters expressed, less eloquently, similar views. But the general attitude towards the peasantry was dying. As a social category it had probably been, until 1945, enshrouded in a more impenetrable cloud of myth than the industrial working class but by the 1960s virtually all the younger leaders of agricultural organisations were defending agriculture as an economic activity like any other, but with its own specific set of problems.

In the first half of the Third Republic the political strength of the agricultural interest seemed overwhelming. The agricultural lobby, broadly defined, had a majority in the Chamber of Deputies and continued to have a majority in the Senate throughout the life of the Republic. The electoral system for both Chambers was biased in favour of rural constituencies. In 1885 a *groupe amical* was founded in the Chamber of Deputies with about 300 members: whilst this group had an active life it always retained over 200 members. Men with very different political persuasions participated – in 1885 there were about 120 monarchists in the group.[1] Representatives of producer interest groups, such as the wine and cider growers co-operated without paying much attention to party labels.[2] But throughout the Third Republic, and to a lesser extent during the Fourth, the agricultural lobby was weakened by the size of its parliamentary representation, which allowed the growth of fissiparous tendencies. Members of parliament tended to promote constituency rather than general agricultural interests and there was little impetus towards a coherent policy favouring agriculture. Even the general tariff of 1892, generally known as the Méline tariff, praised for generations as the legislation which saved French agriculture from the disastrous effects of cheap food imports from the Americas and Australasia, was not originally promoted by the agricultural lobby. An ex-Minister of Finance, Pouyer-Quertier, acting on behalf of industrial groups, realised the necessity of gaining the co-operation of agriculturalists, and founded the *Association de l'Industrie et de l'Agriculture Françaises* in order to promote the protectionist campaign. Méline, generally acclaimed as the 'father of French agriculture' despite minority criticisms of him for atrophying the development of the agricultural sector, was originally concerned to ensure the protection of the textile manufactures of his constituency in Vosges. Although Deputies who represented agricultural constituencies occasionally paid tribute to

[1] P. Barral, op. cit., p. 81.

[2] R. K. Warner, *The Winegrowers of France and the Government since 1875*, 1960.

the theoretical persuasiveness of *laissez-faire* doctrines, not one criticised the practice of protection and the Méline tariff was easily voted by parliament when it came up for renewal.

The great majority of spokesmen for agriculture in the Third Republic desired to limit the role of the State to maintaining protection against food importers and to establish a legislative framework which would encourage individual initiative. The blatantly self-interested nature of this 'liberalism' in domestic policy, which the representatives of agriculture continued to express down to the 1950s, was intermittently revealed by the demands for government support of commodity prices when the market was in danger of collapse. The impression given by the 'agrarian' Deputies of obstinate defence of special interests and lack of a coherent general programme for agriculture provoked occasional criticisms and charges that agriculture was not being properly represented in parliament. These criticisms sometimes came from the agricultural unions which were established after the Law of Associations of 1884 gave them a legal basis.

There was a tenacious struggle for influence over the agricultural unions and other agricultural organisations between the *Société Nationale d'Encouragement à l'Agriculture* founded by Gambetta, generally known as the Boulevard Saint-Germain, and the *Société des Agriculteurs de France* established during the Second Empire and dominated by aristocrats and *hobereaux*, and popularly referred to as the Rue d'Athènes. The officers of the Rue d'Athènes vaunted the social and educational role of the syndicates and, in terms of numbers of unions affiliated, it was the more successful of the two national organisations. The Boulevard Saint-Germain laid greater stress on co-operatives, friendly societies and *caisses de crédit*. The *crédits agricoles* were an important means of political influence: this was quickly realised by Radical politicians who sought to encourage and use them.[1]

There is little doubt that most of the notables who organised the agricultural syndicates affiliated to the Rue d'Athènes were either hostile or indifferent to the Republican regime and certainly hostile to Radical politicians. The social Catholic collaborator of Albert de Mun in the *Cercles Ouvriers*, La Tour du Pin, described the *syndicats agricoles* in 1886 as 'a counter organisation to oppose anti-social influences'.[2] Republican politicians suspected that such a

[1] See especially M. Augé Laribé, *Syndicats et coopératives agricoles*, 2nd edition, 1938.
[2] R. de la Tour du Pin, 'Crise agricole ou crise agraire', *l'Association catholique*, 15 August 1886.

statement was a veiled attack on themselves and that monarchists, having suffered electoral defeat, were seeking revenge and influence in a new field. The unions, however, proclaimed a high-minded apoliticism and ostentatiously refrained from taking sides in elections. Governments did not take this abstention at its face value and watched them carefully. A Minister of Agriculture remarked in 1909 that before the unions were granted subsidies, Prefects were instructed to find out whether they 'were engaged in politics or in agriculture', a statement which provoked vehement protests from the Right. The syndicates undoubtedly had a conservative ideology, denying any conflict of interest between agricultural labourers and property owners, and defending religion, traditions and the established social order. But whether they had any effect on elections is hard to ascertain. Distinguished organisers such as Hyacinthe de Gailhard-Bancel and Henri de Lestapis, both clearly motivated by a disinterested idealism in their work for agricultural unions, were elected to parliament. By participating in syndicates and other agricultural organisations, notables remained in contact with their electoral clientele. Occasionally there were deliberate attempts to wreck the agricultural organisations of political opponents, which is a recognition of their influence. Roger Thabault records that in 1895 a co-operative dairy was organised in Deux-Sèvres by a Radical called Proust. The dairy had numerous members who did not share Proust's political ideas and when the Marquis de Maussabré became Deputy for Parthenay (one of the main towns of Deux-Sèvres) in 1898, he opened dairies in the region: his political supporters called a general meeting of Proust's co-operative and voted its dissolution.[1]

Peasants or farmers who worked with their hands played no role at all before the First World War in agricultural organisations at the national level and scarcely any at the regional level: the number of peasants who entered parliament was very small. The representatives of agriculture in both the parliamentary and the professional organisations of agriculture were therefore representatives in the sense of being brokers or advocates. For this reason they came under attack from a wide range of people, including some Radicals, Socialists, progressive Catholics such as the abbé Trochu, who supported agricultural labourers' unions from the 1890s, and Marc Sangnier's Sillonist movement. The Catholic pioneers were followed in the inter-war period by men like the abbé Mancel who organised in Ille-et-Vilaine a *Fédération des Syndicats Paysans* reserved for *cultivateurs cultivants*.[2]

[1] R. Thabault, *Mon Village*, 1944, p. 153.
[2] P. Barral, op. cit., especially pp. 95, 207.

Other developments in the inter-war period helped to undermine the *syndicalisme des ducs*, as the Rue d'Athènes was referred to by its opponents. Producers' associations became more important especially after agricultural prices started to decline in the 1930s. There was also a ferment of political ideas in the agricultural milieu. Whilst many of these ideas were hostile to the traditional dominance of the conservative notables, they were in other ways very much associated with the Right. Specifically peasant political organisations appeared for the first time. The first was the *Entente Paysanne* founded in 1925 with roots mainly in the centre and south-east of the country: it collapsed in 1932 when the Peasant Bank with which it was associated failed. This was followed by the better known *Défense Paysanne* of Henri Dorgères and the *Parti Agraire* of Fleurant Agricola. They expressed a new assertiveness, cultivated a 'peasant style' and even rehabilitated the term 'peasant' which, since the nineteenth century, had a pejorative sense and was avoided by the notables of agricultural syndicalism. These new leaders, although they had remarkably little doctrine, gave the impression of being pastoral Fascists, hostile to intellectuals, foreigners, urban interests and established politicians. They also had a pronounced taste for direct action. Some peasant leaders were attracted by the example of foreign dictators. Roger Grand, Senator for Morbihan, became an apologist for Mussolini as well as representing the apogee of peasantist doctrine, writing in a book published in 1931:

'It is the peasant household, grouping the agricultural family, fixed to the earth, which alone is eminently valuable for moral progress and social formation. . . . Any social movement . . . which is not desired or accepted by the peasantry will sooner or later be broken by it.'[1]

Rémy Goussault was a rare example of a peasant leader becoming sympathetic to the Nazi regime. Louis Salleron was the best known and most persuasive theorist of the Right on agricultural matters. Although accused of Fascism, he was firmly based in an indigenous counter-revolutionary tradition. In his influential doctoral thesis published in 1937, *Un Régime corporatif pour l'agriculture*, he rejected the Jacobin and Napoleonic centralised bureaucracy and 'liberal' individualism, arguing that the peasantry, ill-adapted to an urban and industrial world, needed a new institutional framework. Some of the main lines of his proposal for a corporate system were embodied in the Peasant Corporation of the Vichy regime, whose statute he helped to draft.

[1] R. Grand, *La Force paysanne*, 1931, p. 24, quoted P. Barral, op. cit., p. 234.

The new 'radical' Right had only modest success in acquiring a following amongst the peasantry in the inter-war period, because there were many competitors in the field. In parliamentary elections the Right and the Radicals could contain, without too much difficulty, the threat which they posed. Socialists and Christian Democrats had solid minority followings and even the Communists, with the help of a shrewd tactician, Renaud Jean, were penetrating the agricultural milieu. The two main national agricultural organisations, the *Société des Agriculteurs de France* and the *Société Nationale d'Encouragement à l'Agriculture*, still existed although they were less dominant than they had been before the First World War. Affiliated to them or operating independently were a large number of syndicates, producer groups, mutual aid societies, chambers of agriculture, and credit associations. All had established leaders who were not easily led and their activities were not easily co-ordinated. André Tardieu, whilst *Président du Conseil*, addressed these words to the Congress of French Agriculture in 1931:

'When one has had some experience of talking to your associations, it soon becomes obvious that, in general, they work separately, without taking notice of one another. Within the bosom of associations, rival local and particularist tendencies combat one another with such force that they continue even when a crisis is at its height.'[1]

The Vichy regime radically altered the situation by suppressing all organisations whether professional or political: the only exception was the *Jeunesses Agricoles Chrétiennes* (JAC), classified as an educational movement for youth, which became very influential in forming a progressive new generation of peasant leaders who gradually acquired control of agricultural organisations after the war. However, Pétain's peasant forbears, his appeal to the peasants of France delivered at Pau, the Peasant Charter establishing the Peasant Corporation, the doctrine of 'the return to the earth' and the practical work of Caziot, the first Minister of Agriculture of Vichy, were appreciated by the agricultural milieu and the regime was widely accepted.[2] Despite the new emphasis on agriculture, there was a remarkable continuity in the men active in agricultural affairs and in the thinking about agricultural matters. The Peasant Charter disclaimed any intention of making an entirely new start. 'The government', explained Caziot, 'refrained from building an entirely new system based on theory; the plan [for the Peasant Corporation]

---

[1] Quoted M. Faure, op. cit., p. 62.
[2] For the war period see M. Cépède, *Agriculture et alimentation en France durant la deuxième guerre mondiale*, 1961.

contained elements of experience acquired in the previous half century at least'.[1]

Elements of Vichy agricultural organisation survived the Liberation. The rarity of the peasant leaders not involved in Vichy caused some disarray in the immediate post-war period and the Socialists attempted to extend their influence through a new national organisation, the *Confédération de l'Agriculture*. But the CGA lost the battle for national leadership to the FNSEA (the National Federation of Agricultural Unions) and by 1949 the latter organisation was firmly in the hands of men who had been involved in Vichy. Another effect of Vichy was to undermine the peasantist ideology or attitude. How far ordinary peasants ever believed that they were the basic element of the nation and were representative of superior moral and spiritual values is very hard to ascertain. But the great period of literature in this vein probably opened with the publication in 1932 of Gaston Roupnel's beautifully written *L'Histoire de la campagne française* and closed with the publication in 1945 of Roland Maspétiol's *L'Ordre éternel des champs*. There were extreme and somewhat ludicrous examples of this literature such as R. Mallet's *Nécessités d'un retour à la terre*, published in 1941 at the height of the Vichy enthusiasm in which the author argued that there were political, economic and moral necessities requiring a policy heavily biased in the agricultural interest. But some of the literature on the peasantry of this period showed considerable subtlety and depth of observation. Charles d'Aragon's novel, *L'Heroïne paysanne*, treats with perception the theme of the new peasant leaders emerging alongside the old rural notables. Roger Thabault's impressionistic but acute account of the effects of opening a village community to outside influences through the railways and education (*Mon Village*, 1944) is partly in the peasantist tradition, partly a reaction against it. Although the peasantist doctrine faded slowly after the war it came under sharp attack or rejection from several directions.

One attitude widespread in the immediate post-war period was that the peasant, far from representing high moral values, was a racketeer who had prospered on the misery of others and grown rich from the proceeds of the black market. Vaunting the social role of the peasantry, therefore, was more than ever before regarded as humbug. Partly as the consequences of the processes of economic planning, more senior civil servants and influential journalists became aware that French agriculture posed serious economic and social problems which would take many years to resolve. The serious press, *le Monde*

[1] Hoover Institution, *La Vie de la France sous l'occupation*, 1940–4, vol. 1, 1957, p. 264.

and *le Figaro*, devoted far more space to specific agricultural problems than *le Temps* or *le Figaro* had done before 1939. More academic attention was devoted to rural communities by electoral geographers, sociologists and social historians, and their writings tended to be matter-of-fact and unsentimental. Most of all, peasantist attitudes were rejected by an increasingly influential minority of peasants. The followers of René Colson, the revered leader of the *Jeunesses Agricoles Chrétiennes* who died in 1951 at the age of thirty-eight, came to the fore in agricultural organisations in the 1950s. They questioned the basis of one of the cornerstones of the peasantist ideology, the sacrosanct rights of private property and the autonomy of the family farm. An even more down to earth generation, represented by Louis Lauga, the Secretary General of the *Centre National des Jeunes Agriculteurs*, arrived in positions of influence in the late 1960s. Lauga and his associates are interested only in practical solutions to the problems of agriculture in a period of rapid social change and do not feel constrained by any doctrinaire considerations.[1] These new attitudes formed part of the different environment of peasant politics after 1945 and together with technical progress, greater indebtedness, an awareness that agricultural incomes were growing more slowly than other incomes and increased rural emigration, produced unprecedented insecurity among the peasantry. The protest vote for the Poujadists in 1956 and, from the late 1950s, annual bouts of agitation with frequent recourse to direct action were expressions of this insecurity.

Industrial France and agricultural France are to some extent geographically distinct. The agricultural population is concentrated south-west of a line from Le Havre to Geneva although this area contains very important urban centres – Bordeaux, Toulouse, Marseilles and Lyons. *Départements* north-east of the line have agricultural populations sometimes as low as 8 per cent and rarely approaching 20 per cent, whereas to the south-west the proportion never drops below two-fifths. The areas of relatively dense rural populations are not necessarily those with the highest rates of rural emigration and partly for that reason the separation between industrial and agricultural France is likely to continue. New demographic patterns emerging in the countryside since the Second World War have influenced political structures.[2] Broadly speaking three 'agricultural Frances' have emerged: the thinly populated areas mainly in the east, the mountainous regions and the plateaux of Lorraine

[1] L. Lauga, *Le Centre national des jeunes agriculteurs*, 1971.
[2] 'Les Transformations des sociétés rurales française', special number, *Revue française de sociologie*, 1965.

and Champagne; the semi-urbanised zones around Paris and the Mediterranean coast; the large mass of the agricultural population in the west of France which is also divided roughly into three regions.[1] The Breton peninsula and its bordering *départements* from Vendée to Calvados contains about a quarter of the population engaged in agricultural activities; the south-west is a more heterogeneous region, containing thinly populated zones, but in the 1960s still had over one and a quarter million people living from agriculture;[2] the third region, the north-west from the Pays de Caux to the Belgian frontier, has about half that number. The other agricultural regions, such as the wine growing area of Languedoc, have significantly smaller populations.

The absolute reduction in the size of the rural population has changed the role and function of the small towns of France.[3] The towns of 5,000 to 20,000 inhabitants in the early Third Republic performed the *fonctions bourgeoises* for populous rural hinterlands. Each town, however small, had a number of professional men – doctors, vets, magistrates, lawyers, bankers and civil servants – as well as tradesmen. The political allegiance of the small town bourgeoisie was far from uniform. During the Third Republic a majority were identified with the Radical Party and fought against the influence of the priest and chatelain in the countryside. But certain forms of political influence and dominance, the last major representatives of which were the Independents and Peasants in the Fourth Republic, disappeared with the decline of this bourgeoisie. The small town is now in a satellite of subordinate relationship to the regional or national metropolis and lacks the partial social, economic and political autonomy it once enjoyed. Both the moderate Left and the Right have been greatly affected by this development. The old style cadre party based on small local elites has, as a consequence, become a much less viable form of political organisation.

The declining numbers of the peasants have also assisted their integration into the life of the rest of the nation. They have become full participants in the market economy; near-subsistence farming is a rarity confined to a dying generation. The changes since 1945 have brought the peasants into closer contact with business, commerce, credit institutions, producer and marketing co-operatives, schemes for regulating markets and for increasing the size of landholding and export services. Collectively the changes have been dubbed as 'the second agricultural revolution' and have encouraged

---

[1] R. Livet, *L'Avenir des régions agricoles*, 1965, pp. 63–8.   [2] ibid., p. 195 ff.
[3] H. Mendras, 'Structures écologiques et sociales', *Economie rurale*, July 1956, pp. 17–19.

the aspiration among the peasantry to become *citoyens à part entière*. Whereas some of the agitation of the 1930s such as Dorgères' campaign against the application of social security legislation to the peasants was a demand for separate treatment, the great agitation of the 1960s represented a desire for genuine equality of treatment for the agricultural sector.

The effects of the changes on the internal politics of agricultural organisations are very obvious: old hierarchies have been challenged and the younger, smaller peasants have effectively wrested leadership from the richer and older. The consequences for electoral politics and for party organisation are much less straightforward. In terms of voting behaviour, the once very pronounced differences between the countryside and the towns has been fading for a long time. The contrast between the Republican areas and the conservative rural areas of the Second Empire and the beginning of the Third Republic became less clear, although it was maintained in some regions such as the west, after the conquest by the Radicals of large numbers of rural constituencies.

After the 1885 election, the Right-wing vote in the countryside was remarkably stable. After the 1898 elections when the Deputies of the Right who publicly acknowledged dynastic allegiance dwindled to a small minority, it became increasingly difficult to distinguish the representatives of the agricultural areas in terms of their general political outlook. There was an agrarian populism just under the surface which had some small electoral successes in the 1930s but the agrarian parties and their more successful post-1945 successor, the *Parti Paysan* were short-lived. After 1945 the parties successful in rural areas in parliamentary elections have tended to change rather quickly, in contrast to the relative stability of the men who have held local government office. At the Liberation the MRP found many votes in the villages and agricultural areas but various Independents and Peasants retained strong positions particularly in the Massif Central, Vendée, Brittany and scattered areas in Lorraine and Franche-Comté. In the 1951 election the CNIP emerged the strongest single party in the agricultural community with about a quarter of the peasant votes. A large number of the CNIP Deputies subscribed to the *Programme d'Action Civique* of the National Federation of Agricultural Unions (FNSEA): this marked the high point of post-war influence of conservatives such as Senator René Blondelle in the agricultural unions.[1] Paul Antier vainly hoped to make the Peasant wing of the CNIP the political arm of the agricultural interest but some members of the FNSEA, foreseeing dangers in tying the agricul-

[1] G. Wright, *The Rural Revolution in France*, 1964, pp. 116–19.

tural lobby to a single party, pressed for the formation of a multi-party farm bloc in the National Assembly. For a time, in the 1951-6 parliament, when the Ministry of Agriculture was held by Antier, Laurens and Houdet, and most of the Deputies associated with the agricultural unions were in the party, the CNIP seemed to dominate the agricultural sector. The weakening of the Vichyite and Right-wing element in the national leadership of the agricultural organisations, the increasing discontent of the peasantry at the grass roots, the political difficulties of the CNIP followed by the change of regime and the electoral success of Gaullism destroyed the possibility that the peasantry would have a linked professional and political representation on the lines of the Communist Party and the CGT. The Gaullists elected for agricultural constituencies were not regarded as representing the agricultural interest in the same way as their CNIP predecessors. Especially in Brittany, there occurred the rather paradoxical situation of the majority of the peasantry in certain constituencies voting for Gaullists in parliamentary elections and rioting against the agricultural policies of Gaullist governments. After the establishment of the Fifth Republic far greater reliance was placed by the peasants on professional organisations and direct action rather than parliamentary influence. Some strong pressure came from parliamentarians on agricultural matters – on one occasion so strong that the government had to ignore a constitutional provision in order to circumvent it – but the peasants realised, like most of the other organised interests, that the influence of parliament was greatly reduced in the Fifth Republic.

The two most obvious features of parliamentary representation of agriculture since 1945 have been that it has never been monopolised by a single party and that the number of Deputies with professional or family backgrounds in agriculture has declined. From a peak in 1951 of sixty-six Deputies with agricultural origins, this number sank to a low point of thirty-two in 1962, to recover slightly to forty-three in 1967 and fall back to thirty-six in 1968. The most remarkable characteristic of the voting behaviour of the agricultural areas is the extent to which they resembled the rest of the country. As Klatzman observed in 1958: 'Everywhere, or almost everywhere, the electoral behaviour of the agricultural voters closely parallels that of the non-agricultural population, above all if, among the latter, the workers are excluded. It is not, therefore, factors internal to agriculture which explain the marked regional differences.'[1] Since 1962 the Gaullist following in the countryside is almost exactly

[1] J. Klatzmann, 'Géographie électorale de l'agriculture française' in J. Fauvet, H. Mendras, op. cit., pp. 39–67.

equivalent to the proportion of rural dwellers in the nation as a whole. The parliamentary Right, therefore, has had and has continued to have a strong rural following, without ever dominating the rural milieu since the early years of the Third Republic; it has had a changing relationship with agricultural organisations which it has never controlled at the national level and over which it now has little influence; notables of a traditional kind continue to be important in local politics in conservative rural areas but the aristocrats, *hobereaux* and rural bourgeoisie who dominated parliamentary elections in the Third Republic have, in most cases, been superseded by Gaullists dependent for their electoral success on the patronage of a powerful political party.

Bourgeoisies: professions, groups and milieux

The profession of arms is the only profession which has been as closely associated with the Right as school teaching has been with the Left.[1] Army officers who have entered parliament have, usually although not always, entered parliamentary groups of the Right. The professions of law, medicine and university teaching have provided recruits for all political movements, except those with an overtly anti-intellectual character such as the Poujadist movement. Although the centre of gravity of the representatives of these professions who have entered parliament since the beginning of the Third Republic has been on the Left, the *professions libérales* as they are usually called, have since the turn of the century been bastions of social conservatism. Many of the professional men who entered the Radical Party, especially after 1914, did so precisely in order to defend 'Republican conquests' and to avoid radical social change. Important financial interests realised, from the first half of the Third Republic, that the moderately Left-wing lawyer, such as Waldeck-Rousseau or Millerand, was a better defender of particular causes and of the general fiscal status quo than reactionaries with no access to political power. Effective defence of established positions and resistance to social change often came from men who were not identified with the Right in politics. This was partly because members of the liberal professions were subject to relatively few constraints in their choice of political allegiance. They could espouse the principles of 1789 and of subsequent revolutions without damaging their career or material well-being. The professional corporations to which they belonged had strong traditions and hierarchies, and were relatively well satisfied with the established social order. A measure

[1] M. Dogan, 'Les Officiers dans la carrière politique: du Maréchal MacMahon au Général de Gaulle', *Revue française de sociologie*, vol. 2, 1961, pp. 88–99.

of their self-satisfaction is that, until the 1960s, few radical criticisms of the nature and organisation of the professions have come from their own members. Threatened by change, they have often manifested a visceral conservatism but no necessarily espoused Right-wing views on general policy matters.

The institutions of higher education through which professional men passed often had a lasting influence on their political outlook. The political atmosphere of these institutions was not static and each succeeding generation modified it. From the time of the Dreyfus affair the *École Normale Supérieure* of the Rue d'Ulm had the general reputation of being Left-wing with leanings towards democratic socialism, the *École Libre des Sciences Politiques* (after 1946, the *Institut National des Sciences Politiques*) was, during the Third Republic and again after about 1962, regarded as fashionable, bourgeois and a moderate defender of the established order. During the Fourth Republic, it was Left-wing Catholic and Mendèsiste in tone and, during the Fifth Republic, moderate Gaullist. The Paris Faculty of Law has supplied a disproportionately large element of the youth sections of monarchist, nationalist and neo-Fascist leagues. The Faculty of Medicine was firmly Republican in the late nineteenth century but seemed to move gradually to the Right (doctors were numerous in *Action Française*). The changed patterns of recruitment and conditions of the medical profession which began to make themselves felt from the beginning of the Fifth Republic, have probably reversed this trend. Educational institutions, with the newspaper press, have been the main communicators of political traditions. They have helped to preserve what Albert Thibaudet called *familles d'esprits* which in his words 'often do not correspond with systems of interests, sometimes do not coincide at all with parliamentary groups'. Traditions of the Right have been encrusted in parts of the educational and cultural establishment for the last century at least. The Académie Française, membership of which is the final accolade of intellectual and social respectability, is the most outstanding example of this. It has never been without conservative priests and soldiers, and its 'party of dukes'.[1] Although the Académie attempts to balance Right and Left in electing new members, the Right often seems to dominate as when it secured the election of Charles Maurras in 1937 and when the overwhelming majority of academicians rallied to the Vichy regime in 1940.

If no cultural or educational establishments, even the *École libre* and the Catholic faculties, have been exclusively Right-wing,

[1] General M. Weygand, *L'Armée à l'Académie*, 1963. Duke de Lèvis-Mirepoix, *Que Signifie 'le parti des ducs' à l'académie?*, 1964.

it is even more striking that no important lobby or interest group has maintained a longstanding connection with any political party of the Right. Financial support for the parties has been organised on an *ad hoc* basis, either through individuals or by committees especially established for the purpose. Employers' organisations have had a natural disposition towards the Right but they have not, unlike individual industrialists, had much influence over parties, individual members of parliament or electoral politics. Since the law of 25 May 1864 provided a legal framework for employers' association, their role has been mainly to provide services for their members, a forum for discussion of common problems and, since the foundation of the *Alliance Syndicale du Commerce et de l'Industrie*, research into fiscal problems, legislation, insurance, transport problems and such matters. The *Confédération Générale de la Production Française* (founded in 1919) commonly referred to as the Rue de Madrid, became a symbol for the 'two hundred families' between the wars. Although in terms of membership (2,000 employers' syndicates and 25 professional sections) it seemed strong, its actual industrial and political influence was very limited. Its most powerful affiliated group, the *Comité des Forges*, which was alleged to control it, was very reticent in political matters. Conscious of its widespread unpopularity, it sought to avoid commitments which would make relations between it and governments difficult.[1] For similar reasons, the most influential individuals in French business have usually avoided public political activities.

The owners or controllers of large manufacturing industry have seldom been Deputies since the turn of the twentieth century. The steelmasters, François de Wendel, Guy de Wendel, Charles Schneider and Jean Plichon in coal, metals and banking were relics of a nineteenth-century practice and found no real successors. Representatives of business in parliament were more likely to have some business interests, rather than have actual control of large firms, or to emerge from small- or medium-sized family firms. Never popular with any large section of the electorate, big business has preferred to exercise pressure on governments discreetly. Both large industry and the employers organisation, the *Conseil National du Patronat Français* (established in 1945 and commonly called the Rue de Penthièvre) have probably had more consistent influence over both industrial relations and government policy after the acceptance by the government in 1945 of broad responsibility for planning and managing the economy.

[1] An excellent general account of the political attitudes of the patronat can be found in H. W. Ehrmann, *Organised Business in France*, 1957.

Regular consultations between government and both sides of industry in the *Commissariat Général au Plan* and in the various consultative committees of the economic ministries, and the representation of the CNPF, as well as the trade unions, in the Economic and Social Council has provided channels of communication with the government and the administration. These somewhat reduce the need to exercise influence through parliament, although they do not dispense with the need for parliamentary goodwill. The large numbers of small commercial and artisanal enterprises in France made *les classes moyennes* a potentially attractive clientele, often wooed by politicians of the Right.[1] For example, in 1936 after the small employers objected to the terms of the Matignon agreements, which Léon Blum negotiated with representatives of the *Confédération Générale de la Production Française* and the *Confédération Générale du Travail* to bring to an end occupation of factories by the workers, the *classes moyennes* began to receive considerable attention. Many marks of solicitude came from politicians and the press. A new organisation, the *Confédération Générale des Classes Moyennes* was established to bring together other groups such as the *Confédération Nationale des Classes Moyennes* and the *Confédération des Cadres de l'Économie Française*. This 'class consciousness' was clearly not spontaneous; there was a deliberate attempt to organise and mobilise a social category which had little sense of solidarity. The Poujadist movement of the 1950s, when in rather different circumstances many small commercial enterprises were actually threatened with extinction, showed that such a campaign could be temporarily successful.

A large number of people continue to run small commerical and artisanal business – 8 per cent of the working population according to the 1968 census. Feeling under severe economic pressure, members of the professional group again became very militant. In 1969, Gerard Nicoud, a young demagogue, organised CID–UNATI[2] to put pressure on the government to legislate in favour of the small business. His campaigns have included mass meetings, demonstrations, tax-strikes, plastic bombing and burning of supermarkets, and kidnapping public officials: some of these activities have brought Nicoud and his followers prison terms. Following the pattern of Right-wing agitators, Nicoud despises predecessors and

[1] For the extensive bibliography on the *classes moyennes* see L. Moulin, L. Aertz, 'Les Classes moyennes; essai de bibliographie critique', *Revue d'histoire économique et sociale*, 1954, pp. 161–81, 293–309.

[2] *Centre d'Information et de Défense – Union Nationale des Artisans et des Travailleurs Indépendants.*

spurns Poujade, although he has fairly amicable relations with Léon Gingembre, the leader of the CGPME. He has refrained from participation in elections but the possibility of his intervention is viewed with some alarm on the Right. Nicoud claims that some Gaullist Deputies are showing 'comprehension' for his cause.

Urban conservatism of the Third and Fourth Republics, outside the capital, was typically based on rather small and isolated bourgeois groups. One or two constituencies in the large cities were usually held by the Right. Marseilles, Bordeaux, Lyons, Le Havre, Nantes, Nancy, Lille (although not Toulouse) regularly sent Deputies of the Right to parliament from the end of the nineteenth century. The Right-wing voters lived generally in the prosperous, residential areas – the *beaux quartiers*. These urban islands could be expanded in circumstances of social and political tension by a 'radical' element demanding constitutional and political change. Turn of the century nationalism, the leagues of the 1930s and the RPF all illustrated in different ways, the appeal of a *droite contestaire* in the urban milieu significantly wider than that of the traditional notables of the parliamentary Right. The notables, although sometimes carried along for a time by these 'surge' movements were usually basically hostile to them. Examples of the urban constituencies which regularly elected conservative notables are the third (roughly the first in the Fifth Republic) constituency of Marseilles which sent representatives of the business circles of the port to the Chamber such as Charles-Roux and Joseph Thierry in the Third Republic and was the main basis for the support of Henry Bergasse in the Fourth Republic. The second and eighth (subsequently tenth) constituencies of Lyons elected men like Edouard Aynard, Alphonse Gourd and Pierre Pays before the First World War and Antoine Sallès and François Peissel after it: Pierre Montel and Guy Jarosson were the most notable continuators of the tradition in the Fourth Republic; the second constituency of Le Havre, the fief of the Ancel family occupied for some time by Louis Brindeau and Paul Bignon's constituency in Dieppe are other examples.

The variety of the local bourgeois societies in these constituencies was considerable. They seldom lived under the shadow of an aristocracy, even at the beginning of the Third Republic. They had an independent and self-confident outlook based on relative affluence and well-established, sometimes very old, families. However, there were among them what many people from Balzac to Tixier-Vignancour have referred to as the *bourgeoisie de tradition*, a group which held to old-fashioned standards and moral values. It was usually contrasted with the *bourgeoisie de l'argent* interested mainly in making money and entirely opportunistic in politics. The stereotype of the *bourgeoisie de tradition*, which owed much to literary models from Balzac to Paul Bourget and René Bazin, was essentially provincial, withdrawn from politics, practising religion, voting for candidates of the Right but privately refractory to the Republican ideal, and profoundly pessimistic about the conduct of public affairs. The references to the *bourgeoisie de tradition*, particularly those made by Tixier-Vignancour and other members of the extreme Right,[1] seem often to refer not to a specific social group but to a state of mind, easier to feel than to define, composed of nostalgia, regrets, sympathies and hostilities. This state of mind has contributed, like the aristocracy in a different way, an element in the politics of the Right. It largely accounts for the *Schadenfreude* with which the collapse of successive Republics have been greeted and to the welcome given by sections of the bourgeoisie to the defeat of democratic, especially Left-wing governments abroad, even though their defeat did not appear in the French national interest.

The author of a monograph on the not particularly conservative *département* of Eure[2] between the wars observed that 'the bourgeoisie greeted with sympathy the advent of Fascism in Italy (October 1922), the substitution of a presidential regime under Hindenburg for the democratic Republic in Germany and the acceptance by the President of the Republic, Alexandre Millerand, of the revisionist cause in his Evreux speech on 14 October 1923'. Later in the period, the victory of the Popular Front in 1936 'exacerbated passions' and the bourgeoisie was Munichois on 'defeatist grounds': at the defeat there was a convergence of *Maréchalisme* and anti-Republicanism and the behaviour of some led to charges that there was an extensive Fifth column in Eure – 'Jean de la Varende, novelist of the Pays d'Ouche, thought it proper to make speeches, under the chairmanship of German officers', condemning France's pre-war allies. After the Liberation the bourgeoisie was quick to denounce the incoherence of the purge of Collaborators. This chronicle could be continued in a similar vein through the Fourth Republic, terminating with a marked sympathy for the French Algeria lobby. There were bourgeois circles in the large provincial cities and in small towns in widely scattered regions such as Compiègne (Oise), Villefranche (Rhône) and Nîmes (Gard), which roughly represented this state

[1] For a recent use of this term by Tixier-Vignancour see his review of the Radical Party manifesto, *Le Monde*, 13 February 1970.

[2] M. Baudot, *L'Opinion publique sous l'occupation. L'exemple d'un département français, 1939–45*, 1960, pp. 2–5, 47, 54, 210–11.

of mind. But the *bourgeoisie de tradition* and the *bourgeoisie de l'argent* are ideal types and difficult to distinguish in practice.

No particular bourgeois society is typical of the French bourgeoisie as a whole but one of the most interesting is the *patronat du Nord* because, for a time, it combined the characteristics of the bourgeoisies *de l'argent* and *de tradition*. The prosperity of this group of families was built on textile manufactures in the *département* of Nord and, to a lesser extent, Pas-de-Calais. It has a remarkable history as a cohesive group of considerable social influence and political power in the nineteenth and twentieth centuries. The great days of the textile industry were over by the end of the 1920s and the great depression brought to an end the semi-autonomous economic status of the north. This partial autonomy had been the basis of the peculiarities and the social authority of the *patronat*. Its disappearance did not, however, destroy the *patronat* whose members either diversified their interests becoming figures of national consequence, or they retrenched and survived in the region, sometimes in reduced circumstances.

The twin pillars of economic expansion in Nord in the nineteenth century were mining and textiles.[1] The ownership and direction of the two industries remained remarkably distinct, a situation which persisted, with certain exceptions, until the post Second World War nationalisation of the coal industry. Coal was first mined at Anzin in 1734: it was and continued to be exploited by members of noble families. At the beginning of the Third Republic (in 1878) the board of the Mines d'Anzin consisted of Baron Chabaud de la Tour, Senator, General and ex-Minister of the Interior, Baron de la Grange, Deputy, Marquis Talhoüet-Roy, Senator and former Minister, Duke d'Audiffret Pasquier, a President of the Senate, Cornelius de Witt, an ex-Secretary of State and Deputy, and Jean Casimir-Périer, a future President of the Republic. Most of these men had noble titles and were the most celebrated names of 'Orleanist' France. Accustomed to sitting in the parliamentary assemblies, they formed an important section of the parliamentary Right for the first two decades of the Third Republic. They were part of a national rather than a local elite and were rarely elected for northern constituencies: very few were elected after the 1880s, although an Audiffret Pasquier survived in an Orne constituency until the Second World

---

[1] The outstanding work on the regional economy is R. Gendarme, *La Région du Nord*, 1954. For the general problem of location of industry in France see F. Coront-Ducluzeau, *La Formation de l'espace économique français*, 1959. L. Gorny, *Les Economies régionales de la France*, 1958.

War. They were very discreet about their monarchist sentiments, if indeed they retained them, after a restoration became improbable. These men also tended to have interests in the related field of heavy industry in the north – iron and steel. In metals, unlike mining, they did not dominate the industry. Paris merchant banks, controlled by Jews and Protestants, as well as industrialists from other regions of France also had interests. By the end of the Second World War the only major firm in metals which was not represented in the north was Schneider. Members of the textile *patronat* have been represented on the board of the great steel combine USINOR, founded in 1947, but there has been almost as definite a separation of control between metals and textiles as between mining and textiles. Until the 1930s the textile patronat seemed content to limit most of its activities to the one industry.

The economy of the north has had other structural peculiarities. The level of agricultural activity continued high (for example in the 1950s although agriculture represented only about 5 per cent of the annual turnover, the *départements* of Nord and Pas-de-Calais were amongst the most productive in the country) and this helped to explain the demographic peculiarity of the region. It was not until some time between the 1954 and 1962 censuses that the proportion of people living in rural communes dropped below 50 per cent and only one eighth of the population in 1954 lived in towns of over 50,000. Until the end of the nineteenth century it was a common practice for workers to combine an industrial occupation, in textiles, with peasant agricultural activities.[1] Agricultural and industrial activities also came together at the entrepreneurial level, particularly in the linen industry where most of the original manufacturers were farmers.

The brusque passage from a rural to an urban environment was attentuated in the northern textile industry and the effects of depressions in the industry could be reduced by a temporary retreat to the land. As a consequence, certain patterns of social behaviour, particularly religious practice, persisted in ways unusual in other industrial areas. Amongst the textile workers, religious practice remained common until the twentieth century. The entrepreneurs of the north, unlike most capitalist entrepreneurs in Europe of the first half of the nineteenth century, were and remained Catholic.[2]

[1] R. Fruit, *L'Agriculture dans la région du Nord*, 1958, p. 74, for the gradual disappearance of the worker peasant.

[2] P. Henry, *Mouvement patronal catholique français*, 1936. R. Talmy, *Un Forme hybride du catholicisme sociale en France. L'Association catholique des patrons du Nord, 1884–1895*, 1962. The archetypal Catholic employer was Léon Harmel at Val-des-Bois, in the neighbouring *département* of Ardennes. See J. Guitton, *La Vie ardente et féconde de Léon Harmel*, 1929.

Although there were traces of sentiments akin to the Protestant ethic – that work is the first duty of man and is closely associated with salvation – there was an unusual disposition to accept theoretical limits on the right to pursue profits. Ideas of social justice, usually of a very paternalist kind, were found among the *patronat* of the late nineteenth century. Traditionalism in social and religious spheres was flanked by conservatism in industrial practice. The textile entrepreneurs of the north were adaptors not innovators and no important invention originates from the area. The location of factories was often not chosen on rational economic grounds and the internal organisation of factories corresponded even less to the ideal type of capitalist organisation.[1] Some had the appearance of great artisanal workshops even in the twentieth century.

The institution of the family seemed to give the textile *patronat* its strength and dynamism.[2] The great names in textiles – Tiberghien, Masurel, Lepoutre, Prouvost, Toulemonde all go back at least to the first half of the nineteenth century and the firm of Motte-Cordonnier has passed from father to son for over two hundred years. Families have been much larger than is usually found in other bourgeois groups: the effect of this has been less to fragment ownership of firms than to increase their number. Fathers tended to set their sons up in business – at one time there were no fewer than eight Mottes in cotton spinning – not only in the north but also abroad, and in some other industries which operated in units of roughly the same scale such as brewing or sugar refining. A complex of family ties linked all the families of the textile *patronat*; to distinguish various branches of families it was customary to add the wife's maiden name to her husband's. Sometimes they were the same and this gave rise to names such as Motte-Motte and Selosse-Selosse. The family networks helped to give a homogeneity to the reactions and psychology of the textile industrialists of the north. They placed great emphasis on independence, especially independence from state control, and on the continuity of the firm.

The same families which dominated the textile industries also controlled the regional banks. The industrialists themselves created the capital necessary to finance most of the locally based industry: the banks were a direct emanation of industry to a much greater degree than can be found in other French regions. This had two main

[1] P. Bruyelle, 'L'industrie cotonnière à Lille-Roubaix-Tourcoing' *Revue du Nord*, vol. 36, 1954, pp. 21–40.
[2] R. Gendarme, op. cit., 107, 108, 179–82, *passim*. J. A. Roy, J. Lambert-Dansette, 'Origines et évolution d'une bourgeoisie. Le patronat textile du bassin lillois, 1789–1914', *Revue du Nord*, 1958, pp. 49–69, 1969, pp. 23–38.

effects: bankruptcies were rare and firms either continued to exist for a long time or were wound up gracefully; the circular form of credit assured to the *patronat* an unusual independence and autonomy of decision until the great depression. In the 1930s, the region became too narrow a context for credit operations and some regional banks disappeared (e.g. Banque Georges Clarin – Lille; Piérard, Mabille et Cie – Valenciennes; Banque Peyt – Dunkirk, etc.). Others became national banks like the Crédit du Nord or were merged with existing national banks.[1] This development, the continued decline of cotton (the lead in man-made fibres was taken in other regions), the dislocation of war and increased government intervention in the economy and the relative economic decline of the north have almost completely destroyed the economic autonomy of the region without altogether destroying the *patronat* as a distinctive social group. Bertrand Motte and others have worked strenuously in the post-war period to create new regional institutions and revive the economy but with only modest success. The defeat of Bertrand Motte in the general election of 1962 marked the end of electoral influence of the textile *patronat*.

Indeed, the electoral dominance of the *patronat* was over by the First World War; leadership passed to the Left and the Socialists from the election of 1919, but there were three or four Deputies who, broadly speaking, could be described as representing the *patronat* after each of the inter-war elections. Most belonged to the *Fédération Républicaine*, like Louis Nicolle, who had interests in textiles, distilling and transport, and Jean Plichon, Deputy for Hazebrouck, who was chairman of the Mines de Béthune and held directorships in other firms engaged in mining, metals and banking. No other extensive industrial group possessed the same sort of political influence over such a relatively large population. The steelmasters in the inter-war period in Meurthe-et-Moselle seemed to be the nearest approach to it.[2] Both Guy and François de Wendel were in parliament; two other steelmasters, Edouard de Warren and Amidou du Clos, and a close associate, Louis Marin, were Deputies. This situation arose from the dominance of only one family, the Wendels, and the political alliance between François de Wendel and Louis Marin. Marin, Deputy from 1905 to 1951, was not dependent politically on the Wendels (although the Left alleged that he was) and he did not come from the *patronal* milieu.

[1] G. Charpenay, *Les Banques régionales, leur vie et leur mort*, 1939. G. Martin, *Les Banques régionales*, 1922. After 1945 the *Crédit du Nord* was the largest non-nationalised deposit bank in the country. J. G. S. Wilson, *French Banking Structure and Credit Policy*, 1951, p. 26.
[2] R. Sédillot, *La Maison de Wendel de mil sept cent quatre à nos jours*, 1958.

The most remarkable feature of the *patronat du Nord*, during their most influential period in the first half of the Third Republic, was the degree to which they preserved political coherence with virtually no public political organisation. The best example of their political coherence was their response to the *Ralliement*. Following the papal advice in *Au milieu des sollicitudes*, the leaders of the textile industry rallied almost to a man, carrying all but one of the Deputies for Nord with them. The hard core of royalists either came from the rural Flemish hinterland or were engaged in independent professional activities: they formed royalist circles and, subsequently, joined *Action Française*. They had quite a following in the region but little influence on electoral politics.

The industrial notables of Nord linked by family ties, neighbourly relations, business interests, membership of the same Catholic circles and committees, conducted their business and political activities along almost exactly the same lines. According to two police reports on the employers' milieu in the middle 1880s when it was still royalist, 'nothing emerges in public from their meetings which take place *en famille* by the fireside'; 'The essential part of the internal life of royalism takes place in the family, professional and religious contexts, impenetrable to the outsider.'[1] Political action was, for the *patronat*, based on communities of interest. Political co-operation took place between men who knew and understood one another very well: political parties and public political organisation were window dressing for private understandings and informal 'non-political' relations. This sort of attitude survived as long as the *patronat*, and elements of it remain in men who have come from that quarter to occupy positions of considerable importance at the national level such as the press barons, who have controlled *le Figaro*, Ferdinand Béghin (also owner of *Paris-Soir* before the Second World War), and Jean Prouvost (also owner of *Paris-Match*), or Bertrand Motte in the National Assembly (chairman of the Independent and Peasant group in 1961–2). The mentality of the *patronat du Nord* survived the economic transformations which destroyed its local political power.

There were always cleavages within the textile manufacturers of the north – between linen and cotton, spinning and weaving and between different family groupings – but there has been no other large employers' group which has had such distinctive common characteristics. The textile industry of Alsace might have had a similar

[1] Quoted A. Bonafous, *Les Royalistes du Nord et le ralliement*, unpublished *mémoire*, 1963, pp. 78–9. Same author, 'Les Royalistes du Nord et le ralliement', *Revue du Nord*, vol. 57, 1965, pp. 29–48.

development if the province had not been annexed by Germany for forty-seven years.[1] Many areas of France had artisanal textile manufacturers in the first half of the nineteenth century which either disappeared or did not develop on the same scale, or were, like the silk manufacturers of Lyons, in a highly vulnerable commercial position. There were few other industries which could support such a range of medium-size firms. Shipping, sugar refining, tanning and brewing could do so but in practice tended to be very dispersed. There were numerous small foundries and forges even after the Second World War but the metals industry tended to be led by the large firms. The domination of François and Humbert de Wendel when the former was President of the Comité des Forges from 1918 to 1940 and Regent of the Bank of France until 1936, and the latter was President and Vice-President of the Comptoir Sidérurgique during the same period and member of the International Steel Entente, has no parallel in textiles until the great expansion of the Boussac empire from the 1930s. Northern textiles up to that time, therefore, represented a kind of archetypal capitalism of small and medium-sized firms with the qualification that competition between them was considered to be a very relative thing. This sort of industrial organisation has had a very wide appeal on the Right, almost at the level of myth. The small or medium-sized firm, with an honest and reliable reputation, which looked after its employees and was owned by the same family for generations, was considered by many as a much preferable form of industrial organisation to the large capitalist enterprise, frequently denounced as 'trusts' by the extreme Right. Antoine Pinay, the tanner of Saint Chamond, represented the former type of industrialist perfectly. He was widely respected, even idolised, on the Right. His colleague and political enemy in the CNIP, and his successor as *Président du Conseil*, Joseph Laniel, owned textile mills in Normandy and, although by mid-twentieth century standards it was only a medium-sized firm, he was denounced as representative of the 'trusts'.

The textile industrialists of the north had very idiosyncratic characteristics. Their political influence, their ideas about political organisation, their attitudes towards political issues were all greatly influenced by the particular economic and social position they occupied in the region. All the urban bourgeois groups engaged in industrial and commercial activity during the Third Republic were similarly enmeshed in unique sets of relationships, commitments and prospects. The *patronat du Nord* is a rather extreme example of the autonomy of an industrial and commercial milieu, which

[1] J. Berger, *L'Industrie cotonnière alsacienne*, 1952.

supported this localism, but it was part of a general pattern. The relatively slow economic growth of the inter-war period helped to preserve this pattern. The external factors tending to break down the old forms of regional autonomy in all parts of France – movement of population and capital, development of national and international firms, rapid industrial growth and economic planning – did not become overwhelming until the 1950s. These changes helped to create a social context in which the unity of Right-wing forces was a much greater possibility.

Conclusion
Why did conservatives coming from different social milieux, although broadly speaking the same class, have such persistent difficulty in co-operating politically? Part of the answer to this question is that class loyalty and identity has been fragmented and sometimes submerged by other loyalties – to smaller reference groups, interest groups and social institutions. The local, restricted and highly specific nature of the loyalties of the French people, particularly if they are of a conservative disposition, has often been exaggerated but the sub-groups which attract loyalty are many and highly complex. A part of the titled nobility preserved an idiosyncratic sub-culture and style of life until the First World War; this has been transmitted in an attentuated form down to the present day. In terms of 'objective' class interest it is difficult to distinguish the nobility from sections of the bourgeoisie at any time since 1830, but the social attitudes of the aristocracy influenced Right-wing politics after the introduction of universal suffrage and contributed to the problems of establishing effective political organisations. Another group whose boundaries are even harder to define, and which rivals the nobility in the antiquity of its origins, is the *bourgeoisie de l'État*, the senior civil servants and the Parisian milieu which has provided a high proportion of the senior administrators of the State. Since the administrative centralisation of the seventeenth century this group has been numerous and powerful; 'democratisation' of recruitment to the senior civil service since the Second World War has only partially undermined its influence. Through a distinguished tradition of public law, the senior civil servants came to embody the 'State' and to regard themselves as guardians of the 'general interest' against the competing claims of political parties and pressure groups.[1] This view of public affairs has made an important contribution to the continuity of the State in circumstances of

[1] B. Gourdon, 'Les Grands commis et le mythe de l'intérêt général', *Cahiers de la République*, vol. 1, 1956, pp. 78–90.

instability of governments and regimes, but it encouraged the denigration of the democratic or representative side of the constitution. A small group of parliamentarians in successive Republics have either come from or been greatly influenced by this milieu and, therefore, have had more in common with senior civil servants than with fellow members of parliament, even those relatively close to them on general policy matters.

Tensions between the *bourgeoisie de l'État* and other bourgeois societies helped to sustain hostility between Paris and the provinces. But the provincial conservative societies, based on towns and regions, have differed from one another at least as much as they have from metropolitan society. Economic expansion and social change have rapidly changed their character. But there remain important divergences of sentiment, tradition and interest between the traditionalist, rural, aristocratic, Catholic groups of some Breton and western *départements*, and the remnants of the traditionalist, Catholic, urban *patronat du Nord*, the steelmasters of Lorraine and the *bourgeoisie Alsacienne*. The burghers of Lyons with interests in a variety of financial, industrial and commercial enterprises have lived in a different environment from that of the professional families living under the shadow of Schneider at Le Creusot[1] or Wendel at Briey where a single firm has dominated a region. Widely dispersed bourgeois groups have possessed common characteristics, sometimes expressed in a common political outlook. The shippers, refiners, maritime insurers, traders of the great ports of Marseilles, Bordeaux, Nantes, Le Havre, Cherbourg and Dieppe, were the last bastion of free trade doctrine in the late nineteenth and early twentieth centuries. But, in general, regional differentiation has been very strong and the factors which have contributed to regional identities have been so great that the geographical location of social groups has been more important than their other characteristics. This has been even more marked in rural than in urban societies.

The peasantry was from the beginning of the Third Republic, and still remains, very divided in its political behaviour. It has not been at any time since the Great Revolution exclusively traditionalist, conservative and Right-wing. From the late nineteenth century, although peasants generally have been less inclined to vote for Left-wing candidates in elections than industrial workers they have voted more to the Left than the rest of the community if the industrial workers are subtracted. The political allegiance of rural communities has shown a remarkable capacity to survive great political upheavals

[1] J. A. Roy, *Histoire de la famille Schneider et du Creusot*, 1962.

and important social changes. The political differences between rural communities can be explained by factors such as the richness of the soil, the climate, the system of land-holding which interact with various human factors – communications, population density, religious practice and historical events. Different rates of economic development, different styles and standards of living, different social patterns, different patois and, occasionally, different languages, helped to preserve regional distinctiveness. Despite Marx's brilliant metaphor comparing the peasantry to a sack of potatoes, a collection of more or less equal but separate units which were incapable of coming together and had to be held together and represented by others,[1] it is an error to regard the peasantry as a social class with common interests. Economic change has reduced the numbers of peasants and, since 1945, given them a greater cohesion and sense of solidarity, but the social cleavages within the agricultural milieu remain sharp.

The very rich – the Rothschilds, the *Haute Banque Protestante*, the great industrialists and *commerçants*, even when, like Wendel, Schneider and Jaluzot, they have been Deputies – have played a secondary role in conservative politics.[2] They have exerted rather negative influence behind the scenes, financed political parties for relatively short periods and have sometimes had some effect on public opinion through control of newspapers. Left-wing governments have never been able to carry through a decisive attack on their interests. But financial power is difficult, in most circumstances, to translate directly into political power and success in elections in France, at least until the Fifth Republic, has not, as far as one can tell, correlated with the expenditure of money. Plentiful funds certainly facilitated campaigning and may, in some cases, have tipped the balance, but only one or two constituencies in the Third Republic could actually be bought by very rich men. Success in elections depended, for all Right-wing candidates in virtually all elections, on the establishment of a personal following in the constituency. To do this it was necessary to be or to become a 'notable'. In the most general terms, the history of the social bases of Right-wing politics since the Third Republic has been the history

[1] K. Marx, 'The 18th Brumaire de Louis Napoleon', *Selected Works*, vol. 1, 1962, p. 334.
[2] Many authors have alleged that they have controlled public authorities behind the scenes. In the inter-war period Raymond Mennevée edited a periodical, *Les Documents politiques, diplomatiques, et financiers*, to document this thesis. Other substantial works based on this view are E. Beau de Loménie, *Les Responsabilités des dynasties bourgeoises*, 1943–63, 4 vols. A. Hamon, *Les Maîtres de la France*, 3 vols, 1936–8.

of the transformation and decline, but not the disappearance, of the notables.

The end of the notables has been many times announced but has not yet happened. Daniel Halèvy wrote a celebrated book about the beginning of the Third Republic entitled *la Fin des notables*, but the electoral politics of the Right through most of the Third and Fourth Republics was the business of notables. To define precisely what is meant by the term 'notable' is far from easy. All kinds of attributes help to support the status of a notable – the number of social relations and contacts, office-holding in associations and societies, a large extra-professional correspondence, a reasonably good income allowing ease of movement, leisure and the offer of hospitality, military and civil decorations, degrees and distinctions. A good professional background in industry, commerce, medicine, the university, public administration, law, journalism or agriculture helps to establish a reputation. Political followings or clienteles have grown up, apparently spontaneously, around men of public standing.

During the Third Republic the notable could, without much specialist knowledge or training, intervene in most of the affairs and problems of his commune or constituency. One of the general reasons for the decline of the notable is that administrative, social and economic changes have made it difficult to be competent over a wide range of local matters. The growing complexity of the social services, increasing intervention of the State in land-use planning and economic development, the establishment of a regional layer in the administration have made it increasingly difficult in some areas for the notable to intervene effectively on behalf of his followers. Economic change, which has come relatively rapidly since 1945 compared with the Third Republic, has worked against the notables: the effort of keeping informed and analysing its implications for a specific locality has become a full-time occupation requiring professional skills. Economic growth has also had effects on the conditions of professional life. Professional careers have become much more time consuming and deprive a greater proportion of men with high social standing of the leisure necessary to participate in public life. In some activities, such as industrial management and university teaching, careers have become more mobile. This has often deprived men of the local roots usually needed to acquire *notabilité*. Finally, the political crises since 1940 have damaged the ability of the notables to provide a lead at the local level. The Vichy experience, Gaullism of the Fourth Republic, the Algerian War and the establishment of the Fifth Republic not only created bitter divisions among moderate and conservative notables, they also undermined the grass roots consensus on which their position rested. When ideological conflict divides the clientele of the notable, his situation becomes very insecure. Differences of view about specific policies can be conciliated and contained but arguments about the course of history are unmanageable.

All these developments have not, however, destroyed the *notabilité* who have shown, in the Fifth Republic, the resilience to resist the Gaullist tide in local, if not national elections. Moreover in national politics, some of the members of the UDR, all the 'Centrists' and most of the Giscardiens are, in the traditional meaning of the term, notables – owing more to their personal status and following than to their party label. The survival of the notable is of great political importance because the basis of disciplinary authority of the Gaullist party would be at risk if a large minority of its Deputies became notables, ensconced in impregnable local positions. The strength of the local implantation of individual Gaullists remains, however, uncertain in most cases.

CHAPTER III

Political Organisation at the Beginning of the Twentieth Century

When modern political parties were established in France in the first decade of the twentieth century, the creation of a large, durable party of the Right seemed a task of overwhelming difficulty and complexity. In this period two types of political organisation – the electoral association and the extra-parliamentary league – competed for influence. Both were ineffective in terms of capturing political power. The leagues had a certain *succès de scandale* but little electoral importance, which partly reflected the distaste of the majority of voters for overt reactionaries. The use made by the parliamentary Right of words such as liberal, popular, democratic, republican and progressive in the titles of their groups and associations showed a marked scepticism about the attractiveness of conservative terminology.

Throughout the Third Republic many moderates earnestly desired the formation of an intelligent, flexible conservative party in accordance with their image of the British Conservative Party. But, in France, the grass roots basis of any electorally important conservative organisation was the stubbornly independent local notable: for the notables, ideological positions of only the most general kind and, more directly, local interests dominated electoral considerations and activities. There was not the remotest possibility that they would or could impose on themselves the discipline necessary to build a well-structured party capable of governing the country. An external force – a charismatic leader, the irruption of the conservative masses into the political arena, the emergence of a bureaucratic authority whether clerical or secular – was required to enforce discipline upon them. All these political phenomena were possibilities, or at least were regarded as possibilities, in the first years of the century.

The charismatic leader was the most effective, and perhaps the only way of recruiting a mass political movement based on the large and mainly passive clientele who voted for Right-wing candidates in elections. The mobilisation of the conservative masses provided at least the possibility of neutralising the divisive influences of the notables and of extending the audience for Right-wing ideas and policies. Napoleon III had appeared to demonstrate that, once in power, a determined leader could use the machinery of government, in particular patronage and the prefectoral corps, to preserve discipline among his followers in the country and maintain a relatively compliant legislature. A leader who was also a national hero therefore seemed, to many members of the Right, a solution to all their problems of discipline, of capture and retention of power. There was an almost constant search by men of the Right for an heroic leader. What characteristics were desirable in such a man and what he should do were matters on which there was no agreement. The cleavages roughly followed the lines of division on the constitutional question. Monarchists wanted a General Monk who would restore the king, nationalists a Cromwell who would, by sending parliament on holiday, install an authoritarian Republic, and 'moderate' Republicans merely wanted a George Washington who would enforce the separation of powers. Opinions were not, however, tidily distributed: the idea of a charismatic leader in politics was anathema to some conservatives of all three constitutional persuasions, as being a revolutionary force of dangerous potential.

General Boulanger had shown, in 1887 and 1888, impressive energies could be unleashed if such a leader emerged. It was partly due to the unfortunate outcome of the Boulangist adventure that Right-wing men in 1900 appeared less enthusiastic in their search for a leader than was the case, for example, in the inter-war period. There were, in fact, few convincing candidates until the holocaust of 1914–18 produced a selection of war heroes one of whom, Marshal Pétain, was to help destroy the institutions of the Republic in 1940.

The Church and political organisation

The Catholic Church in France possessed a range of resources – a sacral authority, a disciplined hierarchical organisation and a capacity for mobilising enthusiasm – which appeared to have considerable political potential. These resources impressed the opponents of the Church more than they encouraged her members or partisans. In effect, attitudes prevalent among both Catholics and anti-clericals circumscribed their using these resources for political purposes. The policy of the Papacy usually discouraged the involvement of the Church in domestic politics except to defend specifically religious interests. Leo XIII was, for example, opposed to the formation of confessional parties and condemned Albert de Mun's attempt to form a Catholic party in 1885.[1] The concordatory regime allowed the government to assist the promotion of conformist or apolitical bishops, to harass the Church if its officials were recalcitrant and to restrict clerical activity in elections. Until the Separation of the Church and the State in 1905, most of the senior clergy found it natural to defer to the temporal power and even support it with their spiritual authority.[2] Many found uncongenial the role of political opposition which the circumstances of the first half of the Third Republic forced upon them. The majority of the clergy also was disposed to defer to those with social power and authority. In those areas where there was a *de facto* alliance between the chateau and the presbytery, it was, in secular matters, rarely an alliance of equals. As the prestige of the aristocracy in rural Catholic areas decreased, it was frequently the case that the secular influence of the parish priest increased through the medium of the mass membership organisations of Catholic Action. Attitudes prevalent among the Catholic laity, which tended to emphasise that 'the kingdom of Christ is not of this world' and therefore that the clergy should devote most of their time to spiritual matters, helped to restrict the political activity of the Church within certain limits. There were very few genuine 'clericals' in France in the sense that there were few who argued in favour of the temporal authority of the clergy, except in certain specialised areas such as education. The vigilance of the militant anti-clericals was also a limiting factor. The anti-clerical *instituteur* who staffed the cadres of the Radical Party held not only that Catholic dogma was unhealthy superstition, dangerous to morals, but also that any intervention by the Church or her representatives was wicked and harmful. The removal of concordatory restraints in 1905 weakened the official pressure which the anti-clericals could bring to bear on the clergy to keep them out of politics, but it did not diminish their resolve to present any such intervention in a light which appeared scandalous.

At the beginning of the twentieth century the bishops and clergy were not and could not be politically inactive because of the sustained

[1] H. Rollet, *Albert de Mun et le parti catholique*, 1947.
[2] See particularly J. Gadille, *La Pensée et l'action politique des évêques français au début de la IIIe République, 1870–1883*, 2 vols, 1967. M. J. M. Larkin, *French Catholics and the Separation of the Churches and the State*, unpublished thesis, 1958. J. MacManners, *Church and State in France, 1870–1914*, 1972.

hostility of the Left, and of its sporadic attacks on the Church since the end of the *ordre moral* in the 1870s. Even in times of relative religious peace any incident, such as a flamboyant intervention by a priest in an election campaign or an immoderate pastoral letter from a bishop, would create a minor political scandal. There were always combative Catholics ready to fight back and turbulent spirits among the clergy willing to become politically involved and to defy anyone, even the Pope himself, if they thought their cause was just. As a corporate body, however, the Church in France was cautious and slow-moving in political matters and usually deeply divided about tactics. Although in the years 1902 to 1906 the hierarchy gave much encouragement to *Action Libérale Populaire* the Church never officially committed itself to support it. Political parties of Catholic inspiration were short-lived and never enjoyed the enthusiastic support of more than a small majority of members of the Church except, perhaps, for very short periods of time. Some had the characteristics of small political sects whilst others had serious pretensions of capturing a majority of the seats in parliament. The first well-known example belonging to the former category was the Christian Democratic Party, which briefly flourished in the latter half of the 1890s under the leadership of the *abbés démocrates* – Naudet, Gernier, Lemire, Six, and Roblot – whose aim was to emancipate the Church from the forces of social conservatism and political reaction.[1] They were followed only by small groups of enthusiasts and faced by the hostility or indifference of the mass of the clergy and laity. At the same time their 'advanced' ideas were too timid to appeal to Left-wing audiences. Deeply divided by cross pressures to which they were subject, the *abbés démocrates* enjoyed a *succès de scandale* and were posthumously honoured as the fore-bears of the *Mouvement Républicain Populaire*. They enlivened political debate, provoked hostility and even hatred on the part of *Action Française* and Catholic ultras but as an electoral force, however, they did not count. Only abbé Lemire in Nord managed to establish an electoral following.

The countryside electoral organisation, contemporaneous with the Christian Democratic Party and also dominated by priests, had quite a different character. The Assumptionist Order set up committees called *Justice-Égalité*, based on the sales organisation of the newspaper *la Croix*, which was controlled by the Order, for the purpose of promoting Catholic and anti-Dreyfusard candidates for the

[1] P. Darby, *Les Catholiques républicains. Histoire et souvenirs, 1890–1903*, 1905. J. M. Mayeur, 'Les Congrès nationaux de la démocratie chrétienne (1896–97–98)', *Revue d'histoire moderne et contemporaine*, vol. 9, 1962, pp. 171–206.

elections of 1898. Although these committees were an embarrassment to Etienne Lamy's *Comité des Intérêts moraux*, which enjoyed the support of the Vatican, they were a resounding failure in all other respects and were quickly forgotten. The two traditions, represented by the *Justice-Égalité* committees and the Christian Democratic Party, were carried on without much of a break; the diocesan unions formed in 1909 were in the former tradition and Marc Sangnier's Sillon, condemned by the Pope in 1910, in the latter. Between these two poles of Christian Democracy and the *catholiques avant tout* lay the large and mainly passive Catholic electorate which disapproved of militant political action unless when directly attacked. This electorate was little stirred by the controversies surrounding the modernist, Sillonist and *Action Française* movements which seemed of great importance to active minorities and troubled the leaders, both clerical and lay, of Catholic opinion. The major structural and organisational problem that the Right faced at the beginning of the twentieth century, and one which it failed to solve, was the integration of the Catholic electorate into the political system in a manner which convinced the majority of its members that they were effectively represented.

The problem was certainly recognised by many of the political organisers of the time who also believed that, during the series of anti-clerical measures culminating in the Separation of the Church and the State in 1905, the times were ripe for mobilising popular enthusiasms and for encouraging the dispersed forces of the Right to work together in a common cause. But defence of religion was not sufficiently popular to stem electoral defeat and no 'federator' emerged to harness the passions unleashed. The considerable efforts made to organise the Right in the five years preceding 1906 produced a spectrum of styles of organisation which persisted well into the Fifth Republic. The *Fédération Républicaine* was the archetypal moderate party, latitudinarian in doctrine, based on small committees of influential men, and on a coalition of not always consistent interests. *Action Libérale Populaire* was, like its successors the *Parti Démocrate Populaire* and the *Mouvement Républicain Populaire*, almost but not quite a confessional party. Also like them, it was a very ambitious and resourceful attempt at party building which was quickly ignored when it began to falter. The *Ligue de la Patrie Française* established the tradition of the nationalist league with an authoritarian programme which, whilst being vaguely anti-parliamentary, was deeply involved in electoral and parliamentary politics. It was also in these years that the most famous of the leagues, *Action Française*, begin its career of subversion by propaganda and propaganda by tumult. Circulating around these basic types of political organisation were a myriad of minor parties and leagues aspiring to replace them.

There were antecedents for nearly all the main organisations of the Right which were established at the beginning of the century, but the immediate aftermath of the Dreyfus affair produced a range of characteristic types in their mature form. The raising of the political temperature by the affair and by the Radical drive for power provoked what André Siegfried described as an *élection de lutte* in 1902, during which national and ideological issues seemed, on the surface at least, to overshadow the parish pump. In this climate men co-operated with greater willingness to establish parties. As well as these contingent factors, there were underlying social changes which were encouraging party organisation in all the countries of Western Europe – urbanisation, improvement of communications and raising of educational standards – which created favourable conditions for mass membership parties and mass political participation. But traditional sociological and political factors combined to delay in France, and particularly in the Right of the political spectrum, the growth of highly structured, mass parties with the potential of winning a majority in the legislature.

The Fédération Républicaine
The first modern political party to be established was on the left, the *Parti Républicain Radical et Radical Socialiste* in 1901, and developments on the Right were to some extent a reaction to it. The Radical Party was a typical ill-disciplined and loosely structured cadre party. The local Radical committees were unused to direction from above and many prominent Radicals remained outside the party neither seeking nor receiving its approval during election campaigns. Also in 1901, shortly after the formation of the Radical Party, an important moderate Republican Party, the *Alliance Républicaine Démocratique*, was set up under the leadership of Adolphe Carnot, brother of Sadi Carnot the former President of the Republic.[1] *Alliance Démocratique* had some of the characteristics of the Radical Party, being a coalition of notables who did not take kindly to party discipline. The Alliance was exclusively an electoral organisation and was almost totally inactive between election campaigns. There was an unsuccessful

[1] The literature on *Alliance Démocratique*, as on other electoral organisations of the period, is sparse. A useful general survey of programmes and constitutions can be found in L. Jacques, *Les Partis politiques*, 1913. See also G. Lachapelle, *L'Alliance démocratique*, 1935. E. Beau de Loménie, *Les Responsabilités des dynasties bourgeoises*, vol. 2, 1948, pp. 328–30. Disappointingly little information is contained in the party newsletter, *l'Alliance républicaine démocratique*.

attempt in 1911 to convert it into a more positive and more structured party, the *Parti Républicain Démocratique*, with permanent committees in *communes* and *départements*. It remained, however, an alliance of a number of political clans led by chieftains who, when elected, joined one of the 'ministerial' groups of the Chamber. By the exiguous standards of French parties, it commanded considerable financial resources but since its leading members were men of substance, this did not assist internal discipline. Many pillars of the Republic belonged to the Alliance including Waldeck-Rousseau, Emile Loubet, Paul Deschanel, Raymond Poincaré and a total of five Presidents of the Republic. At the time of its foundation the Alliance was the most conservative wing of the anti-clerical coalition. Its members held similar views on social and financial questions to the more conservative *Fédération Républicaine* but differed from it on the clerical question. As the religious question ceased to be in the forefront of politics, members of the two groups drifted together as they both emphasised anti-Socialist and *anti-étatiste* themes. In the elections of 1910 and 1914 there was a certain amount of co-operation between the Alliance and the *Fédération Républicaine*. In the 1919 elections the Alliance played a leading role in the formation of the *Bloc National* and from that time until the Second World War there was a close association of the two parties. In its great days, from 1901 to 1914, the Alliance can hardly be classified as a party of the Right because the majority of its members agreed with the Radicals on the religious question and worked with them in government at the expense of their sympathies with the *Fédération Républicaine*.

The *Fédération Républicaine* was the electoral organisation of the *Progressistes*, those moderate Republicans who had refused to follow Waldeck-Rousseau in 1899 in his wish to reopen the Dreyfus case and to implement anti-clerical measures. It was established in 1903 as a result of the amalgamation of three electoral committees – the *Alliance Républicaine Progressiste*, the *Association Nationale Républicaine* and the *Union Républicaine Nationale*. The best known of these was the first, which was led by the former *Président du Conseil*, Jules Méline. All had played obscure and unsuccessful roles in the elections of 1902 and, as comment in the columns of the *Progressiste* newspaper *la République française* amply illustrates, it was that debacle which convinced Republicans of the Right that a more serious effort of organisation at the national level was required.[1]

---

[1] The surviving papers of the *Fédération* in the Thierry papers and in the offices of the *Républicains sociaux* give the impression that it was itself rather a feeble organisation.

The stated aim of the Federation was to 'unite all Republicans in order to put into practice the principles of the French Revolution, as they were formulated in the Declaration of the Rights of Man and of the Citizen'.[1] However, the formal constitution of the party indicated that it was not a very democratic organisation. It was administered by a general council of fifty members or more, a fifth of whom were renewed annually. Every two years this council elected its bureau consisting of a president and at least six vice-presidents, a secretary-general and a treasurer. The general council could delegate all or part of its powers to a central committee composed of twelve members (in effect to the office-holders of the Federation). The president could, on his own initiative, speak for the whole Federation. The oligarchy of the office-holders was supported by the position accorded to the founder members: there was a graded membership of *membres fondateurs, sociétaires, participants et adhérents* who paid annual subscriptions of five hundred, one hundred, twenty and five francs respectively. The small subscription necessary to become a member was designed to attract recruits but the largest subscribers, who were also the founder members, were clearly intended to have the most influence in the running of the organisation.

The annual conference which the leaders were constitutionally obliged to call, gave a fairly clear picture of the nature of the party. At the conference the amount of influence the delegates could collectively bring to bear on the leadership was limited by the requirement that the assembly should split into sections to discuss special fields of the Federation's activities. The plenary session was devoted to speeches by the leadership and the vote, never the discussion, of resolutions presented by the provincial delegations. As many as a thousand delegates attended these conferences which opened with a presidential speech and closed with a banquet.[2] An attempt was generally made before and during the conference to invest the proceedings with some significance but there was no life in them because no delegate ever went beyond the terms of reference defined by the leaders. The only objection made to this was voiced, not by a rebel from the floor of the conference, but by Jules Méline, the grand old man of the Federation. At the 1912 conference, Méline made an ineffective plea for greater activity by the general council and by the rank and file membership. But it was difficult to stimulate genuine political debate within the Federation. The conferences did not attempt to plan specific courses of action or

[1] Fédération Républicaine, *Programme et statuts*, 1904, p. 1.
[2] See reports in the press, *le Temps*, 23 November 1906, *la République française*, 10 December 1908, 23 November 1909.

formulate binding policies; consequently, there were no open disagreements despite the deep divisions within the leadership on some matters such as protection. Before 1914 the name of Méline, more than that of any figure in national politics, was associated with high protective tariffs yet, within the Federation, there was an influential group of free-traders led by Joseph Thierry, Paul Beauregard and Edouard Aynard. This fundamental difference was glossed over. For example, Thierry at the 1909 conference turned to Méline and said:

'Have we not always differed on economic questions? Have we not always fought on different sides? But this does not prevent us from co-operating in a spirit of mutual confidence and esteem. . . . It is the same for all of us: we have particular aims which do not correspond with the programme of the party: we can have different views on concrete questions. But we are fully in accord, and this is the main point, on the essential moral basis of our programme.'

The conferences indicated the moment when *Progressistes* began to accept policies and developments which they had previously rejected as undesirable. One example is the acceptance of the law of Separation of Church and State by the conference of 1906. The programme approved by the congress of 1909, which Joseph Thierry hailed as a great innovation, contained a list of measures – an obligatory old age pension scheme, sickness and unemployment assurance, a code of labour and social law, and profit sharing – which had not previously been supported.[1] Thierry wanted to give the Federation a progressive image so that 'young people are not frightened away by the rigidity of our programme'. Most members, however, gave the impression that they viewed such reforms without enthusiasm.

The lack of published information about the Federation is a sign of its weakness: it produced neither a party bulletin nor, at election times, a list of candidates whom it supported. This was not due to a desire for secrecy: it supplied information to those who asked for it. The affairs of the *Union du Commerce et de l'Industrie*, the fundraising organisation which worked closely with the Federation, were shrouded in greater obscurity. It did not, however, make any secret of its function and the banquets of the union ended with rousing appeals by the President (usually the same man as the President of the Federation) for the election fund.[2] Most of the raising and spending of the money for the Federation, as for the *Centre National des Indépendants et des Paysans* after the Second World War, was apparently done in a very informal way.

[1] Manuscript of speech in Thierry papers.
[2] See appeal of P. Beauregard, *le Monde économique*, 30 March 1912, p. 290.

The Federation was not an impressive organisation. Its prestige was directly related to the influence of its leaders. It was headed by a divided oligarchy, lacked militancy and militants, had a limited appeal and a programme unlikely to make converts. As a consequence during the ten years after the foundation of the party, its prestige was on the wane. After the First World War the party was revived by the energetic leadership of Louis Marin and it was often called the *Parti Marin*.[1] Its influence did not spread much beyond certain limited regions such as Marin's locality, Lorraine, the sphere of influence of the Marquis de La Ferronays in the west, and Brittany, Normandy and Anjou. It was almost without representatives in the Paris basin and in the south-west. At no point in its history did it have the appearance of a party which could dominate the country, and during the inter-war period it moved further to the Right.[2] After 1919, many Deputies of the Federation were aristocrats, some had connections with the extra-parliamentary leagues, and its young recruits such as Xavier Vallat, Philippe Henriot and Jacques Poitou-Duplessy gave a more extreme tone to the party.

Action Libérale Populaire
In its early years, this was a more formidable and interesting organisation than the *Fédération Républicaine*. Its parliamentary antecedents went back to 1893 when Jacques Piou, Count Albert de Mun and Baron Armand Mackau formed the *Droite Républicaine* group, following the publication of the papal encyclical, *Au milieu des sollicitudes*. The *Droite Républicaine* changed its name to *Action Libérale* in 1899, immediately after Waldeck-Rousseau in his Toulouse speech made it clear that he did not want *rallié* support for his ministry. The parliamentary group published a programme for the elections of 1902 signed by Piou and de Mun.[3] After the elections they organised the party *Action Libérale Populaire* – the first party to be modelled on the statute of association required by the Law of Associations of 1901. Its purpose was proclaimed to be the defence of

'. . . public liberties by all legal means within the constitutional framework, particularly by electoral propaganda: the promotion of legislative reforms; the creation and development of social institutions and programmes; the improvement of the lot of the working class.'[4]

---

[1] For the later history of the Federation see W. D. Irvine, *The Republican Federation of France during the 1930s*, unpublished thesis, 1972.

[2] A. Siegfried, *Tableau des partis en France*, 1930, pp. 182–4.

[3] E. Flornoy, *La Lutte par l'association*, 2nd edition 1907, p. 37.

[4] Action Libérale Populaire, *Programme et statuts*, 1903.

This definition of aims illustrated that the founders of the party were more aware of social problems and more convinced that the action of the government could help to solve them than were the leaders of the *Fédération Républicaine*.

On the other hand, *Action Libérale* was very similar to the Federation in having an oligarchic constitution. The central committee of the association was a co-optive body and the President (according to article 7 of the statutes) was 'invested with the widest powers' to direct the administration and the policy of the party. The annual conference, composed of the founding members, delegates from the local sections and affiliated organisations did little to temper the oligarchic nature of this constitution. A graded membership supported it: the party comprised affiliated groups or committees established or approved by the central committees, *membres sociétaires* paying a life membership of 500 francs or an annual subscription of not less than twenty francs, and *membres adhérants* subscribing not less than one franc annually. But the annual conferences, unlike those of the *Fédération Républicaine*, gave the impression of having a purpose and a meaning. The sections of the conference heard a great number of detailed reports on specialist topics. Because there was a considerable divergence of view on social questions, few concrete proposals emerged but the work was well prepared and apparently taken very seriously.

The officers of the party continually stressed that *Action Libérale* differed from the other political groups of the time. At the 1907 conference, Louis Laya, one of the secretaries of *Action Libérale*, echoed many speeches made by the party leaders, saying that *Action Libérale* was not

'. . . a simple electoral committee, an occasional grouping which goes into abeyance between elections. It is above all an association . . . in other words it is an attempt to create a powerful, active and disciplined union . . . achieved by feelings of solidarity and through economic institutions, within the general framework of a political programme.[1]

Despite resounding declarations such as this, there were only two organisations which could be described as 'economic institutions'. These were the *Union des Caisses Rurales et Ouvrières* whose founder and President was Louis Durand, a more reactionary Catholic than usually found in *Action Libérale*, and the *Union Fédérale des Patrons Industriels et Commerçants* which among other activities, ran employ-

[1] Action Libérale Populaire, *Compte-rendu du congrès national de 1907*, 1908, p. 37.

ment agencies. These agencies, according to opponents, pursued discriminatory employment policies. There were other affiliated groups engaged in social good works such as Albert de Mun's *Cercles Ouvriers*, the *Association de la Jeunesse Catholique Française*, *Jeunesse Libérale*, the *Ligue Patriotique des Françaises*, and the *Union des Travailleurs Libres*. Research on social questions was encouraged by the *Cercle d'Études Sociales* which had several provincial sections. The affiliated groups were intended to help establish the party and spread its doctrines throughout the country. Detailed memoranda were drawn up on the methods of forming local committees and obtaining financial support. The propaganda effort of the party was considerable; a large number of pamphlets were published, especially between 1903 and 1906, on the religious question, Freemasons, strikes, social policy, fiscal policy, agricultural matters and a range of other subjects. Although affirming a resolute commitment to the Republican form of government, *Action Libérale* espoused the cause of constitutional reform and gave wide circulation to a lavishly produced pamphlet on constitutional revision.[1]

Action Libérale was the creation of Jacques Piou, strongly supported by Albert de Mun. Piou, President of the party until his retirement in 1919, was a subtle politician, an accomplished parliamentary tactician and, on occasion, an effective orator. He had a strong belief in the importance of a party organisation, often repeating the rather banal slogan 'We will triumph through organisation'. As late as 1914 *Action Libérale* was called the best organised of parties by a contemporary political observer.[2] The organisation was greatly helped in its early years by the support of many priests and the fringe organisations of the Church such as the *Association de la Jeunesse Catholique Française*. It was a Catholic party in the sense that it was composed almost exclusively of Catholics. Piou steadfastly refused to call it a Catholic party on the grounds that 'the establishment of such a party is, at least for the moment, impossible' and was moreover not particularly desirable, because the religious question was 'only one of the many problems facing the country'.[3] No appeal to Catholic principles was made in the programme of the party and although defence of religious liberty was given a prominent place this was, Piou explained, because it was the liberty most threatened. Many individual members of the party did not share this reticence and, for the majority of political commentators at the time of the Separation, *Action Libérale* was *the* Catholic party.

[1] Action Libérale Populaire, *Projet de constitution libérale*, 1907.
[2] P. G. La Chesnais, *Statistique des élections législatives de 1914*, 1914, p. 7.
[3] E. Flornoy, op. cit., p. 7.

However, both Piou and de Mun apparently assumed that it could attract a non-Catholic clientele and would perhaps become the majority party in the country.

The first election the party fought as an organised force, that of 1906, resulted in a decisive defeat. From that moment, the morale of the party was shaken and the ensuing attacks from the extreme Right were not effectively countered. Many charges were made villifying the motives and condemning the tactics of Catholic Republicans. The attacks were mainly directed at Piou and not at de Mun, whose name commanded too wide a respect. Before the election of 1906, the Cassagnac brothers and Jules Delahaye conducted a campaign in *l'Autorité*, accusing Piou of misappropriating money contributed by Catholics to fight the common enemy. This kind of attack might not have been important had there not been an apparent shift in Vatican policy.[1] The Liberals tried to deny that there had been a change whilst the extreme Right tended to exaggerate its significance. The change could be described as one of emphasis rather than substance: Pius X, although he said that he was carrying on the policy of his predecessor Leo XIII, stressed the necessity of unity among Catholics rather than their acceptance of the regime. In so far as this appeared to encourage specifically Catholic political organisation, it was a blow to the officially non-confessional *Action Libérale Populaire*.

The so-called lifting of the *consignes de ralliement* encouraged initiatives such as the proposal in 1908 by the monarchist from Vendée, Count Xavier de Cathelineau, to form a coalition of Catholic organisations regardless of their position on the constitutional question. The most cogently argued appeal in favour of an *Entente catholique* was made by Emile Flourens, an ex-Minister and former nationalist Deputy. Flourens asserted that a party had ruled France for thirty years with the sole aim of de-Christianisation and this basic fact must not be obscured. Although he admitted that there were good historical and tactical reasons for the divisions within the Right, they encouraged indifference, abstention in elections and disastrous disputes. More controversially, he suggested that it was ridiculous to refuse the support of any supporters of religious liberty whatever their views on the constitutional question. His argument was that the Republic might be the best form of government when it governed well but when it oppressed consciences it was unreasonable to condemn those who preferred another regime.

Between 1909 and 1914 twenty-one diocesan unions were formed.

[1] In the encyclical *Gravissimo officii*, issued in 1906. See R. Cornilleau, *Le 'Ralliement' a-t-il échoué?*, 1927, pp. 22–3.

Some candidates whom they supported won seats in the Chamber of Deputies. But they were not particularly active political groups because most of the bishops did not wish to be directly involved in political activity.[1] The great defender of the diocesan unions, Jacques Rocafort, impatient at their relative lack of success, accused *Action Libérale Populaire* of obstructing them. Despite their modest achievements, the very existence of the diocesan unions was an acute embarrassment to *Action Libérale*. Organisations such as the *Ligue de la Résistance Catholique* had previously claimed to be 'more Catholic' than *Action Libérale*, but they had never attracted much episcopal sympathy nor had the tacit support of the Papacy. The diocesan unions eroded the prestige of *Action Libérale*: Jacques Piou wrote that 'desertions multiplied within the ranks' and speculated whether the Vatican had completely disowned the movement.[2] De Mun made a discreet enquiry in Rome asking whether Piou and himself should retire from politics in order to make room for more acceptable leaders. The Vatican replied in a private communication that they both still enjoyed the favour of the Pope. The scurrilous attacks on Piou's personal reputation, which would have been diminished by a public expression of papal support, continued to damage his political effectiveness. To counter these attacks, he seemed on occasions to be trying to outbid the extremists by the violence of his language. But he fought a losing battle. After a second major electoral defeat at the 1910 general elections the party had few resources with which to fight back.

Despite all the attempts to provide *Action Libérale* with a doctrine and a comprehensive programme transcending the issues raised by the *Ralliement* and by the revival of anti-clericalism during the Dreyfus affair, the party gradually declined as they ceased to be the central issue of political debate. If the Liberals had maintained or increased their numbers in parliament the party would possibly have developed away from its constricting origins. Electoral success was also the *sine qua non* of keeping the public support of the Vatican and of influential French Catholics. As it turned out, the number of Liberal Deputies steadily declined from the time of the formation of the parliamentary group until its official disappearance in 1919. The party played some part in the formation of the *Bloc National* in 1919, although Piou was forced to stand down. The party newspaper continued publication until 1933, but *Action Libérale* was regarded as a relic from the past of little importance.

[1] See C. Guignebert, *Le Problème religieux dans la France d'aujourd hui*, 1922.
[2] J. Piou, *D'une guerre à l'autre*, 1932, p. 244.

The groups in the Chamber of Deputies

The organisation of electoral parties in the first decade of the century was paralleled by a more clearly defined group system in the Chamber of Deputies. Although, from 1900 to 1914, the parliamentary groups had little internal life and were linked only in a very loose and informal way with the electoral organisations, they illustrated the balance of forces within the parliamentary Right.[1] There was an interesting and significant tendency to proliferate groups in the indeterminate zone where the government majority and the opposition of the Right coincided and, indeed, overlapped – between the *Gauche Démocratique* (the Poincaré group) and the *Républicains Progressistes* (the Méline groups). These were the two main strands of moderate Republicanism which had become separated during the Dreyfus affair and its aftermath. Two groups emerged with little *raison d'être* other than to keep the way open for reconciliation between the two sides of the schism. In 1898 the *Union Démocratique*, which led towards the *Gauche Démocratique*, was formed and in 1902 the *Union Républicaine*, sympathising with the *Progressistes*, came into being. The division between ministerial majority and the opposition in the first three parliaments of the twentieth century roughly fell between these groups: for example most members of the *Union Démocratique* voted in favour of, and all members of the *Union Républicaine* voted against, the Law of the Separation of Church and State in 1905. Membership of more than one of these adjacent groups (*double appartenance*) was very common. The formation of the *Groupe Républicain Nationaliste* after the elections of 1902 added – besides the *ralliés* of *Action Libérale* – another non-royalist element to the Right. The Republican loyalties of the Nationalists like those of the Liberals were suspect, partly for the same reason: about half of the fifty-nine members (in 1902) of the Nationalist group were former monarchists. The monarchists disappeared as an indentifiable parliamentary force in 1902 when their group went out of existence: the surviving monarchist Deputies became 'Independents'. Although not all the Independent Deputies were monarchists, nearly all voted consistently with the Right. When, in 1910, membership of a group became essential for selection to the standing committees of the Chamber the monarchists revived the *Groupe des Droites*. Since *double appartenance* was officially no longer possible the Nationalist group ceased to be viable and the Nationalist Deputies dispersed among the other groups of the Right.

[1] Lists of members of groups were published for the years 1899–1912 in G. Bonet-Maury and R. Samuel, *Annuaire du parlement*. From 1910 they were published in the *Journal officiel*.

THE MEMBERSHIP OF GROUPS IN THE CHAMBER AT THE BEGIN-
NING OF EACH PARLIAMENT, 1902–1920

	1902[a]	1906[a]	1910	1914	1920
Union Républicaine	33	46	29[b]	—[c]	—
Progressiste	106	79	80	37	—
Action Libérale	81	64	34	24	—
Nationaliste	59	29	—	—	—
Droites	—	—	19	16	—
Indépendants	41	34	21	46	29
Entente Républicaine Démo-					
cratique	—	—	—	—	186
Non Inscrits	—	—	—	—	26

[a] The total number of members of the Right is exaggerated because Deputies with *double appartenance* are counted twice. The actual membership of the groups in these years is hazy because membership carried no rights or obligations.

[b] It went out of existence in 1910 but was reformed as a result of a split in the *Groupe Progressiste*.

[c] It adopted a new name – *Fédération Républicaine*.

When Deputies changed their groups they generally did so immediately after an election. The groups were formally reconstituted
at the beginning of each parliament and it was the natural time to
make a change. The changes made in 1906, 1910 and 1914 were, in
nearly all cases, moves to the Left. This drift had little significance
except in cases of movement of Progressists into the *Union Républicaine* in 1906 and from *Union Républicaine* into *Gauche Démocratique* in 1914: on these occasions a change in group presented a
change in tactical position. At other times changes reflected no more
than a desire to belong to a group with a progressive sounding
name – encouraged by the apparent lack of popular appeal of
reactionaries. The names of the groups of the Right, therefore, tended
to give a much less conservative impression than the behaviour and
views of their members warranted.

In the 1906–10 parliament some attempt was made to organise
the opposition of the Right through inter-group co-operation.
There was a strong feeling among Deputies of the Right that they
were not adequately represented on the grand standing committees
of the Chamber of Deputies: study groups parallel to the official
committees were therefore established. The study groups were given
the tasks of examining the proposals made by the official committees
and of preparing their own bills. The chairmen of groups of the Right
began to meet every Thursday morning to consider matters which
the study groups put before them and to discuss matters of common

interest. Within two years, however, the meetings of the study groups and of the chairman of groups ceased to take place. More successful, because it achieved limited but concrete results, was the *Groupe Républicain de l'Egalité devant la Loi* whose chairman was Baron de Belcastel (*Action Libérale*) and in which all the most prominent Republican members of the Right participated. The purpose of this group was to protest against arbitrary conduct by civil servants; when a serious complaint was established a delegation went to see the appropriate Minister. Although this seems to have been a relatively successful activity, there are no reports of the committee's activities after 1912. There were other ostensibly non-political groups composed almost entirely of Right-wing Deputies, but these were not deliberate attempts to integrate the opposition of the Right. On the Right of the Chamber the tendency, apparent in the first decade of the twentieth century, to fragment into a number of loosely organised, ill-disciplined groups continued until the Fifth Republic. From time to time there were more or less short-lived attempts to set up a federation of these groups; the more practically minded members of the Right, recognising the difficulties of organising a federation, set up groups (*groupes amicaux*) with limited objectives on which men holding a variety of views on general political questions could agree.

The Ligue de la Patrie Française

The mundane programmes and rather drab electoral politics of the *Fédération Républicaine, Action Libérale Populaire* and their associated parliamentary groups did not have much appeal for the intellectuals who became politically involved during the Dreyfus affair. The purer, more militant posture of the extra-parliamentary leagues had much greater attraction for them. The affair was the great formative experience of *ligueur* politics. Déroulède revived his *Ligue des Patriotes* in September 1898, Jules Guérin founded the *Ligue Antisémite* in 1897, Colonel Monteil set up the *Ligue de la Défense Nationale* early in 1899 and the *Jeunesse Royaliste*, an older organisation, acquired a new reputation through its involvement in street demonstrations. On the left wing of nationalism several organisations were founded – *Parti Rochefortiste*, the personal following of the ex-communard pamphleteer Henri Rochefort, *Comité Central Révolutionnaire, Jeunesse Blanquiste* and *Parti Républicain Socialiste Français*. The activities of these groups were restricted mainly to street demonstrations, breaking up Dreyfusard meetings and plotting in effect to overthrow the Republic. They were compromised in Déroulède's ludicrous attempt at a *coup d'état* in 1899, when he tried to persuade the General leading the troops at the funeral of the President of the Republic, Félix Faure, to march on the Elysée. One league not discredited, because it was not involved, was the *Ligue de la Patrie Française* founded by three Paris *lycée* teachers, Syveton, Dausset and Bourgeois who wished to challenge 'the claim of the [Dreyfusard] *Ligue des Droits de l'Homme* that it represented the intelligence of France'.[1]

In the vacuum left by the discredit of the other leagues, *Patrie Française* won a remarkable victory at the Paris local elections of 1900. The Nationalists became the largest group in the Paris city council, with a total of thirty-six councillors. The Nationalists managed to attract voters from Right-wing Radicals and moderate Republicans and to divide Paris politically on fairly clear socio-economic lines. Nationalism was not, therefore, a revival of Boulangism which drew support from both extremes, although it was often interpreted as such in the contemporary press. The *Patrie Française* won thirty-nine seats in the parliamentary elections of 1902, although few of its adherents elected in provincial constituencies owed their success to the League's patronage. Nationalism appealed to different audiences in different areas. It was, perhaps, only in constituencies in the east of France that there was a 'patriotic' vote by people primarily concerned by the effects of the anti-militarism of the Dreyfusards on national defence. In the slogan of the *Patrie Française*, 'national and social defence', social defence was usually the most important element. A strong government, a more authoritarian social system and resistance to collectivism was certainly the programme which appealed to the nationalist electorate of Paris.

Although, in general, the election of 1902 was a modest success for the *Patrie Française*, the radical, non-Catholic wing of the League fared very badly and the group was faced with the choice between 'impotence or absorption by the Right'.[2] The provincial notables who dominated the parliamentary group were completely identified with the Right. This caused tension between them and the small minority of anti-clerical Parisian Nationalists. There were other serious problems facing the League. Its constitutional programme was an uneasy compromise between anti-parliamentary *plébiscitaires* and conservatives with no taste for Bonapartist adventure. The latter deserted the League in large numbers when Lemaître made a speech in favour of universal suffrage in elections for the Presidency

[1] D. R. Watson, 'The Nationalist Movement in Paris, 1900–1906', St Antony's Papers, No. 13, 1962, p. 60.

[2] L. Fatoux, *Les Coulisses du nationalisme*, 1903, p. 38.

of the Republic. He caused quite as much offence on the religious question, when he said that 'he no more wanted three hundred Catholics in the Chamber than he wanted three hundred Radicals'.[1] Basic doctrines and principles were not the only cause of division; tactical considerations were also in dispute. Henri Vaugeois and his friends walked out of the League when it refused to countenance illegal action against the regime. Maurice Barrès, the most respected nationalist intellectual of the time, ceased to be a member of the League in 1902 because, he said, its electoral success would only have the effect of replacing Waldeck-Rousseau by Ribot and Méline, 'the other side of the same coin'.[2] Perhaps the main tactical weakness of the League arose from the ineffective leadership of Jules Lemaître. One of his closest associates, Léon Fatoux, resigned from the League and wrote a bitter account, published in 1903, of the confusion which reigned in its affairs. In 1905 the suicide of the League's treasurer, Gabriel Syveton, under a cloud of financial scandal marked the end of *Patrie Française* as an important political organisation. Lemaître was converted to monarchism. The Parisian Nationalists who had commenced their career on the extreme Left, such as Rochefort, Tournade and Emile Roche, became by 1906 virtually indistinguishable from the rest of the Right. The few working-class areas which voted Nationalist in 1900 were reclaimed by the Left by the elections of 1906. The League lingered on in Paris in 1912, occasionally organising meetings addressed by prominent nationalists such as Gauthier de Clagny, Admiral Bienaimé and Lucien Millevoye, but there was little life in it.

The league was particularly interesting because despite its nationalist emblem it had scarcely anything to say about foreign affairs, even about revenge on Germany. It represented a rather confused and incoherent mood, expressed by a multitude of minor parties in the three succeeding decades. It illustrated the need, felt by *déraciné* intellectuals and sections of the urban middle and lower middle classes for a Right-wing radicalism. In Paris at least, the nationalist electorate differed from that of the Boulangist movement. Boulanger managed to assemble a genuine coalition of Right- and Left-wing voters whereas the nationalist vote was that of the traditional Right extended to lower middle-class groups which were alarmed by working-class agitation, syndicalism and socialism. The *Patrie Française* was a movement with the potential of making large inroads in the Radical vote. The lack of effective leadership, of discipline, of appropriate political traditions and, perhaps above all,

[1] J. Piou, *D'une guerre à l'autre*, 1932, p. 171.
[2] M. Barrès, *Scènes et doctrines du nationalisme*, n.d., p. 95.

the absence of a sufficiently severe economic crisis were decisive constraints on its development.

The Ligue de l'Action Française

As well as being the most extreme of the successor groups to the *Ligue de la Patrie Française*, *Action Française* also had the most elaborate and coherent doctrine. Founded by Maurras, Pujo and Vaugeois as an association for propaganda, it never lost its original character through a history which lasted almost half a century. *Action Française* exercised an extraordinary fascination over intellectuals of the Right and the Left who tended to exaggerate its importance. The best scholarly work on the movement, written by Eugen Weber, does not escape this error:

'. . . between 1899 and 1944 [it] provided the fundamental doctrines for practically the whole Extreme Right in France and the nationalist and traditional groups in Belgium, Italy, Portugal, Spain, Romania and Switzerland as well as the theoretical background of the National Revolution of Vichy.

The literary and political influence of the *Action Française* was immense: its columns were responsible for launching Proust, Bernanos and Céline to public favour, others from office – even into jail – for shaking the foundations of several cabinets and, at one time, of the Republic itself.'[1]

Exaggeration promotes debunking which in the case of *Action Française* usually involves treating its leading figures as café intellectuals and their activities as low farce.[2]

There are no objective measures of the kind of influence *Action Française* was exerting. Whether it was responsible for the political and literary developments mentioned by Weber are questions to which there are no definitive answers. *Action Française* was certainly involved to some degree in these developments and the writings of Maurras fascinated at least two generations of French intellectuals. Since Maurras despised electoral activity this cannot be regarded as a significant test of the influence and importance of the League. But its following in the country remained a small and electorally insignificant minority. A handful of members of the League were returned to the Chamber but only Léon Daudet (in 1919) was actually elected on an *Action Française* ticket. Maurras was a theoretician and propagandist rather than a man of action; his aim was to

[1] E. Weber, *Action Française*, 1962, p. vii.
[2] For example, A. Mirambel, *La Comédie du nationalisme intégral*, 1947 and E. Tannenbaum, *Action Française*, 1962.

educate and to spread ideas rather than to take power directly. On the night of 6 February 1934, the reproach of the young activists – that he was more interested in getting out the next edition of the paper than in taking power – was a justified comment on his whole career. Although he frequently discussed the possibility of a *coup d'état* he never seriously tried to mount one.

The framework of *Action Française* was created between 1899 and 1908. The *Revue de l'Action française* was established first, followed by the League in 1902, then in 1906, the *Institut de l'Action Française* with its chairs for teaching the doctrine, and finally the daily newspaper in 1908. The doctrine was established by Maurras at approximately the same time in a series of articles and books centred on three main areas – constitutional, international and religious affairs. The basis for the great reputation of Charles Maurras was laid and two personal qualities – stubbornness and the ability to write – helped to further it. He regarded literary style as a matter of considerable importance: before he became immersed in politics, he had campaigned in favour of classical clarity in art and literature, reacting harshly against what he considered romantic anarchy. Many readers and admirers, even among those who utterly rejected his doctrines, were attracted by his economical and elegant prose. The importance which he accorded to style gave a dimension to his personality and to *Action Française* which might otherwise have left an unrelieved impression of rigid and humourless fanaticism. The persuasiveness of his doctrines depended to a great extent on the brilliance of their presentation. Inevitably he attracted attention as an oddity, erecting an ideology around the hereditary principle in a country where Republican democracy seemed firmly entrenched and, as an atheist, defending the Church in a society where non-believers were almost invariable anti-clerical. The clear and apparently logical statement of his theories, formulated in a manner which made them almost impossible to refute by an appeal to evidence, gave him the kind of intellectual status which inhibited people from dismissing him as a crank.

The literary distinction of Maurras gave a quality to the pages of the newspaper *Action française* which to some extent relieved the rabid and, in Léon Daudet's case, earthy polemics of its political comment. The effectiveness of Maurras as a political propagandist relied heavily on his ability to shock. *Action française* was launched by a scandalous article defending the action of Colonel Henry, the intelligence officer who forged evidence to support the guilt of Dreyfus and committed suicide when his crime was discovered. Throughout his long career, Maurras continued to outrage by defending apparently indefensible actions when performed in causes of which he approved. The very violence of his language was also a cause for scandal. It eventually earned him a prison term in 1936, for incitement to murder, after a violent attack on Léon Blum by *Action Française* militants. He used the most extreme epithets to describe political opponents calling them crooks, traitors, deserters, pederasts, prostitutes and all kinds of animals, a habit which his collaborator, Léon Daudet, carried to even greater lengths.

All observers have remarked on the stubbornness of Maurras: this helped to make him an excellent controversialist and a persistent, if not a dynamic organiser. Most of his organisational energies were devoted to the newspaper and there is much truth in the disillusioned comment of an ex-member of *Action Française* that the movement was 'no more than a newspaper'.[1] Maurras never entrusted the running of the paper to a subordinate and it was a very onerous task. The paper did not pay for itself through sales and advertising – it was a costly publishing operation partly because of the never ending law suits in which it was involved. Financial difficulties were experienced from the beginning. Fund raising activities for the paper appeared to grow as the circulation increased, because the price of the newspaper was held at an uneconomic price to avoid losing readers. The production costs, therefore, rose proportionately faster than sales revenue. Also the economic conditions for newspaper publishing deteriorated during and after the First World War. Some individuals contributed large sums such as the ubiquitous perfume manufacturer, François Coty, in the period 1924–6, but the directors of *Action française* appeared to prefer small contributors because they did not seek influence over policy. The small subscribers were rewarded by the satisfaction of seeing their names printed in the columns of the newspaper. The movement promoted other fairly costly publishing ventures such as the *Revue de l'Action française* devoted to more considered articles, the *Almanach* containing chronicles of the year, articles and useful information, the Sunday edition of *Action française* which became *Action française agricole* before going out of existence towards the end of the 1920s, and a range of pamphlets on a wide variety of subjects, sometimes printed in very large runs.

The most active and famous element of the League was a by-product of the publishing activity of the movement. The street vendors of the newspaper were organised at the end of 1908 into the Camelots du Roi under the Presidency of Maxime Réal del

[1] E. Weber, op. cit., p. 188. See chs 10 and 14 of Weber's excellent book for a fuller account of the problems of the newspaper and the League.

Sarte and the general direction of Maurice Pujo. The Camelots quickly established a reputation for activities other than those of selling newspapers. They organised the 'tactics of tumult' previously used spasmodically by Réal del Sarte and other young men of *Action Française*. The Camelots broke up lectures in the Sorbonne, and created incidents in national theatres and riots at the Paris cemetery of Père Lachaise. They were particularly active in the Latin Quarter, although many of them were not students. They came from a heterogeneous social background ranging from wealthy young aristocrats to working-class youths. The exact numbers which either the Camelots or the Commissaires (the less well known shock troops of the League) could mobilise for demonstrations is impossible to estimate. In the early days they were clearly not very great; for example, in 1908 they were in considerable difficulties when Republican students organised to defend Professor Thalamas whom the Camelots tried to prevent from lecturing in the Sorbonne because they considered him as a traducer of the reputation of Joan of Arc. The determination which they showed during this campaign and Maurrassian propaganda in favour of a *coup d'état* helped recruitment. They never became a major threat to public order on a national scale but they were a force to be reckoned with in the Latin Quarter.

The propaganda success of the newspaper and the success of the Camelots in the streets gave *Action Française* control of the royalist cause in France. The takeover was completed with the ousting in 1910–11 of the Count de Larègle and the old-fashioned royalists from the political bureau of the Pretender. The monarchist aristocrats frequently had little taste for the new plebeian and aggressive monarchists of the *Action Française* but they had no political resources with which to resist the Maurrassian offensive. For over a quarter of a century the *Action Française* was reluctantly accepted by the Pretender until, in 1936, the Count de Paris speaking on behalf of his father, the Duke de Guise, stated that the movement did not represent his ideas. Whilst the Pretender's endorsement lasted any royalist who did not support the movement seemed anomalous.

Action Française also tried to take the Catholic Church into its embrace. For more than twenty years it gradually extended its influence within the Church. Polemical attacks on anti-clericals, Freemasons, Protestants, and especially on progressive Catholics such as members of Marc Sangnier's Sillon movement (condemned by the Vatican in 1910), recommended *Action Française* to numerous priests and laymen. Praise for the values of hierarchy and order, represented by the Church, and the alleged indissoluble union between the Church and the 'true' France also appealed to a large minority of Catholics. Catholic supporters of Maurras conveniently overlooked his attitude towards the religious element of Catholicism which he regarded as partly useful and partly dangerous mythology. Although obviously reluctant to condemn such a vigorous scourge of the enemies of the Church in France, the Vatican could not, in the long run, ignore the atheism of Maurras. Many French Catholics regarded him as a true and valiant defender of the Church which made his doctrines potentially subversive of Catholic orthodoxy. The papal condemnation drafted in 1914, delayed by the First World War, and finally published in 1926, caused many crises of conscience, refusals of absolution and the disciplining of priests – one Jesuit cardinal returned to the mother house of his province as a simple priest. Maurras argued that the condemnation was ill-founded and that he was condemned for opinions which he did not hold. But he could not escape the anomalous position (although the ban on Catholics reading *Action Française* literature was eventually lifted) of being a defender of the Church which condemned him. Exactly a decade after the papal condemnation the irony was complete: he became a monarchist whose 'king' rejected him.[1]

Action Française was an expression of a socio-political climate at the very end of the nineteenth and the beginning of the twentieth centuries. At an intellectual level, it was the most coherent and total reaction against the political arguments in favour both of revision of the Dreyfus case and of Combiste anti-clericalism. Maurras believed that the fundamental questions of French politics had been posed during the great controversy over the revision of the Dreyfus case: his celebrated remark after his condemnation for Collaboration in 1946 – 'It is the revenge of Dreyfus' – illustrated the permanence of this conviction. In this sense, *Action Française* was a creature of its time, perhaps to a greater degree than any of the other political movements established in the early years of the century. It achieved its largest audience in the years immediately after the First World War, although throughout the inter-war period Right-wing candidates in parliamentary elections found its support embarrassing. The movement set out to elaborate and teach a doctrine: the achievement of political influence by this method is not rapid in any circumstances. The chauvinistic atmosphere of the First World War made politicians and the public at large particularly susceptible to the doctrines of integral nationalism. The harassment of those who were or who might have been in favour of a compromise peace, such as the Radical politicians,

[1] E. Renauld, *L'Action française contre l'Eglise catholique et la monarchie*, 1936.

Malvy and Caillaux, earned *Action Française* the sympathy of President Poincaré and Georges Clemenceau who both had some correspondence with Maurras. Interest in the movement was encouraged by the vaguely anti-democratic feeling of the *esprit ancien combattant* and the fear of Communism stimulated by the Russian Revolution. The newspaper was more widely read and the positions adopted by *Action française* commanded national attention. The various scandalous happenings associated with the movement in the 1920s – the assassination of the war hero Marius Plateau, the death of Philippe Daudet, Léon Daudet's imprisonment and his escape from La Santé – all helped to keep the movement newsworthy. But the leaders of *Action Française* seemed to prefer celebrity to power intellectual influence to revolutionary action. There was no attempt to make a direct challenge to the regime, in the manner of the Fascist movement in Italy. The patterns of thought and action had been set before the First World War. The new conditions of the inter-war period did not produce any marked revision of the Maurrasian strategy. Some members of *Action Française* continued to act within the same framework even after the Second World War.

The men of the Right in the first years of the twentieth century showed resolution and inventiveness in political organisation, and, particularly on the extreme Right, showed no lack of energy in ideological debate. Great and compelling common interests were, however, absent; nothing was pushing them towards unity. In practical policy matters such as income-tax, industrial accident insurance and old age pensions the Right showed little ability to organise opposition in the country to match its delaying tactics in parliament. The league against income-tax was a one-man effort, organised by Jules Roche, although a rather wooden opposition to any attack on the rights of property was the only important common view held by the very diverse clienteles of the Right-wing groups and parties.

Nationalism, the new political phenomenon at the beginning of the century, had shown that it was possible to increase the following of the Right in some urban, particularly Parisian constituencies. But the decisive electoral battle for the Right was fought in the countryside. In the rural areas, there was very little which the new party organisations could do to assist the rural notables. Two major developments of the second half of the nineteenth century, the railways and universal primary education, had exposed rural communities to external influences. The notables, for the most part, were neither disposed nor well equipped to react to the changing social circumstances engendered by these developments. The slow process of integrating the peasantry into the rest of the national community created aspirations to which this generation of conservative notables seemed hostile. The rural vote therefore tended to ebb away from them. Their persistent lack of success in parliamentary elections led, in the years before 1914, to a lassitude and a feeling that they were somehow, inexplicably, being excluded from the key centres of power.

CHAPTER IV

Aspirations and Initiatives in the Inter-war Years

The basic patterns of Right-wing politics in the inter-war period were established in the months preceding the elections of 1919: the vague but repeated demands for political 'renewal', the pro-liferation of organisations and movements in which great hopes were briefly placed, the obsessive fear of Communism and the per-sistent, though often half-hearted, quest for unity of the 'national' parties. The aspirations to change the structure of politics and to build new types of political movement were encouraged by the social effects of war, the rapid change of the personnel of politics and the absence of strong party machines. None of the leagues or parties of the Right was strengthened by the war. The extra-parliamentary organisations, *Action Française* and the *Ligue des Patriotes*, gained prestige by 'patriotic' activity but had only skeleton organisations at the armistice and, in any case, were not capable of uniting a large body of Right-wing opinion. The electoral organisations, in decline before 1914, did not show much sign of revival in 1919. Despite this very obvious organisational weakness, the moderate Right won its first electoral victory for over two decades.

This electoral triumph cannot be explained in terms of the activities of men of the Right. Victory in war had strengthened their loyalty to the Republic and they were, therefore, more readily accepted as moderate conservatives, neither suspected nor accused of being reactionaries in revolt against the institutions of the country. The Russian Revolution and the severe bout of industrial unrest in France in 1919 created fears which also helped the Right-wing cause. So, too, did the desire for change. Since the Socialists had made considerable gains in the elections of 1914 and the Right had been badly beaten, the election slogan of *Sortez les sortants* was now mainly directed at the Left. The relative unity of the Right, under the banner of the *Bloc National*, contrasted with the divisions of the Left and was certainly an important symbolic factor in the election campaign. The unity was, of course, superficial as the very vagueness of the programme of the *Bloc National* indicated. The national committee of the Bloc had little influence over the composition of the lists of candidates in the *départements*, which were established by local bargains, and had no sanctions to impose on dissident members of the coalition. Most Right-wing candidates earnestly desired the existence of this kind of national co-ordinating body, but there was no compelling reason why they had to accept its discipline. This failure to create a strong central organisation in the relatively favourable conditions of 1919 was reflected in the following two decades in the scepticism which greeted all the subsequent attempts at reviving or emulating the *Bloc National*.

THE STRENGTH OF THE GROUPS ON THE RIGHT OF THE CHAMBER OF DEPUTIES AT THE BEGINNING OF EACH PARLIAMENT, 1919–1936

	1919	1924	1928	1932	1936
Républicains de Gauche	16	38	64	42	44
Action Républicaine et Sociale	46	—	—	—	—
Démocrates (Démocratie Populaire)	—	14	19	17	13
Action Démocratique et Sociale	—	—	28	18	—
Entente (Union) Républicaine Démocratique	183	104	102	—	—
Républicain et Social	—	—	—	18	18
Centre Républicain	—	—	—	35	—
Fédération Républicaine (Fédération Républicaine et des Indépendants d'Union Républicaine et Nationale)	—	—	—	41	59
Républicains Indépendants et d'Action Sociale et Groupe Agraire Indépendant	—	—	—	—	39
Non-Inscrits	21	28	38	—	—
Indépendants d'Action Économique, Sociale et Paysanne	—	—	—	7	—
Indépendants	29	—	—	16	—

Note: The names in brackets indicate a change of title. Some groups such as the *Groupe du Parti Social Français* founded in 1937 with eight members were established in the course of parliaments and had short careers and are not included in the table. Also excluded is the *Gauche Démocratique*, most of whose members were elected in *Bloc National* lists in 1919: it was a group containing many *ministrable* Deputies and its general political complexion is hard to define.

Although the new political organisations which flourished in 1919 did not make a permanent impact on the politics of the Right, some important new formations were established during the following decade. They can be assimilated to the basic type of organisation described in the previous chapter but they had original features. The broad lines of strategy followed by Taittinger's *Jeunesses Patriotes* and La Rocque's *Croix de Feu* were analogous to those of the *Ligue de la Patrie Française*. They attempted to turn anti-parliamentary sentiments and fears of 'red' revolution to electoral advantage; the *esprit ancien combattant*, however, added a new and paramilitary dimension to the post-war leagues. Nationalist and neo-Fascist organisations proliferated but the most interesting and original – Doriot's *Parti Populaire Français* and the *Cagoule* conspiracy – did not appear until the 1930s. In terms of programme, Raymond-Laurent's *Parti Démocrate Populaire*, had novelty but, although its ambience was that of a university seminar of progressive Catholics working out their ideas, its organisation was recognisably in the tradition of *Action Libérale*. Raymond-Laurent and his collaborators wanted to present their party as belonging to the Left but their claims failed to convince contemporaries. Another politician, Henri de Kérillis, firmly committed to the Republic, to electoral and parliamentary processes, charted a new, although not strikingly successful, course: he established a propaganda centre around which, he hoped, the unity of the parliamentary Right would be established. The agrarian movements led by Fleurant Agricola and Henri Dorgères were curious, time-bound phenomena. Espousing some of the most reactionary propaganda themes, they were symptoms of a new assertiveness in some agricultural communities and they added an original dimension to the political landscape of the 1930s.

The new groups of the inter-war period emphasised basic dilemmas concerning the aims of political action. The men of the Right were torn between moderation and intransigence, between 'liberal' values and an immoderate desire for a strong State. There was also tension between attachment to the existing social order and desire for change, stimulated as much by the First World War as by the great depression. According to the circumstances, to the general climate of opinion and to the balance of forces in parliament and in the street, the Right alternately gave the impression of timid and defensive conservatism and of aggressive innovation, without the two strands being entirely separate. The organisations and most of the men of this period suffered an almost complete discredit among the generation which succeeded them; their successors, however, did little more than synthesise their ideas and practices.

The Jeunesses Patriotes

The link between *Patrie Française*, the *Ligue des Patriotes* and the *Jeunesses Patriotes* was not only of attitude and tradition, it was also personal. Maurice Barrès had been a member of *Patrie Française* and the President of the *Ligue des Patriotes*. The *Jeunesses Patriotes* were formed as a youth branch of the latter. All three leagues engaged in activities which, even when they were not overtly anti-parliamentary, had anti-parliamentary implications. Despite this, on many occasions they acted as supporting organisations in electoral campaigns. All had a very varied membership although the number of people involved was relatively small. The constituent meeting of the *Jeunesses Patriotes* held on 10 April 1924 was a graphic illustration of this. A student of the École Normale, Henri Simon, brought along his monarchist and anti-democratic friends: Provost de la Fardière came with Bonapartist supporters, and Edouard Soulier and his associates represented a strand of Republican nationalism. The founder and only President of the League, Pierre Taittinger, had been a Bonapartist. He had been encouraged by the Bonapartist son of a Prefect of the Second Empire, Le Provost de Launay, to fight the election of 1914 in Charente Inférieure; in 1917 he married the daughter of a banker, Jules Guillet, who had Bonapartist connections, and he was on friendly terms with Bonapartist notables such as Prince Murat and the Cassagnac family.[1]

The war, in which he was wounded twice and mentioned in dispatches four times, was for Taittinger the great formative experience. He retained Bonapartist connections in Charente Inférieure (he was elected Deputy there in 1919) but after the First World War made no mention of Bonapartist opinions. He considered that the 'generation of the Front' had an essential political role and, in 1919, with others of similar persuasion such as Joseph Barthélémy, Jean Fabry and François-Marsal, helped to form the *Parti Républicain de Réorganisation Nationale*, one of the ephemeral parties whose aim was the rejuvenation of French politics.

In most respects Taittinger was a typical Right-wing Republican member of parliament who conscientiously performed the usual constituency duties in Charente Inférieure and maintained strong connections with the area, even after 1924 when he had abandoned his constituency there for one in Paris. He was active in the Chamber, becoming a specialist in colonial matters and chairman of the Committee for the Colonies: he was never a Minister although Tardieu offered him a portfolio. This unwillingness to seek or accept office

[1] J. Philippet, *Les Jeunesses patriotes et Pierre Taittinger*, unpublished *mémoire*, 1967, pp. 8–12.

distinguished him from the other Deputies in the parliamentary group, *Fédération Républicaine*, which he had joined despite an antipathy for Louis Marin. Although forceful and energetic he was not an 'apprentice dictator' in the same sense as the other leaders of minor leagues of the Right. Undoctrinaire and quite willing to associate with nationalists of all tendencies, he allowed considerable autonomy to local leaders in the *Jeunesses Patriotes* as an 'army of order' which would promote unity at the grass roots. The tactics adopted to achieve this end were of a commonplace kind – in June 1924 a parade was held in honour of Joan of Arc, in September another parade on the anniversary of the battle of the Marne, in October a *Jeunesses Patriotes* commando disrupted a revue in which Clemenceau was ridiculed, in November a demonstration was organised against an exhibition of paintings which allegedly denigrated war veterans and, in the same month, a meeting of the League of Rights of Man was broken up. The two events which gave the *Jeunesses Patriotes* the greatest publicity in 1924 were the demonstration against the transfer of the ashes of Jaurès to the Panthéon and the skirmish with the Communists at a by-election meeting in the 18th *arrondissement* of Paris during which four *Jeunesses Patriotes* were killed. These incidents stimulated recruitment to the League although it suffered a setback in 1925 when Georges Valois, the ex-syndicalist and ex-member of *Action Française* founded the *Faisceau* with the financial backing of François Coty. Taittinger tried to ignore it and the Paris evening paper which he edited, *la Liberté*, did not even mention it. But later he admitted:

'It was a terrible blow for the *Jeunesses Patriotes*, then expanding rapidly, to be faced with this formidable and powerfully supported competitor. We were a youthful army, rich in idealism but poor in financial resources and enjoying little press support. Although most members remained loyal, some supporters, despite our warnings, joined the *Faisceau*.'[1]

The foundation of the *Faisceau* brought to the surface the kind of objections and tensions expressed by Antione Didier, the first leading member of the *Jeunesses Patriotes* to resign. Didier, a Vice-President of the League, explained that he resigned because the League was too much influenced by members of parliament and the values of the parliamentary system.[2]

[1] *Le National*, 23 August 1936. This newspaper is the main source of published information on Taittinger and the *Jeunesses Patriotes*. There remain very useful collections of material in private hands, relating to the League.
[2] *Le Nouveau siècle*, 22 December 1925.

There was a sound basis to Didier's criticism for the period 1926 to 1929 when the League was little more than a boisterous group of supporters for a particular parliamentary majority. The policy of the League, as expressed through its weekly paper *le National*, evolved from rather passive acceptance of Poincaré in 1926, to strong support for the *Union Nationale* electoral coalition in 1928 and finally, in 1929, to the eulogistic admiration of Poincaré. Calculations about electoral advantage clearly played an important role in this change. The main activity of the League from October 1927 was the preparation of *bonnes élections*. Taittinger trying to minimise, by making vaguely anti-parliamentary remarks, the tensions this caused:

'The present parliamentary system is anachronistic and harmful. If we vote, it is not to help the system but to use it to the advantage of *la Patrie*.'[1]

The League also tried, with some degree of success, to maintain its reputation for militancy by violent confrontation with the Communists. But the allegations that the *Jeunesses Patriotes* were participating fully in 'the system' carried weight especially after the party newspaper published a list of no fewer than 496 names of 'candidates who merited support' in the 1928 election campaign.[2] The nature of this support was specified by a private circular in which two categories of candidates were distinguished. The first were to be helped actively with propaganda, stewards to keep order at meetings and other forms of material help. The second category, to be assisted merely by the endorsement of their candidature, was very much larger than the first. However, the act of approving candidates in five constituencies out of six created the impression that the League was much more concerned with the general composition of the new Chamber than with any other consideration.

Dissension broke out within the *Jeunesses Patriotes* shortly after the elections of 1928. Pighetti de Rivasso, the President of the *Phalanges Universitaires*, the organisation which provided the bulk of the shock troops in Paris, resigned and published an attack on Taittinger, accusing him of perverting the patriotic idealism of youth for electoral advantage. Maurras took up the attack causing a complete breach between the *Action Française* and the *Jeunesses Patriotes* until some relations were re-established in the February riots of 1934. Taittinger retorted sharply by saying that the programme of the *Jeunesses Patriotes* had never included the destruction of parliament and the regime. He showed by his behaviour that he

[1] *Le National*, 12 December 1927.
[2] *Le National*, 22 April 1928.

had no intention of being deflected from the course he had chosen. The formation of the Tardieu government in November 1929 marked the most ministerial phase of Taittinger's career. Four associates of the *Jeunesses Patriotes* entered the government – Pernot (Minister of Public Works) and Héraud, Sérot and Ober-kirch (Under-Secretaries of State). This identification with the government caused a decline in the activities and membership of the League. Taittinger was very much aware of the dangers inherent in his strategy. In October 1930 he proposed that the League should disengage itself from electoral activities: a new party, the *Parti Républicain National et Social*, would take over these activities and the League would concentrate on direct action.[1] The PRNS was not a great success: its influence was mainly restricted to the Paris region and two *départments*, Loiret and Charente Inférieure, where Taittinger had a personal following. The party was not welcomed by the established formations of the Right but, since it soon became apparent that it would not provide damaging competition, only Maurras and Coty remained openly hostile to it during the 1932 election campaign.

Although the party did not make much impact, the *Jeunesses Patriotes* prospered. Henry Provost de la Fardière, in his periodical *le Brin de Houx*, revived the original harsher tones of the League before the Poincaré period and also tried to give the movement a firmer doctrinal base. Increasing street violence in the course of 1932 encouraged new recruits and a more militant posture;[2] in the last two months of the year *le National* ran a series of articles on the coming 'national revolution'. The *Jeunesses Patriotes* were enthusiastically committed in the riots of February 1934. But from those incidents a very formidable rival emerged, Colonel de la Rocque and his *Croix de Feu* movement. Taittinger remarked two years afterwards:

'Colonel de la Rocque's great merit was that he knew how to extract the maximum advantage from the situation. Also, it should be emphasised that the mass circulation press suddenly dropped

[1] *Bulletin de liaison des Jeunesses patriotes*, No. 3, October 1930. Taittinger remained a member of the *Fédération Républicaine* until May 1931 when he resigned under the mistaken impression that Marin had accepted *Action Française* support for a meeting to protest against the Austro-German customs union.

[2] The membership of the League is hard to estimate because the only evidence are the claims made by the League itself. These were 200,000 at the third congress in February 1930, 320,000 at the fourth conference in March 1931; Pierre Taittinger in his evidence to the parliamentary committee of enquiry into the events of February 1934 claimed that the membership was 240,000.

its customary reserve and persuaded the public that a new force had emerged to thwart the revolution.'[1]

The tactics adopted by La Rocque damaged Taittinger's movement. Taittinger alleged that La Rocque wanted the leagues dissolved so that he could impose his leadership on the whole of the Right through a new party. He seems to have had some grounds for his suspicion: in January 1936, La Rocque refused his offer, made through an intermediary, of the leadership of the *Front National*, which had been set up as a response to the *Front Populaire*. La Rocque's snub effectively marks the end of Taittinger's influence although he continued to be active. In March 1936 he launched an unsuccessful appeal to Pétain to lead the Right.[2] He participated in the *Comité d'Entente et d'Arbitration Electorale des Républicains Nationaux*, organised by Kérillis, and in the *Front de la Liberté* established in April 1937, mainly on Doriot's initiative. But in the four years preceding the Second World War, the *Jeunesses Patriotes* and the *Parti Républicain National et Social* were in rapid decline.

In the absence of any notable success, Taittinger's willingness to play both the parliamentary and the anti-parliamentary game appeared vacillating and equivocal. A conciliatory attitude towards rivals and a frequently expressed desire to co-operate were not particularly attractive to the sectarian activists of the extreme Right. La Rocque became more popular amongst the moderates because he was aiming at similar ends with an apparently greater chance of success. Dissensions broke out within both the League and the Party in 1938 over both Munich and domestic policies. Taittinger's organisations contained a higher proportion than other groups of the Right of old-fashioned nationalists who were irredeemably anti-German and who considered that national unity in face of external threat was more important than partisan success. Such dissensions were, in any case, a typical feature of the periods of declining political fortunes of Right-wing formations. The war terminated the activity of the League and the Party and marked their final dissolution. Apart from sustaining Taittinger's personal career and achieving a good deal of publicity, they left few traces.

The Croix de Feu *and the* Parti Social Français
La Rocque used basically the same strategy as Taittinger but with

---

[1] *Le National*, 23 August 1936.

[2] *Le National*, 14 March 1936. P. Machefer, 'L'Union des Droites: le PSF et le Front de la Liberté, 1936–1937', *Revue d'histoire moderne et contemporaine*, vol. 17, 1970, p. 118.

considerably greater panache and, for a time, posed a genuine threat to the political status quo. Exactly how La Rocque became involved in ex-servicemen's politics, and for what motives, remains unclear. Nothing in his early career indicated a political vocation. He came from a minor aristocratic family: his father was a General with monarchist leanings and his two brothers served in the entourage of the Count de Paris. La Rocque never apparently considered that a monarchist restoration was possible or even desirable, although there was an attempt to compromise him with the monarchist cause. His military career, much of it spent in Morocco, was moderately distinguished; he was decorated for bravery in the First World War and served briefly on the staff of Marshal Foch.[1] On retirement with the rank of Colonel of the Reserve in 1926, he was given a job by Ernest Mercier, an electricity magnate with Right-wing views. He soon became involved in the affairs of the *Association Nationale des Combattants de l'Avant et des Blessés de Guerre cités pour Action*, commonly known as the *Croix de Feu*. This association was founded in November 1927 by Maurice d'Hartoy with the financial support of François Coty. The original founders resisted Coty's attempt to politicise the association and Coty was probably responsible for introducing La Rocque to the League and assisting his rapid promotion.[2] There are unsubstantiated allegations that Tardieu helped him: although Tardieu almost certainly paid La Rocque to organise demonstrations on his behalf two years later, it is improbable that Tardieu was meddling in the affairs of an obscure ex-servicemen's league in 1928.

As soon as La Rocque became influential in the League the tone of its pronouncements became more political. The newspaper of the association, *le Flambeau*, contained an increasing number of statements that the *Croix de Feu* were prepared to do battle in the streets to save the country from revolution. Declarations such as these quickly brought forth charges of Fascism from the Left, which were rejected in phrases which became almost a litany of the movement in the decade that followed:

'We are not Fascist. But if Fascist means Frenchmen good and true who oppose traitors and lunatics stabbing the country in the back, then we are Fascists. If Fascist describes supporters of order and discipline freely consented to, then we are Fascists. But if

[1] For biographical details see E. and G. La Rocque, *La Rocque tel qu'il était*, 1962. P. Rudeaux, *Les Croix de feu et le PSF*, 1967.

[2] See A. Kupferman, *François Coty, journaliste et homme politique*, unpublished thesis, 1965.

Fascism refers to repression, to brute force, defending special interests, to persecution of opinions, to regimentation and militarisation of the nation, then we are not Fascists. If necessary we will go into the streets to assist the army and the police to re-establish order. Our league is useful to everyone because it embodies French patriotism and courage.'[1]

In so far as he articulated them clearly, La Rocque's views were those of a rather old-fashioned moderate Republican but there were elements of Fascism in the style of the *Croix de Feu* and in its equivocal attitude towards violence.

The declared readiness to fight Communists in the streets was an undoubted spur to recruitment: in the year 1929–30, membership almost doubled from 8,000 to 15,000. By 1933 it was 60,000, including supporting organisations such as the *Briscards* and the *Volontaires Nationaux*. Circumstances helped this growth: it was a new movement at a time when the effects of the depression were becoming apparent in France. But it was also due to the leadership of La Rocque. He inspired trust and admiration among the rank and file of the movement, appearing more respectable than other leaders of Right-wing leagues and more in harmony with the times than the ageing leaders of *Action Française*. Although a poor writer and a dull orator, he nonetheless gave the impression of energy and integrity. The pageantry and excitement of the carefully stage-managed rallies inspired the ordinary members of the movement. But La Rocque was distrusted and came to be despised by many of his closer associates. A large number left him and, in 1935, the entire leadership of the *Volontaires Nationaux*. With most of them he was cold, distant and dictatorial: they felt bitterly that he had perverted a valuable movement.[2] The apostates made several efforts to discredit him and he was eventually forced to react when, in 1937, one of them, Pozzo di Borgo, accused him of having received government funds in return for organising demonstrations. He brought a libel case against Pozzo di Borgo but the evidence of one of the Ministers involved, Tardieu, was decisive and La Rocque lost.[3] The polemics surrounding this libel action exposed deep

---

[1] *Le Flambeau*, 1 November 1929, quoted J. Plumyène, R. Lasierra, *Les Fascismes français*, 1923–63, 1963.

[2] P. Chopine, *Le Colonel de La Rocque, veut-il la guerre civile?* 1937, p. 14. F. de Hautecloque, *Grandeur et décadence des Croix des feu*, 1937, pp. 22–5.

[3] *Le PSF devant la cour d'appel. Plaidorie de Me Andriot, déclaration de La Rocque*, n.d. F. Veuillot, *La Rocque et son parti comme je les ai vu*, 1938, pp. 14–35. For an anti-La Rocque view, P. Chopine, *La Verité sur le PSF et le comte de La Rocque*, n.d.

internal dissensions within La Rocque's movement and between it and the other movements of the extreme Right. Although the Right as a whole clearly suffered some discredit, La Rocque and his party were remarkably unscathed by the incident.

La Rocque embarked on the same strategy as Taittinger. Never wholly accepting nor rejecting the Republic, he attempted to use the system whilst, at the same time, appearing to reject it. He never took steps to mount a *coup d'état* but attempted to mobilise the activist temperament of the *anciens combattants* to create a new style of conservative party. Between 1930 and 1936 the *Croix de Feu* were organised as, and had the mystique of, a paramilitary organisation. By the end of that period an 'army' of approximately half a million strong, members of the *Croix de Feu, Briscards, Volontaires Nationaux* and *Equipes de Propagande* were organised into sections, platoons and companies ('centuries') and kept in a constant state of alert. Despite the torchlight parades, the show of discipline, the cult of action and the high degree of mobilisation, the level of violence was not high. Some of the nocturnal motorcades through provincial towns were intended to intimidate but La Rocque did not seek physical confrontation with his opponents. Typical of his activities was the holding of a counter demonstration on the Champs Elysées when the Communists were meeting at Bastille. In February 1934 the League went into the streets 'to shout its disgust at the scoundrels who dishonoured the Republic'[1] but on 6 February when the most violent demonstrations took place La Rocque, apparently deliberately, kept his men inactive.

La Rocque was a reticent and enigmatic figure. It is not clear whether all his tactics were consciously worked out: his closest confidants, Noël Ottavi and Jean Ybarnégaray, remained unusually discreet. There was, however, an intelligible thread running through them. By consistently refusing to co-operate with other leagues and refraining from anti-Republican pronouncements during the paramilitary phase of the *Croix de Feu*, he seemed to be deliberately maintaining the option of abandoning direct action for electoral politics. In the course of 1935, when an alternative to the Popular Front was being demanded in the Right-wing press, La Rocque decided to exercise that option by participating in the local elections and by conniving at the dissolution of the leagues. In December 1935 the Chamber debated a government proposal for powers to ban political leagues, Jean Ybarnégaray, the spokesman of the *Croix de Feu*, said: 'To the extent that our organisations are paramilitary, we are ready to have them dissolved.' This statement and the

[1] F. de Hauteclocque, op. cit., pp. 14–15.

acceptance of the decree of 18 June 1936, which disbanded the *Croix de Feu* was interpreted by La Rocque's enemies as a loss of nerve. It is equally plausible to assume that La Rocque considered that continuance of direct action, if it resulted in a serious and violent confrontation with the Left, could exclude him permanently from power. A speaker at the Radical Party conference in November 1935 paid an ironic compliment to La Rocque: 'Do not let us forget to salute the real initiator of the Popular Front – Colonel de La Rocque.' Direct action thus encouraged the unity and militancy of the Left but seemed unlikely to defeat it.

A nationwide poster campaign was conducted by the *Croix de Feu* in September 1935, typifying the Popular Front as *la ruine, la révolution et la guerre* but La Rocque seemed to think that the time was not ripe for engaging the battle.[1] Before the elections of 1936 he published a directive to the *Croix de Feu* telling his followers to restrict themselves to 'creating a barrier against disorder'.[2] A handful of members and sympathisers of the League were elected but there were no official candidates. Immediately after the election he founded the *Parti Social Français* to take the place of the banned League. The new party was not compromised by the electoral defeat of the Right and benefited from the absence of an effective opposition to the Popular Front government. Membership grew enormously: in 1938 the party claimed two million members, in 1939 three million. These figures are unreliable but the PSF was clearly a mass party which would have made a considerable impact in the 1940 elections had they taken place.[3]

The transition from league to party was smoothly managed but many of the hard-line activists did not join the new organisation. There remained a militant element in the *Equipes de Propagande* attempting to play the same role within the PSF as the *Camelots du Roi* within *Action Française*. But the party was concerned to avoid the sectarianism of the extreme Right. The first manifesto, printed in a run of a million copies with the emblem of the Republic on its cover, had an exalted, but neither an extreme nor Fascist tone. It contained a wish to unite as many people as possible:

'Frenchmen and Frenchwomen of all conditions, of all classes, of all opinions, the *Parti Social Français* awaits your help in the common task of public safety and national renaissance.'

[1] ibid., p. 29.

[2] *Croix de feu. Parti Social Français. Tracts politiques, 1934–1939.* G. Vallin, 'Le Parti Social Français', *Sciences politiques*, August 1937.

[3] P. Marabuto, *Les Partis politiques et les mouvements sociaux sous la Quatrième République*, 1947, pp. 222–5.

The statutes of the party were very similar to those of the *Alliance Démocratique* and included a statement of loyalty to the Republic. The party evoked the spirit of Republican patriotism and claimed the heritage of the *France de Valmy*. The constitutional programme was anti-parliamentary only in the sense that the post-war Gaullist programme was anti-parliamentary. It had authoritarian implications but was very definitely not Fascist:

'A President of the Republic with effective rights of dissolution and the right to communicate with parliament.

A single cabinet for each legislature.

The President to appoint the Prime Minister and have the right of countersigning the acts of the government.

Regulation of parliament (an age limit, reduction of the number of Deputies, strict incompatibility rules).

Members of parliament not to have the right to propose increases in expenditure.

Creation of a consultative National Economic Council representing the professions.'

The programme caused alarm because of the studied vagueness about how these aims were to be achieved.

The vagueness was probably no more than fence-sitting and gave point to Maurice Pujo's amusing tag *Monsieur-je-ne-suis-pas:*

'I am neither royalist nor Bonapartist, but I am not a Republican in the usual manner.

I am not a Socialist but neither am I a supporter of capital.

I am neither of the Right nor of the Left.'[1]

The programme of the PSF was designed to avoid alienating potential support; even on the reforms of the Blum government the party usually avoided outright condemnation. A long policy statement on the forty-hour week suggested that it was possibly inequitable, harmful to production and to the smaller firms, and that it ought to be preceded both by an international agreement and by other domestic social reforms.[2] But the party did not demand its repeal. The positive social and economic programme was equally vague. A corporatist theme was omnipresent but how industrial, agricultural and professional corporations were to be established, organised and administered was never worked out. Policy statements usually terminated with a flourish about measures being implemented by the

[1] M. Pujo, *Comment La Rocque a trahi*, n.d.
[2] Service de Propagande du Parti Social Français, *Parti Social Français et la semaine de 40 heures*, n.d.

relevant 'organised profession' *en dehors de toute ingérence étatiste ou politicienne.*[1] This theme, together with flattery of the peasantry and autarchic economic arguments gave the party a somewhat reactionary tone.

One element commonly found in the programmes of reactionary organisations was conspicuously missing. La Rocque refused to have anything to do with anti-Semitism, and he had several Jews in his entourage including his private secretary. Other organisations of the extreme Right, and some elements within his own party, tried to make him declare his position. However, he consistently described it as a religious matter on which his movement had no opinion and was embarrassed when confronted with cries of *A bas les Juifs*, during a visit to the Algerian sections of the PSF. Some of the propagandists of the party, however, made anti-Semitic remarks. Michel Aucouturier, for example, asserted: 'Behind socialism there is Freemasonry and Jewry: Jewish-Masonic high finance and everything is said.'[2] La Rocque, by steering clear of religious matters, managed to get the support of anti-clericals as well as well-known Catholics such as François Veuillot. The Catholic hierarchy were, on the other hand, very cautious and seemingly intent that the Church should not be compromised in any way. The Assembly of Cardinals and Archbishops issued a statement in 1936 calling on the clergy not to participate in political parties and leagues: referring specifically to the *Croix de Feu*, the clergy were advised that they need not resign from the movement but they should refrain from playing an active role in it. The episcopate raised no doctrinal objections to the programme of the league or the PSF but the style of the movement was clearly a cause of concern.

The equivocal attitude to violence alarmed both the moderate and the extreme opponents of La Rocque's movement. In a pedestrian book, *Service Public*, published in 1934, La Rocque wrote:

'Disapproving of violence is not the same as fearing it. One can reject its use but at the same time not exclude the possibility of having to face and defeat violent men. Confronted by the instigators, paymasters and thugs of the Common Front and their criminal manoeuvres, it would be unforgivable if we did not prepare effective means of defending good Frenchmen and of crushing attempts at revolution.'[3]

La Rocque seemed sincere in asserting that he would not counten-

[1] Parti Social Français, *Le Paysan sauvera la France avec le PSF,* 1937, p. 26.
[2] M. Aucouturier, *Au Service des Croix de feu,* 1936, p. 235.
[3] Colonel de La Rocque, *Service public,* 1934, pp. 261–2.

ance the use of violence except as a response to its use by other people. The paramilitary organisation of the *Croix de Feu*, the motorcades of the local sections of the PSF and the demonstrations of disciplined force were intended to have a propaganda effect, to dramatise the movement and its leader. The typical evening rally at a chateau of a sympathiser, commencing with the arrival of a leader in a large car, strikingly illuminated, surrounded by praetorian guards and received by a torchlight parade, was designed to stimulate the enthusiasm of members of the movement and impress potential supporters. Demonstrations and parades helped to maintain an atmosphere of constant excitement but they were also inflammatory and provocative.

Without the simulated ambience of adventure and violence La Rocque would not have made such an impressive impact, admired even by a sceptical observer such as Henri de Kérillis. All methods of propaganda were used – the short film, recordings, simple dramatic posters, the party newspaper *le Flambeau* which had reached a circulation of 400,000 (very high by French standards) at its peak, a mass circulation newspaper *le Petit Journal*, acquired in 1937, and an abundance of brochures. This propaganda was disseminated both by the propaganda services within the *Croix de Feu* and the PSF and by a large number of fringe organisations – charitable associations, university centres, rambling and athletic clubs. Some had analogies with Nazi front organisations: an association of Frenchmen living abroad, societies for *Préparation et éducation sportive*, a civil defence corps and a federation of aero-clubs run by the pioneer pilot, and La Rocque's close collaborator, Jean Mermoz. The most ambitious project was a trade union federation, the *Confédération des Syndicats Professionnels*; one million members were claimed in 1938 but it has little industrial impact and was not, as it was intended to be, a significant rival to the CGT. Even the Communist Party could not equal the PSF in the range and variety of its fringe organisations: perhaps only *Action Libérale Populaire* during the Third Republic had an equivalent number within its orbit. The *Parti Social Français* was, until the *Rassemblement du Peuple Français* in the late 1940s, the most successful drive towards mass mobilisation of a 'moderate' and conservative clientele.

This drive had authoritarian anti-parliamentary implications and caused widespread alarm. After La Rocque had ceased to be a political force of any consequence, his opponents exacted their revenge. The outbreak of war was the effective end of the *Parti Social Français* because La Rocque loyally supported the government until the fall of France and Marshal Pétain thereafter. The party was allowed to continue its activities in the unoccupied zone but relations between La Rocque and the Vichy authorities were not close. There was never the slightest suggestion that La Rocque favoured collaboration with Germany: he opposed Laval, the attempt to set up a *parti unique* by Déat, Doriot and others, and policies such as the direction of labour to Germany. Many of his supporters, including his deputy, Charles Vallin, opted for de Gaulle and the Resistance. Eventually La Rocque himself was arrested for Resistance activities and deported to Ravensbrück.[1] In poor health when liberated in 1945, he was immediately imprisoned without charge by the provisional government, being released only to die. Although apparently harsh treatment for a man who had always maintained that power should be acquired only by legal means, the men of the Resistance could not forget that Hitler, after the abortive putsch of 1923, had said exactly the same thing. His end was pathetic and there was something ludicrous about his general political posture – he was always announcing battles which he never fought unless his hand was forced. The formulae on which the *Parti Social Français* was based were potentially successful; an emotional nationalism without excessive chauvinism, a vaguely authoritarian constitutional programme, a relative willingness to consider social reforms, and a mass political movement, complemented by a range of ancillary organisations, providing its members with a sense of participation and adventure. The amalgamation was a more formidable synthesis than had been previously achieved. La Rocque attempted to impose unity on the 'nationals' from the outside and never compromised to gain the support of any group or individual.

The Centre de Propagande des Républicains Nationaux
Henri de Kérillis had a similar general aim and identical views on most of the main policy issues, but he attempted to promote the unity of the Right by very different tactics. Kérillis played a minor but interesting role in the politics of the inter-war period. Coming from a background of the minor provincial aristocracy, he joined *l'Echo de Paris* after his demobilisation in 1919. At that time the paper was dominated by the influence of Maurice Barrès and Kérillis remained his faithful disciple. In the early 1920s his articles were mainly on foreign and colonial policy, with the alienation of the French working class from the political system, forming a third and lesser theme. He supported the conventional nationalist view that France must remain the strongest military power in Europe and

---

[1] Service de Documentation du Parti Social Français, *Le PSF après quatre années d'ostracisme et de persécutions*, 1945.

enforce the provisions of the Treaty of Versailles to the letter. Throughout the inter-war period he held that Germany was the largest threat to French security and that French foreign policy must be mainly directed towards obtaining safeguards against it. On colonial matters he was unconventional, being hostile to the cultural assimilation of the colonies and to the concept of overseas France. He took the view that the overseas possessions had specific ethnic and cultural characteristics: they perhaps could not and certainly should not become 'French'.[1] Although tinged with racialism his attitude could easily have evolved into acceptance of independence of colonial territories.

From the middle of the 1920s he paid a number of visits to Britain, usually in the company of Paul Reynaud, to study Conservative Party organisation. He acquired a considerable admiration for the party, particularly for its propaganda directed at a mass audience and for its ability to attract working-class votes. His desire to put into practice in France the lessons he had learned from the Tories was motivated, at least in part, by his detestation of the Communists to whom he attributed almost demonic qualities. Only propaganda, he thought, could emancipate the workers from the 'slavery' of Communism.[2] A Paris by-election which he fought with Paul Reynaud in 1926 convinced him that the Right lagged far behind even its non-Communist opponents in the techniques of propaganda and he established the *Centre de Propagande des Républicains Nationaux*. He argued that the Right feared the masses and relied too much on individual leaders and provincial notables. In a democracy, according to Kérillis, the Right had to mobilise the masses in order to avoid electoral defeat. To this end the Right must utilise 'true propaganda (which) is not agitation but education'. His view of propaganda was similar to that of the extra-parliamentary leagues: 'Propaganda should not consist of lectures on the art of war or sociology or finance, but on the presentation of clear themes supported by "obvious facts".'[3] That such a platitude made an impression is a reflection of the turgid and clumsy public relations of the parliamentary Right. The 'moderate' Republican notables were not very receptive to Kérillis's arguments, partly because of his youth and lack of status. He retaliated by calling them 'Louis-Philippards', selfishly defending their material interests in a narrow-minded way. He was a member of the *Fédération Républicaine* but

---

[1] See especially *l'Echo de Paris*, 23 February 1925.

[2] For the development of his ideas on propaganda see H. Cartier, H. de Kérillis, *Faisons le point*, 1931.

[3] O. Gaudry, *Henri de Kérillis*, unpublished *mémoire*, 1966, p. 46.

his relations with it became so bad that at one point in 1931 Louis Marin, the Secretary General of the Federation proposed that Kérillis be excluded. The proposal was withdrawn but relations remained strained.

The most successful period of Kérillis's propaganda centre was between 1928 and 1933. It received apparently quite generous financial support from *l'Echo de Paris*, private sources, firms and public subscriptions.[1] The country was divided into four regions each with an autonomous committee to manage the distribution of propaganda literature. This was distributed free to various organisations – *Jeunesses Patriotes*, *Ligue des Patriotes*, *Fédération Républicaine*, *Alliance Républicaine Démocratique*, *Parti Démocrate Populaire*, *Redressement Français*, *Union des Intérêts Economiques* and the *Associations Paroisselles*. Others received the propaganda materials by paying a graded subscription. The centre published a press bulletin which, in its hey-day, was taken by over two hundred journals, and a periodical called *Documents* mainly devoted to articles on propaganda techniques. In association with these activities, Kérillis organised a federation of newspapers whose editorial persuasion was Republican nationalist. He also established (in 1927) a school for orators on the lines of the Conservative Party school in Britain and a team of semi-professional orators, associated with this school, toured the country.

Kérillis aroused suspicions among the notables of the parliamentary Right because he had greater ambitions than the provision of posters, brochures and periodicals. He hoped that conservative Republicans would unite around the propaganda centre because it was the most articulate spokesman of their cause. An early practical expression of this ambition was a service to arbitrate disputes over candidates in elections which he set up within the propaganda centre. He also tried to mobilise broad movements of opinion behind particular campaigns: an example was the petition, for which three million signatures were collected, calling for the return of Gaston Doumergue to power, which he organised in February 1934. He managed to assemble a broad electoral coalition for the Paris region in 1936 – the *Comité d'Entente et d'Arbitrage Electoral des Républicains Nationaux pour la Région de Paris* – consisting of National Radicals, *Fédération Républicaine*, *Union Nationale des Anciens Combattants*, *Parti Démocrate Populaire*, *Alliance Démo-*

---

[1] Subscribers of less than 500 francs seem to have provided most of the funds according to lists published in *l'Echo de Paris* but for allegations of the dominance of large subscribers see H. Coston, *Le Retour des deux cent familles*, 1960, p. 23.

cratique and representatives of the newspapers *le Figaro, le Gringoire, le Jour, la Liberté, l'Ami du peuple* and *l'Echo de Paris*. Fear of a Popular Front victory brought this disparate group together but their co-operation did not survive the election.

The anti-parliamentary Right clearly regarded his centre as a threat and Kérillis was frequently attacked in the columns of *Action française*. Most of the established parliamentary figures seemed to regard it as no more than a convenient source of propaganda material. Its activities were very unevenly spread over the country: some important cities, where there were large conservative electorates such as Marseilles, Lyons, Strasbourg and Bordeaux, were scarcely touched by the centre. Its main influence was north of the Loire, in the Paris region, in certain provincial towns and in those rural areas which traditionally voted for Right-wing candidates. Whatever personal influence Kérillis had, and it was always limited because he was regarded as a lightweight, rapidly evaporated after 1936. He had been in broad agreement with the rest of the Right on issues of foreign policy in 1935 when he had strongly supported Mussolini over Ethiopia, but he was much more alarmed by the remilitarisation of the Rhineland in 1936 than were his colleagues. He opposed appeasement of Germany and, with his old associate Paul Reynaud, was one of the few members of the Right to oppose Munich. This foreign policy position was attractive neither to the financial supporters of the propaganda centre nor to the audience which it was trying to reach. Isolation on foreign policy would probably have been decisive but the work of the centre was made much more difficult by the success of men like La Rocque and Doriot.

In the atmosphere which surrounded the Popular Front victory (which seemed to alarm Kérillis very much less than the threat from across the Rhine) the violent words of the extra- and anti-parliamentary Right had a much wider appeal. Kérillis had some respect for La Rocque because he understood the necessity of 'conquering the masses' and of constant mobilisation of Right-wing opinion. During the war Kérillis called La Rocque's followers 'Fascists without knowing it',[1] but the *Parti Social Français* came close to the notion of a large 'national' party which Kérillis had been advocating since 1925. Kérillis was certainly more perceptive than most of his colleagues on policy matters but his tendency to despise other leaders of the Right was not compensated for by outstanding personal qualities of his own. His judgement deserted him during the war when, choosing New York as a place of exile, he became bitterly

[1] *Pour le Victoire*, 3 October 1942. H. de Kérillis, *Français, voici la vérité*, 1942, p. 63.

anti-Gaullist. He decided not to return to France after the liberation and finished his life as a farmer in the United States.

The Parti Démocrate Populaire[1]

Kérillis was in a secular tradition of moderate Republicanism: religious concerns and the affairs of the Church seemed to interest him little. He distributed propaganda to parish associations and regarded the traditionally Catholic areas of the country as electoral bastions on which a large conservative party could be built. The political debates of militant Catholic circles raised issues which did not concern him. He regarded the *Parti Démocrate Populaire*, founded in 1924, as a minor irritant although it was the only Catholic formation to acquire a significant electoral following during the inter-war period. The Party claimed the heritage of four movements established in the period before 1914 – the *Sillonist*, the *Parti Démocrate Chrétien*, the *Semaines Sociales* and the *Association Catholique de la Jeunesse Française*[2] – but it did not succeed in attracting many of the major figures who had been involved in these movements and came to resemble *Action Libérale Populaire*, whose example it rejected, more than any of them. It commenced as an ambitious attempt by a new generation of political leaders – men such as Robert Cornilleau, Champetier de Ribes, Alfred Bour and Raymond-Laurent – to convert the Catholic electorate to more progressive, 'Left-wing' political and social policies. Some Christian Democrats such as Francisque Gay, who as editor of *l'Aube* was to be an important influence behind the founding of the *Mouvement Républicain Populaire*, held aloof because they thought that the time had not yet come for a progressive and reforming mass party of Catholic inspiration. This judgement proved correct not only because the maximum number of Deputies it achieved was twenty-one (in the 1928–32 parliament) but also because it appeared to be another ineffectual attempt to establish the Republican credentials of Catholics.

As a generator of ideas, the party was very lively, more so than its much larger and more successful successor, the *Mouvement Républicain Populaire*. These ideas were developed in the columns of the official party newspaper, *le Petit démocrate*, and a number of reviews associated with the party – *les Cahiers de la nouvelle journée*, *la Revue des jeunes*, *la Vie intellectuelle* and *la Politique*. The four

[1] See especially R. E. M. Irving, *Christian Democracy in France*, 1973, pp. 41–51. M. Prélot, 'Histoire et doctrine du Parti Démocrate Populaire', *Politique*, July–December 1962, pp. 307–40.

[2] Raymond-Laurent, *Le Parti Démocrate Populaire; un effort de dix ans, 1924–1934*, 1935, pp. 11–36.

'cardinal points' of the party's programme related to economic and social reform, foreign affairs, civic education and constitutional reform.[1] An expressed willingness to co-operate with the Socialist Party to promote economic and social reforms came to nothing, except for a brief flirtation with Léon Blum, because the clerical question lay awkwardly between them and because their perspective on social questions was very different. In foreign policy the party was 'Briandiste', supporting international organisations and *détente* in Europe, an attitude which aroused considerable hostility in nationalist and traditionalist Catholic circles. This eventually led to support for appeasement (the parliamentary group, after deep internal dissensions unanimously voted for the Munich agreements) and for Marshal Pétain in 1940, thus causing another division between generations of Christian Democrats. Only those who opposed Pétain, or who subsequently retrieved their reputation by Resistance activities like Reille-Soult, won the favour of the founders of the *Mouvement Républicain Populaire*.

The presence within the party of two distinguished professors of Public Law, Marcel Prélot and Maurice Hauriou, contributed to the high quality of the discussion within the party on constitutional matters. This question was given a prominence unusual among Republican parties during the Third Republic.[2] The 1929 party congress held at Nancy was devoted to *Réforme de l'Etat Républicain* and the ideas expressed there were developed in numerous articles and several books. The main themes of the constitutional programme were the importance of bringing professional and social groups into government through a form of corporative system, decentralisation of administration, regional democratically elected assemblies, proportional representation in elections, a strict separation of powers and devices to ensure greater governmental stability. This programme was influential in moulding the constitutional ideas of both the *Mouvement Républicain Populaire* and the Gaullists.

The PDP was in the mainstream of Catholic political action in France but it remained a minor political party. It achieved modest parliamentary strength because members of certain lay and clerical Catholic elites moved to the Left. Its electoral support was localised: in 1924, eleven out of fourteen, and in 1928 fourteen out of twenty-one Deputies came from either Brittany or Alsace. Local notables led rather than followed the opinions of their constituents. The election of Reille-Soult in the Tarn or Michel Walter in Bas-Rhin

[1] Raymond-Laurent, op. cit., pp. 47–8.

[2] J. Molinier *Le Parti Démocrate Populaire et la réforme de l'état*, unpublished *mémoire*, 1966.

did not give grounds for believing that their traditionally minded electors had changed their views. Reille-Soult inherited his seat from Bonapartist and Right-wing Catholic predecessors and was elected in 1919 only because his elder brother, who was very much a man of the Right, was killed in the war. Most of the Deputies of the party were elected with the help of traditionally Right-wing electorates: for example, out of a total of seventeen Deputies in 1932, thirteen were elected with the help of Right-wing votes against candidates of the Left and only four were elected against candidates of the Right. The party failed 'to destroy the sophistry which links religious convictions with political reaction and social conservatism'[1] and was simply squeezed between the conservatives and the anti-clericals. George Bidault's electoral failure in an Orne constituency in 1936 was typical – he was attacked by the Left as a clerical and by the Right as a *chrétien rouge*. It was for this reason that the great majority of the seventy federations in the *départements* were electorally insignificant. The exceptions, apart from Brittany and Alsace, were in scattered areas where a strong local leader was present – Neyton in Isère, Demagny in Seine-et-Oise, Diligent and Catrice in Nord.

The party presented a well-meaning but rather blurred and in-effectual image, not least because of the behaviour of its members in parliament. Anti-cartellist in 1924 because of the anti-clerical platform of the Herriot government, its members participated in various Rightward tending ministries led by Poincaré and Tardieu down to 1932; between 1932 and 1938 there was no participation in governments but the group more frequently supported coalitions of the kind led by Flandin or Laval than those led by Herriot or Sarraut. Moderately Left-wing rhetoric was accompanied by moderately Right-wing tactics. The vilification and occasional physical violence directed against the party by *Action Française* and other organisations of the extreme Right established the party's claim to be anti-reactionary and at least a potential threat to the bases of the support of reactionaries. Accompanied by the slow but steady rise of the Catholic trade union movement and the polemical writings of some Catholic intellectuals such as Mounier and the group around the short-lived *Sept*, the party helped to create the impression that Catholic opinion was moving into a period of change. This impression was not nearly enough to convince the democratic Left that the time had come to co-operate with men who flaunted their Catholic allegiance.

[1] R. Cornilleau in *le Petit démocrate*, 20 September 1924. This was a frequently repeated sentiment.

The Parti Populaire Français

Expressing an analogous dissatisfaction with the status quo but with a very different character were the various attempts to establish a genuine French Fascism commencing with Georges Valois and culminating with Jacques Doriot. Valois started and finished (on his death in a German concentration camp) his political career as a syndicalist. He was converted to monarchism by Maurras and by the conviction that the working class would be better protected by a King than by the Republic.[1] After the First World War, with the support of Maurras, he launched two 'social' movements, the *Confédération de l'Intelligence et de la Production Française* (1920) and the *Etats Généraux de la Production* (1922). Neither was a success and by 1924 he was looking elsewhere: he founded a newspaper, *le Nouveau siècle*, with a view to organising the exservicemen. He broke with *Action Française* in November 1925 when *le Nouveau siècle* was converted into a daily. Valois and the leaders of *Action Française* were almost certainly competing for Coty's financial support at this time which added bitterness to the conflict.[2] Valois made the break irreparable by establishing an overtly Fascist party, *le Faisceau,* and in December 1925 wresting control of the publishing house, the Nouvelle Librairie Française, from *Action Française.* Valois, like the young men of the 1930s, Rebatet, Brasillach and Thierry Maulnier, did not break with Maurras for doctrinal reasons but because he had a low opinion of Maurras as a leader and man of action. Valois proved as ineffective as the ageing theoretician. Coty's financial support lasted little more than a year and Valois lacked stature and qualities to attract a mass following.

The emulators of Valois had no more success than he had, until 1934 to 1936 during the period of the rise of the Popular Front. Valois had claimed in 1926 to be the first French Fascist but Jacques Doriot's *Parti Populaire Française* was the only serious drive towards a French Fascist party.[3] Until the defeat of France, it denied being Fascist, but it had the essential components – virulent anti-Communism, social radicalism, anti-parliamentary authoritarianism, vague anti-Semitism (although it was not part of the official programme until the defeat), a leadership cult, a disciplined team of militants and a popular clientele. The last two characteristics marked

[1] G. Valois, *La Monarchie et la classe ouvrière,* 1910.

[2] A. Kupferman, *François Coty, journaliste et homme politique,* unpublished thesis, 1965.

[3] This is also the judgement of J. Plumyène, R. Lasierra, op. cit., p. 110, and D. Wolf, *Doriot: du communisme à la collaboration,* 1969. The latter work contains an excellent and exhaustive account of all aspects of Doriot's career.

the PPF off from its predecessors. Doriot managed to attract supporters from the most diverse social groups and from very varied
political backgrounds, welding them for a short period into an
intimidating political force. Like La Rocque, Doriot demonstrated
the weakness of the established parties of the Right and showed that
some but not all the conditions of the success of a Right-wing
radicalism were present during the Popular Front period.

A son of a blacksmith in Oise, Doriot left home at the age of
seventeen to find a series of jobs around Saint-Denis, the north
Paris suburb with which all his political career was linked.[1] After a
period in the army as a conscript, during which he witnessed both
Belà Kun's soviet republic in Hungary and D'Annunzio's *coup de
main* in Fiume, he returned to Saint-Denis and joined the Communist
Party. By a series of chances, he had an extraordinarily rapid career.
After a visit to the Soviet Union, he was elected a Deputy for Saint-
Denis in 1924. He then gained a national reputation and a short
term in prison for supporting the Moroccan revolt of Abd El Krim
in 1925.[2] It was apparently during a visit to China in 1926, where
he had been sent by Stalin as an emissary of the Comintern, that
Doriot had his first doubts about the leadership of the international
Communist movement exercised by the Kremlin. He did not reveal
these misgivings and went on to become a major figure in the French
Communist movement in the late 1920s. A skilful tactician, a forceful
orator and possessing a solid local power base in Saint-Denis,
his chances of eventually becoming leader of the party looked good.
But his growing scepticism about the tactics dictated by Moscow
caused him to become a premature partisan of a Popular Front
with the Socialists: differences over tactics during the troubles of
February 1934 brought matters to a head and Doriot was excluded
from the party on 27 June 1934.

From 1934 to 1936, although professing very anti-Communist
views, he preserved the appearance of a Left-wing dissident without
a clearly defined programme or doctrine. Just after the victory of the
Popular Front in the 1936 elections, he took his decisive step in the
direction of Fascism at the celebrated *Rendez-vous de Saint-Denis*
of 28 June at which he founded the *Parti Populaire Français*. By
bringing together nationalism and socialism, he hoped to gather
around him the *forces disponibles* – all those who were disillusioned
by the established parties, whether of the Left or Right.[3] Most of

---

[1] P. Drieu La Rochelle, *Doriot ou la vie d'un ouvrier français*, 1936.
[2] P. Semart, *La Guerre du Rif*, 1926. M. I. Sicard, *Doriot et la guerre du Rif*,
1943.
[3] A significant number of young politicians and intellectuals with various

those who came to the *Rendez-vous de Saint-Denis* were fascinated by the Italian and the German experience and saw in Doriot a great popular tribune who could similarly mobilise mass enthusiasms in a national and anti-Communist cause. Some like Drieu La Rochelle openly proclaimed a Fascist ideology, whilst others such as Jouvenel, Fabre-Luce, Suarez and Marion were more circumspect.[1] Leroy-Ladurie, through an intermediary, and Pierre Pucheu brought the support of large industrial and financial groups alarmed by the Communist threat implicit in the electoral victory of the Popular Front. Militants in various Right-wing organisations – including nearly all the leading members of La Rocque's *Volontaires Nationaux* – joined Doriot in the hope of more active and determined leadership. Both the militants and the leadership of the *Parti Populaire Français* contained a preponderance of men who had previous political experience in either the Communist Party or the Rightist leagues. The respectable bourgeoisie would be attracted to such a party only if there seemed imminent danger of a Communist revolution and the workers' takeover of the factories in 1936 provided a temporary spur to recruitment in that milieu. But traditionally Right-wing areas like Brittany were impervious to the party's influence and the main areas of recruitment were the large cities. The size of the party is hard to estimate precisely.

The party itself consistently claimed 250,000–300,000 whilst hostile estimates put the figure as low as 15,000. The most reliable estimates give figures for the most prosperous period as 10,000–15,000 militants, 50,000–60,000 active members and perhaps 300,000 'within the sphere of influence' of the party.[2] The acquisition of this kind of following within eighteen months of the foundation of the party was a considerable achievement. But the expansion of the movement was limited by the presence of other organisations, notably La Rocque's *Parti Social Français*, which immobilised many thousands of men who might otherwise have joined Doriot. Doriot was aware of this and encouraged the attempt to form an alliance of

backgrounds – Radical, Socialist, Communist and *Action Française* – were, in the middle 1930s, seeking a radical new regrouping and making various contacts with one another. See P. Andreu 'Le Complot des Acacias', *la Science historique*, February–August 1955, pp. 97–9. On the *rendez-vous* itself see especially D. Wolf, op. cit., pp. 155–76. On the programme which emerged from it, J. Doriot, *La France avec nous*, 1937. P. Marion, *Programme du Parti Populaire Français*, 1938.

[1] Until the defeat of France the PPF refused to accept the description of Fascist. G. M. Thomas, *The Political Career and Ideas of Paul Marion*, unpublished thesis, 1959, p. 237.

[2] D. Wolf, op. cit., pp. 216–21.

the 'national' parties, the *Front de la Liberté* in 1937. Also the obvious slowing down in 1937 of Doriot's drive for power inhibited recruitment and weakened loyalties. There were important defections such as that of Pucheu in 1938, whose departure had a disastrous effect on the party's finances. The intellectuals, at first regarded as a great asset for the party, were not taken into the leader's confidence and the majority of them deserted Doriot within two years of the foundation of the party. This was partly because Doriot ran the party as a despot. He introduced the principle of democratic centralism, censored articles written in the party controlled press, and administered the party with a kitchen cabinet, ignoring the national council and other formal institutions established by the party constitution. This was the style of Fascist dictators and might not have had ill-effect if Doriot had provided authoritative leadership. However, he seemed to become more erratic, perhaps as a result of the change in his personal fortunes.

The Blum government removed him from his post as mayor of Saint-Denis after the so-called 'massacre of Clichy', whereupon he resigned his parliamentary seat. He was well beaten in the ensuing by-election (10,565 to 6,504 votes) by the Communist candidate. Without the administrative responsibilities of the mayoralty of a large industrial town, enjoying the support of the majority of its citizens, Doriot came to appear as a rootless political adventurer without any solid political base. He acquired a taste for food and drink and became very fat. Leaving doctrine to the intellectuals of the party, who were eclectic in the extreme, he never evolved a coherent set of principles for the activity of the party. His policy line wavered, particularly in the field of foreign affairs (*ni Berlin ni Moscou* in 1937, pro-Munich in 1938, anti-German nationalism in 1939, Collaborationist at the defeat). Even though this wavering caused trouble within the party he did not regard consistency in policy matters as important. As a result of his experience in the Communist Party, he became convinced that the majority of people were gullible and easily led. He regarded politics as the plotting and manoeuvres of teams or conspiracies of men, of which the Communist Party was the most dangerous. The main object was to acquire power and keep it: the substance of policy was secondary. He had no strategic vision and this led him in 1940 to accept the German victory as definitive and, when the Germans invaded Russia, to throw in his lot with the Nazis. He engaged in the paranoid and obscure world of the Paris Collaborators, attempting in 1942 to seize power. He helped to establish and subsequently joined the *Légion Française contre le Bolchévisme* and fought on the eastern

Front. Finally, he became a member of the puppet French government in exile in Germany and was killed by a strafing allied aircraft in 1945. Many of his followers suffered execution, exile, imprisonment and disgrace during the purge of the Liberation period. Some re-emerged: those who had broken with him in the 1930s such as Maurice Duverger and Bertrand de Jouvenel were not compromised to any appreciable degree; Leroy-Ladurie became an important figure in the CNIP; Pierre Poujade was to lead the most extraordinary protest movement of the Fourth Republic. Those who had followed him into the adventure of Collaboration, if they reappeared at all, had to wait for the revival of the activist extreme Right of the 1950s. But Doriot had no real heirs; he was a plebeian demagogue of great vitality whose career illustrated the disorder of the political system between the wars.

The Parti Agraire *and the* Front Paysan
Extremist demogogy was not, however, the preserve of the urban, largely Paris-based leagues. Fleurant Agricola and Henri Dorgères established fluctuating, but sometimes large and impassioned, followings in the countryside. Both were influenced by a general climate of ideas – Fascism and populism in other European countries and the *ligueur* politics of the French urban milieu – but their activities and successes are more readily explicable in terms of a revolt against the existing agrarian organisations and against the parliamentary representation of agriculture. They were representative of a particular and transitory stage in the development of peasant politics in France. They led a grass-roots revolt against the notables who ran the agricultural associations, unions and co-operatives and against the paternalistic attitudes of most of the Deputies who represented agricultural constituencies. In the virtual absence of a genuine peasant elite, despite the attempts of certain Catholics to educate one, sections of the peasantry turned to brokers of protest, just as in the past they had elected professional men to parliament as brokers of political influence. The new demagogues, although not peasants themselves, voiced in aggressive terms the bitterness and frustrations of the peasantry faced by sharply declining prices for agricultural produce. Their message was simple and direct, aimed at impressing a relatively unsophisticated audience. 'Wheat, milk, wine and cattle have no political opinions and there is no radical, socialist, monarchist or clerical way of cultivating the land', asserted Fleurant Agricola as a justification for establishing the first party exclusively devoted to the defence of peasant interests.[1]

[1] *La Voix de la terre*, 1 March 1929. On the *Parti Agraire* see Pierre Barral,

Fleurant was an ex-*lycée* teacher and an organiser of agricultural co-operatives who, with two lawyers, Noilhan and Casanova, as his most important assistants, founded the *Parti Agraire* in 1928 on a banal programme of defence of property and the interests of those who worked on the land. This programme and, more important, Fleurant's style of presenting it, attracted support in the poorer agricultural areas, particularly in the Massif Central. The electoral successes of the party were limited to one seat in 1932 and eight in 1936, with several other sympathisers in parliament, but the impact of the party was greater than the impression given by this record. Like the *Jeunesses Patriotes*, it combined electoral politics with direct action, becoming better known for the latter. Disorders were frequently associated with the meetings of the party and these sometimes took a fairly serious form as, for instance, when the party's supporters broke into the Prefect's office in Chartres in 1932. The party occasionally descended on the capital for meetings and demonstrations: these gained much publicity, especially after the meeting which attracted 10,000 to the Salle Wagram in 1933, when the party supporters showed that they were much more capable than were urban demonstrators of dealing with police horses. The party was not, however, an efficient political instrument because of internal discords. These turned on control of finances, personality clashes and ideological differences. The sources of money were very obscure but it is probable that a considerable proportion came from the Radical Deputy Louis Louis-Dreyfus, a rich banker and wheat merchant.[1] For this reason, the original anti-capitalist, anti-monopolist themes of the party propaganda were played down. No serious allegations of corruption were made against Fleurant but some of his associates such as Casanova were suspected of over-enthusiastic business methods. Fleurant was, on the other hand, an ineffective leader, obscuring with rhetoric the genuine dilemmas of his movement. The party split early in 1936 after bitter disputes within it: the split was consecrated by differences in attitude towards the Popular Front's proposals for organising the wheat market by establishing the *Office du Blé*. Noilhan set up the *Parti Républicain Agraire et Social* which was slightly more to the left than Fleurant's party, accepting some forms of State intervention: the only candidate

Les Agrariens français de Méline à Pisani, 1968, pp. 237–40, *passim*. G. Wright, *The Rural Revolution in France* 1964, pp. 49–55. G. Le Normand, *Le Parti Agraire*, 1932. H. Noilhan, *La République des paysans*, 1932. M. Braibant, *D'Abord la terre*, 1935. Confédération Générale des Paysans Travailleurs, *Que veut le Parti Agraire?*, 1935.

[1] P. Barral, op. cit., p. 238.

of Noilhan's party elected in 1936 was invalidated. Fleurant himself died shortly afterwards and was posthumously honoured by the post Second World War *Parti Paysan* as the great forerunner.

Dorgères was a more forceful and significant leader than Fleurant, with whom he had somewhat uncertain relations.[1] He is alleged to have been a member of the *Parti Agraire* until 1930 but after that date was alternately a rival and an ally. As a demagogue and agitator his talents outstripped those of Fleurant's and rivalled those of Doriot, with whom he shared a humble background although not an apprenticeship in extreme Left-wing politics. Son of a butcher in the Nord, born in 1897, he worked as a journalist first on the *Echo des syndicats agricoles du Nord* and then on the *Nouvelliste de Bretagne* before coming to prominence as the editor of the *Progrès agricole de l'Ouest*, an obscure Right-wing local paper published in Rennes which he turned into a successful regional daily in the middle of the 1920s. His first major campaign was typical of the anti-State, populist style in which he specialised. In 1928 he set up *Comités de Défense Paysanne* to protect the peasantry against new proposals for social insurance which were being debated in parliament and which involved an increased burden of taxation on the peasantry. After a major public meeting held at Vannes in December 1928, the committees multiplied rapidly particularly in Normandy and Brittany but also in other regions to the north of the Loire such as the Paris basin, Lorraine and Nord. Excepting a lively development in Vaucluse, the Dorgèriste movement did not have much success in the south of the country and therefore did not overlap to any appreciable extent with the *Parti Agraire*.

When the law on social insurance was voted on 22 April 1930, Dorgères organised a highly successful boycott of it, describing it as a 'machine for centralising and drawing off capital which should fructify in our farms and in our villages instead of being used up in goodness knows what luxury enterprise where its power of reproduction will be lost'.[2] Dorgères earned his first short prison sentence for his part in a demonstration aimed at preventing the confiscation of the goods of a peasant who refused to pay compulsory insurance contributions. Using this campaign as a springboard to broaden his activities, he was instrumental in forming the *Front Paysan* in 1934 with a programme of improving prices for agricultural produce, protection of the French market and a 'reform of the State on the

---

[1] H. Dorgères, *Haut les fourches!*, 1935. *Au XXème siecle, dix ans de jacquerie*, 1959. L. Gabriel-Robinet, *Dorgères et le Front paysan*, 1937. J. M. Royer in J. Fauvet, H. Mendras, *Les Paysans et la politique*, 1958, pp. 153–81.

[2] *Le Progrès agricole*, 19 March 1933.

basis of the family as the profession'. The participants in this alliance, as well as the *Comités de Défense Paysanne*, were the *Parti Agraire*, the *Union Nationale des Syndicats Agricoles*, which were associated with the conservative *Société des Agriculteurs de France* and led by Leroy-Ladurie, and certain specialised producer groups such as the *Association des Producteurs de Lin*, the *Confédération des Producteurs de Fruits à Cidre* and the *Association Générale des Producteurs de Blé*.

The *Front Paysan* was never welded into an effective unity but it made Dorgères a celebrity. In the course of 1935 he attracted a great amount of publicity by a striking by-election campaign in Blois, an eight month prison sentence for inciting a tax strike, the publication of a book *Haut les fourches!* and the formation of the Greenshirts (the *Jeunesses Paysannes*) whose mission was 'expeditions of reprisal against those who have dared to trouble peasant meetings'. The Left accused him of Fascism and of collusion with Doriot and La Rocque when he organised the market gardeners' strike of 1936. On this occasion *l'Humanité* and *le Populaire* alleged that he was trying to sabotage the Popular Front, starve the capital into submission and create conditions for the coming to power of the leagues. However, although Dorgères tried on all occasions to be as intimidating as possible, he seemed to lack a political strategy. His political ideas were of a rudimentary kind: 'The State is rotten; incompetent civil servants and corrupt parliamentarians sacrifice the interests of agriculture to industry and Jewish finance. Faced with this shameful system, the peasantry is the only healthy force in the country, the only element of the nation remaining in contact with the realities of French life.'[1] He envisaged the abdication of the leaders of the existing system followed by a peasant revolution. It is doubtful whether Dorgères regarded these ideas as anything more than useful myths which would give his young peasant followers more self-confidence and help to efface the paralysing inferiority complex which they had inherited.

Dorgères' ideal came near to realisation in the Vichy regime. The Republican regime abdicated and was replaced by a man proud of being the son and brother of peasants. The *Révolution nationale* both enhanced the status of the peasantry and apparently excluded its enemies from power. Dorgères gave enthusiastic support to Pétain, helped to prepare the law establishing the peasant corporation, became a National Delegate for Propaganda and a National Councillor, and converted his newspaper *le Cri du Sol* into a semi-official organ for the agricultural section of the community. This identification with Vichy caused difficulties at the Liberation but he re-

[1] *Haut les fourches!*, 1935.

embarked on a public career which eventually brought him into both conflict and co-operation with Pierre Poujade.

In the 1930s and indeed throughout his political career Dorgères was a publicist and agitator rather than either a coherent theorist or a political organiser pursuing a single-minded quest for power. Like the leader of the *syndicats jaunes*, Pierre Biètry,[1] for an earlier and Pierre Poujade for a later period, he was taken up by the press as a bizarre, newsworthy figure. As a journalist who ran a series of successful publications which occupied an important place in agricultural journalism, he knew how to exploit this celebrity. Using extreme statements and a certain amount of violence to gain attention, he was most effective in mounting short campaigns on specific grievances. A buccaneering, resilient character, he found it very difficult to work harmoniously with others and preserve stable alliances, as his relations with Fleurant in the 1930s and Poujade in the 1950s illustrate. His campaigns were revealing of a social climate. In part they were manifestations of a traditional *jacquerie* and in part an expression of a new uncertainty about the place of the peasantry in French society.

The Cagoule

The careers of Dorgères and Doriot were, in different ways, symptoms of deep social tensions. An even more sinister symptom of underlying disorder was the conspiracy of the *Cagoule* or hooded men.[2] The name was an attempted joke by Maurice Pujo in *Action française*, in order to make Left-wing suspicions of a 'Fascist' plot appear ridiculous. However, the first clear and public indication that a genuine conspiracy was afoot came from the columns of *Action française* which, on 29 July warned its readers against the recruiting activities of clandestine organisations. La Rocque followed, publishing a statement in November 1936:

'We have received incontrovertible information from different sources concerning the establishment in Paris and the provinces of organisations calling themselves defence groups or some such

[1] G. Mosse, 'The French Right and the Working Classes: les Jaunes', *The Journal of Contemporary History*, vol. 7, 1972, pp. 185–208.

[2] The main works on the Cagoule are P. Bourdrel, *La Cagoule: 30 ans de complots*, 1970. H. Charbonneau, *Les Mémoires de Porthos*, 1967. J. Debû-Bridel, *L'Agonie de la Troisième République*, 1948. J. Désert, *Toute la verité sur l'affaire de la Cagoule*, 1940. P. M. de La Gorce, *The French Army*, 1963. Commandant G. Loustaunau-Lacau, *Mémoires d'un français rebelle*, 1948. A. Mahé, 'La Cagoule', *Le Crapouillot*, No. 20, 1963. S. Arbellot, 'La Cagoule', *le Document*, February 1938.

similar name. We urgently warn our friends against the provocative activities frequently hidden behind these initiatives.'[1]

La Rocque issued an even stronger warning in January 1937.[2] The police had only to read the columns of the Right-wing press to get the impression that something odd was happening, but they moved with caution. However, outrages such as the blowing up of the offices of the employers' association in the rue de Madrid and the assassination of the Italian anti-Fascists, the Rosselli brothers, were clearly the work of political terrorists and could not be overlooked. The first arrests were made in December 1937 and January 1938. The police uncovered evidence of a tolerably serious conspiracy – seven substantial arms caches in central Paris, a field hospital and a dungeon in the suburbs, and a large number of documents relating to the *Cagoule* in an office in the rue de Provence.

Most of the Left was predictably delighted that a group of reactionaries had behaved in a fashion which coincided with the Left-wing caricatures of them. The Right was divided: *Action Française* suspected a diversionary tactic by the police and the Popular Front government whilst the *Parti Social Français*, perhaps better informed, was anxious to dissociate itself completely from the affair. The *Fédération Républicaine*, less suspect of complicity, protested strongly 'against the flagrant attack on personal liberty constituted by these arrests, some of which seem motivated entirely by political considerations'. The Federation emphasised that the accused, 'who have unblemished records, have been treated with less consideration than common law criminals or recidivists'.[3] A committee of support for the 'imprisoned patriots' was formed which attempted to mobilise Right-wing support for the accused.

The investigations proceeded slowly, the police making themselves slightly ridiculous by searching the most unlikely places for arms. However, the death of four soldiers at Villejuif on 27 January 1938 during the clearing of an arms cache illustrated the seriousness of the search. But the *juge d'instruction* took almost two years over his task, finally presenting a bulky dossier to the public prosecutor on 6 July 1939. Most of the principals in the case were mobilised before or on the outbreak of war and the trial did not open until 11 October 1948. Forty-nine were in the dock but sixteen accused had died, including some of the most important figures such as Duseigneur, Deloncle and Moreau de La Meuse, and another thirteen

---

[1] *Le Flambeau*, 14 November 1936.
[2] ibid. 23 January 1937.
[3] Quoted P. Bourdrel, op. cit., p. 212.

were in exile, including probably the only man who had a comprehensive picture of the ramifications of the *Cagoule*, Dr Félix Martin, the head of Intelligence for the conspiracy. The evidence presented during the thirty-nine sessions of the court was not particularly enlightening: it confirmed what many of the more sober newspaper accounts had made common knowledge ten years previously. The accused were determined to reveal as little as possible and also, by constant reference to contacts with the army, to make any condemnation of the *Cagoule* also appear as a condemnation of the army. The extent and importance of clandestine networks within the army cannot be established with any great accuracy but there is no doubt that the *Cagoule* caused considerable alarm to the government. Léon Blum said at the trial, without any trace of rancour:

> 'The *Cagoule* was a real danger. After we had dissolved the leagues, secret societies carried on their work continuing the attempts at subversion of 6 February 1934. . . . If intervention in Spain had brought us to the brink of war, we would have seen in France a movement analogous to the one which Franco led against a legally constituted government, and having support in the same quarters.'

The seizure of power was perhaps technically possible, but politically it was quite out of the question. Neither the general political situation nor the character of the conspirators gave grounds for believing that the *Cagoule* could conquer and retain power.

There were three main groups described under the general heading of the *Cagoule*: the *Comité Secret d'Action Révolutionnaire* (CSAR) led by Eugène Deloncle, the *Union des Comités d'Action Défensive* (UCAD) created by General Duseigneur and Duke Pozzo di Borgo, and the anti-Communist networks in the army which, under the code name *Corvignolles*, were co-ordinated by an aide and literary collaborator of Marshal Pétain, Commandant Loustanau-Lacau. Deloncle was the most determined conspirator, a very able man but excessively paranoid. A graduate of the Polytechnique, briefly a naval officer (his father had been a sea captain), he was a much decorated artillery officer during the First World War. After the war he embarked on a successful business career, becoming a director of shipping, petroleum and engineering firms. This success was reflected in a spacious style of life with a flat in the 16th *arrondissement* of Paris and a villa at Le Touquet, which contrasted oddly with the extremism of his politics. He was an *Action Française* militant but became disillusioned by the inactivity of the leaders of the league. An admirer of Leninist and Masonic techniques of organisation, he determined to fight his opponents with what he considered to be their own method, a clandestine organisation of highly disciplined and fanatical activists who would seize power by violence. The *Cagoule* was, according to Deloncle, a *franc-maçonnerie retournée au bénéfice de la nation*[1] with a whole paraphernalia of ceremonies, rituals and signs of recognition. The codes, passwords, couriers, disguises and alibis gave a farcical air to the enterprise. The central figures of the conspiracy were, however, well educated men who had made careers in business, medicine, law and journalism.

The CSAR had a structure based on the organisation of the French general staff, and its plan of operation was carefully thought out. An elaborate attack, making maximum use of the Paris sewers and underground passages in the city, was planned to seize the strategic point of government. Deloncle and his associates drew up a black list of ministers and Left-wing politicians who were to be incarcerated. The arms discovered in the Paris region (20 machine guns, 250 sub-machine guns, large quantities of revolvers and explosives, which were allegedly supplemented by arms caches hidden in the provinces and in neighbouring countries) and the estimate made at the 1948 trial of the number of men involved (put at 5,000 ready for action and another 7,000 in reserve in Paris), probably gave Deloncle the logistic capacity to attempt a coup. The political support which the CSAR could muster was, however, very limited, even among the circles of the extreme Right. Clandestine organisations are by their nature restricted in their proselytising activities. UCAD was a slightly more public organisation than the CSAR. General Duseigneur toured the country in the year following the 1936 elections trying to establish local 'defence' committees to resist Communist revolution. This activity quickly became known and does not appear to have been successful. When the *Cagoulard* leaders were arrested in the autumn of 1937 very few provincial networks were uncovered, presumably because they were few, very informal and autonomous.

An even more serious weakness was the lack of real co-operation between the civilian conspirators and the army. Both the opponents and the participants in the *Cagoule* had an *ex post facto* interest in exaggerating the co-operation between UCAD, the CSAR and army officers. Joseph Darnand, the leader of the Vichy *milice*, asserted during his trial in 1945 that the network he directed in Nice, the *Chevaliers de la glaive*, was an extension of military intelligence.[2] This is implausible, because the most active of the military conspirators Loustanau-Lacau, although he had plans to have a civilian extension to his networks, denied that they came into existence.

[1] Interview in *le Gerbe*, 25 September 1941.
[3] J. Delperrie de Bayac, *Histoire de la Milice*, 1969, pp. 23–30.

According to Loustaunau-Lacau, he was able to recruit 10,000 military participants in the *Corvignolles* without difficulty. He insisted that the sole function of the networks was the reporting of Communist activity within the army.[1] He certainly met Duseigneur in 1936 and Marshal Franchet d'Esperey introduced him to Deloncle in 1937. He refused to co-operate with either, except in the very restricted way of exchanging information through intermediaries about Communists. His view was that Deloncle was trying to promote civil war and for that reason he advised officers in touch with the CSAR to keep their distance. This attitude was also based on prudence: Loustaunau-Lacau probably thought that Deloncle had little chance of success and that his conspiracy would be quickly broken.

Some military leaders were undoubtedly out of sympathy with the civilian politicians in the middle and late 1930s. Some, such as Franchet d'Esperey, were more or less openly disaffected. Loustaunau-Lacau testified after the war that three members of the *Conseil Supérieur de la Guerre* (whom he refused to name) were aware of his activities and it is quite possible that Pétain was one of them. The favour which many *Cagoulards* enjoyed at Vichy raised suspicions, resurrected at his trial, that Pétain was one of the leaders of the *Cagoule*. This favour was probably no more than that extended to Right-wing men who were not identified with the Third Republic. In the hallucinatory atmosphere of the plotting of the late thirties, it was impossible to identify who was involved in what, and the mysteries still persist. There was a moral rupture between the Army and the Republic in the 1930s and by 1940, the shift of the French military from a role as an apparently passive instrument of the political power to a position of great importance in national affairs was well under way.[2] But it is highly improbable that more than a handful of disaffected officers were actively contemplating a putsch. Civil military relations in the 1930s had become such a tangled web that the great majority of senior officers were probably genuinely baffled by the situation. There is plenty of evidence of seditious talk but little of organised conspiracy. No professional soldier was in the dock in the 1948 trial of the *Cagoulards*.

The strong group loyalty of the *Cagoulards* survived despite the different paths taken by *Cagoulards* during the war. They were found among the ranks of the Collaborators, the *milice*, the entourage of Pétain, as well as the Resistance. Maurice Duclos, an arms runner

[1] See his statements at the trial of the *Cagoulards* in 1948, especially the sittings of 24 January and 6 February.

[2] P. M. de La Gorce, *The French Army*, 1963, pp. 216–82.

for the *Cagoule*, served in the Free French Intelligence during the war. He emigrated to South America after the war but reading of the *Cagoule* trial in the newspapers he returned to take his place alongside his comrades in the dock. He was one of the eleven who were given an unconditional acquittal for distinguished war service. Despite the various options chosen, the accused were anxious not to incriminate each other. They insisted that the *Cagoule* was essentially a defensive organisation which would not have been mobilised unless a Communist rising had occurred; it is possible that many of them believed this to be the case at the time and others had subsequently convinced themselves of it.

By 1948 the *Cagoule* had ceased to be a serious political matter. The sentences were light except for the assassins of the Rosselli brothers, who had been murdered allegedly in return for arms supplies from Italy. Only one of the conspirators remained active, Dr Félix Martin, the director of the *deuxième bureau* of the *Cagoule*. Clandestine action had become a way of life for him: after rallying to Vichy he had been imprisoned for plotting against the regime; he became involved with veterans' organisations and the Algerian lobby in the Fourth and Fifth Republics, being arrested in 1957, after the Barricades affair in 1960 and again after the Generals' putsch in 1961. He was held for several months but in every case released without trial. Compulsive plotters like Martin, Collaborationist activities of men like Jeantet and Deloncle who seemed to live in a fantasy world, and the ignominious collapse of the conspiracy by the arrests of November 1937 all combined to give an air of absurdity to the *Cagoule*. There was certainly an atmosphere of unreality about the affair, difficult to explain except in terms of a collective psychosis: the analysis of the political situation was as wrong-headed as the conspiratorial activities. But the *Cagoule* was a symptom of a situation in which Right-wing men despaired of a weakening regime and feared the disintegration not only of the institutions of the State but also of the very fabric of the nation. Similar symptoms persisted until the period of war, internal revolution and colonial adventure passed. Conspiracy and the attitudes which go with it were temptations which assailed even the professionally successful and socially secure until the end of the Algerian War.

In parliamentary and electoral terms, all the ambitions and activities to change the party system and reform political institutions amounted to very little. The new men and organisations made very little difference to the types of men who were elected and to their activities when they were in parliament. There was a fairly clearly defined inter-war generation of leading Right-wing personalities. Only Louis Marin, Laurent Bonnevay and Raymond Poincaré had significant parliamentary careers behind them in 1919. Tardieu, Laval, Flandin and Mandel all had careers which were more or less delimited by the two wars. Only the conservative Radical Henri Queuille and the Independent Paul Reynaud were major ministerial figures of the parliamentary Right who had important careers after 1945. The leading parliamentary figures took note of the cries coming from those who practised their politics in the streets; they were well aware of the attempts to build new kinds of political movement. They were sometimes alarmed by the implications of these developments but they were, in no real sense, part of them. The kind of electoral and parliamentary activities in which they were engaged did not relate much to extra-parliamentary effervescence. The leagues could be a noisy nuisance in the election campaigns; individuals occasionally suffered from their activities. They were a factor, along with the tensions produced by the domestic and international situation of France, in the creation of an atmosphere which encouraged sectarianism in politics. A simple indicator of fissiparous tendencies present at the parliamentary level was that in January 1920 there were ten groups in the Chamber of Deputies and in May 1939 there were twenty. Six or seven of these groups could be assigned to the Right. One was the outgrowth of an extra-parliamentary league – the *Groupe du Parti Social Français* with a membership of eight. The leagues and the other extra-parliamentary activities of the Right were expressions of the malaise and insecurity felt by most sections of conservative opinion in the inter-war period. The men who committed themselves to the leagues were convinced, if briefly, that they had the answers to the ills of the country. They regarded most of the parliamentary conservatives as indecisive time-servers. But, collectively, the leagues and the other organisations had no unity or fixity of purpose, they were blown hither and thither by events and intimidated by their opponents. Their political foresight was certainly no better than that of the parliamentarians who voted full powers to Pétain in 1940.

CHAPTER V

The 'Party of Independents' and the Parliamentary Right during the Fourth and Fifth Republics

The origins

Immediately after the Liberation there was a second *ralliement* of broad sectors of the Right to the Republic and, subsequently, to the practice of *gouvernement d'assemblée*. It was undemonstrative and unenthusiastic. Jacques Rueff, an economist internationally renowned for his support of a return to the gold standard, told the *journées d'études* of the *Centre National des Indépendants* in 1950: 'We do not underestimate the faults of the parliamentary regime but the lesson of history is before us. We must choose between parliament and the police.'[1] His remark encapsulated a widespread attitude. Some conservatives, particularly those who joined the Gaullist *Rassemblement du Peuple Français*, capitalised on anti-parliamentary feeling in the country by condemning the *régime des partis*. But even those who had been involved in *ligueur* politics in the 1930s could not justifiably be charged with trying to subvert parliamentary institutions as such. Almost without exception the 'moderates' – a term often used to describe conservative Deputies – believed that the constitution of the Fourth Republic ought to be reformed. However, until the Algerian War caused widespread doubts about the ability of the regime to endure, the two most common attitudes found amongst them were either cynical reconciliation with the system or active support of it. Accepting the necessity of parliamentary institutions, the moderates also realised, perhaps more forcibly than ever before, the desirability of some sort of unity amongst themselves for electoral purposes. The disciplined organisations of the 'Marxist' parties (the SFIO and the PCF) and the MRP gave the impression that political influence, and even survival, depended on a greater degree of organisation than the moderates had previously possessed.

[1] 'Journées des Indépendants et Paysans', *Unité paysanne*, November–December 1950.

These were the vague sentiments on which Roger Duchet based his party building enterprise during the first parliament of the Fourth Republic.

Although Duchet's career as Secretary General of the *Centre National des Indépendants et des Paysans* was punctuated by repeated disputes with his colleagues, he aroused few prejudices and hostilities when he began his self-appointed task of constructing a broadly based conservative movement. His previous career was middle of the road: mayor of Beaune since 1932, President of the Radical federation of his native *département*, the Côte-d'Or, in the 1930s and an unsuccessful Popular Front candidate in the elections of 1936, he was neither compromised by association with Vichy nor identified with the militant Resistance during the Second World War. When the Fourth Republic was established he was elected Senator for the Côte-d'Or. Believing somewhat prematurely that the Radical Party was a relic from the past, and that the clerical issue was dead, he considered that moderate Radicals need no longer be divided from Marin's *Fédération Républicaine*. He was therefore convinced that a new initiative in party organisation was required. He did not join the new groups established in the Liberation period such as the *Parti Paysan* founded in July 1945 under the prestigious but ineffectual chairmanship of Michel Clemenceau. He had not been a member of the moderate pre-war electoral parties *Alliance Démocratique*, *Fédération Républicaine* and *Parti Social Français* (renamed *Réconciliation Française* in 1944) and did not become associated with them when they were revived after the war. Lack of strong public commitment to political principles and the absence of party ties were virtues when he began his attempt to federate the moderates.

In the parliamentary elections of November 1946, the various parties of the Right polled one and a half million votes and won eighty seats.[1] This was a good result in view of the disorganisation of the Right and the cloud of opprobrium which hung over it for the wartime behaviour of some of its prominent members. When the new parliament met, Duchet formed a group of Independent Senators and Deputies and then conducted an opinion survey to discover what impact this move had on the public. Not surprisingly, he found it had very little. The parliamentary Right was at this time divided into approximately the same number as before the war but with different titles – the *Parti Républicain de la Liberté* (the largest,

[1] For a general account of conservative groups during the Fourth Republic see M. Merle, 'Les Modérés' in M. Duverger (ed.), *Partis politiques et classes sociales*, 1955, pp. 241–76. P. M. Williams, *Crisis and Compromise*, 1964, ch. 11 and references there.

with approximately thirty Deputies),[1] *Républicains Indépendants*, *Union Démocratique*, *Action Démocratique et Sociale*, *Républicains Populaires Indépendants*. These groups had little parliamentary influence: some of their members occupied ministerial office during the first parliament of the Fourth Republic but, with the exception of Maurice Petsche, Minister of Finance in six governments between 1949 and 1951, they were all in minor and technical posts. Some of the moderates, notably Garet, Jacquinot, Kir, Lalle, Pinay, Roclore, Rollin and Temple adopted pro-government positions, behaving much like the *radicaux de gestion* of the Third Republic. By contrast, a group of members of the *Parti Républicain de la Liberté* adopted oppositionist and even anti-'system' attitudes: the prominent ones included most of those who rallied to the *Rassemblement du Peuple Français* – Barrachin, Bergasse, Bouvier O'Cottereau, Frédéric-Dupont, July, Sesmaisons and Rousseau – and were elected on the Gaullist ticket in the 1951 election. This was a strategically important and influential group because it helped to give the RPF a very Right-wing tinge, thus limiting its appeal to Radical and Socialist voters. Although many Gaullist defections came before the 1951 election – mainly Radicals, but also René Pleven and conservatives like Pierre Montel – the Barrachin-Bergasse group was the first to desert after the 1951 election on the occasion of Pinay's investiture in 1952. Between the *ministrables* and the 'Gaullists' gravitated a number of smaller groups which were even less consistent in their attitudes. The moderates were easily the most inchoate segment of the National Assembly in terms of voting behaviour in the first parliament, although they were rivalled by the Gaullists in the second (1951–5) after General de Gaulle had withdrawn from politics, and surpassed by the Radicals in the third parliament (1956–8). The pressures to unify the parliamentary Right in one group were not strong. It was generally thought that the divisions were regrettable but inevitable.[2] On the other hand, most moderates recognised the desirability of some kind of flexible extra-parliamentary organisation to prepare for elections.

Duchet approached the problem of party building in an essentially traditional way, but he made use of a modern technique – the opinion survey. He sent a questionnaire to all the mayors of

[1] J. Laniel, 'Le Parti Républicain de la Liberté', *Revue de Paris*, May 1946. Laniel claimed over-enthusiastically that the PRL was 'a strongly equipped party with a modern organisation, supported by militants of quality'.

[2] There were occasionally optimistic assertions that the Right had learned the lessons of the past and was rejecting indiscipline and individualism. See, for example, E. Borne, 'Du côté de la droite classique', *La Vie intellectuelle*, June 1955.

France, asking general questions about private enterprise and traditional liberties. About 7,500 mayors replied expressing 'liberal' conservative views; Duchet proceeded to make personal contact with them by a grand tour of the country, urging them to set up 'centres' of Independents in each *département* and to stand for elective office. Duchet was frequently criticised by men ranging from Gaullists to the extreme Left for basing himself on the local notables. His defence was that conservatives as well as their opponents genuinely feared that a Right-wing party with a mass membership would have Fascist tendencies: only de Gaulle could overcome this fear and even he was accused of sponsoring a neo-Fascist movement when the RPF commenced recruiting large numbers of members. Local notables approached by Duchet were appreciative of his efforts: in some cases, it relieved them of a 'political isolation which had become intolerable' or it gave them 'the indispensable support of a national organisation in the local electoral struggle'.[1]

The statutes of the *Centre National des Indépendants*, dated 6 January 1949 and signed by René Coty (elected President of the Republic in 1953), Jean Boivin-Champeaux and Roger Duchet made it clear that the gentlest of discipline was to be imposed by the national organisation of the party on the almost completely autonomous centres in the *départements*. At the national level, the party was intended to be little more than an electoral clearing house, arbitrating disputes about candidatures, giving support to sympathetic candidates of other parties, providing propaganda materials and other useful services. The origins of the CNI, the bringing together of a number of heterogeneous groups, were very similar to those of the *Fédération Républicaine* in 1903. Both organisations had the objective of preventing conservative candidates in elections damaging each others' interests. Duchet wanted to group all 'liberal' conservatives – all those between the Radical Party and the Maurrassian or neo-Fascist Right who were not sufficiently tempted by Gaullism to join the RPF. He always had in mind the possibility of attracting Gaullists if the RPF failed. Duchet tried to avoid the Right-wing label: 'For the old distinction between "men of the Right" and "men of the Left", we prefer to substitute men of the future and men of the past.'[2] Political opponents were well used to this kind of language: it was a commonplace of moderate Republican discourse since the days of Jules Méline. The Left emphasised and sometimes exaggerated the Right-wing careers and attitudes of Duchet's associates.

[1] These phrases were used by Duchet and frequently repeated by local notables, in interviews with the author.
[2] *La France indépendante*, 20 May 1950.

Daniel Mayer, for example, turning in the National Assembly to the *Républicains Populaires Indépendants*, one of the groups Duchet was trying to federate, said: 'Your party drinks from the gutters into which have drained Drumont, Maurras and *Gringoire*.'[1]

In the early years of the party, no congresses were held, only 'study days'. The first of these *journées d'études* in November 1949 illustrated the loose structure of the movement. There were no delegates in the normal sense, merely participants who listened to a variety of views and took no decisions. The opening declaration of the first issue of the party newspaper, *France Indépendante* on 22 April 1950 made a virtue of indiscipline:

'[The Independents] are men who oppose the omnipotence of committees and parties. They do not accept orders and instructions from anyone. They account for their votes only to their electors and to their own consciences.

The Independents have not formed and will not form a party. They do not have and will not recognise a leader. With neither a rigid programme nor an intransigent doctrine, they are, however, agreed on certain great principles and a few major reforms . . . : constitutional revision, single member constituencies, the fight against political and economic *dirigisme* and for strict financial orthodoxy.'

More precise objectives and a well-defined programme would have been divisive at a time when the task of federating the diverse strands of the Right had just begun.

Duchet won two important tactical successes during the preparation for the 1951 general election, absorbing the *Parti Républicain de la Liberté* (PRL) and partially integrating the *Parti Paysan*. During the parliamentary debate on the new electoral system of *apparentements* (permitting alliances between national lists of candidates), Joseph Laniel visited Duchet on behalf of the PRL to say that the party could not, as a consequence of defections to the RPF and lack of organisational drive, form the thirty lists necessary to qualify as a national list.[2] Duchet insisted on the dissolution of the PRL and Laniel was compelled to accept this condition as the price of co-operation. The Peasants, who joined the CNI to form the *Centre National des Indépendants et des Paysans* in February 1951, retained

[1] *Assemblée Nationale – Débats*, 3 March 1950.
[2] R. Duchet, 'Le Mouvement des Indépendants, son histoire', *La France indépendante*, 12 September 1953. R. Duchet, *Pour le salut public*, 1958, pp. 169 ff. Centre National des Indépendants, *Le Centre National des Indépendants, son histoire*, n.d.

their separate identity and were allocated a fixed number of seats on the central committee of the party. The marriage should have been fairly equable because the Peasants drew their electoral strength mainly from the poorer agricultural *départements* south of the Loire, and particularly from the Massif Central, areas where the Independents had little following. There was not, therefore, an obvious clash of electoral interest but, from the beginning, there was tension between them.

The *Parti Paysan* had been founded in July 1945 by Paul Antier, the first Deputy to join de Gaulle in 1940, a member of the Constituent Assemblies in 1945 and subsequently a Deputy for Haute-Loire. He was supported by men such as Camille Laurens, who had been prominent in the Peasant Corporation of Vichy, and influential members of pre-war peasant organisations such as Jacques Leroy-Ladurie. There were three main motives behind the establishment of the party: it was an act of piety by the surviving members of the *Parti Agraire* and its leader Fleurant Agricola: an attempt to create a political wing for the agricultural lobby and thus a political complement to the *Confédération Générale de l'Agriculture*; and a reacrion of defence provoked by the manifest hostility towards the peasantry in some urban milieux. In the party manifesto, published in July 1945, and in the party newspaper *l'Unité paysanne*, whose first number appeared in October 1945, these motives were made quite explicit. They were placed in a context of a programme of defence of the family farm, government support of agricultural markets and a 'peasantist' ideology which gave the peasants a fundamental place in the life of the nation. The party expressed defensive attitudes and the feeling that the peasantry was misunderstood by the rest of the French people. There was a long history, Antier explained, of social prejudice against peasants and lack of informed interests in agricultural problems, which had been exacerbated by suspicions that the peasants had lived a comfortable existence during the war. The spokesmen of the *Parti Paysan* alleged that the peasants were less well organised to defend themselves than other social groups; the Communist Party, in association with the *Confédération Générale du Travail*, was regarded as a model of militant, disciplined and effective defence of a class interest:

'The peasantry, like the working class, is a giant because it is quite as numerous – but it is a mutilated giant. It has only one arm, the professional association: the political arm is missing. . . . The history of the peasantry over the last hundred years, composed of misery, humiliation and defeat, is explained by this. Lacking an arm the peasantry was defeated in the past and it will continue to be defeated in the future if this condition is not put right.'[1]

Articles frequently appeared in *l'Unité paysanne* urging a closer association of syndicalist and political action, and deploring the indiscipline of peasant organisations. But despite the inferiority complex and the dissensions, the electoral fortunes of the party prospered, far exceeding the performance of the *Parti Agraire* in the 1930s. Four Deputies were elected to the first Constituent Assembly (Camille Laurens was invalidated for his association with Vichy after a bitter debate but he was subsequently re-elected); eight to the first National Assembly and another ten joined the Peasant group before the 1951 election: in that election, forty-seven Peasants were elected out of a total ninety-nine successful candidates on CNIP lists, making the Peasant wing of the party relatively the more successful.

There were some strange parliamentary 'Peasants'. André Boutemy, Senator for Seine-Maritime from 1952 to 1959 and the distributor of funds for the *Conseil National du Patronat Français* in the 1951 election, was a member of the *Parti Paysan*. Jacques Isorni, Pétain's lawyer elected Deputy for Paris in 1951, was refused admission by the Independent group and joined the Peasant group of the National Assembly. Despite these oddities, there were important distinctions between the Independents and the Peasants. After the 1951 elections, two-thirds of the Peasant Deputies came from south of the Loire and three-quarters of the Independent Deputies from the north of that river. The core of the *Parti Paysan* was in its original heartland, the *départements* of the Massif Central – Haute-Loire, Lozère, Puy-de-Dôme, Cantal and Ardèche. In this region it had some of the characteristics of a mass populist movement. With perhaps 25,000 militants in 1951, it was quite ready to engage in direct action if there was enough grass-roots hostility to government policy. This contrasted with the style of most Independent notables who, whether urban or rural, were brokers and spokesmen of interests, almost completely lacking support organisations with militant members.

Duchet was, therefore, the manager of an uneasy coalition of men with varying political attitudes defending different and sometimes conflicting interests. The common principles of his coalition in the 1951 election campaign were new and negative. Anti-Communism and *anti-étatisme* were the keynotes of the CNIP manifesto issued in May:

[1] Quoted R. Barillon in J. Fauvet, H. Mendras, *Les Paysans et la politique*, 1958, p. 135.

'Since the Liberation, the Independents and Peasants have been amongst the rare members of parliament who have never compromised with the Communists. They have criticised a constitution and an electoral law which inevitably led to a dictatorship of the parties. They have been amongst those who have obstinately rejected *dirigisme*, bureaucracy and ruinous nationalisation. They condemned the financial experiments which destroyed savings and credit which, in turn, led to ruinous fiscal policies.

They wanted and still desire the revision of the constitution to restore governmental authority and to give the Senate real power. They demanded and continue to demand the restoration of fundamental freedoms, especially those of the press and of education. They requested and continue to request a return to financial orthodoxy and genuine social justice. They wanted and still want a reconciliation of Frenchmen in a strong and rearmed France.

To defend this policy the *Centre National des Indépendants et des Paysans* will sponsor and support lists over the whole country, and group all those who, whilst conserving their liberty of vote, demand a new majority of Public Safety. In face of the Communist peril, they wish to be the first to appeal for the union of all liberals, moderates and national Republicans. The considerable success of Independent and Peasant candidates in the last local and Senate elections qualify them to make this appeal for concord and unity.'[1]

A slightly longer manifesto was published just before the elections in June 1951, but it did not stray beyond these general platitudes. Nothing was included which could possibly alienate any non-Gaullist conservative voter.

The content of the manifesto was not a controversial issue within the CNIP, but there was much argument over the composition of the lists of candidates in the constituencies. The drawing up of lists was sometimes an arduous and always an idiosyncratic business. Some lists were eclectic, including candidates apparently very much out of sympathy with the general political tendency of the Centre; François Mitterrand was, for example, on a list patronised by the CNIP in Nièvre. In arbitrating disputes over the composition of lists for this election, Duchet seemed concerned almost exclusively with maximising the possibility of success. He nevertheless created antagonisms which endured to the end of his career as Secretary General of the party. By his adroit management he also led the CNIP into 'the system'. After denouncing as 'immoral' the electoral law of 1951, Duchet made maximum use of *apparentements* with national

[1] *La France indépendante*, May 1951.

lists of the 'Third Force' parties. These included the Socialists, previously condemned with almost as much venom as the Communists. This compromise paid substantial electoral dividends.

The party entered the elections with neither militants nor professional organisers. It inspired little confidence or loyalty in the electorate, even among those who voted for its candidates. In answer to a question posed in a survey by the French Institute of Public Opinion (IFOP) in 1952: 'Does the party you voted for have your full confidence?' the ranking of the parties was Communist voters 62 per cent 'full confidence', Popular Republicans (MRP) 51 per cent, Socialists 48 per cent, Radicals 37 per cent, CNIP 31 per cent. Other questions asked showed that CNIP voters participated less in public meetings, in sticking up posters and in proselytising than voters of other political persuasions.[1] The vote for CNIP candidates increased only slightly. As a result of better discipline and the efficient use of the new electoral law the number of successful candidates increased by a quarter. It was Duchet's personal triumph.

A party of government?

The result of this electoral success and the manner in which it was achieved were threefold. Firstly, Independents and Peasants were called on to play a major role in government. Secondly there was a bandwagon effect; individuals and groups joined the CNIP. Thirdly, there was a general strengthening of the party organisation.

The 'Third Force' parties had only a bare majority over the Gaullists and the Communists. Consequently the leading figures of the CNIP – Antier, Duchet, Jacquinot and Pinay – were offered and accepted office. The party made its major impact on public opinion through the 'Pinay miracle' in 1952–3, the ten months in office as *Président du Conseil* during which Antoine Pinay apparently halted the inflationary spiral for the first time since the war. Shortly after Pinay relinquished office, Jacques Fauvet, the political editor of *le Monde*, wrote: 'Roger Duchet gave the Independents unity, Antoine Pinay has now given them popularity.' But the participation of the Independents and Peasants in government was not uniformly profitable.

Five months after the election of 1951, the Radical Minister of Finance, René Mayer, clashed with the Minister of Agriculture, Paul Antier, the Peasant leader, over a tax increase and other fiscal measures. Antier's objections to Mayer's programme were perhaps partly based on sympathy for the Gaullist cause, but they were

[1] *Sondages*, 1952, No. 3.

strongly supported by the majority of Peasant Deputies and by the National Federation of Agricultural Unions (FNSEA). However, when Antier resigned he was immediately replaced by his main rival within the *Parti Paysan*, Camille Laurens. Antier, supported by Jean Raffarin, Deputy for Vienne, thereupon established his own parliamentary group, the *Groupe Paysan d'Union Sociale*, with a membership of twenty-one. Antier explained that he stood by the promises given in the election and believed in the necessity of co-operating with other groups to defend the interests of agriculture, but close association with the 'Independent-Peasants' in parliament was impossible.[1] This split, the result of disagreement over tactics and the clash of personalities, was to some extent related to social differences – the Antier Peasants were more truly agrarian than the Laurens Peasants. It weakened the CNIP but surprisingly did not cause a schism.

Antier and his friends pressed for still more autonomy for the *Parti Paysan* within the CNIP in order to undermine the position of Laurens. The factional struggle was not very popular with the militants of the *Parti Paysan* and there were various attempts to paper over the division at the party congresses of 1952, 1953 and 1954. In parliament, the rivalry between the two men sustained different tactics on the part of the two groups of Peasants. The Antier faction was anti-European opposed to the European Defence Community, and Mendèsiste: Raffarin accepted office in the Mendès-France administration. The Laurens faction was pro-European and opposed Mendès with increasing bitterness. After the fall of the Mendès government, the Antierists became involved with the Poujadist movement. A higher proportion of the Laurens faction managed to maintain their distance from Poujade. In the long run, in the Antier-Laurens feud, Antier was the less successful. Only fourteen of his followers were elected in 1956, most of them on CNIP lists, after a pre-election reconciliation. There was little direct clash between the 'Peasant-Peasants' (Antier) and the 'Independent-Peasants' (Laurens) and the 'Independents' (Duchet-Pinay). The battle between Leroy-Ladurie and Laniel in the Calvados was unusual. It was simply the case that Antier had a smaller following than Laurens among the Peasant notables. Although the CNIP tamely approved the brief alliance which Antier made with his rival demagogues, Poujade and Dorgères in 1957, this further reduced his parliamentary following to a low point of four. His parliamentary career came to an end in 1958 when he lost his seat. Camille Laurens

[1] On divisions within the peasants see D. MacRae, *Parliament, Parties, and Society in France, 1946–1958*, 1967, p. 135.

went on to win a Pyrrhic victory taking over the office of secretary general of the CNIP in 1962 when the party was in rapid decline.

The tension within the *Parti Paysan* was tenuously related to the cleavage between the Resistance and Vichy; Antier was identified with the former and Laurens with the latter. The influence of war-time experience was, however, much stronger in the Independent wing of the CNIP. The second Independent *Président du Conseil*, Joseph Laniel, former member of the *Conseil National de la Résistance*, represented the Resistance strand; he favoured neo-Gaullists such as Jacquinot and discriminated against the Vichyite elements in the party, and against Pinay's friends. Although there were eight members of the CNIP executive committee in both the Laniel and the Pinay governments only one member sat in both. The Laniel government was in most respects a failure. The international prestige of France reached a low point with the military disaster of Dien Bien Phu in Indo-China and with an apparent snub to Laniel by Churchill and Eisenhower at the Bermuda conference. His government had also to cope with the most intense bout of industrial unrest since 1947. Divisions within the party were brought into the open when seven Independent Deputies who, at that time, were close to Pinay – Pierre André, Anthonioz, Chamant, Jarrosson, Jacquet, Guichard and Moreau – abstained on Laniel's finance bill. The Laniel section of the Independents did not gain any prestige or subsequent advantages from this period of office. Indeed, the experience probably hardened the anti-government wing of the parliamentary Right and added a further element of division in an already complex situation.

On the major issues of policy during the second parliament – European integration, German rearmament and colonial policy – the Independents and Peasants were split, usually into different groupings. After the Pinay ministry, there was a gradual accretion of a hard core of forty Right-wing Deputies who were to be involved in the defeat of successive governments in the third parliament.[1] The *ministrable* element of the Right was balanced by a roughly equal number of oppositionist, anti-government Deputies. The composition of the opposition tendency was very heterogeneous. It included representatives of some economic interests such as Denais whose connections with big business went back to the Third Republic, Pierre André, spokesman for the steel industry, Marcellin, linked with the *Petites et Moyennes Entreprises*, and Liautey, 'the Deputy for the *bouilleurs de cru*'. Nationalists like the Lyonnais Deputies, Jarrosson and Montel, and the more extreme members of the Gaullist

[1] M. Duverger, 'Les Quarante', *le Monde*, 22 November 1957.

group, the URAS, such as Kauffmann and Wolf, were gravitating towards them. Only a man outside or apparently outside 'the system', such as Pinay, could persuade most of these Deputies to support a government. The outsider called on in 1954 to extricate France from Indo-China, Pierre Mendès-France, was not at all to their liking and their opposition to him became progressively more extreme. Legendre and Barrachin led the attack and their behaviour was described by Léon Noël, a Gaullist Deputy and the first President of the Constitutional Council in the Fifth Republic, as 'snarling virulence'.[1] This attitude was not, however, shared by all the Independents. Mendès-France had a small following amongst them, as he had among all non-Communist groups. These mendèsiste Independents, above all, approved of his decisive style of government.

Pinay and Duchet returned to office in the Faure government of 1955 and thus shared some of the responsibility for Moroccan and Tunisian independence. This cut them off, in Duchet's case only temporarily, from the hard-line nationalists within their own party. Pinay briefly left the CNIP in the Autumn of 1955 because of attacks by extremists on the Faure government's North African policy and threatened not to return whilst they remained in the party. Even Pinay's prestige could not stem the rising nationalist sentiment wounded by military defeat in the Far East and the liquidation of French presence there, by the movement of the North African Protectorates towards independence and by the revolt in Algeria.

Despite the emergence of mortal divisions within the party, the CNIP in some respects prospered during the second parliament. The Gaullists who voted for Pinay, after briefly forming their own party, Action Républicaine Sociale (ARS), joined the CNIP in 1953. This amalgamation caused difficulties, mainly associated with Edmond Barrachin, the chairman of the ARS group in the National Assembly. He had been elected in 1946 on the PRL ticket, rallied to the RPF in 1947 and vigorously attacked his erstwhile colleagues, the non-Gaullist conservatives. In the 1951 election, Barrachin and most of his friends had been elected in competition with CNIP lists. After the fusion in 1953, reconciliation of the electoral interests of some members of both groups was awkward. Barrachin was also a self-important man who liked the prestige of being chairman of his own group. His personal habits caused irritation: despite fairly modest origins, he moved in fashionable circles and was a member of the Jockey Club. This conflicted with the more plebeian style of the provincial Deputies who made up the great majority of the Independents. In 1954, Duchet achieved another, more modest, amalga-

[1] L. Noël, Notre dernière chance, 1956.

mation with the CNIP when he persuaded the majority of the members of the great moderate Republican party of the Third Republic, the *Alliance Démocratique*, to join the CNIP. The Alliance had previously participated in the amorphous and rather unsuccessful electoral formation, the *Rassemblement des Gauches Républicaines*. The *Alliance Démocratique* continued to exist as a minor and unimportant political party, kept in being by Senator Georges Portmann, apparently for sentimental reasons.

The central organisation of the CNIP was strengthened in a variety of ways. Funds, although never very large, became more plentiful and were usually provided by the personal friends and contacts of the Secretary general. No large industrial or financial group gave continuous support. The banker, Christian Wolf, who had previously financed movements of the extreme Right, was reputed to give large sums after the success of the Pinay government. The external signs of improvement in the party's fortunes were obvious from 1951. Duchet obtained new party headquarters in the rue de l'Université, equipped with a separate set of offices for the Independents and the Peasants, a large room for meetings, a documentation service and a bar. Regional propaganda centres were established, the party newspaper published regional editions, and pamphlets were produced, often defending the record of CNIP ministers but also on general policy matters such as constitutional reform. These activities encouraged movement away from the modest purpose of being an electoral clearing house towards the creation of a party with a specific programme and a more disciplined parliamentary group. In 1954, for the first time, a party congress was held, in addition to the *journées d'études*. Although the proceedings of this congress were hampered by the presence of various extremist delegates, including monarchists and Poujadists, an attempt was made to improve parliamentary discipline: a motion was passed to expel members who persisted in joining a government after two-thirds of the parliamentary group had decided against participation. Expulsion was not a very intimidating sanction and the motion mainly reflected resentment at those who had joined the government of Mendès-France. The idea of a detailed party programme was also briefly discussed at the 1954 congress. Raymond Beaujeu subsequently argued the case for it in the columns of *France indépendante:*

The Independents have the urgent task of drawing up a programme which should be both dynamic and concrete; in other words it should represent the aspirations of all Frenchmen. The doctrine of neo-liberalism is a starting point but its relevance to present realities should be made explicit. This is a difficult and important task, requiring both intelligence and common sense.[1]

Two other themes prominent in the CNIP statements in the middle 1950s were identical to those featured in the propaganda of the extreme Right at the same time – the 'defence of Christian civilisation' and an increasingly intransigent nationalism. The first, as well as being an anti-Communist slogan, was also the outcome of the largely unsuccessful attempt to outbid the MRP for the Catholic vote. It was associated with the second theme by way of the charge that support for 'third world' nationalist movements was a cover for Communist subversion.

The difficulties of framing a detailed programme for the CNIP were much the same as those faced by its predecessors, the *Alliance Démocratique* and the *Fédération Républicaine*. United by common antipathies to Communism and to government intervention in the economy, the views and beliefs of its members were neither generally shared nor very specific. The 'defence of Christian civilisation' many times repeated could not hide the religious indifference of Duchet and many of his friends; few people were persuaded that the Independents were more genuinely concerned with the interests of religion than the devout Catholics of the MRP. The nationalism of the CNIP was unconvincing, not only because of the wartime sympathies of some of its members but also because the defence of French North Africa seemed to coincide too closely with material interests. Even economic 'liberalism' lacked conviction because the Peasant wing of the CNIP was constantly calling for government support of agricultural commodity prices. The members of the CNIP believed very strongly in the rights of private property. 'Defence of legitimate interests' was more frequently given by CNIP voters than by others as a reason for party preference. But there was no clear-cut distinction between the CNIP, Radicals and Gaullists on the sanctity of property rights.

Despite the lack of distinctive principles and positive aims, a party programme appeared in 1955 signed by Pinay, Antier (who was temporarily co-operating for the forthcoming election) and Duchet. Although much longer and more detailed, it was very similar to the manifesto issued for the 1951 election. Designed to avoid alienating any section of the party and any potential voters, it gave an equivocal impression. The party went into the election campaign in a rather unhappy condition. The leadership was divided by personal rivalries and by differences over policy. In certain regions electoral support was being undermined by a dangerous and disruptive rival, the

[1] *La France indépendante*, 26 July 1955.

Poujadist movement. There had already been symptoms within the CNIP of the possible emergence of a populist, protesting Right rejecting both the local notables and the Paris political establishment. The turbulent and disruptive behaviour of some Peasant Deputies had much in common with that of the Poujadists and fed on the same frustations. Faced by an energetic and charismatic rival, the Peasants and some of the Independents were compelled to make the unpleasant choice between joining forces with or outbidding Poujade. Poujadism was only a temporary disturbance in the political system but it damaged the electoral cause of the CNIP and weakened the cohesion of the party.[1]

In the 1956 election, the electoral system did not work to the advantage of the CNIP as it had done in 1951. The fading of the Gaullist challenge on the Right was, from the electoral point of view, a mixed blessing. Although it provided an opportunity of gathering votes which had gone to the Gaullists in 1951, the parties of the moderate Left were no longer willing to co-operate with 'reactionaries' in order to save the Republic. Moreover, as a Right-wing protest movement, Poujadism was a more direct threat to the CNIP than the RPF had been. The CNIP found itself in a complex situation owing to the relative absence of potential allies, the difficult integration of the conservative Gaullists, the renaissance of the extreme Right both within and outside the party, and the uncomfortable fact that Antoine Pinay's following in the country was not co-extensive with the party. Despite its recruitment during the second parliament, the CNIP returned only 97 Deputies, two fewer than in 1951. After the election, all the CNIP Deputies came together for the first time in a single parliamentary group, the *Indépendants et Paysans d'Action Sociale* (IPAS). *France Indépendante* claimed that it was the largest and most important 'national' party ever elected. In an attempt to make it even larger, Duchet tried to attract Poujade into a working relationship but abandoned it because of Poujade's naïvety and unreliability.

The breakdown of the Fourth Republic

In the new parliament the Republican Front, led by Mendès-France and Mollet, claimed victory and the IPAS was temporarily excluded from government. In 1956 and 1957 the attitude of the Independents and Peasants to the government headed by the Secretary General of the Socialist Party, Guy Mollet, was mixed and very complex in

[1] For Poujadism, see below pp. 276ff. For the elections of 1956 see M. Duverger, F. Goguel, J. Touchard, *Les Elections du 2 janvier 1956*, 1957. P. M. Williams, *French Politicians and Elections, 1951–1969*, 1970, pp. 46–7, 58–9, 61–2.

detail. The popular estimation that they disapproved of the government's domestic policies but refrained from all-out opposition because they were well disposed to its North African policy, was a fairly accurate general impression. The internal politics of the IPAS were, however, confused and even general support for the government's Algerian policy vacillated.[1] The nationalist wing gained confidence and influence as time passed: the moderates, for the most part, fell silent. All were, to some extent, carried along by the nationalist mood of the country which accompanied the Suez expedition and events such as the kidnapping of the Algerian nationalist leader Ben Bella. When Mollet announced, in February 1956, his famous triptych – 'Cease-fire, elections, negotiations', the majority of the IPAS seemed in hesitant agreement. In the first year of the Mollet government, the majority of the Independents appeared willing to contemplate the possibility of internal political and administrative reforms for Algeria, whilst the presence of the Socialist hard-liner Robert Lacoste, from February 1956, as Governor General of Algeria, seemed a guarantee of maintaining French Algeria.

It is difficult to identify the precise position of the moderate leaders of the IPAS in the period 1956–8. Jacques Isorni accused some of them of double dealing throughout the third parliament because, he alleged, they encouraged rank and file members of the IPAS to vote against the financial and Algerian policy of governments whilst they themselves abstained or voted in favour. There is little evidence for this charge but the moderates seemed to want to escape responsibility. Pinay, Barrachin, Bergasse and Marcellin sent an open letter to Mollet, published on 26 January 1957, complaining that the government's proposal to hold elections in Algeria constituted 'a serious threat to the nation'.[2] The difficulties of financing the war provided the opportunity for the majority of the IPAS to move into opposition. In July 1956, the group had approved the proposal of Ramadier, the Socialist Minister of Finance, to finance the war by a loan but inevitably the government had to raise new tax revenue. When, in May 1957, tax increases were announced, the central committee of the CNIP opposed them. In the same month the government was defeated with the help of IPAS defections. This was the culmination of frustration in the parliamentary Right, not only about the political orientation of the government and its financial

---

[1] The most informative works on the Independants and the Algerian War are I. R. Campbell, *Political Attitudes in France to the Algerian Question*, unpublished thesis, 1972; T. A. Smith 'Algeria and the French Modérés: the Politics of Immoderation?', *Western Political Quarterly*, vol. 18, 1965, pp. 116–34.

[2] *Le Figaro*, 26 January 1957.

policies, but also over the inconclusive nature of the Algerian War.
The government which followed, headed by the Radical, Bourgès-
Maunoury, won the temporary support of the IPAS by maintaining
Lacoste in Algiers and giving office to the ex-Radical André Morice,
who was also a resolute supporter of French Algeria. In September
1957, Bourgès-Maunoury proposed an outline law (*loi cadre*) to
establish new and relatively liberal institutions for Algeria, first at
the level of the *communes* and then in the *départements* and regions.
Duchet supported this proposal even though it was attacked by the
Algerian Deputies. Duchet's position was made very difficult by
Paul Reynaud, who also supported the outline law; Reynaud announced his conversion to the eventual independence of Algeria,
the outcome predicted by the more extreme defenders of French
Algeria if the outline law was implemented. After Duchet came under
attack from the nationalist members of the IPAS such as Montel and
Legendre, the group split: fifty-three members voted against the
outline law and brought the government down. At this point Duchet
irrevocably committed himself to the cause of *Algérie française* and
commenced on a path which wrecked the CNIP and his own political
career.

Duchet had previously been saying that the regime was in a state
of crisis; but during the Bourgès-Maunoury ministry, and the thirty-
six day ministerial crisis which followed its fall, he became convinced both that the tide of opinion was running strongly in favour
of keeping Algeria French and that some kind of government of
'Public Safety', not based on the shifting sands of parliamentary
majorities, was feasible. The impression that the government had
little control over the course of events was fostered by the acceptance
of the Anglo-American good offices mission after the unauthorised,
but unpunished, bombing of the Tunisian village of Sakiet by the
French Army in Algeria. Also the victory of *Algérie française*
candidates in by-elections in Marseilles, Nièvre and Paris in the first
three months of 1958, and the proliferation of anti-parliamentary
activist groups encouraged the belief that the days of the regime
were numbered. Unlike Pinay and Reynaud, who clearly believed by
early 1958 that both parliament and opinion in the country were
moving towards a more, rather than a less, liberal position on Algeria,
Duchet held the view that the future lay with the supporters of
French Algeria. This divergence of views led to an open split between
the leaders of the CNIP and relations between Reynaud and Duchet
broke down completely.

The crisis which followed the fall of the Gaillard government in
April 1958 demonstrated that there was no majority in parliament for

any *Algérie française* leader. Opposition to the regime and, in some cases, to parliamentary institutions, intensified amongst some sections of the IPAS and the activist groups outside parliament. Informal networks of contacts were established between Deputies, administrators, army officers and the activist groups. The French Algeria lobby was joined by dissidents from the MRP, the Radical Party and from Gaullism. As usual, Duchet looked for new allies and potentially the most important from his point of view was the nationalist wing of the MRP.

The roots of this tendency within the MRP went back to the origins of the party: emerging from the Resistance, the emotional patriotism of a section of the movement needed little impetus to be transformed into an instransigent nationalism. Also, its electoral success in the Liberation period was partly the consequence of the weakness of the organisations of the Right and the absence of an official Gaullist Party. The MRP managed to retain some of its conservative clientele acquired at that time. Throughout the 1950s, the traditionally Right-wing voters of the west of France sent about a dozen *droitiers* in the MRP to the National Assembly and elected some very conservative Senators such as Montais de Narbonne and Jaouen from Vendée. Although these men did not prove to be last ditch defenders of French Algeria they were susceptible to nationalist arguments. But the decisive influence on the Rightward drift of a section of the MRP was administrative responsibility for the more politically advanced overseas territories.

Although immediately after the war very few members of the MRP were either interested in or well informed about, colonial questions, experience in office developed a number of commitments. The intransigents were always a minority in the party, outnumbered by a coalition of those like Teitgen, Buron and Pflimlin who developed a more liberal approach based on experience of responsibility for Black Africa, and the trade union, peasant and *mendèsiste* sections of the party who were all mainly interested in other policy areas. Those who shared in responsibility for Madagascar and Indo-China – Paul Coste-Floret, Letourneau, Bidault – and those who had close links with the army – Dupraz, Mercier and Halbout – became leaders of the nationalist tendency as it emerged in the 1950s, but they were not agreed about Algerian policy. The hard line French Algeria tendency became an identifiable faction after the debate on the outline law for Algeria in 1957. In 1958 Bidault established a political movement, *Démocratie Chrétienne*, based on this faction. In the ministerial crisis of 1958, Pierre Pflimlin, the MRP mayor of Strasbourg was rejected by Georges Bidault and the great majority of the IPAS as being too liberal on Algeria. But even at the height of the agitation over Algeria, most of the nationalist wing of the MRP preferred not to be associated with 'reactionaries' and Bidault was alone in voting against Pflimlin's investiture. If Duchet ever harboured a serious intention of persuading a significant minority of the MRP to integrate with the IPAS it was a rather vain hope.

At the very end of the Fourth Republic, the liberals on Algeria in the IPAS, such as Reynaud, Bettencourt, and Mutter were out on a limb. Even Pinay opposed participation in the Pflimlin government. Opposition to the four members of the IPAS who joined the government reached the level of threats when Rogier warned Mutter, Minister for Algerian Affairs, that there would be riots if he set foot in Algeria. But the prospect of civil disorder and intervention by the army in metropolitan France alarmed most of the parliamentary Right. After the *Gouvernement Général* in Algiers was stormed by a mob with the connivance of the army the majority of the IPAS supported Pflimlin when he declared a state of emergency. Pflimlin invited Pinay to join the government but the IPAS demanded too high a price – the reappointment of Lacoste – for Pinay's participation. The majority of the IPAS once again moved into opposition when it became clear that the government was not going to survive.

The establishment of the Fifth Republic
The Right voted almost unanimously for de Gaulle as the last *Président du Conseil* of the Fourth Republic, but except for the Gaullist tendency within the IPAS, represented by Louis Jacquinot, support for his return was late and half-hearted. Jacquinot, a wartime Gaullist, was unconditionally in favour of de Gaulle in 1958 and he remained so for the rest of his career. Paul Reynaud, who had appointed de Gaulle to a junior post in his government in 1940, supported him in 1958 because they shared similar views about constitutional reform, a matter about which Reynaud felt strongly. Reynaud was appointed chairman of the consultative committee on the constitution of the Fifth Republic, but he failed in his attempt to become chairman of the National Assembly. Within eighteen months of the establishment of the new Republic, Reynaud became highly critical of its President. He continued to support de Gaulle over Algeria but opposed him on constitutional and foreign policy issues. Pinay helped de Gaulle back to power as a last resort but was very influential in rallying the pro-government wing of the IPAS to a Gaullist solution during the May crisis. However, it soon became clear that an association between Pinay and de Gaulle could only be temporary. Duchet had never been tempted by Gaullism: he had

created the CNIP in the teeth of Gaullist opposition and profited from the disintegration of the RPF. He rallied late to de Gaulle and his support remained conditional upon de Gaulle's resolve to keep Algeria French. Others were even less well-disposed: Tixier-Vignancour said in the investiture debate that he had been declared ineligible for elective office by voting in favour of a prestigious soldier in 1940 and he was not going to make the same mistake again! The almost unanimous support given by the IPAS in June 1958 to de Gaulle quickly evaporated.

Disillusionment within the CNIP started during the protracted negotiations which preceded the parliamentary elections of November 1958. In the month before the election, de Gaulle vetoed common action between Soustelle (attempting to negotiate on behalf of the UNR), Duchet, Morice and Bidault. Soustelle and Duchet had the biggest battalions in these discussions and the veto was a grave setback to the French Algeria lobby, leaving Duchet alone with two stage armies, the dissident Radicals under Morice and the potentially larger group of the followers of Georges Bidault. Bidault, however, turned out to be a broken reed. After the MRP had officially rejected an alliance with Morice and Duchet, he apparently believed that he could get enough loyal supporters into the National Assembly, by distributing his own *Démocratie Chrétienne* investitures, either to dominate or to divide the MRP group. Only about half a dozen Deputies were elected with *Démocratie Chrétienne* investiture and the MRP *droitiers* became very unreliable allies when both the bishops and their constituents made it clear that they were unsympathetic to *Algérie française* extremism. A few *droitiers* joined the intergroup, *Association Parlementaire pour la Démocratie Chrétienne*, which Bidault founded in May 1959, but they did not follow his lead. By contrast, the CNIP was very successful in the 1958 election, increasing its poll by almost $1\frac{1}{2}$ million to $4\frac{1}{2}$ million votes, and the number of its Deputies to 129. This success was to a large, though incalculable, extent due to the enthusiastic public support which CNIP candidates gave to the new Republic and to de Gaulle personally.

Pinay was appointed Minister of Finance in the first government of the Fifth Republic but the Independents and Peasants showed no inclination to be docile supporters of the government. In January 1959, Pinay announced a programme of devaluation, a balanced budget, reduction in certain subsidies and social security benefits, abolition of some pensions and tax increases. A meeting of the IPAS parliamentary group passed a motion describing the measures as 'excessive, inopportune and ineffective' and Duchet made clear that the party bore no responsibility for them.[1] Only thirty-one IPAS Deputies voted for the 1959 budget, which indicated a fairly sharp decline in Pinay's influence within the party. Duchet was motivated partly by electoral considerations: in the imminent municipal elections the CNIP were in a strong position and he wanted to make capital out of the unpopularity of the Pinay programme. He was also becoming alarmed by de Gaulle's policy in Black Africa and by his reluctance to talk of 'integration' of Algeria into France.

Like many of his colleagues in the CNIP, Duchet was in close touch with the Deputies from Algeria. This influenced his attitudes, because their numbers made them potentially valuable parliamentary associates. The electoral arrangements of 1958 gave a total of seventy-one Deputies to the Algerian *départements* and, when elected, sixty-one combined to form their own 'administrative' parliamentary group; nine joined the UNR and one the Socialists. During the 1959 parliamentary session, the Moslems and a few Europeans, expecting speedier reforms in Algeria, left the group: the extremists, Lagaillarde Vignau and Vinciguerra also departed, leaving about forty-five members headed by Marc Lauriol and Philippe Marçais to form the *Unité de la République* group.[2] His main contacts were with Lauriol who, although firmly opposed to any moves towards Algerian independence, was a relatively moderate man.

When, on 16 September 1959, de Gaulle announced his policy of self-determination for Algeria, there were four main tendencies within the CNIP. Ministers such as Jacquinot, Broglie and Giscard d'Estaing and prominent Deputies such as Reynaud, Mondon and Anthonioz approved the general direction of the government's Algerian policy. A block of Deputies and Senators of approximately the same size as the pro-government tendency were so unsure of the government's intentions, of the morale of the army and of the feeling of the country that they took up no public position. The cautious and pragmatic defenders of the Algerian connection such as the ex-Minister and Deputy for Marseilles, Henri Bergasse, did not withdraw support from the government until 1960 when it became clear that the government was moving towards complete independence for Algeria. The hard core defenders of *Algérie française* – Lacoste-Lareymondie, Legendre, Jarrosson, Le Pen, Vaschetti, Fraissinet and François Valentin, chairman of the Defence Committee of the National Assembly, made up the fourth tendency.

[1] *Le Monde*, 9 January 1959.
[2] R. Brunois, *Le Groupe pour l'Unité de la République et ses séquelles*, unpublished *mémoire*, 1962.

The pro-government and the French Algeria tendencies were the most active and clearly defined. Certain divisions in the 1958–62 parliament tended to isolate both of them as, for example, the October 1959 motion approving the government's policy of self-determination for Algeria, the request for special powers in February 1960 to deal with the Barricades rebellion and the subsequent demand, in April 1960, for amnesty of those involved, and the so-called 'Salan amendment' proposed by Valentin in November 1961 reducing the length of military service, which was interpreted as a gesture of sympathy for the OAS. The hard core *Algérie française* tendency was less numerous, at least in terms of consistent voting behaviour, than the pro-government tendency. But the period 1960 to 1962 was remarkable for the willingness of the extreme Right on matters such as the nuclear strike force, the *force de frappe*, and issues of economic policy, to resort to the *politique du pire*. This was the first time since the first decade of the twentieth century that this tactic was pursued with any degree of consistency.

The most important impression given by the voting record of the IPAS group in the first parliament of the Fifth Republic is lack of unity and common purpose. Duchet tried to dragoon the party into disciplined support of French Algeria. He used the party newspaper to give the impression that the CNIP solidly supported the cause. But he failed in his attempt to manipulate the committees of the party. At the National Council coinciding with the Barricades rebellion in January 1960, Reynaud, Barrachin and others withdrew after Duchet sent a message on behalf of the party to Marc Lauriol, assuring him of full support from the CNIP for the protests of the Europeans of Algeria. Another message was dispatched by Duchet to the President of the Republic requesting a solemn assurance that Algeria would remain French. Duchet thus identified himself with the ultras. He participated in the two *Colloques de Vincennes* in Spring and Autumn 1960 with Soustelle, Morice and Lacoste and began to turn his back on the CNIP. Although not directly involved, he was popularly identified with the *Front National de l'Algérie Française* formed in July 1960 by hard core *Algérie française* Deputies – Le Pen, Lacoste-Lareymondie, Caillemer, Thomazo, Senator Lafay and other prominent extremists – Tixier-Vignancour, Isorni, Dides and Sauge. The general attitude of these men was well-expressed by the short and violent manifesto of the Front:

'It is impossible to rescue Algeria and to save the country without smashing the system and its organisations, cadres and ideologies. Encouraged and directed by the Communist Party and with the complicity of some of those in government, the system prepares to launch the final assault to destroy the army and national independence. . . .'[1]

The central committee of the CNIP rebelled against Duchet in July 1960 by issuing an acid communiqué stating that it could not allow its representatives to belong 'to certain movements of the extreme Right whose aggressiveness and imprudence compromise the cause which they claim to defend'. Even in his own *département* of the Côte-d'Or, Duchet's authority was rejected. All the Independent Deputies of the *département*, Lalle, Japiot and Roclore took a moderate pro-government line; only the colourful and eccentric mayor of Dijon, Chanoine Kir, had a voting record which could possibly be construed as support for *Algérie française* extremism; but he was personally hostile to Duchet. The municipal council of Beaune, where Duchet was mayor, showed its distaste of the French Algeria lobby by sending a message of sympathy and support to President de Gaulle after the Barricades affair of 1960. Duchet's cause was not, however, hopelessly lost because the majority of the provincial notables in the CNIP were still faithful to the cause of French Algeria. At the National Congress of the CNIP in December 1960, 70 per cent of the delegates voted a motion hostile to the government's Algerian policy although the Congress remained cautious in its attitude to the referendum of January 1961 on self-determination for Algeria because it feared desertions from the party. This caution was paralleled in other parties. Only a few of the former *Algérie française* members of the MRP, such as Alfred Coste-Floret (Haute-Garonne) and Raymond-Clergue (Aude) with large numbers of *pieds noirs* constituents, campaigned against the government in the referendum.[2]

The break-up of the CNIP
After the massive pro-government majority in the referendum, critics of Duchet within the CNIP gained confidence and determination. Anthonioz and Mondon described Duchet and his associates as unrealistic and, in March 1961 mounted a coup against him. The central committee resolved that the executive power of his office should be reduced, that measures should be taken to ensure that all shades of party opinion were represented in *France Indépendante* and that membership of 'extremist organisations' should be pro-

[1] *L'Année politique 1960*, 1961, p. 75.
[2] For a calculation of the importance of *pieds noirs* constituents see *l'Express*, 5 July 1962.

hibited. After the putsch of the four Generals in Algiers in April 1961, the internal situation in the party reached the point of acute crisis. A petition was signed by forty Deputies requesting Duchet's resignation after he refused to send a message of support to President de Gaulle. Following more pressure, he 'voluntarily' withdrew from office in May. In a rather farcical episode later in 1961, Duchet attempted to reoccupy his office and resume his functions, stating that he would call a meeting of the National Council to resist Algerian independence to the bitter end. *Algérie française* sentiment lingered on in the CNIP, even after Duchet's departure: at a *journée d'études* held immediately after the conclusion of the Evian agreements between the French government and the Algerian nationalists, a motion was passed calling for the maintenance of Algeria and the Sahara within the framework of the French Republic. Most of those who voted for it were making a quixotic and sentimental gesture but only four Deputies – Reynaud, Mondon, Paquet and Roclore – voted against it. At the end of March, the central committee and the national council passed motions allowing a free vote on the referendum in April 1962 approving the Evian agreements.

During this referendum campaign the confusion existing within the CNIP was again given wide publicity. The pro-government tendency composed of Jacquinot, Giscard d'Estaing, Broglie, Mondon, Marcellin and others actively campaigned for the government. Many did not commit themselves, including Bertrand Motte, chairman of the IPAS, Antoine Pinay who prudently went abroad, and some members of the *Algérie française* tendency such as Trémolet de Villiers and Frédéric-Dupont. Duchet called for abstention. The neo-Fascist Le Pen and his friends campaigned for a 'no' vote. More unity was achieved for the referendum in Autumn 1962 on de Gaulle's proposal to change the system of electing the President of the Republic from a small electoral college to universal suffrage. The various frustrations felt by different groups of the IPAS over European, foreign, defence, fiscal and agricultural policy as well as bitterness over Algeria produced a great welling up of hostility to President de Gaulle's high-handed behaviour over the constitutional reform.

In a final vain show of party unity, the IPAS decided to enforce voting discipline to defeat the Pompidou government in October 1962. Although the motion obtained the necessary two-thirds majority of the parliamentary group, the Independent Ministers and their friends refused to accept it as binding because they alleged it was an act of revenge on those who had previously supported the government over Algeria. Jean Chamant and Raymond Mondon organised a study group (quickly nicknamed *les studieux*) within the party which was the basis of the *Républicain Indépendant* parliamentary group formed after the elections of Autumn, 1962.[1] For the referendum campaign, the CNIP joined the *Cartel des Non*, composed of the major parties of government of the Fourth Republic, the Radicals, Socialists, MRP and the CNIP. After de Gaulle had won a comfortable, although not massive, majority in the referendum, the Gaullists went on to win a crucial victory in the parliamentary election. This election was a major disaster for the CNIP: only 29 Deputies were elected compared with the maximum membership of the IPAS of 121 in the previous parliament. Not sufficiently numerous to form a parliamentary group, they split three ways: 7 joined the *Centre Démocrate* (composed mainly of MRP Deputies), 4 went to the *Rassemblement Démocrate* whose largest single element was Radical, and the remainder joined those elected on *Rassemblement des Républicains Indépendants* lists to form the *Républicain Indépendant* group, committed to supporting the government and the regime.

The Independents were, therefore, reduced to utter confusion over the Algerian question and were destroyed as a major political party almost immediately after the declaration of Algerian independence. The tensions created by the Algerian War were unmanageable. Nearly all the CNIP Deputies were elected in 1958 on *Algérie française* platforms; most of the provincial notables and local councillors, in so far as the congresses and the study days provide reliable evidence, were deeply committed to keeping Algeria in the French Republic. But the majority of conservative voters did not share this commitment and demonstrated massively in two referenda that they would follow de Gaulle in granting independence to Algeria. This placed the party manager, Roger Duchet, in an impossible position. He had to cope with a group of about twenty extremist Deputies – neo-Fascists like Le Pen or men with close family, financial or constituency connections with the European settlers of Algeria – who traded on nationalist sentiments within the party. Duchet did not have the temperament of a reactionary fanatic and was never a genuine part of the extremist wing but he was carried along by it.

Duchet's course of action in the five years from 1957 to 1962 led to a spectacular disaster. This was not entirely due to his lack of political foresight. The change in his position from being an arbitrator of disputes within the CNIP to a little trusted spokesman of a particular interest was undoubtedly based on a miscalculation. He considered wrongly that there was an *Algérie française* majority in the country between 1957 and 1960. This misjudgement was based

[1] J. C. Colliard, *Les Républicains Indépendants*, 1971, pp. 39 ff.

on his own very wide but peculiar contacts with grass roots opinion via the local notables of the CNIP. The parliamentary elections of 1958 seemed to produce a clear majority of Deputies who supported French Algeria. Duchet was also guilty of the wishful thinking characteristic of most politicians when the exact state of opinion is unclear. However, all alternatives open to him were unattractive. Consistently voting for the government could have led to the absorption of the Independents into the Gaullist Party. Supporting the government on Algeria, the main issue of the day, and refusing support on a number of others was likely to make the Independents a mere satellite group, susceptible to pressure. Fence-sitting and making vague pro-*Algérie française* statements was risking extinction – if the government's Algerian programme failed, others would take advantage of it; if it succeeded the party could claim no credit. There was a real dilemma: no consistent tactic could have been imposed on the party because of the deeply held divergent views of its members, but its reputation and continuing prestige depended on a credible and defensible policy being pursued by its Secretary General.

Duchet had built the CNIP by piecing together a number of groups and he saw no reason why he should not go on collecting such groups until he had created a conservative party with a parliamentary majority. From 1957, the most obvious recruits were the factions within the other major parties, committed to the cause of French Algeria. If Lacoste could be attracted from the Socialist Party (the most unlikely of all the possibilities), Morice from the Radical Party, Soustelle from Gaullism and Bidault from the MRP, not only would they have brought up to fifty Deputies with them but they would have also provided ministerial talent and nationally-known leaders. But the number of people both inside and outside parliament who would follow these men declined as it became clear that *Algérie française* was a lost cause. When Duchet's own position within the CNIP became difficult he thought less of attracting the leaders of the French Algeria lobby into the party but of submerging the CNIP in a wider alliance in order to bring pressure to bear on his opponents within.

Duchet was a conservative politician, unsympathetic to de Gaulle, who was making his dispositions in case the government's Algerian policy came to grief and in the hope that it would do so. In the three or four years after 1958, the constant threats of a civil and military revolt in Algeria and of the assassination of de Gaulle made a radical change in the political orientation of the country an imminent possibility. Both Duchet's personal reputation and the fortunes of his party would have been less damaged if he had adopted a more opportunistic course on Algeria, like Giscard d'Estaing or Antoine Pinay.

A renewal

After the electoral debacle of 1962, there was a move to reform the CNIP; Duchet was replaced as Secretary General by Camille Laurens and a largely ineffective attempt was made to reduce the powers of his office.[1] The name of the party newspaper was changed from *France Indépendante* to the *Journal des Indépendants* but, despite the aspiration to express all tendencies within the CNIP, it remained primarily the organ of the Secretary General and the group of journalists in the central office. In 1963, the central committee was abolished and Pinay was elected chairman of a *Groupe d'Etudes et de Liaison* to examine the problems of reorganisation and to redefine the aims of the party. The study group operated very much as a central committee. Members of parliament continued to control the most important posts. They were in a majority on the study group and on the central committee when it was re-established in 1964; they held all the seats on the executive committee which met weekly and applied the general directives of the central committee or the national council. The attempts to co-ordinate the different levels of the party – Senate, Assembly, *conseils généraux* in the *départements* and municipal councils – gradually petered out. Several *journées d'études* were held in 1963 but none in subsequent years: even national council meetings became less frequent. The drive to re-invigorate the party was, therefore, unsuccessful.

The party continued to do well at the local level: in the cantonal elections of 1964 and the municipal elections of 1965 the CNIP retained most of its positions. This local strength was reflected in the Senate where the Independent Republican group (affiliated to the CNIP) still had eighty members in the middle 1960s. Senators showed less interest in party matters than Deputies and their loyalties were often obscure. In 1964, for example, the election of François Schleiter, former *chef de cabinet* to Louis Jacquinot, as President of the Senate group was taken as an indication that the group was moving towards a more pro-government position. But soon after his election Schleiter, apparently as a gesture of independence vis-à-vis the Gaullists, renewed his association with the CNIP. Practically the only issue which united all the Senators in his groups was the defence of the prerogatives of the upper house. Although formidable in

[1] J. Bourdin, 'La Crise des Indépendants', *Revue française de science politique*, vol. 13, 1963, pp. 443–50.

numbers, the Senate group was not therefore a base upon which the party could be revived as a national political force.

The exodus of the Gaullist and pro-government Independents after 1962 simplified the internal situation of the CNIP. But, as a French Institute of Public Opinion (IFOP) poll in 1963 indicated, there was a division between the majority of CNIP supporters who opposed the government and the regime from a moderate 'centrist' position and the minority who opposed them from an extreme Right position. Even in a situation of declining activity and membership, this distribution of opinion made it virtually impossible for the party to agree on major decisions about strategy, such as the candidate to support in the 1965 presidential election. After a move to draft Antoine Pinay had failed, the CNIP officially decided to support Jean Lecanuet, the ex-President of the MRP. The party was rewarded with four seats on Lecanuet's campaign committee, the *Comité de Démocrates*. An extreme Right minority led, or at least represented, by Lacoste-Lareymondie supported Tixier-Vignancour. Some quietly made their peace with the Independent Republicans and with the regime. The ex-Secretary General, Roger Duchet, made an unsuccessful political comeback, founding the *Union pour le Progrès* in 1964 on the basis of what he called the *nouveaux notables*. He announced his support for General de Gaulle and, in return, enjoyed some favour in government circles. The failure of the *Union pour le Progrès* illustrated Duchet's lack of political credibility.

The presidential election of 1965 showed once again the attraction of General de Gaulle for the conservative electorate. As a consequence the leadership of the CNIP seemed to lose faith in the future of the party. A new broad grouping to fill 'the democratic void and to combat both Gaullism and the reviving Popular Front' was frequently urged in the *Journal des Indépendants*. The basis for such a federation never emerged. The elections of 1967 and 1968 confirmed the decline of both the CNIP and of Lecanuet's Democratic Centre in which most of the leading members of the CNIP had placed their hopes. After the 1968 election the moderate Deputies in the parliamentary group *Progrès et Démocratie Moderne*, numbered only thirty-four, including three *apparentés*. This inchoate group was the successor to a major part of the defunct Radical, MRP and IPAS groups. The allegiance of PDM Deputies was often vague. Approximately six, led by Pierre Abelin, were identified with the *Centre Démocrate*, about the same number were close to the CNIP, three held posts in the *Centre Républicain* of André Morice, some such as Pierre Sudreau were not connected with any political party and the most numerous tendency, comprising about fifteen, were members of *Démocratie et Progrès* led by Duhamel and Pleven, both of whom entered the Chaban-Delmas government in 1969. PDM Deputies naturally looked in different directions for a way out of their unpromising political situation. Some, together with the CNIP leadership outside parliament, gravitated towards the *Républicains Indépendants* who had grown and prospered since the split in 1962. These *Giscardiens* and the CNIP were *frères ennemis*, close in general political position but divided on tactics. For about two years after the parting of the ways in 1962, despite mutual recrimination, ties were maintained between them. Both respected the old moderate Republican tradition of loose organisation and discipline. This facilitated personal contacts between members of the two groups. Neither side wanted to create an unbridgeable barrier which would prevent an eventual reunion. In July 1970, the Secretary General of the CNIP, Camille Laurens, took an important step towards a reunion when he approached Giscard d'Estaing for a working relationship with the Independent Republicans. The outcome of this approach could only be to the advantage of the stronger party.

The motives were varied of the Independents who chose, from 1958, to give support to the government on all major matters of policy whilst reserving the right to criticise the detail of policy.[1] Some Independent Republicans were disposed to support any non-Socialist government in order to moderate the excesses to which, according to a certain strand of conservative opinion, all governments are prone. These Deputies and their supporters in the country valued stability and continuity in government and consequently approved the new regime. Such traditional attitudes combined with important tactical considerations. Polarisation of the party system between the Communist Party and the Gaullists, predicted by André Malraux during the RPF period, would have destroyed the political positions of the Independents. Those who chose to support de Gaulle's constitutional amendment in 1962 were, in part, trying to maintain diversity within the government majority and to prevent the complete domination of the government by the 'unconditionals' of Gaullism. They were also much concerned with their own careers. The original leaders of the Independent Republicans were either *ministrables* who wanted to retain or acquire office or old Gaullists –

[1] The main published works on the Independent Republicans are M. Bal, 'Les Indépendants', *Revue française de science politique*, vol. 15, 1965, pp. 537–55. J. Charlot, *The Gaullist Phenomenon*, 1971, pp. 109–19. J. C. Colliard, op. cit. M. C. Kessler, 'M. Valèry Giscard d'Estaing et les Républicains Indépendants', *Revue française de science politique*, vol. 18, 1968, pp. 77–93.

such as Raymond Boisdé, Jean de Broglie and Raymond Mondon – who found it difficult to return to the fold because they had broken the discipline of the RPF. Provided that the *Union pour la Nouvelle République* (or its successors) did not win an absolute majority of the seats in the National Assembly without them, support for the government gave them the certainty of office and did not necessarily exclude them from alternative coalitions if the UNR suffered electoral defeat.

Jean Charlot argues that Georges Pompidou, as Prime Minister in 1962, made a tactical error in allowing the Independent Republicans to establish an independent group in the National Assembly.[1] However, as well as remembering the old adage 'divide and rule', Pompidou was probably impressed by the disciplinary problems which almost certainly would have arisen if the Independent Republicans had been integrated into the UNR. The original group of thirty-five Deputies who formed the Independent Republican group in the National Assembly were, for the most part, experienced parliamentarians with a highly developed sense of survival. Thirty-two out of the thirty-five had been Deputies in the previous parliament and eleven had sat in the Palais Bourbon since 1951. Loyalty to a group and acceptance of party discipline by these men were unlikely in any circumstances in which these attitudes conflicted either with the possibility of acquiring office or with the certainty of electoral success. Their acknowledged leader Giscard d'Estaing, the Minister of Finance in the Pompidou government from 1962 to 1965, in the Chaban-Delmas government from 1969 to 1972 and subsequently in the Messmer government never tried to exercise discipline over them. On important occasions the parliamentary group failed to follow his lead and Independent Republican ministers publicly dissociated themselves from his views when he adopted positions critical of President de Gaulle between 1966 and 1969.

His statements on matters of party organisation were even more circumspect than those of Roger Duchet in the early years of the CNIP. Until his abrupt departure from office in 1966 he reiterated a simple theme: 'We do not seek to be a party. We do not pretend to dictate our law to imaginary militants. We are a meeting-place [*rencontre*] and a movement.'[2] He fully accepted the traditional moderate Republican repugnance for party discipline. The extra-parliamentary organisation of the group, until 1966, was the rudimentary *Comité d'Études et de Liaison* founded mainly on the initiative of Raymond Mondon on 6 May 1962. Like the CNIP in

[1] J. Charlot, op. cit., p. 109.
[2] *Le Monde*, 5 February 1964.

its first years, the Independent Republicans held no congresses, only 'study days'. Modest resources were devoted to propaganda and publicity for the activities of the group and, in particular, to building up its newspaper, *France rurale et indépendante*, for which a circulation of 40,000 was claimed in 1965.

The origins of the Independent Republican Party were, therefore, very similar to those of the CNIP. A group of conservative parliamentarians (an Independent Republican group in the Senate was established in 1966) wished to escape the unpopularity of the previous regime and were not attracted by the existing political parties. They grouped together under the leadership of a skilful manager to ensure their own political survival. Both the CNIP and the RI tried to diversify their activities and to strengthen their organisation. In the case of the Independent Republicans the first significant diversification came with the establishment in 1965 of the clubs *Perspectives et Réalités* organised by Michel Poniatowski under the sponsorship of Giscard d'Estaing. By the end of the decade, guided by an active Secretary General, Charles-Noël Hardy, the clubs numbered about forty with three thousand members, mainly young professional people.[1] The activities of the clubs received a good deal of press attention and were an important part of Giscard's strategy of transforming his movement into a youthful, dynamic and forward-looking party in accordance with the image he had created. The *Jeunesses Républicaines Indépendantes* was mainly composed of students in university towns. Other clubs were organised such as the *Club Sigma* and the *Club Tiers Monde* but they have remained of very minor importance. The clubs *Perspectives et Réalités* were founded at a time when the clubs of the social democratic Left enjoyed a vogue but they had no competitors on the moderate Right. They proved to be popular amongst people who objected to parties of the more formal kind.

The clubs predated the establishment of the Independent Republican Party, the *Fédération Nationale des Républicains Indépendants*, registered in June 1966. The Federation preserved the loose structure of the liaison committee which preceded it but was intended as a more impressive platform for Giscard d'Estaing after his dismissal as Minister of Finance. The central organisation of the Federation was kept firmly under control of Giscard and his friends. The constitution of the Federation made Giscard's position invulnerable because no grass roots revolt could be organised to overthrow the President: the Federation held no congresses (until 1971), only

[1] Fédération Nationale des Républicains Indépendants, *Les Animateurs des clubs perspectives et réalités*, n.d.

'federal councils', had no national membership and no organised recruitment, although like Duchet twenty years before, the President launched an appeal to the mayors of France. Giscard d'Estaing and his associates were, in effect, self-appointed and self-perpetuating. The federations in the regions and the *départements* enjoyed great autonomy, but the corollary was that they had little control over the national leadership. The Deputies posed little threat to the party hierarchy. They represented divergent and even conflicting interests.[1] In different areas the political circumstance of the Deputies and their supporting committees varied considerably, depending on the manner in which the Deputy had been elected and the local political traditions. A challenge to the leadership required a degree of political cohesion which was not present in any significant group of Independent Republican Deputies. The Deputies disliked pressure both from the national leadership and from organised groups of militants in their constituencies. They were mainly interested in preserving their independence and, therefore, not disposed to run a candidate for the Presidency of the Federation against an established national figure such as Giscard.

Both Giscard and his followers were searching for a presidential as much as, and perhaps more than, a parliamentary majority. Their intention was to create a *structure d'accueil pour l'après-Gaullisme*[2] in the country as well as in parliament. Giscard never made any secret of his long-term ambition of running for the Presidency of the Republic. The parliamentarians realised that, under the existing constitution, their hopes of ministerial office were directly dependent on a well-disposed individual occupying the Presidency. This attitude helps to explain why, despite serious divergences of view between Giscard and the majority of the Independent Republicans in the National Assembly in the period from 1966 to 1969, the party managed without great difficulty to stay together.

Giscard did not hide his irritation when dismissed from the Ministry of Finance after the presidential election of 1965. De Gaulle's dissatisfaction with him was probably based on three things: Giscard used office to gain personal publicity and make a national reputation; some Independent Republicans had backed Lecanuet at the first ballot of the elections and Giscard had made no attempt to bring them to heel; de Gaulle apparently blamed his poor showing at the first ballot partly on the deflationary 'stabilisation plan'

---

[1] These tendencies freely expressed their points of view in the party publications: *Réponses, France rurale et indépendante, France moderne*.

[2] Article by Claude Krief in *le Nouvel observateur*, 28 January 1965.

administered by Giscard between 1962 and 1964. Giscard retaliated by becoming more and more critical of the government, and in a famous statement in 1967 he attacked the 'lonely exercise of power' by President de Gaulle. He also sought to create the impression that on matters such as European and social policy he was more liberal and forward-looking than de Gaulle. On European policy at least, his position was very different to the government's: in a major speech at Metz in June 1966 he declared himself in favour of a European bank, currency and Senate. He wanted to appear as an alternative to the Gaullist government without becoming identified with the opposition. His support for the government he described as 'Oui mais . . .' in January 1967. This allowed him to escape the opprobrium of unpopular government policies and, at the same time, avoid responsibility for provoking government instability. It produced serious discord among the Independent Republicans: Raymond Marcellin, a minister in the Pompidou government and subsequently Minister of the Interior from 1968, threatened to leave with his followers (who came mainly from his own *département* of Morbihan). The Prime Minister prevailed upon him to stay on the grounds that he would be more useful to the Gaullist cause as a member of the Independent Republicans.

The results of the 1967 parliamentary elections showed that Giscard's tactics did no electoral damage to the FNRI. According to the opinion polls, Giscard made a considerable impact on television in the campaign and the party made modest gains.[1] The number of Deputies in the group increased from 33 at the end of the second parliament to 42, and they held the balance of power in the short third parliament. Giscard d'Estaing was elected Deputy and subsequently elected to the chairmanship of the finance committee of the National Assembly. Despite occupying this crucial position, his influence over the general policy of the government was not appreciably increased. He could not threaten to bring down the government because de Gaulle was unlikely to be intimidated and direct responsibility for ending de Gaulle's tenure of office would have been in conflict with Giscard's general political strategy. The situation was, however, transformed by the events of May 1968, which Giscard considered a great national crisis. In the elections of June 1968, the parliamentary representation of the Independent Republicans increased by nearly a half and at the beginning of the fourth parliament numbered 61. But the group no longer held the balance of power because the Gaullist UDR held 292 seats and

[1] J. C. Colliard, op. cit., pp. 90–9. J. Charlot, 'Les préparatifs de la majorité' in *Les Elections législatives de mars 1967*, 1970.

therefore had an absolute majority. This increase in numbers gave the group new confidence, although not sufficient confidence to follow Giscard when he moved a decisive stage further into opposition in 1969.

Giscard opposed the referendum on President de Gaulle's complex bill, put to the country in April 1969, for reform of the Senate and the establishment of new regional institutions. Over three-quarters of the Independent Republican Deputies were in favour of a 'yes' vote in the referendum, mainly for tactical reasons. They attributed the electoral success of 1968 to fear of revolution and Communism, and considered it prudent to pursue a rigidly anti-Communist line. Charles Deprez, Deputy for the Hauts-de-Seine, claimed, in a fairly typical statement, 'if the "noes" win it will render a great service to the Communists'.[1] Giscard on his own initiative as President of the *Fédération Nationale des Républicains Indépendants* and with the support of most of the regional federations, published posters all over France:

'This referendum is not a modern and reasonable means to commit the future of France. It is not in such a way that the country ought to be governed. This is why, to the only question asked, which is to approve by a single response the whole of a bill, in so far as I am concerned, I reply with regret but with certainty, in the negative.'

The defeat of the proposal in the referendum and de Gaulle's immediate resignation was followed, after some hesitation, by Giscard's support for Georges Pompidou in the ensuing presidential election. This successful manoeuvre gave him a claim to office and, after an unsuccessful attempt to persuade Pinay to lend his authority to an inevitable devaluation of the Franc, Giscard was invited to the Ministry of Finance in the Chaban-Delmas government in June 1969.

The Independent Republicans had become an incubus within the government majority. Their leader was of quite a different stature to the first Secretary General of the CNIP. He came from a distinguished family of moderate Republicans and civil servants: his father was a very distinguished *Inspecteur des Finances*, and both his grandfather and great grandfather had been Senators.[2] His relations and relations by marriage were widely spread through public administration, business, politics and the aristocracy. He was, in that sense, a representative of the *grandes familles* but he

[1] *France moderne*, 22 April 1969.
[1] For biographical details see M. Bassi, *Valèry Giscard d'Estaing*, 1968. A. P. Lentin, 'Valèry Giscard d'Estaing' in C. Angeli *et al.*, *Les Héritiers du Général*, 1969, pp. 143–58.

cultivated the common touch, occasionally travelling second class in the metro, eating in modest restaurants and playing the accordion at Independent Republican gatherings. His career was very rapid after he had graduated from the highly prestigious Ecole Polytechnique and the Ecole Nationale d'Administration. He was an *Inspecteur des Finances* in 1954, deputy director of Edgar Faure's *cabinet* in 1955 and elected, at the age of twenty-nine, to the National Assembly in 1956, succeeding to his grandfather's seat in Puy-de-Dôme. In the last parliament of the Fourth Republic he tried to assemble around himself a very heterogeneous 'inter-group' of 'Young Turks' ranging from neo-Socialists to members of the radical Right. He rallied quickly to de Gaulle in 1958 and, showing flexibility on the Algerian question, he entered the Debré government as Secretary of State for Finance. He was promoted Minister of Finance in January 1962 at the remarkably early age of thirty-five. His career added lustre to the Independent Republicans by contrast with that of Duchet, who was never considered as having the qualities of a senior minister. Giscard d'Estaing, young and forward-looking, was aiming for the highest offices in government. The Independent Republican organisation was an instrument for furthering his ambitions and the main stages in the development of the movement corresponded with the necessities of his career.

The *Fédération Nationale des Républicains Indépendants* was, despite the clear difference in the quality of leadership, the successor party to the CNIP. The effective life of the latter spanned about a decade and a second generation of leaders never emerged, as they had in *Alliance Démocratique* and the *Fédération Républicaine* during the Third Republic. The party was destroyed as a serious political force by political circumstances and by the politics of *opéra bouffe* surrounding Duchet's eventual exclusion from the Secretary General's office. The leading figures in the party in the 1970s had been prominent in the 1950s, despite claims that young people were rallying to it. In 1970 the main claim made by the CNIP to be a national party of consequence was its alliance with the Independent Republicans. In July, Camille Laurens, the Secretary General of the CNIP said at a national council meeting that the Independent Republicans had two 'privileged' allies, the *Union des Démocrates pour le République* and the CNIP: 'Certainly we do not pretend that we are the equal of the UDR: but if we are placed in parallel with that organisation today, it indicates that the CNIP has become once again, and will remain, an element of a certain weight.'[1] The immediate results of the rapprochement were not substantial – the

[1] *Journal des Indépendants*, 15, July 1971.

joint publication of a brochure on communal administration and the occasional joint investiture of an electoral candidate such as Philippe de Bourgoing who stood, in September 1970, for the Senate in Calvados in opposition to a UDR candidate.[1] The absorption of the remnants of the clientele of the CNIP by the FNRI seemed only a matter of time. There was not a strong enough bond among the men of the CNIP either to resist or to come to terms with the Gaullists. Social and economic conservatism, coupled with a rather suspect nationalism was not sufficient to give the members of the CNIP, who co-operated mainly to obtain short-term electoral advantage, the sense of identity on which great and durable political enterprises are based.

In the Fifth Republic, the Independent Republicans played a similar role to that of the Independents and Peasants in the Fourth Republic. They were a focus for conservatives who wished to rally to the new regime and to gain access to political power. The previous career of some of the conservatives made a new political organisation imperative. The Independent Republicans maintained just sufficient voting discipline in parliament to retain their status as members of the government majority. When their votes were no longer necessary to preserve that majority after 1968, and particularly after the departure of President de Gaulle in 1969, the Independent Republican Deputies showed a certain *esprit de fronde*. For example, in the 1971 parliamentary session they voted with the opposition of the Left against government bills on local government reorganisation and on higher education. These expressions of independence served both to accentuate the conservative tendencies of the UDR, fearing loss of support on the Right, and to attract the so-called 'Centrists', the survivors of the Radical Party and other minor groups on the fringes of the government majority. In August 1971, the Secretary General of the FNRI, Michel Poniatowski, a specialist in putting out not always discreet feelers, called for a 'grand federation of the Centre' and for recruits to the party 'whether they belong to the majority or not'.

Although claiming, as Giscard d'Estaing said to a seminar of Independent Republican cadres in June 1970, that '. . . we belong to the majority and this choice is definitive for the septennate of President Pompidou' the FNRI sought to maintain a distance between itself and the UDR as part of the strategy to become the 'majority of the majority'. There was also an attempt, in preparation for electoral battles to come, to turn the FNRI into a more cohesive party. Five years after its foundation, exactly the same period which the CNIP

[1] *Journal des Indépendants*, 14 September 1971.

took to arrive at the same point, the FNRI held its first national conference in the Autumn of 1971. Christian Bonnet, Deputy for
Morbihan, defined the doctrinal base for a party programme. The
'liberalism' which he expounded differed little from the 'neo-
liberalism' of the CNIP; both parties expressed a fervent anti-
Communism. The congress was, like the CNIP congress of 1954,
conceived of as an important stage on the path towards creating the
great French conservative party.

There were, however, important differences between the two parties
mainly because they were operating in a different political context.
The speech made by Giscard d'Estaing to the 1971 conference was
widely interpreted as a declaration of his candidature for the
presidential election of 1976. It was a reminder that the leader had a
different constituency to members of parliament and that this gave
him a dominant position. The denunciation of the principle of the
'single candidate of the majority' in each parliamentary constituency
illustrated the constraint which the UDR, the larger and more disciplined ally, placed on the FNRI. Both Giscard and Poniatowski
refused to accept the notion in their own constituencies in 1967 and
1968, although the FNRI accepted it for the 1973 parliamentary
elections. Whilst Giscard d'Estaing and his associates could hope
for a breakdown of discipline within the UDR, it is also possible that
the greater strength and organisational drive of the UDR will keep
the FNRI in its position of a subordinate partner and eventually
integrate it. Once again holding the balance of power in the National
Assembly, after the 1973 elections, the decisive moment for the
FNRI probably will come a decade after its foundation, in the Presidential election of 1976.

The willingness of Giscard d'Estaing to use contemporary methods
of publicity and new forms of organisation, such as the clubs, are
a thin veneer which does not obscure his identification with the
moderate Republican tradition. The main themes of the tradition
have changed little since the end of the nineteenth century. Its principal slogan remains *la liberté de l'homme* and the more disturbing
aspects of economic liberalism are hidden by declarations of good
intentions about helping the under-privileged and those who have
not benefited from economic expansion. Support for government
stability is accompanied by the apparently contradictory hostility to
disciplined voting by members of parliament. The inevitable consequence of voting discipline would be, according to the Independent
Republicans, a polarisation of the political system in which the
Gaullists would be confronted by a united Left. Giscard d'Estaing
favours the preservation of at least four major parliamentary

groups. On the constitutional question, like most of his moderate Republican predecessors, he believes in a degree of separation of powers. His success shows that there is still a place in French politics for a party representing these basic ideas.

CHAPTER VI

The Extreme Right after the Second World War

The 'internal exiles'

At the Liberation, the extreme Right was more isolated within the political community than ever before. Its members were widely regarded as having followed a path which, from the riots of February 1934 to the declaration of Montoire in 1940, had led 'from blackmail to treason'.[1] Vichy, Collaboration and the purge at the Liberation were crucial and disastrous episodes for the extreme Right, deeply marking those involved for the rest of their political careers.[2] Many paid heavily for their wartime activities at the Liberation and the summary executions, death sentences, prison terms and general opprobrium greatly reduced, without totally interrupting, the activities of the extreme Right. The number of summary executions will probably never be known precisely because of the disordered condition of the country, but estimates range from 4,000 to 100,000. Some, like the law student nephew of Joseph Darnand, the chief of the *Milice*, suffered because of their connections rather than for any actions imputed to them. When the purge was put on a legal footing, not only did the courts deprive many of the leaders of Collaboration of their lives and their subordinates of their liberty, but all means of political defence were denied to them: their newspapers were seized and their organisations proscribed.

Some of the leaders of the extreme Right such as Maurras and Pujo seemed genuinely outraged by their treatment at the Liberation.[3] Humbler members of *Action Française* had every reason to be surprised because like the *avocat*, Henri Castille, future Vice-President of the Paris municipal council, they had abstained from

[1] L. Ducloux, *Du Chantage à la trahison*, 1955. English translation 1958.
[2] For an interesting personal testimony on the experience of the war, see H. Charbonneau, *Le Roman noir de la droite française*, 1969.
[3] S. M. Osgood, *French Royalism since 1870*, 1971, p. 182.

all political activity during the war and yet were imprisoned, often for long periods, without trial. Their supporters rallied to the defence as best they could. A clandestine publication entitled *Documents nationaux*, edited by Georges Calzant formerly President of the *Action Française* students' organisation and a prominent member of the *Camelots du roi*, appeared in 1944, first in duplicated form and then printed in Switzerland, to defend the role of the leaders of *Action Française*. Other clandestine news-sheets defending the record of the Vichy regime more generally, such as *Questions actuelles* (apparently the first), were circulated almost immediately following the Liberation. The Paris-based Collaborators were necessarily more circumspect. *Combattant européen*, their first publication, came out in 1946. It revived the title used by the *Légion Française contre le Bolchévisme* and was openly racialist, as well as being both anti-capitalist and anti-Communist. It was followed by other ephemeral and badly produced periodicals such as *les Cahiers de la Révolution européenne* and *les Idées et les faits*, which repeated themes of collaborationist propaganda such as 'Europeanism' and support for the formation of a national Socialist revolutionary party.

The only post-war French Fascist of intellectual distinction, Maurice Bardèche, made an early and notorious reputation with two books published in 1947 and 1948 – *Lettre a François Mauriac* and *Nürnberg ou la terre promise*. In the former, he pursued a line of argument, first used by Alfred Fabre-Luce in *Au nom des silencieux* (1946), that the Vichyites and Collaborators had preserved the French race from extinction and that the men of the Resistance were guilty of lies and illogicality. In *Nürnberg ou la terre promise*, Bardèche attacked allied war propaganda (alleging that some of the evidence about concentration camps had been fabricated), the authority of the Nuremburg war crimes tribunals and the collusion of the Western powers with Communism. The seizure of this book, and Bardèche's imprisonment in 1948, attracted much publicity and provided a focus for the persecution complex of the extreme Right. A noisy campaign was organised to defend Bardèche on the grounds that his freedom of expression had been infringed; after his release he became a cult figure preaching Fascist doctrine to a small band of devotees. He was unlike the proto-Fascist leaders of the leagues of the inter-war period for whom the conquest of power posed essentially empirical problems. For Bardèche, the appeal and persuasiveness of Fascism were unrelated to specific circumstances. In this respect, he was the continuation of the 'literary' Fascist tradition of the 1930s which Paul Sérant described as 'Fascist romanticism', represented by writers such as Drieu La Rochelle and Thierry Maulnier.[1] He had been associated with the pre-war generation since 1930 when he made his debut in journalism in the little review *Réaction*, but he had not been particularly committed to political action until the closing days of the war. In the post-war period, through the columns of *Défense de l'Occident*, a monthly which he took over in 1953, and in his best-known book *Qu'est-ce que le fascisme* (1961) Bardèche elaborated a 'purified' national Socialism which, like the writings of Drieu and others, was intended as an ideological defence of certain cultural and moral values against the threats posed by mass society and proletarian revolution. He attempted to excise all the accretions to German national Socialism which circumstances had, in his view, forced upon the Nazi leaders. Co-operation with large-scale capitalism and the establishment of extermination camps came into this category. Many of his main proposals were similar to those advanced in Drieu La Rochelle's book, *Socialisme fasciste* (1934) – the suppression of large private fortunes, compulsory co-operation between labour and capital, the *führerprinzip* and the institution of an elite corps such as the SS to embody in their noblest form the ideals of the national Socialist system. He tended, like most of his French predecessors, to use a romantic rather than the pseudo-scientific language of the Nazi racialists to defend the superiority of the Indo-European race.

As well as defending Fascist doctrine, Bardèche also fostered the memory of his brother-in-law, Robert Brasillach, shot at Fresnes in 1946 for treason. He had been friendly with Brasillach since the late 1920s when they had been students together at the Ecole Normale Supérieure. They had jointly written a history of the cinema, a subject which remained of abiding interest to Bardèche. He founded a *Société des Amis de Robert Brasillach* and published a number of his writings posthumously, culminating in a complete edition of his works in the 1960s. This tireless activity did something to restore Brasillach's literary reputation in other than Collaborationist circles. In 1970, for example, *le Monde*, after a silence of a quarter of a century, published an extended review of his work. Bardèche retained a certain scandalous reputation as an intellectual oddity and as the standard bearer of a particular point of view. However, he has scarcely belonged to the realm of political action because he has never transcended the role of the leader of a coterie devoted to the most unpopular cause in France.

The first organised groups of the extreme Right after the Liberation were those of Vichyites who sought to re-establish their cre-

[1] P. Sérant, *Le Romanticisme fasciste ... ou l'œuvre politique de quelques écrivains français*, 1959.

dentials as patriotic Frenchmen. The men prominent in them were not necessarily, in origin, members of the extreme Right. Their main periodical *Les Ecrits de Paris*, which began publication in January 1947, had contributors with Socialist, Radical and Christian Democratic backgrounds as well as others with *Action Française*, neo-Fascist and various extremist careers. Pierre-Etienne Flandin, the moderate Republican, *Président du Conseil* of the Third Republic and under Vichy, was the President of the association of Deputies and Senators of the Third Republic made ineligible by their vote of full powers to Pétain in 1940. In the post-war period he was compelled to associate with the extreme Right, and seems to have acquired some of their attitudes partly because until the Cold War was well under way, there was virtually no one urging a reconciliation between the Vichyites and the Resistance. Exceptions were André Mutter[1] in the columns of *Paroles françaises*, the official journal of the *Parti Républicain de la Liberté*, and the rump of La Rocque's *Parti Social Français* (renamed *Réconciliation Française*) whose members had followed a variety of courses during the war. These voices had little influence. A more effective initiative, concerned almost exclusively with individual cases, was the *Comité Français pour la Défense des Droits de l'Homme*, founded by Jean Ebstein. Before the war he was a militant in the *Union Royaliste d'Alsace* and a founder of the *Comité de Co-ordination des Mouvements Anti-Marxistes* after the 1936 victory of the Popular Front, but he was one of the first to rally to the Resistance. He was therefore well-qualified to form a committee to bring together Resisters and Vichyites to publicise miscarriages of justice. His committee also urged both the abolition of the special tribunals set up to carry through the purge and the passing of a general amnesty.

The *Union des Intellectuels Indépendants* and its off-shoot, the *Union pour la Grande Amnestie*, had similar policies but unlike Ebstein's committee they were composed exclusively of Vichyites and had no links with the Resistance. Both the *Comité Français pour la Défense des Droits de l'Homme* and *Union pour la Grande Amnestie* disbanded when the general amnesty came into effect in 1953, but the *Union des Intellectuels Indépendants* still survives. The latter brought together academicians, intellectuals, ex-ministers and ex-members of parliament who felt discriminated against by the dominant political forces of the Fourth Republic. It was a club of the counter-establishment whose members gradually lost their

---

[1] Mutter was a regional official of the *Fédération Républicaine* before joining the *Parti Social Français* in the late 1930s. During the war he was a leader of *Ceux de la Résistance* and a member of the *Conseil National de la Résistance*.

reputation for treasonable conduct as the Resistance parties lost prestige. They occupied roughly the same position in the political system as the Legitimists at the beginning of the Third Republic, although their electoral following was much smaller. Rather more quickly than their Legitimist predecessors, they came to be regarded as an ineffective group of old men by a younger generation of activists.

It was not unusual for men involved at an early stage in Vichy but who adopted a reserved position after 1942 to resume their political careers. Antoine Pinay and Camille Laurens were prominent examples. On the other hand, it was very rare for Collaborators or those who remained loyal to Vichy until the end of the war to do so. Alfred Fabre-Luce, whose involvement in Collaboration was probably relatively slight, after being a rather unpopular editor of *Rivarol* in 1954–5, became a highly successful freelance journalist whose articles on current politics were accepted by both *le Monde* and *le Figaro*. Charles Spinasse, a close associate of Léon Blum, one of the most prominent journalists of Collaboration, after years of ostracism became a *conseiller général* of Corrèze. It is difficult to find other examples of a successful return to public life even at these modest levels. Of those who remained loyal to and active in the Vichy regime until the very end, only Henri Dorgères made a significant comeback.[1] Acquitted of major charges of treason at the end of the war because he was never closely identified with Collaborators such as Laval and Darnand, he was nevertheless sentenced to ten years 'national indignity'.

Dorgères did not wait until the general amnesty of 1953 made him re-eligible for elective office, before re-entering politics. After running a small advertising agency to pay his debts, he bought in 1949 one of the oldest agricultural journals in the country, *la Gazette agricole*, and resumed his activities as a propagandist. The style he adopted differed from that of the 1930s, although his themes were much the same – the progressive impoverishment of the peasantry, the iniquity of the co-operatives, of the *lois sociales* (accident insurance, social security and pensions), and of government regulation of the markets for agricultural products (particularly the *caisses de garantie*). His approach was more moderate and he often suggested improvements in existing institutions and arrangements. Finding allies was the main problem which he faced in re-acquiring influence. The National Federation of Agricultural Unions (FNSEA) had achieved

[1] J. M. Royer in J. Fauvet, H. Mendras, *Les Paysans et la politique*, 1958, pp. 157–81. P. Barral, *Les Agrariens français*, 1968, pp. 238–40, 251–5. G. Wright, *The Rural Revolution in France*, 1964, 126–7, 136–8.

the unity of peasant organisations; and the *Parti Paysan* (which later merged with the Independents in the *Centre National des Indépendants et des Paysans*) united former members of the *Parti Agraire* such as Paul Antier, of the *Front Paysan* led by Leroy-Ladurie and of the Vichy Peasant Corporation such as Camille Laurens, giving a semblance of unity to the peasants at the political level. Dorgères tried to infiltrate and divide both these coalitions, making use of networks of old followers who remained loyal to him. His first important, although unreliable, ally was Paul Antier who, after his resignation as Minister of Agriculture in 1951 was isolated within the CNIP by his bitter rivalry with Camille Laurens. As in the 1930s when Dorgères allied himself with Lemaîgre-Dubreuil, leader of the taxpayers' league, he also looked beyond the agricultural milieu and, in the early 1950s, made temporary alliance with Léon Gingembre, the Secretary General of the *Petites et Moyennes Entreprises* (PME). In 1954, he was attracted to Pierre Poujade but their first contacts led to resentment and bitterness. The Poujadist movement was, however, so explosive that Dorgères had to come to terms with it in order to retain his own following. Partly because of his age and his past, and partly because of his relative moderation when he recommenced political activity in the late 1940s, he could only play a subordinate role during the great expansion of the Poujadist movement in 1955 and 1956. In 1956 he was elected, with his close associate Jean Bohun, Deputy for Ille-et-Vilaine. In 1957, when the Poujadist movement had started to fade, he formed a short-lived *Rassemblement Paysan* in alliance with Pierre Poujade and Paul Antier. This was a personal triumph for Dorgères and once again he was taken up by the Right-wing press as an important figure, without becoming the national celebrity that he had been in 1935–6. He had established a position of equality with Antier and Poujade but unwisely tried to impose his superiority: he claimed 50 per cent of the seats on all committees of the *Rassemblement* for his nominees and, in the acrimony which followed, the *Rassemblement* disintegrated. In 1958 he rallied briefly to de Gaulle, but was not re-elected to the National Assembly. He continued to run a small party, the *Convention Paysanne*, edit a newspaper and attend the occasional meeting to honour the memory of Marshal Pétain, but effectively he went into semi-retirement. His most widely noticed action was the publication of his memoirs of the 1930s, *Dix Ans de jacquerie*.[1] His post-war career was a less effective repetition of his pre-war activities; agitation had become a way of life which he found difficult to abandon. He found a following amongst sections of the peasantry

[1] H. Dorgères, *Au XXème siècle, dix ans de jacquerie*, 1959.

because the old rallying cries still moved them and because his insistence on the theme of the progressive impoverishment of the peasantry seemed justified by the relative decline in the income of those engaged in agriculture. The policies of successive governments were little understood by the less well-educated peasants and the general economic position of agriculture was incomprehensible to them: they felt threatened by all change and the simple aggressive language of Dorgères expressed their feelings.

Although few of the *dernière heure* Vichyites managed to emulate Dorgères and reacquire a measure of political influence, nostalgia for Vichy persisted. The cult of the person of Marshal Pétain was carefully cultivated by the *Association pour Défendre la Mémoire du Maréchal Pétain*, and aspects of Collaboration were defended in the columns of *Rivarol, Défense de l'Occident* and other publications. This nostalgia had little political significance: and the passage of time was healing the bitter divisions. This was shown by the growing indifference of public opinion to the demands of the Vichyites to successive governments that the body of Marshal Pétain should be transferred to Douaumont (to lie among those who had fallen at Verdun in 1917). The main interest aroused by these requests after 1958 was whether General de Gaulle would support them as a symbolic gesture to indicate that the time of reconciliation had arrived. He chose to ignore them.

The great stimulus to extremist activity was not nostalgia or the alleged injustice of the post-war purge, but decolonisation and, to a lesser extent, economic modernisation. In the period 1954 to 1962 a myriad of groups of the extreme Right came into existence of a variety which exceeded that of the 1930s.[1] However, except in Algerian *départements* and, at the very end of the Fourth Republic, in Paris, they were not strong enough to make the public shows of force achieved by the pre-war leagues. At the time, they were considered as an important threat to democratic institutions. But they were ill-disciplined, unstructured, lacking stable membership and coherent programmes, and, for the most part, excellent examples of the paranoid style in French politics. The Poujadist movement which had a meteoric rise in the period 1954 to 1956 was not typical of these groups for two reasons: it was only loosely involved

---

[1] The most exhaustive list of these groups is in E. Seuillard, *Les Groupements de l'extrême droite actuelle en France*, unpublished *mémoire*, 1960. An interesting, although somewhat partial, account by an author involved in extremist politics is F. Duprat, *Les Mouvements d'extrême droite en France depuis 1945*, 1972. See also, H. Coston, *Partis, journaux et hommes politiques d'hier et d'aujourd'hui*, 1960.

in the colonial problem, although trying unsuccessfully to make use of it; and it succeeded in acquiring a large electoral following which the other groups failed to do.

The Poujadist Movement

Poujadism started as a tax strike led by Pierre Poujade in July 1953 in his native *département* of Lot. It was highly publicised because like Dorgères's Greenshirts in the 1930s it was bizarre, unusual and colourful. The established politicians were made acutely aware that it was based on genuine economic and fiscal grievances. Although attempts were made to diversify its appeal to other social groups, it appealed essentially to shopkeepers and artisans.[1] The rapidity of its success was remarkable. A week after the formation of the *Union de Defense des Commerçants et Artisans* (UDCA), it captured a majority in the elections of the Chamber of Commerce of Lot. The surrounding *départements* were organised and Poujade embarked on the 'conquest of Paris': he wrote an open letter to the President of the Republic, lobbied members of parliament and organised mass meetings. The size of these meetings caused alarm – estimates of one at Versailles on 24 January 1955 gave the numbers of participants variously between 130,000 and 200,000. The government and members of parliament were concerned by the threat to public order and by the possible effects of movement on the imminent general election. Timely tax concessions were made in March 1955. Although the movement became involved in court cases and in various internal dissensions, its impetus did not seem to be affected. It won important successes in the 'social' elections of November 1955 and in the following months elected its entire list to the Paris Chamber of Commerce. Poujade, with the help of young and dynamic recruits such as Le Pen, Demarquet and Chevallet, turned the UDCA into a political party, *Unité et Fraternité Française*. They went on to conduct a tumultuous campaign for the parliamentary elections of 1956. Using the banal slogan *sortez les sortants*, populist propaganda themes such as condemnation of large capitalists and *les trusts apatrides*, nationalist attacks on the government parties for liquidating the empire and violent denunciations of the 'sectarians' of the Left, the Poujadists won two and a half million votes and fifty-two seats in the National Assembly.[2] The extent of this success was

[1] Many peasants voted for Poujade. He claimed 400,000; S. Hoffmann, *Le Mouvement poujade*, 1956, p. 335 estimates 350,000; J. Klatzmann in J. Fauvet, H. Mendras, op. cit., p. 48, estimates 14.5 per cent; but no peasant was elected as a Poujadist Deputy.

[2] For the basis of Poujadist electoral support see M. Duverger, F. Goguel, J. Touchard. *Les Elections du 2 janvier 1956*, 1957, pp. 477–82.

almost entirely unexpected, although the craven behaviour of some members of the CNIP indicated that they were, to some extent, aware of the threat posed by Poujadism. Neither the opinion polls nor experienced political observers had foreseen the size of the Poujadist vote. The appeal of the movement transcended its original sociological base, at least in the centre and the south of the country.

The campaign which Poujade had conducted, cynically exploiting every discontent which came to hand, did not provide a satisfactory basis for parliamentary action. The new parliament unseated eleven Poujadist Deputies for electoral fraud, allowing their opponents to take their places without ordering new elections: only Jean Chamant, later a Gaullist Minister in the Fifth Republic, refused to accept the seat of a disqualified Poujadist but he won the subsequent by-election. This process did not reflect much credit on the established parties but Poujade was quite unable to oppose it effectively or to exploit the discredit of parliament. Indeed he seemed unable to plan any parliamentary strategy at all. Although he had managed to intimidate a number of conservative Deputies in the previous parliament, he was not able to control his own followers. He turned on the neo-Fascist element in his movement, disowning for example Chevallet, the founder editor of *Fraternité française*, refused to ally himself with the most able tactician of the extreme Right Tixier-Vignancour, and astonished his associates by opposing the Anglo-French Suez expedition. The ultra-nationalist wing which contained all the relatively able Poujadist Deputies, notably Le Pen, Dides and Demarquet, rejected his lead over Suez. The others were of quite unusual mediocrity, most of them unable to make a speech or formulate a proposal. Alarm about the Poujadist phenomenon soon turned to derision: the Poujadist electorate melted away with Poujade himself receiving only half the votes in the Paris by-election in 1957 that the Poujadist candidate had obtained in the general election of the previous year. Feeling his influence draining away, Poujade attempted an alliance with his rival demagogues, Henri Dorgères and Paul Antier. The collapse of that alliance was followed by the complete disintegration of the Poujadist movement when, at the congress of *Unité et Fraternité Française* in 1958, Poujade disowned the Deputies who were still members of his party. Poujade, unlike most of his followers, opposed the return of de Gaulle in 1958.[1] Although he continued to run a newspaper and a skeleton

---

[1] This was because he thought he had been double-crossed by the Gaullists, F. Duprat, op. cit., p. 78. See also J. P. Sauvage, *Le Poujadisme de 1958 à 1968*, unpublished *mémoire*, 1970.

political party, he never regained a significant following. Eventually he even reconciled himself to de Gaulle.[1] Most of these who had joined his bandwagon disappeared from politics. Only two ex-Poujadists were re-elected to the National Assembly in 1958, one as a Gaullist, the other as a member of the CNIP. Some of the others reappeared from time to time, such as Le Pen in the entourage of Tixier-Vignancour for the presidential election of 1965, but none went on to play any major political role.

Poujadism was somewhat different from the other demagogic movements of the extreme Right. Although Poujade had a Maurrassian father and joined Doriot's PPF as a young man, the protest on which his movement was based and the milieu from which it sprang were not exclusively Right wing. The extreme Right elements were obvious enough. Poujade attracted ex-servicemen and neo-Fascist associates such as Chevallet, Demarquet, Dides and Le Pen who saw in him a great popular tribune who would overturn 'the system'. Some of his electoral support came from the most reactionary corners of France such as Vendée and 'little Vendée' in the Bouches-du-Rhône, although in Vendée, at least, Poujadism could be interpreted as a weakening of reactionary tradition of the area.[2] Part of the anti-regime, authoritarian protest vote which went to the Gaullists in 1951 was attracted to Poujadist candidates in 1956. The defence of economic backwardness was the most overtly reactionary of the Poujadist propaganda themes. But there was no consistency in Poujadism: it was anarchic, populist, 'radical' in the tradition of Alain, and too ill-disciplined to be a genuine Fascism. However, the Poujadist movement helped to elect a sufficient number of the extreme Right to disrupt sittings and bring an atmosphere of violent agitation to the National Assembly.

In the last two years of the Fourth Republic, the precise strength of a tendency which could be labelled as extreme Right is very hard to assess. Prior to 1956 there were up to fifty Deputies who had been associated in some way with extremist movements. But involvement in *ligueur* politics in the 1930s, as François Mitterrand's youthful royalism indicates, did not necessarily imply a continuing commitment to extremist positions. A large proportion of the members of the Independent and Peasant groups made extreme nationalist remarks from time to time and some even made anti-Semitic jibes,

[1] Allegations were made that he was bought by the Gaullists, F. Duprat, op. cit., p. 95.

[2] See M. Duverger, F. Goguel, J. Touchard, op. cit., pp. 178–80, 206–7, 401, 404, *passim*. S. Hoffmann, op. cit., pp. 190–2. P. M. Williams, *Crisis and Compromise*, 1964, pp. 166–7.

but they were not overtly anti-parliamentarian. A minority of the CNIP, the most notable being Pierre Montel, had connections with *intégriste* Catholic circles and ex-servicemen's organisations. But Deputies of the extreme Right were very few in numbers if current membership of 'extremist' political parties is taken as a definition of belonging to the extreme Right. In 1951 five members of *Réconciliation Française*, the successor party to La Rocque's *Parti Social Français* were elected – Aimé Paquet, Guy Petit, Philippe Olmi, Pierre de Léotard and Joseph Dixmier. Others were claimed as sympathisers such as the political chameleon, Bernard Lafay, who gave an emotional eulogy of La Rocque in a speech at the Mutualité on 6 July 1951. But these men developed very different views on policy issues: Aimé Paquet was, for example, a 'liberal' on Algerian policy whereas Joseph Dixmier was a hard core defender of *Algérie française*. The Pétainistes also put up candidates in the 1951 election on lists called *Union Nationale des Indépendants Républicains*. Jacques Isorni, who was encouraged to stand by Pierre-Etienne Flandin, and whose list included members with impressive Resistance credentials, was elected in Paris. Roger de Saivre in Oran and Paul Estèbe (a member of Pétain's personal staff until 1943 when he was arrested by the Germans) in Gironde were also successful. All these men were conservative by any standard. They disapproved of the workings of the institutions of the Fourth Republic, and by the middle of the 1950s were very firmly opposed to any concession to the Algerian nationalists. But it is very difficult to distinguish them by their general political attitudes or their positions on particular policies from conservatives who had quite different careers and associations. From 1956 the ultra-nationalist wing of the Poujadist movement with their would-be mentor, Jean-Louis Tixier-Vignancour, added a more strident, militant and genuinely anti-parliamentary element to the Right in the National Assembly. They contributed significantly by innuendo and abuse to the atmosphere of fear and insecurity of the last two years of the Fourth Republic. They did not last long: Tixier, Demarquet and Dides were not re-elected in 1958 and Le Pen lost his seat in the electoral holocaust of the extreme Right in 1962. In 1958, it is true they were briefly replaced by other men of similar temperament such as the ex-Prefect of Police, Jean Baylot, the lawyer agitator, Jean Biaggi (organiser of the riots against Guy Mollet in Algiers in 1956 and founder of the *Parti Patriote Révolutionnaire* in 1957) and Pierre Lagaillarde, an ex-paratrooper and former student leader in Algiers. The tense atmosphere of 1958 permitted their election but did not provide a springboard for durable careers: they all lost their seats in 1962. The attempts of the extreme Right to gain a foothold in the National Assembly were therefore notably unsuccessful in the long run. After the loss of Algeria, despite the persistence of counter-revolutionary traditions in some regions of the country, the extreme Right had no heartland to fall back on. The militants of the extreme Right were quite numerous in Paris, but not numerous enough to be an effective force in parliamentary elections. No effective leader emerged in 1958 or 1962 to rally a protest vote.

The Algerian War

The extra-parliamentary organisations of the extreme Right in the years from 1954 to 1962 are cloaked in deep and sometimes impenetrable obscurity. From the beginning of 1956, when the authority of the regime began to crumble, there were many reports of subversion and plotting. Some conspiracies existed only as far-fetched rumours and, although others had serious implications, there was a very high proportion of 'mythomanes' and of men with an interest in either exaggerating or obscuring their own role in this area of clandestine political activity. Unstable personalities were attracted by the fantasy and unreality of much of the scheming. Intimidation, terror and murder culminated in the Secret Army Organisation campaign in 1961 to 1962; all this put great personal strain on many of those involved, and helped to form unbalanced and apocalyptic views. As the end of the crisis approached there was a perceptible change of mood: desperation turned into apathy in many sections of the activist Right. The army, which seemed so thoroughly politicised in 1958, after a relatively modest purge and a rapid conversion, from anti-subversive to a nuclear strategy, reverted to political discretion after 1962. Even those soldiers imprisoned for acts of revolt and indiscipline did not conserve much of their activist temper.

There were only a small number of men involved directly in the *Algérie française* agitation who were both reliable and perceptive.[1] It is therefore doubtful whether it will ever be possible to write more than the most piecemeal history of the groups and organisations of the Algerian lobby. The impunity with which they operated and the connivance of some sections of the police forces, the extraordinary inadequacy of the evidence presented at some of the trials about what actually happened suggest that the police archives will not

[1] An example of such a man is the anonymous author of *OAS*, 1964, in the series *Archives* published by Juillard. This contains an important collection of documents. Also on the *OAS* see M. T. Lancelot, *L'Organisation de l'Armée Secrète*, 2 vols, 1963. J. Susini, *Histoire de l'OAS*, 1963.

furnish the material for an illuminating conspectus. A selection of the groups does, however, give a fair indication of the types of activity and the range of people involved. Amongst those which received the most attention were the *Centre d'Etudes Politiques et Civiques, Jeune Nation, Mouvement d'Action Civique et Sociale, Mouvement de la Jeunesse Combattante et Syndicaliste, Mouvement Populaire Français, Mouvement Populaire du 13 Mai, Mouvement pour l'Instauration d'un Ordre Corporatif, Comité de Vigilance pour l'Indépendance Nationale*. There were many others – *Union de la Jeunesse Nationale de la France, Comité de Jeunes Patriotes, Parti Patriote Révolutionnaire, Ligue Nationaliste, Centre National d'Action Civique, Front National Français*: there were probably over a thousand in total. Some were very secretive about their existence and were hardly known outside the circle of their own members. The study groups led the most public existence. The *Centre d'Etudes Politiques et Civiques*, whose honorary President until his death was General Weygand, had none of the attributes of a clandestine society. Its connections with financial and industrial milieux were unusual, and it was disliked by members of other groups because of these associations. It was execrated after 1958 by some of the most extreme because it was hostile to de Gaulle only by implication. After 1960, its official position was a 'realist' support of the government's policy in Algeria. But it had strong North African connections and there were many personal contacts between its members and activist defenders of *Algérie française*. The first President of the Centre was Alfred Pose, the director of the African section of the Banque Nationale du Crédit Industriel, and its members included men such as Victor Berger-Vachon, one time President of the Algerian Assembly. The industrialists who participated in the Centre covered a wide range of activities from the traditional family firm in the textile industry to the technologically advanced and modern sectors. Between these limits could be found men whose interests were in publishing, cement, engineering, and distilling.

The Centre was founded in 1954 and published two periodicals (*Cahiers du CEPEC* and *Courrier du CEPEC*) as well as a series of occasional papers on specialised topics. The brochure defining the aims of the Centre stated that:

'The spiritual development of the managers of the economy requires a political culture and a civic conscience as well as moral and social education.'[1]

The Centre did not produce propaganda for a mass audience but

[1] *Centre d'Etudes Politiques et Civiques*, Brochure, 1954, p. 2.

for one which it considered to be the elite of the nation. It had some interest in change and reform, but it was very much the intellectual Right of the employers' movement. It had strong personal and intellectual associations with the technocratic element of the Vichy regime. For example, Louis Salleron, the architect of the Peasant Corporation in the Vichy period, was an active member. The political aims of the organisers of the Centre remained enigmatic. Beneath its apparently reasonable and unemotional propaganda there was an ambition to group the movements of the Right under its intellectual leadership. As a network of influential contacts with the organisational potential to expand rapidly in a variety of directions, the Centre d'Etudes possessed resources for a major political role if events had been favourable.

The other study groups of the extreme Right were of a very different character. One which achieved considerable notoriety because of its penetration of the officer corps was the Centre d'Etudes Supérieures de Psychologie Sociale founded by a bizarre figure, Georges Sauge.[1] It operated on the intégriste fringe of the Church, following a policy line more in keeping with the nineteenth-century syllabus of errors than with the sentiments of the majority of French Catholics in the mid-twentieth century. It was viewed with distaste even by conservative Catholics because of Sauge's Manichaean view of the world. But he appealed to some officers working in psychological warfare who felt the need for an aggressive ideology to combat Algerian nationalism and the international Communist movement which they were convinced lay behind it. Several members of the study group, including army officers, subsequently joined the OAS; whether Sauge was himself a member is not clear. He was arrested twice in 1960, but no charges were preferred against him. The activities of his group were bounded by the Algerian affair (although his lettre d'information did not cease publication until 1964) and in this respect it differed from a group with which it had some affinity, the Cité Catholique. The Centre d'Etudes Critiques et de Synthèse, the full title of Cité Catholique, represented a tendency with a long history within the Church.[2] The ultras or the intégristes, as they were usually called, enjoyed some influential ecclesiastical support. Although not all of the intégristes were members of Cité

---

[1] W. Bosworth, Catholicism and Crisis in Modern France, 1962, pp. 184–5, 336. J. Maître, 'Catholicisme d'extrême droite et croisade anti-subversive', Revue Française de sociologie, vol. 2, 1961, pp. 107–17.

[2] The periodical Verbe was associated with Cité Catholique and is an essential source for its doctrines and positions. See also H. Fesquet, 'Verbe, revue de la Cité Catholique, renie les principes de la révolution', le Monde, 9 July 1958.

Catholique, it represents their view that the Algerian War was the last of a long series of occasions on which their bitter enemies, the liberal or progressive Catholics, had shown a lack of judgement and appreciation of the true interests and teaching of the Church. In some respects similar to *Opus Dei* in Spain, with its heterogeneous membership and quest for secular influences, it was on the other hand very much less successful. Both *Cité Catholique* and Sauge's association had the characteristics of a Freemasonry of the Right: their members believed with unshakeable conviction in the rectitude of their cause and placed great importance on intelligence networks and secrecy.

These and other study groups attempted with various degrees of persistence and success to establish consistent doctrines and policy positions. In this emphasis they were unlike the groups involved in direct political action. The main function of the programme of these latter groups was to exacerbate political conflict, raise the temperature of debate by aggressive slogans, and encourage the polarisation of opinion to the benefit of those who proposed extreme solutions to the country's problems. They were devoted more to propaganda by deed than the slow process of political education.

Jeune Nation and the groups which later emerged from it epitomised the activism of the extreme Right during the decolonisation period.[1] *Jeune Nation* first received widespread public notice in October 1954 when the newspaper of the Communist Party, *l'Humanité*, accused members of the movement of wrecking a delivery truck and destroying 25,000 copies of the newspaper. The first congress of *Jeune Nation* was held in the following year (November 1955) and, after a brief career of subversion, it was banned on 15 May 1958. Its programme, as developed at the 1955 congress and in subsequent pronouncements, was overtly Fascist; it called for a national revolution, the suppression of elections and parties, the exclusion of *métèques* from positions of political and economic responsibility, punishment of those responsible both for the death of Frenchmen since 1940 and for the loss of colonial territories, abolition of *capitalisme apatride*, the establishment of a corporate system, the restoration of dignity to the army, opposition to Russian and American materialistic imperialism and the construction of a Europe from 'Brest to Bucharest'. The movement adopted the Celtic Cross as its insignia and under the leadership of Dominique Venner and the four Sidos brothers (whose father, a militant in the leagues of the extreme Right of the 1930s had become a Vichy *milicien* and was executed at

[1] For a partisan account of *Jeune Nation* and its successor groups, see F. Duprat, op. cit., pp. 56–7, 70–4, 87–93, *passim*.

the Liberation), it specialised in violent direct action. Various terrorist acts were ascribed to it, such as a bomb placed in the lavatory of
the Palais Bourbon in February 1958.

As the regime weakened, the strength of *Jeune Nation* seemed to
grow. Over three thousand supporters could be assembled for mass
meetings and, as its confidence in organising public demonstrations
increased, the government became alarmed. *Jeune Nation* was heavily
involved in the plotting which accompanied the end of the Fourth
Republic. Some of its members took part in the storming of the
government headquarters in Algiers on 13 May and in the demonstrations on the Champs-Elysées which followed. The government
took action against it – after banning its participation in the fête of
Jeanne d'Arc on 11 May, the Pflimlin government dissolved it by
decree on 15 May. Publicity for the movement continued through a
publishing house, the *Société de Presse et d'Edition de la Croix
Céltique*, and a periodical, *Jeune Nation*, the first number of which
appeared in July 1958. This publication was frequently seized because of articles defending *Algérie Française* activists and attacking
the head of state. Eventually it ceased publication in the final stage
of the Algerian conflict because of internal divisions within the editorial board. Many contributors were also actively involved in the
Secret Army Organisation.

Jeune Nation, however, was reincarnated in two new movements.
The Sidos brothers went separate ways; Jacques was sentenced to
ten years' imprisonment for OAS activities; François founded, with
Dominique Venner, the review *Europe-Action* which became the
basis of the political movement of the same name; Pierre founded
Occident in 1964. The organisers of *Europe-Action* had all been
heavily committed to the cause of French Algeria. The publisher,
Suzanne Gingembre, was the wife of the treasurer of the OAS;
Dominique Venner had been condemned to a three-year sentence
for plotting against the State; Jacques de Larocque-Latour had
served a prison term for subversion. Dominique Venner, the principal theorist of the group, attempted to grapple with the implications
of defeat in the struggle to keep Algeria French. In his view it marked
the end of the European colonialism: the Portuguese territories in
Africa were unimportant; without colonies to divide them, the
characteristics and interests common to the European peoples were
more obvious. The European peoples had the same external rivals
and enemies, and the same internal forces sapped their morale. As
European civilisation was becoming more unified it was crucially
important, Venner argued, for Europeans to co-operate to defend
their superior values against those who, in the name of equality and

liberty, promoted the interests of the Third World and of Communism. His arguments were tinged with racialism – *Europe-Action* opposed coloured immigration into France and dwelt at length on crimes committed in France by Algerians. The periodical was particularly insistent that France should end her economic aid to ex-colonies. Pierre Sidos attacked *Europe-Action* for being 'apatride' and materialistic although, by adopting the conventional extreme Right theme of defence of the West against Communism, *Occident* had a Europeanism of its own. This and other doctrinal differences between *Europe-Action* and *Occident* were little more than pretexts for a family quarrel of unusual intensity. Tactical positions often seemed to be chosen to emphasise the differences between them; for example, in the Presidential elections of 1965, *Europe-Action* was for and *Occident* against Tixier-Vignancour.

In October 1964, as a response to the establishment of *Occident* as a political movement, *Europe-Action* founded 'support committees', ostensibly to promote circulation.[1] These were successfully established in large cities which had nationalist and *Algérie française* traditions such as Paris, Lyons, Toulouse and Marseilles, and attracted support from members of defunct organisations such as the *Parti Patriote Révolutionnaire* (Biaggi's party), the *Parti Nationaliste* and *Jeune Nation*; the *Fédération des Etudiants Nationalistes* also joined forces for a time with *Europe-Action*. It appeared at this time to have wider support and to be more intelligently led than *Occident*, but the latter eventually attracted more attention. Both engaged in a certain amount of propaganda by deed, attacking opponents' meetings and assaulting newspaper vendors. This gained the attention of the national press in the relatively fallow years of Right-wing activism in the middle of the 1960s.

In 1968 *Occident* gained international renown. Its threats to clear the 'Bolshevik vermin' out of the Sorbonne caused the rector of the University of Paris to call in the police to disperse Cohn-Bendit and his followers, a decision which sparked off the events of May 1968. Disorder or the threat of it has always been an important stimulus to Right-wing activists. But in 1968 the belief was too widely held that the riot police were a better instrument to cope with students' riots than *Occident* or other strong arm men of the extreme Right. The atmosphere of the Latin Quarter and other university centres carried along some of the extreme Right groups in the general spirit of 'contestation', whilst others felt impotent to challenge the dominant

[1] A. Laurens, 'Nouveaux visages de l'extrême droite', *le Monde*, 1, 2, 3 March 1965. W. R. Tucker, 'The new look of the extreme Right in France', *Western Political Quarterly*, vol. 21, 1968, pp. 86–97.

leftist forces. *Occident* did not attract many followers even among those Right-wing university students determined to do battle with the *gauchistes*. It was dissolved by the government in 1968 but its members continued to be active and publicity seeking. Pierre Sidos attempted to stand as a presidential candidate in 1969, but the constitutional council refused his candidature. The disorders of May–June 1968 revived the Maurrassian rather than the proto-Fascist Right. *Jeune Nation* and its successor groups belonged to the generation of the Algerian War and they continued to bear the marks of their defeat in that struggle when a younger generation of activists, like public opinion at large, had lost all interest in it.

During the Algerian War, *Jeune Nation* had many emulators. One example was the *Mouvement National Révolutionnaire* founded in 1956 by Jean Daspre. Like *Jeune Nation*, it was first noticed in the press following a violent demonstration, on this occasion against Mendès-France in 1957. The movement differed in some respects from *Jeune Nation*. It was more anti-Semitic, although the only reason for this seemed to be the disposition of its leader. Daspre was also in much closer contact with the extreme Right in other countries, particularly Italy and Portugal. Although its activities and membership are obscure, it attracted publicity through the violent tone of its newsletter (circulated to all Deputies and to the national press). This earned for it the probably undeserved reputation of spokesmen of the *ultra* milieu. Its membership was very diverse – a small student following in Paris and Marseilles (where Daspre himself had been a student); a peasant agitator, formerly an important member of the Poujadist movement, Léon Dupont, and some of his followers from Ardennes and eastern France; representatives of the old *ligueur* tradition such as Guy Charles-Vallin, son of La Rocque's deputy; an Algerian connection through Antoine Cozzolini; and even a former Gaullist, Georges Adam, who was the MNR chief of the Paris region. Although there was some attempt to give the movement a structure and a programme, it remained primarily a network of *Algérie française* supporters in metropolitan France. It was banned during the Barricades affair in Algiers in January 1960 because of its enthusiastic support for Ortiz and Lagaillarde. It had no successor group and Daspre faded into obscurity.

Some other organisations stated that their origins and purpose were exclusively to defend the cause of French Algeria. One of these was the *Mouvement Populaire du 13 mai* (MP 13), founded in the summer of 1958 by General Chassin (who had melodramatically taken to the maquis in May 1958) and Robert Martel. It was the public wing of a clandestine network called the 'Grand O' which had the reputation before and during the events of May 1958 of being the new *Cagoule*.[1] For a short period MP 13 was considered to be of some importance because of the notoriety of its leaders and its potential for direct action in Algeria where it had a relatively large popular following. Robert Martel had a long career of political conspiracy reaching back to the Third Republic and was the President of one of the *colon* organisations, the *Union Française Nord-Africaine*. Chassin had a distinguished military record as an air-force general and possessed a flair for self-advertisement: he stood against Chaban-Delmas in the second constituency of Gironde in November 1958 with the slogan Cha-Cha-Cha (Chassin chassera Chaban) but was decisively defeated. Early in 1959, after the death of his wife, Chassin withdrew from the association leaving control to Martel. Martel was a reactionary in the *intégriste* Catholic and corporatist tradition: he was also strongly anti-Gaullist.

Martel's views caused divisions very quickly in the movement: in the referendum of September 1958 its members were allowed freedom of vote because they would not follow Martel's absolute hostility to de Gaulle. Martel finally destroyed MP 13 because he could not resist being in the thick of conspiratorial activity. Although he suspected that the whole affair had been provoked by the government both to compromise the partisans of French Algeria and to obtain full powers, he went to join Ortiz and Lagaillarde on the barricades in Algiers in January 1960.[2] The Algerian sections of MP 13 were dissolved by the government, the metropolitan branch split, Martel went into hiding and, after the end of 1960, little was heard of the movement. It had a fairly elaborate structure for a party which effectively lasted only two years – an annual congress, a national executive committee composed half of representatives of the professions and half of the regions, nine regional committees with authority over sections in the *départements* and *communes* and, under the title of *Conseil National des Métiers*, a number of fringe or front organisations. The pretentiousness of this structure illustrates the seriousness with which the leaders regarded the possibility of a 'national revolution' at this time.

With the possible exception of the Vichy period, the eight years of the Algerian War were the most favourable historical context which the extreme Right had enjoyed during the twentieth century. Although the fears that it might seize power have, with hindsight, seemed exaggerated, its resources were considerable and its activities

[1] M. and S. Bromberger, *Les Treize complots du treize mai*, 1959, pp. 9, 81–4, *passim*. J. R. Tournoux, *Les Secrets d'état*, 1960, pp. 73–88, 180–95.
[2] M. and S. Bromberger *et al.*, *Colonels et barricades*, 1960, pp. 46, 72, 102.

alarming. It had the support of important elements in the army and most of the European population of Algeria, intelligence networks within the administration, shock troops capable of intimidating opponents and an issue, at least until 1959–60, on which to mobilise mass enthusiasm. The Secret Army Organisation led by General Salan, supported by other army officers such as General Jouhaud and Colonels Broizat, Argoud and Gardes and by civilians such as Jean-Jacques Susini, Pierre Lagaillarde and Maurice Gingembre, was the apotheosis of the French Algeria extremism. It engaged in plastic bomb attacks, assassinations and, finally, when it knew the cause was lost, a scorched earth tactic. Although it lasted little more than a year, from the summer of 1961 to the summer of 1962, and had the specific purpose of preventing Algerian independence, there was an attempt to give it a general political and constitutional programme. But the OAS, like the whole of the extreme Right, laboured under the serious handicaps of sectarianism, lack of able leadership and the usually passive, but very real hostility of the great majority of the French population. Paranoia was a prominent feature in the mental universe of the OAS and of the extreme Right as a whole. Conspiracies, betrayals and persecution were identified in the most unlikely places.[1] The extent of the paranoia was justified by the knowledge that the extreme Right was a small minority whose ideas were detested and whose activities were repellent to the great majority of their fellow citizens.

The feelings of persecution and extreme suspicions of the motives of others made co-operation between individuals and between groups of the extreme Right almost impossible. It was very difficult for relatively competent leaders to establish themselves. When the principal parliamentary defenders of French Algeria – Duchet, Bidault, Morice and Soustelle – tried, in 1959, to organise a broad movement, called the Rassemblement de l'Algérie Française, based on the Colloques de Vincennes, they were automatically suspect both because of their past and their presumed future intentions. The only type of man not suspect in the circles of the extreme Right was the unpolitical or politically naïve army officer. It was, therefore, virtually impossible for a politically skilful leader of impressive personal stature to emerge as federator of the extreme Right-wing groups. Within groups, paranoia encouraged factionalism; even the smallest and the most para-military were split by acrimonious personal feuds. The justified fear that police informers had penetrated the organisation

[1] See works on *OAS* referred to above, p. 280, footnote 1, and F. Carreras, *L'Accord FLN-OAS*, 1967. Morland, Barange, Martinez, *Histoire de l'Organisation de l'Armée Secrète*, 1964.

fed the fires of mutual suspicion. The failure to win the struggle to keep Algeria French stimulated further dissensions between and within the groups.

Algerian independence was a serious blow for the extreme Right: many activists had been involved in clandestine activities which ended in prison terms, exile or silent obscurity. The organisations which withered included not only those specifically devoted to the defence of French Algeria, but also others which predated the terrorist phase of the struggle and had more comprehensive programmes. The trials of the leading OAS figures, Salan, Degueldre, Bastien-Thiry aroused no great popular indignation, even when Bastien-Thiry was executed for his part in an attempted assassination of General de Gaulle. As after the collapse of Vichy, an earnest desire to forget the whole episode was apparent, despite Soustelle's assertion that 'the page has not been turned'.[1] On the extreme Right there was a deep sense of injustice and an emotional campaign was conducted on behalf of those imprisoned for subversive activities. The legal counsel of the most prominent of those involved in the OAS had a great public relations success: just as Jacques Isorni became nationally known as defence lawyer for Marshal Pétain, so Tixier-Vignancour acquired a similar reputation as counsel for Salan, Bastien-Thiry and others. There were, however, differences between the two men. Isorni was unknown before he obtained his celebrated brief: Tixier-Vignancour had a career going back to 1936 when he was first elected as Deputy for Basses-Pyrénées.[2] He went on to become Under-Secretary of State for Information at Vichy, successfully practised at the Paris bar after the war, specialising in cases with political overtones, and was a brilliantly obstructive Deputy for Basses-Pyrénées in the last parliament of the Fourth Republic before he acquired a national reputation and following in the 1960s.

Tixier-Vignancour's bid for the Presidency[3]

Tixier-Vignancour's announcement on 22 April 1964 that he would be a candidate at the presidential elections of 1965 marked the effective end of his involvement in the Algerian question. Parallel to this

[1] J. Soustelle, *La Page n'est pas tournée*, 1965.

[2] Some biographical details can be found in the campaign biography, J. Mabire, *Histoire d'un français, Tixier-Vignancour*, 1965. He published a selection of his pleas in 'political' trials, J. L. Tixier-Vignancour, *J'ai choisi la défense*, 1964.

[3] See F. Costa, *L'Extrême droite et les élections de 1965*, unpublished *mémoire*, 1966. A. Christnacht, *Aspects de la campagne présidentielle de M. Tixier-Vignancour*, unpublished *mémoire*, 1967. Y. Madiot, *L'Extrême droite et l'élection présidentielle de décembre 1965*, unpublished *mémoire*, 1966.

announcement, an attempt was made to federate the various strands of the extreme Right in a *Bureau de Liaison de l'Opposition Nationale*. This initiative languished because of the usual factionalism and because of personal opposition to Tixier-Vignancour by Pierre Poujade and others. Tixier based his campaign upon a personal organisation, the *Comité National Tixier-Vignancour*, whose central offices he inaugurated on 5 November 1964.[1] At the peak of his campaign, 52,000 members were claimed and eighty committees established in the *départements*. Tixier's propaganda drive was of impressive energy. In the eighteen months before the election he spoke in every town with a population over 50,000 and, in the summer of 1965, he took a caravan the whole length of the French coastline from Dunkirk to Menton, addressing meetings in all the resorts. A propaganda periodical, *T-V Demain*, was published monthly in the last ten months before the election in runs of over 80,000. Tixier-Vignancour asserted that the funds for his campaign came entirely from subscriptions and from the revenue raised from the sale of books and recordings (particularly of his defence of OAS terrorists).

At the beginning of his campaign Tixier-Vignancour was, as he had been since 1936, unequivocally identified with the extreme Right. His entourage in the *Comité T-V* included the extreme Right ex-Deputies Le Pen and Lacoste-Lareymondie. Other committee members were Colonel Thomazo, an important conspirator in 1958 who had left the UNR over Algeria, and Dominique Venner of *Jeune Nation* and *Europe-Action*. As well as these individuals, a number of extreme Right groups publicly announced their support. They included *Europe-Action*, *Fédération des Etudiants Nationalistes*, *Union des Intellectuels Indépendants*, *Fédération des Français d'Algérie*, *Amis d'Antoine Argoud* (the OAS leader) and *Convention Paysanne* (led by Henri Dorgères). He also had the support of *Rivarol* and the *Action Française* weekly, *Aspects de la France*. By no means all the extreme Right rallied to Tixier-Vignancour's candidature: some periodicals contented themselves by being merely anti-Gaullist, whilst others, including some with the largest circulations such as *Carrefour* and *Minute*, seemed completely indifferent to the outcome of the election. There were a few eccentrics who rallied to de Gaulle and even to Mitterand (for example ex-Captain Sergent, a leader of the OAS).[2] The main rival to Tixier and the candidate who most damaged his electoral strategy was Jean Lecanuet, the President of

[1] *Candide*, 10, 17 December 1964.
[2] A. Laurens, 'Les Grandes manœuvres de l'opposition nationale', *le Monde*, 2 March 1965.

the *Mouvement Républicain Populaire*. On the extreme Right Isorni, Soustelle, Poujade, Antier, Sauge as well as the conservative wing of the Church represented by *La France Catholique* preferred Lecanuet to Tixier-Vignancour (who was not a character who appealed to the devout).

Early in his campaign Tixier attempted to widen the basis of his support by refusing to accept the extreme Right label.[1] He was supported in this by the journal *l'Esprit public*, founded as a monthly in 1960 by Philippe Marçais, a Deputy from Algeria. *L'Esprit public* was the main platform of the exiled ex-Prime Minister Georges Bidault. Although defending French Algeria with such virulence that it was suspected of being the public arm of the OAS, *l'Esprit public* condemned racialism in all its forms, and claimed that its social policy was Left wing and its international policy in line with the MRP. Articles attacking Catholic priests and laity who held liberal views on Algeria and a serialised biography of Tixier-Vignancour by Jean Mabire gave the impression of a preponderance of extreme Right-wing views, although it drew its inspiration from Lyautey and the heroic aspects of French colonialism. From 1963 the journal, and from 1964 the movement, the *Rassemblement de l'Esprit Public*, was primarily concerned to prepare the ground for a return to France of Georges Bidault and to secure for him a central place in the political life of the country. Tixier-Vignancour hinted that, if elected President, he would make Bidault his Prime Minister. Bidault probably had no illusions about Tixier-Vignancour's chances of success, but regarded the presidential campaign as an opportunity to keep his own name before the public eye and prepare the climate for his return to France. As it turned out, the students in May 1968 were unwittingly more effective than Tixier-Vignancour in creating conditions which permitted the dropping of charges against Bidault.

In addition to enlisting the support of the *Esprit Public* group, Tixier tried to take over the mantle of Pinay by claiming to be the candidate of the 'liberal' and of the 'national' opposition. Although he neither abandoned the symbols nor ceased to mention the names which the extreme Right applauded, he progressively took up the traditional moderate Republican themes. This strategy was destroyed when Jean Lecanuet decided to stand and the majority of the prominent figures in the CNIP rallied to his candidature. Tixier was therefore thrown back on his original clientele: despite a vigorous campaign he obtained only one and a quarter million votes or 5 per cent of the votes cast, compared with Lecanuet's 17 per cent. He received as high a proportion of the extreme Right-wing vote as

[1] See especially, *le Monde*, 29 May 1965.

it was perhaps possible for a single candidate to gather and a high proportion of the votes of the *rapatriés* from Algeria.

It was not a very encouraging result but, like his rivals Lecanuet and Mitterrand, he attempted to use the Presidential campaign as a springboard for establishing a permanent political organisation.[1] His motley alliance of monarchists, nationalists, neo-Fascists and political adventurers, united only in detestation of both de Gaulle and Communism, did not survive the election. Apparently undismayed, Tixier founded in 1966 the more narrowly based *Alliance Républicaine pour la Liberté et le Progrès*. As the name of the party suggests, he was trying to establish himself more in the mainstream of the moderate Republican tradition and to defend what he called the *bourgeoisie de tradition* against the *bourgeoisie de l'argent*. But his party failed to make any impression in the parliamentary elections of 1967. His personal evolution away from extremism however, continued: he moderated his opposition to Gaullism and, in 1969, supported Georges Pompidou. The reasons for this evolution are fairly clear. Both the exploitation of scandal and 'political' court cases had sharply diminishing returns in the immediate post-colonial period. Excepting the campaign of amnesty for those sentenced for terrorist or subversive activities during the Algerian war, there was no issue on which the extreme Right could launch a campaign. Algerian *rapatriés* reverted to traditional 'socio-economic' voting behaviour. Marginal economic groups, partly as a result of the Poujadist debacle, did not seek political spokesmen but took to direct action on their own account in defence of their interests. The quiescence of the Communist Party and increasing prosperity caused the old *ligueur* tradition to decay in bourgeois circles. One important stimulus of nationalist extremism, the wounded sentiments felt during the humiliations of the twenty-five years preceding 1962, was removed by de Gaulle's arrogant assertion of French independence in foreign policy. Many militants of the extreme Right felt that the world was changing rapidly around them and that they were becoming 'forgotten men'.

The 'events' of May 1968

In this situation, the oldest of the activist groups of the extreme Right, the monarchists, emerged as the best able to survive and attract young recruits. Durability, a consistent doctrine and a refusal to become totally committed to short-term objectives help explain the modest revival of an apparently archaic movement. The

[1] 'Les forces politiques au lendemain de l'élection présidentielle', *Revue française de science politique*, vol. 16, 1966, pp. 161 ff.

first official national organisation of Maurrassian inspiration in the Fourth Republic was the *Service de Propagande et des Amis d'Aspects de la France*, founded almost contemporaneously with the newspaper. This changed its name in 1955 to *Restauration Nationale, Centre de Propagande Royaliste et d'Action Française*. Various other *Action Française* organisations were established or revived in the decade after the first issue of *Aspects de la France* in 1947 – *Cercle Fustel de Coulanges, Association d'Anciens Combattants Marius Plateau, Institut de Politique Nationale, Association Professionnelle de la Presse Monarchique et Catholique* (whose President was the former Vichy Minister, Xavier Vallat) and *Institut d'Action Française*.[1] No organisational links tied these groups together and tensions within and between them similar to those of the inter-war years reappeared over the religious question (some leaning towards the defence of the Church for secular reasons, whilst others belonged to the *intégriste* tendency within Catholicism), over general strategy (the dogmatists were almost mystics in their belief that they bore witness to millennial political truths, whereas the activists wanted to involve the movement directly in the issues of the day) and over the person of the Pretender who showed no desire to tie his political destiny to the fortunes of relatively obscure extremist organisations.

These tensions lay behind the split in 1954, led by Pierre Boutang and Michel Vivier. In 1955 Boutang and his friends produced a rival newspaper *la Nation française* and established *Cercles de la Nation française* to rival the *Restauration Française* movement. Although there were also personal issues behind the split, Boutang was the leader of the 'revisionist' wing. He wished to reinterpret the Maurrassian doctrine in the light of post-war experience as well as to bring the monarchist movement closer to the Count de Paris. A political theorist of considerable subtlety, he attracted an impressive range of contributors to his newspaper such as the Duke de Lévis Mirepoix, Louis Salleron, Philippe Ariès, Louis Pauwels, Gabriel Marcel, Paul Sérant and Roger Nimier. Not all were convinced monarchists but all wished either to express fidelity to the commitments of their youth or to maintain a valuable political tradition. Boutang and the Count de Paris earned hostility on the extreme Right because they came to accept the principle of self-determination for Algeria and gave qualified support to de Gaulle. The Pretender, after his return to France (following the abrogation in May 1950 of the law of 1883 which exiled claimants to the French throne) maintained his own political bureau and published until January 1967 a newsletter, *Bulletin mensuel d'information*. He had social relations with many of

[1] S. M. Osgood, *French Royalism since 1870*, 1971, ch. 11.

the leading figures of both the Fourth and the Fifth Republics and presented himself as a figure who could be accepted by the great majority of moderate Frenchmen in a situation of grave crisis. His political statements were moderate and well-informed, completely lacking the sectarian extremism and bitterness inseparable from the *Action Française* tradition. His political tactics, however, appeared on occasion both comical and pathetic because of the improbability of a restoration of the monarchy.[1]

The *Association Générale des Légitimistes de France* which pressed the claims of Jacques-Henri de Bourbon, Duke of Anjou and of Segovia, descendant of the second grandchild of Louis XIV, and the *Cercle Louis XIV* whose candidate for the throne was Xavier de Bourbon-Parme, also a descendant of Louis XIV, were usually regarded as frivolous oddities even by royalists. All the pretenders, but particularly the Count de Paris, were given publicity in the popular press. They were celebrities treated much in the same way as sportsmen, film stars and the very rich. The opinions and person of the Count de Paris were accorded some respect by Republican officials and leading politicians, but he had little influence in any political milieu. *Restauration Nationale*, on the other hand, was capable of mobilising genuine enthusiasm in the aftermath of the events of May 1968.[2]

The main characteristics of *Restauration Nationale* were much the same as those of *Action Française* in the Third Republic. Pierre Pujo, editor of *Aspects de la France*, and son of the founder member of *Action Française*, Maurice Pujo, defended the purity of the doctrine of Charles Maurras. *Restauration Nationale*, like the *Ligue de l'Action Française*, refused to commit itself seriously to battles which had to be fought within the framework of the existing constitutional system or to allies who accepted that system. A typical example of this was its position during the presidential campaign of 1965. Anti-Gaullism and the opportunity to make propaganda encouraged *Restauration Nationale* to support Tixier-Vignancour during this campaign, even though in principle it opposed 'plebiscitary democracy' exemplified by the system of direct election for the Presidency of the Republic. The attitude of the movement was summarised at the 1964 congress of the movement by Bernard Mallet, the President of the *comités directeurs de l'Action Française:*

'Firstly, we realise – and Mᵉ Tixier-Vignancour realises it too – that nothing good can come out of an election by universal suffrage.

[1] L. Bourdier, *Le Comte de Paris: un cas politique*, 1965.
[2] P. Grover, *Histoire de la Restauration Nationale*, unpublished *mémoire*, 1970.

Secondly, our first duty is to use all our resources to work for the re-establishment of the monarchy. However, the election of one candidate rather than another is not a matter of indifference to us, because we are citizens. But the nature of the process means that the election is not central to our preoccupations as Frenchmen desirous of building the future of our country on durable foundations. We are happy to see Me Tixier-Vignancour, in deciding to stand, publicise throughout the country certain truths. We are supporting him at his meetings ... but our militants ought not to desert indefinitely their specific combat, in other words the process of education and propaganda in all the traditional forms of *Action Française* ... our militants who have limited time at their disposal, ought not to deflect their energies from the main objective – the re-establishment of the monarchy.'[1]

This lukewarm support never became more enthusiastic, despite previous involvement in the common cause of *Algérie française*. There were, of course, some monarchists who followed the lead of the Pretender, the Count de Paris, and refused any involvement with Tixier-Vignancour.

After the election, *Restauration Nationale* quickly disassociated itself from Tixier-Vignancour and ceased to participate in electoral politics. Its attitude in the 1969 electoral campaign was in marked contrast to that of 1965: *Aspects de la France* stressed that *Action Française* felt no need to choose between two forms of Republic. The criticism directed at Alain Poher, the Democratic Centre candidate, were, however, particularly severe. Pierre Juhel, the Secretary General of *Restauration Nationale*, in a sentence which recalled the deep animosity towards Christian Democracy going back to the days of the Sillon, remarked: 'The Christian Democrats are the worst, opposed as they are to any political revival of France.'[2]

The monotonous repetition of Maurrassian teachings about the nefarious activities of the *métèques*, intellectual anarchy, and integral nationalism brought modest returns after the events of May 1968. In the student milieu, both in the *lycées* and the universities, *Restauration Nationale* appealed to some of those who were alarmed by the disorder and who were intensely hostile to the *gauchistes* whether anarchist, Trotskyite, Maoist, situationist or of any other sect. *Restauration Nationale* had more appeal after May 1968 than other movements of the extreme Right because it was better organised and was intellectually more respectable. As well as having a long

[1] *Le Monde*, 3 March 1965.
[2] ibid., 28 February 1970.

continuous history and a coherent view of the university, it was also prepared to engage in direct action. In order to recruit and maintain the allegiance of several hundred young people, *Restauration Nationale* worked hard on study groups and propaganda activities. The condition of the universities was the principal area of concern after 1968. There were frequent denunciations of 'the university corrupted by democracy' and 'colonised by Communists' in which 'the children of Edgar [Faure] were aware only of drugs and eroticism'.[1] *Restauration Nationale* called for a 'third force' in the university between the *gauchistes* and the university authorities to wreck the Faure law reforming the universities. The dismantling of the Faure law was necessary, according to *Restauration Nationale*, to restore order in the universities.

The slogan commonly used by *Restauration Nationale, monarchie populaire*, hinted at the anti-capitalist theme which had been voiced in all movements of the extreme Right since the beginning of the Third Republic. This tradition was reinvigorated by the events of May 1968. Some of the militants of the extreme Right came to denounce capitalist and 'consumer' society with as much force as the 'new' Left. One group (*Pour une jeune Europe*) attempted a synthesis between the ideas of May and the traditions of the Right. Members of another (*Jeune Révolution*) ranked the Gaullists before the Communists among their enemies and hinted that they did not feel very hostile to the *gauchistes*. The neo-Fascist extreme Right was aware that some of its better known recruits in the past had come from the extreme Left and it had no reason to reject recruits coming from that source. Also the absence of rich supporters, such as Mercier and Coty in the inter-war period, Christian Wolf in the decade after the Liberation and the rich *colons* of the period of decolonisation in North Africa, gave a freer reign to the anti-capitalist sentiments on the extreme Right.

Only a tiny number of *gauchistes* drifted towards the Right: a handful were to be found in *Ordre Nouveau*, one of the groups to be founded in the wake of the events of May 1968, by the Paris lawyer and university teacher, Jean-François Galvaire. The name *Ordre Nouveau* caused some confusion, but there were no connections between it and the monthly review of the same name founded in 1933 to which Denis de Rougemont, Daniel Rops and Robert Aron contributed. Although the *Ordre Nouveau* group of the 1930s included some who found Fascism appealing, it was very different in style to the extremism of Galvaire. Despite several successful meetings in the period 1969 to 1971 and guerilla activities within the

[1] Undated propaganda leaflet.

universities, *Ordre Nouveau* did not succeed in replacing the *Restauration Nationale* as the organiser of the biggest meetings and the most frequent confrontations with the revolutionary Left in a variety of untidy skirmishes.[1]

Conclusion

The history of the extreme Right in the quarter of a century after 1945 is a confused record of feuds, violence and inefficiency. The Right-wing men of revolutionary temperament who formed a bewildering array of associations, parties and leagues, scarcely seemed, at times, to be engaged in political activity but in a form of sociodrama involving elaborate fantasies about what had happened or what could happen. The difficulty which some had in distinguishing between fantasy and reality gave them a pathological appearance. They have an important place in the history of Right-wing politics because they illustrate traditions, ways of feeling and interests which were scarcely expressed by the electoral parties of the Right. A large number of people gained their political initiation in them because of the virtual absence of youth movements attached to the parliamentary parties of the Right. During the Fourth Republic men such as Bergasse in Marseilles and Raingeard in Nantes encouraged young people to work for and enter politics in the Independent interests, but at the national level the youth movements run by the Gaullists and the Independents were derisory until around 1965. In the middle of the 1960s there was a change when the Gaullist *Union des Jeunes pour le Progrès* and to a lesser extent Giscard d'Estaing's club, *Perspectives et Réalités*, acquired a genuine popular following. But prior to these developments, movements of the extreme Right played an influential role in political education. This tended to weaken both the authority of the parliamentary Right and loyalty to the constitutional order in Right-wing milieux. These consequences distorted perceptions of political action and political processes because, in contrast to the parliamentary Right involved in careers, compromises and manoeuvres in defence of sectional interests, the groups of the extreme Right represented a 'purer', less corrupt form of politics. As the participants saw it, they defined and defended certain basic truths and principles.

The overall influence exercised by the groups was similar to that of the literary figures of the Right. They contributed to a rather diffuse atmosphere of questioning, dissatisfaction and insecurity – but they were neither trusted nor followed by the conservative electorate. Although many of the leaders, particularly of the study groups, often

[1] For a contrary view see F. Duprat, op. cit., pp. 235–8.

had long careers in political agitation, they attracted a youthful following despite the fact that they had little new in programme or in doctrine. The only novel aspect of the post-1945 extreme Right was its Europeanism. Even this had its forerunners among the 'romantic' Fascists of the inter-war period and it had been a Collaborationist propaganda theme during the Second World War. Some groups such as *Occident*, which had a clear paternity in Collaboration, claimed that a new European nation was emerging, stretching from the Atlantic to the 'marches of the East'. Others defended a new cultural entity *européenne et multinationale* in a vague, somewhat contradictory manner. The sources of this Europeanism were various, the most potent being the almost inevitable Manichaean view of the world. In the case of the extreme Right the battle between good and evil was the clash of international Communism with 'the West'. As a consequence, the conviction developed during and after the war that the 'national' forces had to be organised on an international level in order to organise effective resistance. Only the Maurrassian *Restauration Nationale* stood out against this tendency, insisting that European union would mean domination by Germany. For the extreme Right, other than the Maurrassian, *la France seule* had become an archaic slogan.

Closer contacts and modern communications made it more difficult to found a racialist position on the biological or cultural differences between the French and other European nationalities, whereas a 'white man's' racialism remained potentially a persuasive ideology. Antipathy towards America, based on mistrust and xenophobia, was also an influence behind this Europeanism. America was the home of 'the international money power' and international trusts: behind the distasteful liberal ideology of official America, alleged the propagandists of the extreme Right, lay an imperialist drive towards domination of the European nations.

The extreme Right drew upon a fund of ideas which were already commonplace at the beginning of the twentieth century. The forms of organisation and the patterns of activity also had venerable antecedents. The agitators of the Fourth and Fifth Republics were in the *ligueur* tradition established before the turn of the century by men such as Déroulède and Guérin; the clandestine conspirators against those Republics were recognisable as descendants of the nineteenth century *ultras* of legitimist conspiracy and their twentieth century successors in the *Sapinière* and the *Cagoule*. After 1945 the traditions of polemic and behaviour were, however, manifest in a very different environment. The wartime experience had identified them with defeat. The international climate of the Cold War between

Churchill's Fulton speech and the death of Stalin, although stimulating, was not as encouraging to the extreme Right as the presence in other European countries of Fascist, Nazi and nationalist dictatorships in the 1930s. The process of decolonisation and the Algerian War gave the extreme Right an issue to exploit, a 'heartland' among the settlers of Algeria, and an opportunity to brand its opponents with the charge of incompetence and treason. But, although the Algerian crisis brought some army officers to the point of *pronunciamento*, a genuinely revolutionary situation seemed more remote than it had been during the economic depression of the inter-war period. The transference of power to de Gaulle in 1958 was neither a revolution nor even a situation which allowed the extreme Right more than indirect and temporary influence.

Economic growth and rapid social change in the years after the immediate post-war recovery caused outbursts of anger from those who were adversely affected and created, in the short term, fertile conditions for the agitator and the demagogue. But the conditions which, for example, fostered Poujadism did not persist long enough in the same form to become the basis of a reactionary assault on the existing social order and political institutions. The agitators therefore either faded like Poujade and Dorgères, shouting the same wild slogans to a vanishing audience, or changed their tactics like Léon Gingembre, Secretary General of the small- and medium-size business association, to extract maximum advantages for their clientele by more or less regular styles of negotiation. The poor record of the brokers of protest persuaded aggrieved groups like peasants, Algerian *rapatriés* and shopkeepers to adopt syndicalist attitudes and trust those leaders who made specific sectional demands on their behalf. The aggrieved groups did not, however, eschew the typical extremist methods of violent demonstration, excess of language and, even, in the case of the shopkeepers, arson and the kidnapping of government officials.

Increased social and geographic mobility, which helped to diminish traditional social distance and hostility, weakened the bases of political extremism in the Fifth Republic. On the other hand certain political developments sustained it. The apparently revolutionary protest movement of May 1968 rekindled the kind of fears which stimulate reactionary fervour. The attitudes and emotions of the extreme Right cannot be accommodated in the existing parliamentary parties. Since 1962 the highly disciplined Gaullist Party, the Giscardian Independents and the Democratic Centre have not provided attractive havens for the maverick Right. Dissatisfaction with the status quo and distaste for any practical alternative to it is still the most common motive for joining groups and associations of the extreme Right. The complex and rich intellectual tradition of the extreme Right also helps to explain its attraction. The 'texts' of this tradition, the writings of Barrès, Maurras, Bourget, Thierry Maulnier, Brasillach, Fabrègues, Rebatet, Coston, Bardèche and many others are as important in the life of the groups of the extreme Right as the great socialist 'texts' are on the revolutionary Left. The literacy of the extreme Right in France, by comparison with other countries, is perhaps its most outstanding feature and its greatest contribution to political life in France.

CHAPTER VII

Gaullist Parties

The Gaullist Party of the Fifth Republic, presenting itself as a party of the 'Centre', eventually succeeded in attracting most of the votes of the Right-wing electors. But this result was not achieved by the rallying of Right-wing politicians to the Gaullist banner. De Gaulle's political successes were achieved in the face of intermittent, but occasionally very active opposition of Right-wing notables. The most fortunate and astute managed to join or ally themselves with the Gaullists in the Fifth Republic before the Gaullist electoral success destroyed *la droite classique*. But, in the course of a political career spanning three decades, the relations between de Gaulle and conservative politicians, other than a small cohort of loyal followers, were frequently hostile and always complex. De Gaulle's reputation, his following and the general political situation were very different on the three occasions, in 1940, 1947 and 1958, when he offered his leadership to the country. Moreover, the three great periods of Gaullism – the Resistance, *the Rassemblement du Peuple Français* and the Fifth Republic were not themselves homogeneous and their significance changed over time. The outstanding personality of de Gaulle and the consistency of some of his attitudes give a somewhat misleading appearance of unity to Gaullism. The variety of the forms of Gaullism virtually ruled out a uniform attitude towards it by the non-Gaullist Right.

The great and perilous commitment of June 1940 remained until the end of his life the most notable of his achievements in the eyes of his compatriots. In a survey, conducted in November 1970 by the French Institute of Public Opinion, the replies to the question 'What in your opinion is the most outstanding moment in the career of General de Gaulle?' were:[1]

[1] J. Charlot, *Les Français et de Gaulle*, 1971, p. 30. This volume contains the most important opinion polls relating to de Gaulle and Gaullism.

	percentages
The 18 June appeal	27
His role during the war	22
The Liberation (entry into Paris)	9
Return to power in 1958 (establishment of Fifth Republic)	11
Solution of the Algerian problem	8
Events of May 1968	5
Resignation in 1969	4
Period as President of the Republic	4
His whole life	3
Other moments (when he said '*Vive le Québec libre!*', when he placed an embargo on arms to Israel, etc.)	1
No opinion	6

The *gaullistes historiques*, who joined him early in the war, frequently followed him until retirement or death but these *gaullistes de toujours* were very few in number. The 7,000 men under his orders in July 1940 were obscure men, with the exception of a handful such as Catroux, Governor General of Indo-China, Legentilhomme, Commander-in-Chief of Somaliland, Eboué, Governor of Chad, and Rear-Admiral Muselier. The numbers of 'Free French' multiplied many times before the Liberation but the majority joined after the German invasion of the Free zone in 1942 when the outcome of the war was easier to predict. The external, unlike the internal, Resistance was not a movement in which great political reputations were made. The soldiers – Koenig, Hautecloque, Juin and Leclerc – became national heroes by feats of arms but the civilians, perhaps with the exception of Jacques Soustelle and Maurice Schumann, had little opportunity to acquire an independent reputation. *Gaullisme de guerre* was, therefore, more exclusively based on the personality of Charles de Gaulle than the subsequent manifestations of Gaullism.

In the early days, de Gaulle had no very clearly defined political profile. He had the traditional, Catholic background of an army officer.[1] Brought up in Paris, he came from a family of the *petite noblesse d'épée de province* and, although arrogant, until 1940 he tended to show a conventional respect for established authority. The themes of his early wartime speeches were those of an exalted patriotism. He was a rigid defender of national sovereignty in his

[1] Of the many biographies of de Gaulle, the best account of his background is J. Lacouture, *De Gaulle*, 1965, English edition, 1970.

relations with wartime allies, particularly the British government, and his attitude towards the empire was precisely expressed in a short sentence: 'National unity and imperial unity are not separable.'[1] Anti-democratic views could be inferred from his absolute condemnation of the defects of the Third Republic. Until 1942, he hardly mentioned the Republic: the motto *Liberté, Egalité, Fraternité* was replaced in the Free French movement by *Honneur et Patrie*. The anti-German statements of de Gaulle encouraged xenophobia among some of his followers. There were even hints of anti-Semitism by Gaullists in such propaganda statements as: 'All these recently naturalised Frenchmen (*français de fraîche date*) do not think as Frenchmen and contribute to the ruin of national sentiment in our country.'[2]

Until about the end of 1941, Gaullism, in so far as it can be classified in the domestic French political spectrum, seemed to belong to the nationalist Right. However, recruits to the movement from the Right and from the elites of the country in administration, politics and business were conspicuously lacking. The Resistance in 1942, and especially the internal Resistance, was composed mainly of people with relatively humble backgrounds – trade unionists, workers and men of the Left. De Gaulle, recognising their aspirations, began to make speeches in which the themes of social and political democracy were prominent: '. . . France betrayed by her elites and privileged classes, has begun a revolution, the greatest in her history . . . those people who imagine that, after the last shell has been fired, they will find a France politically, socially and morally similar to that which they knew before are committing a signal error'.[3] De Gaulle also recognised the necessity of co-operation with the Communists after they clearly became the most important element in the internal Resistance, and this encouraged socially progressive statements by Gaullists. Until 1942, the nationalism of the Free French movement and that of the Vichy regime had similar features, but in the last two years of the war there was an increasing divergence. Gaullism became progressive on social questions and anti-Communism was almost entirely excluded from its propaganda.

At the Liberation the prestige of de Gaulle was based on the exemplary patriotic act of 1940 and on his successful leadership of the internal and the external Resistance. His experience during the war as head of a national resistance movement and then of a provisional government, without any kind of electoral mandate and with the very

[1] BBC broadcast, 26 March 1943, *Discours de guerre*, vol. 2, 1945, p. 43.
[2] H. Michel, *Les Courants de la pensée de la résistance*, 1962, p. 93.
[3] ibid., pp. 103–6.

slight political experience as Under-Secretary of State in the Reynaud government, was without parallel in modern French history. He evolved a distinctive style of leadership of a semi-presidential and somewhat authoritarian character, different from that of most of the men who had held the office of *Président du Conseil* in the Third Republic. He could not maintain this style for long after the end of the war. At first he shared some of the euphoric optimism of the Liberation period, writing in his memoirs that 'It was possible to believe in the renewal of political unity around my person'. But he brusquely withdrew from office in January 1946, dissatisfied with the pattern of relations emerging between government and parliament – '. . . once the danger had passed, the parties reappeared. Everything was called into question.'[1] This resignation provided a focus for the 'plebiscitary pool' in the country which, as a consequence of the dislocation of war, was much larger than it had been in the Third Republic. The fluidity of party allegiance was illustrated by the *Mouvement Républicain Populaire* which, claiming to be the *parti de la fidelité* to General de Gaulle, attracted nearly five million votes in less than a year after its foundation. In the immediate post-war period, a large proportion of the MRP votes, with some Socialist, radical and conservative votes, were available to de Gaulle if he appealed for them.

The Rassemblement du Peuple Français
De Gaulle's first act of political opposition (the Bayeux speech of June 1946, outlining his views on the constitutional question) was quickly followed by the founding of the first Gaullist party. Without the public authorisation of de Gaulle, René Capitant set up the *Union Gaulliste pour la IVème République*. Like its successors, the Gaullist Union claimed not to be a party. Article 3 of its programme stated that it was 'a *rassemblement*, above political parties, composed of combatants and Resisters, of all Frenchmen determined to devote themselves to the building of the Fourth Republic in the spirit of 18 June'.[2] The Gaullist Union made little impact in the country. In the parliamentary elections of November 1946, the results obtained by Gaullist Union lists, with the exception of those in Alsace and Moselle, were mediocre: they received only 147,000 votes over the whole country. The union effectively came to an end with de Gaulle's Bruneval speech on 30 March 1947 in which he hinted at a major new political initiative: 'The day is approaching when, rejecting the sterile games and reforming the badly-built framework

[1] *Mémoires de guerre*, vol. 3, 1955, p. 242.
[2] Union Gaulliste pour la IVème République, *Programme et statuts*, 1946.

in which the nation is going astray and the State is abdicating, the immense mass of Frenchmen will gather together with France.' This cloudy statement was followed by the much more direct appeal in his Strasbourg speech at the beginning of April, and the official foundation of the *Rassemblement du Peuple Français* in the middle of the same month.[1]

De Gaulle had much the same programme as Tardieu for reform of the State and modernisation of the country, and he headed a political movement which came close in form and ambience to the *Parti Social Français* of La Rocque. De Gaulle unintentionally attracted much the same conservative and Catholic audience as his less famous predecessors. According to the opinion polls the Right and the MRP had been unhappy about his withdrawal from power in January 1946:[2]

	All	PCF	Soc.	Rad.	UDSR	MRP	Mod.
Pleased by the departure of de Gaulle	32	83	42	23	17	9	9
Unhappy about his departure	40	6	25	31	49	39	71

The beginning of the Cold War made some sections of moderate and conservative opinion look with favour on a possible return by de Gaulle. Any credible counterweight to the Communist Party was potentially attractive to a broad range of social groups. Both the membership and financial resources of the RPF reached their highest levels when the Communist threat seemed most immediate. The RPF also appealed to feelings of disgust with the working of the parliamentary system. It was anti-parliamentary in the sense that the PSF had been and that Tardieu had become at the end of his career: all three opposed a system in which an executive was dependent on unstable coalitions of parliamentary groups. Their constitutional programmes, containing demands for a strong State and an independent executive, had authoritarian, plebiscitary implications. The RPF, like the PSF, aroused great enthusiasm, mobilised many thousands of people and attracted a somewhat violent, *fascisant* element. The ambience of the RPF appealed to those who wanted to 'take down their beret', nostalgic for the direct action of the authori-

[1] For general accounts of the history and structure of the RPF see R. Barillon' 'Le RPF' in M. Duverger (ed.), *Partis politiques et classes sociales*, 1955. C. Purtschet, *Le Rassemblement du Peuple Français, 1947–1953*, 1965. P. M. Williams, *Crisis and Compromise*, 1964, pp. 132–47.

[2] J. Charlot, op. cit., p. 27.

tarian and nationalist leagues of the inter-war period. A doctrinaire of the extreme Right, writing at the beginning of the Fifth Republic, placed the RPF in the tradition of 6 February 1934, the *Croix de Feu*, the *Révolution Nationale* and the Poujadist movement. A small minority within the RPF regarded the movement in this way. A fraction of the neo-Fascist youth such as Jean-Jacques Susini, the organiser of the Gaullist students of Algiers, later a Poujadist and leader of the Secret Army Organisation, was attracted to the RPF.

Presided over by a general, recently the leader of a national resistance movement, and staffed almost exclusively by men who had fought in the war, the RPF had some of the features of veterans' organisations. Adulation of the leader and a *cocardier* nationalism, expressed particularly strongly in the field of colonial policy, were prominent characteristics of the movement. Its authoritarian organisation in which all major policy decisions were taken by the President, was also in the *ancien combattant* tradition. The *esprit ancien combattant* was, however, much less obtrusive in the RPF than it had been in the *Croix de Feu* or the *Jeunesses Patriotes*. The veterans' section of the RPF was set up at the beginning of 1948 with high-sounding words from its chairman: 'The veterans' section, desired by General de Gaulle, will be, above all, the cohort of his most valued followers, united around him in the task of renewing and re-establishing [the authority of] France. Exemplary militancy was attributed to the veterans: 'Our group must be, within the RPF, the most important, the most dynamic, the most homogeneous and, also, the most vigilant in the recruitment of the cadres of the RPF'.[1] The chairman said that General de Gaulle expected much of the ex-servicemen. De Gaulle, at least in public, gave no special role or aims to the *anciens combattants* section of the RPF. Particular categories of men who served in the Resistance were obviously very useful to de Gaulle, such as the former members of the Free French intelligence service, the *Réseau de la France Libre*. Not all these intelligence agents were Gaullists in the post-war period but they nevertheless had very strong group loyalty based on the experience of shared danger. They were scattered through the security services of the State, the civil service, the armed forces, politics and a variety of private activities. The Secretary General of the RPF, Jacques Soustelle, who had been head of the intelligence services during the war, had at his disposal a network of contacts which only the Communists could rival.

No coherent *esprit ancien combattant* emerged after the Second

---

[1] *Rapport pour la commission des anciens combattants du RPF*, 1948, quoted C. Purtschet, op. cit., p. 148.

World War because of the gulf separating the various categories of combatants of the 1939–45 conflict. None of them had much in common with the 1914–18 veterans. Ex-servicemen's organisations, in general, were weak until a younger generation emerging from colonial wars provided a new impetus. The ex-servicemen's section of the RPF, despite a commitment to avoid overlapping with other ex-servicemen's organisations, soon reverted to the conventional practice of making a long list of demands on the public purse for various categories of ex-servicemen.[1]

The collective effect of professional and social sections of the RFP which, as well as veterans, included workers, civil servants, teachers, liberal professions, peasants, commerce, intellectuals, sports and families, was to give the movement the appearance, which de Gaulle wished to avoid, of a normal political party. These sections elaborated detailed programmes on behalf of the groups they represented. The RPF claimed not to have a programme and denied that its members had a common ideology: the *compagnons*, so it was argued, came from diverse intellectual horizons and political backgrounds, because the movement had the grand ambition of uniting all Frenchmen behind the basic objective of re-establishing the State through constitutional reform. But the internal pressures coming from the professional and social sections were compounded with external influences. The movement was compelled to draw up 'objectives of government' which in any other party would have been described as a programme or an electoral manifesto. In addition to detailed recommendations, the RPF had established, by the *Assises* (the Gaullist term for party conference) of Lille in 1949, a general policy platform containing three main elements.[2] These were a 'new State' which was based on de Gaulle's constitutional proposals made in his Bayeux speech of 1946, 'Association capital-travail' which, by involving the worker in the prosperity of the firm for which he worked, would achieve the old conservative dream of ending the class war and finally the 'allocation-education' which was a formula for giving State aid to private, mainly Catholic schools, in order to end the clerical–anti-clerical feud. The last theme caused considerable controversy within the movement at the *Assises* of Marseilles, at the National Council at Saint-Maur in 1948, and at the *Assises*

[1] 'Les Anciens combattants et la nation', *Défense de l'occident*, Nos 56–7, 1958. R. Rémond 'Les Anciens combattants et la politique', *Revue française de science politique*, vol. 5, 1955, pp. 267–90.

[2] 2ᵉᵐᵉˢ *Assises de Lille, 11–12 février 1949. Discours, motions, rapports*, n.d. Rassemblement du Peuple Français, *L'Allocation éducation*, 1950. Rassemblement du Peuple Français, *Association capital-travail*, 1950.

of Lille in 1949, resulting in the departure of some of the more *laïc* members of the movement.

The claim not to be a party like the others was credible in the early days of the movement when Jacques Soustelle said that recruits were joining at the rate of ten thousand a day and candidates supported by the RPF obtained six million votes in the municipal elections of 1947. The high-water mark of the RPF as a great new 'surge' movement was the meeting at Vincennes on 5 October 1947 when an estimated half a million people were present. But the extraordinary elan and the naïve enthusiasm of the first period disintegrated into the troubles and setbacks typical of mass movements of the Right in France. Large meetings after Vincennes tended to be troubled by violence. This reached alarming proportions when, in September 1948, a Communist was shot dead by a Gaullist steward at Grenoble. The responsibility for the rise of violence was shared with the Communists but the presence of an extremist element within the RPF was clearly demonstrated when, in June 1949, a Gaullist mob tried to storm the prefecture of Saint-Etienne. Conservative alarm about violence was a contributory factor to the first electoral setback. In 1948 the RPF failed to translate their victory at the local elections of 1947 into a majority in the indirectly-elected upper house of parliament, the *Conseil de la République*.

The morale of the RPF was shaken by this setback. An internal reorganisation took place, culminating with installation of a new *conseil de direction* in June 1949 dominated by parliamentarians. The only non-parliamentarian newly promoted to it was Marcel Prélot previously a *Parti Démocrate Populaire* Deputy subsequently elected an RPF Deputy in 1951, and UNR Deputy and Senator in the Fifth Republic. The endemic indiscipline of parliamentary groups of the Right invaded the highest councils of the Gaullist movement. There were also defections: amongst the first was Senator Giacobbi, too much imbued with the mores of the Radical Party from which he came, to accept the discipline de Gaulle wished to impose; and amongst the most notable was Colonel Rémy who had a very distinguished Resistance record and who departed at least partly, because his initiative to reconcile Vichyites and Gaullists was abruptly disowned by de Gaulle.[1]

Despite the apparent degeneration of the RPF into a political party like the others and the decline of enthusiasm, it remained an impressive political force. Huge crowds gathered at its meetings. It was staffed by men from an unusually wide range of social backgrounds and was backed by considerable financial resources through the

[1] Colonel Rémy, *et al.*, *Pétain, de Gaulle*, 1952.

Union Privée pour l'Action Nationale du Général de Gaulle (UPANG). But its only hope of success was the speedy and massive rejection of the existing political order at the polls. Differences over specific policy issues, commonplace among other political parties, progressively weakened the cohesion of the RPF as the prospect of overturning the Fourth Republic receded. Unless swept to power by a popular vote, it was compelled to choose between two unsatisfactory tactics – the *politique du pire*, intransigent opposition to all governments and all their policies to destroy the existing constitutional order, or, alternatively, to become an essential element of the government majority by penetrating 'the system', to compel its partners to accept de Gaulle's return. The first tactic involved voting consistently on the same side as the Communists. This was repugnant to most Gaullist Deputies and could have produced a revolutionary situation of doubtful outcome. The great mass of the Gaullist electorate was certainly opposed to any complicity with the Communists and strongly in favour of the preservation of order. Entering 'the system' was an equally divisive tactic because it would (and eventually did) expose the different priorities among Gaullist Deputies, between those who gave greater importance to the preservation of the social status quo than to the restoration of General de Gaulle and those who had the reverse order of priorities.

In 1951, the RPF had to choose between these alternatives after obtaining 4¼ million votes and 120 Deputies elected to the National Assembly. Some Gaullist Deputies thought that the moment had come to transform the movement into an ordinary conservative party and seek alliances with other groups in order to get into the government. General de Gaulle was as resolutely opposed to participation in coalition governments as he had been to forming alliances with other parties in the election. The tactics of intransigence, imposed by him on the parliamentary group of the RPF, had a temporary success. Strong support from the RPF to the Barangé bill for State aid to Catholic schools broke the Socialist-MRP alliance which had been the axis of all government majorities since 1947. A crisis of the regime seemed possible, but a section of the Gaullist group, growing weary of constant opposition and, perhaps, even of de Gaulle's leadership, fell for a conservative temptation. In March 1952, despite a strong personal appeal by de Gaulle to the combined Assembly and *Conseil de la République* groups, the Gaullists split over their attitude towards the investiture of the Independent, Antoine Pinay, as *Président du Conseil*. The Gaullist group in the National Assembly officially decided to abstain but twenty-seven Gaullist Deputies voted for Pinay. The breach of discipline was all the more serious since without Gaullist votes Pinay would not have had a majority.

In July 1952, General de Gaulle tried to reimpose discipline over the parliamentary group, and, at the same time, gave it more influence over policy. After new arrangements had been accepted by a special National Council meeting at Saint-Maur, the Deputies who voted for Pinay made the secession final by founding a parliamentary group, *Action Républicaine et Sociale* (ARS) under the Presidency of Edmond Barrachin.[1] Almost immediately afterwards, the 'loyal' Deputies implicitly disavowed the decisions of Saint-Maur by asking their executive committee (bureau) to prepare new rules for voting and discipline, and requesting that the committee should not be appointed by General de Gaulle but elected by secret ballot. In May 1953, after a series of skirmishes, secessions, threats of schisms and a heavy defeat for the Gaullists in local elections, de Gaulle withdrew from the direction of the movement and gave freedom to his followers. The loyalists formed the *Union des Républicains d'Action Sociale* (URAS) with, in the hallowed tradition of the parliamentary Right, freedom of vote on all questions. The number of controversies over personalities and policies is perhaps the most surprising aspect in the history of a movement which placed such a high value on unity. The breakdown of loyalty to the person of de Gaulle, impatience with Jacques Soustelle as Secretary General and with the leaders of the parliamentary group, the struggles (usually envenomed by personal rivalry) between 'liberals' and 'conservatives' over social, educational and colonial policy, and the always contentious issue of investitures, provide the *petite histoire* of the RPF. The increasing importance of personal rivalries was an index of the disintegration of a movement based on the cult of one heroic leader and committed to total victory over its opponents.

Some Vichyites considered the RPF as a possible instrument for their own political rehabilitation.[2] They joined the movement as ordinary members but did not succeed in penetrating the leadership. Their position was made very difficult in 1950 when Colonel Rémy, a leading member of the RPF, suggested a more respectful treatment of the imprisoned Marshal Pétain. He advanced the argument of 'the shield and the sword' – that Vichy had been necessary to limit the damage of defeat and was complementary to the Resistance: he helped to revive the belief of many Frenchmen during the war that there was collusion between Pétain and de Gaulle. Rémy was

---

[1] R. Guespin, *L'Action républicaine et sociale, mouvement politique*, 1953.

[2] Even Paul Marion in Fresnes prison advised his friends outside to vote for the RPF. H. Charbonneau, *Le Roman noir de la droite française*, 1969, p. 315.

immediately disavowed by de Gaulle who maintained a rigidly hostile attitude to the Vichy regime until his death, rejecting for example, the demand to transfer Pétain's coffin to Douaumont so that his body could lie amongst those of the soldiers under his command at the battle of Verdun.

RPF Deputies with Vichy associations were rare (Frédéric-Dupont was an example) but virtually all conservative politicians engaged in electoral politics considered coming to terms with RPF at some time during its history. Although Left-wing Gaullists such as Capitant and Vallon were members, the RPF certainly had the appearance of a Right-wing movement. The majority of de Gaulle's followers considered that he was above party politics but he was more identified with the Right during the RPF period than before or since. As Roger Frey remarked in 1958: 'For reasons ... which did not coincide with the unifying will and vocation as an arbitrator of General de Gaulle, the old RPF grouped the main elements of the French Right'.[1] The RPF electorate was not, however, as intransigent as de Gaulle in opposing the regime and this influenced the behaviour of RPF Deputies. The dissatisfaction with the Fourth Republic which Gaullist voters clearly felt was not sufficiently deep and bitter to produce revolutionary sentiments. The RPF briefly and imperfectly articulated the desire for greater stability in government and for the electorate to have direct influence on the choice of government rather than allow coalition governments to emerge from obscure parliamentary bargaining. The satisfaction of these desires was important in establishing the Gaullists as the majority party in the Fifth Republic, but as an opposition party without immediate prospect of forming a government the constitutional programme of the movement seemed utopian. Other parties, such as the CNIP, competed with rival schemes for reform.

The newspapers of the Left often represented the RPF as an aggressive nationalist movement attempting to instal an authoritarian dictatorship, but the main attitudes of the Gaullist electorate as recorded by the opinion polls, were fairly typical of moderate conservative views found in other countries.[2] There was a great respect for, but not unreasoning adulation of, the leader: in 1951, 68 per cent said that they had full confidence in him but only 18 per cent admitted that they voted primarily for de Gaulle. Gaullist voters were very anti-Communist: 55 per cent held that the greatest danger to the parliamentary regime was the Communist Party; 75 per cent wanted to make the party illegal, and almost all thought

[1] *Combat*, 23 October 1958.
[2] J. Purtschet, op. cit., pp. 324–9.

that it received subsidies from the Soviet Union. Nationalist and imperialist attitudes were also common: a majority were, for example, in favour of energetic pursuit of the war in Indo-China. Malraux's description of the Gaullist electorate as 'the rush hour crowd. in the metro'[1] conveyed the correct impression that the Gaullists were roughly a cross-section of the community in terms of age and social category. Women were slightly over-represented, comprising 53 per cent of the Gaullist voters in 1951, and the industrial working class and the retired were somewhat under-represented.

The Gaullist clientele was not, therefore, typical of movements of the radical Right. The cadres who staffed the party differed from both the professional agitators and activists who organised a movement like Doriot's PPF and the ex-army officers who assisted La Rocque. Many students and intellectuals of the extreme Right were hostile to de Gaulle because they considered that his ideas had little in common with their own. They held against him some of his actions in the recent past, particularly those concerning individuals. They reproached him for allowing the execution of Pierre Pucheu in 1943 after the Vichy Minister of the Interior, and former member of Doriot's PPF, had rallied to Algiers; they thought that the execution in 1945 of Robert Brasillach, the Collaborationist journalist and poet, was an unnecessary act of revenge. They also considered that, despite the anti-Communist position of the RPF, de Gaulle had assisted the rehabilitation of the Communist Party during the war and its electoral success at the Liberation. Jean-Louis Tixier-Vignancour wrote: 'In 1945 the masterpiece was complete. Thorez was in power and Weygand in prison. . . . Communism was reintegrated into the nation and the traditional framework of resistance to Communism was broken.'[2]

All senior positions in the RPF were held by men who had been prominent in the Resistance. Although not all *Compagnons de la Résistance* were Gaullists, members of the RPF maintained the *esprit de la Résistance* by addressing one another as *compagnons* on all public occasions. The rank and file of the movement shared in the emotional patriotism of an heroic resistance movement; common experiences and shared danger were bonds, which survived political differences, between active members of the Resistance. The cohesion of the inner circle of Gaullists, comprising about fifty men, was based on the wartime experience and on loyalty to the person of General de Gaulle as a leader of quite outstanding qualities. This loyalty broke down only in exceptional cases. The Gaullist inner

[1] Quoted R. Barillon in M. Duverger (ed.) *Partis politiques et classes sociales*, 1955, p. 277.

[2] J. L. Tixier-Vignancour, *La France trahie*, 1956, p. 18.

circle maintained networks during the period of the General's
retirement from politics and helped to bring him to power; it was
also a vital factor in the long-term electoral success of the Gaullist
Party in the Fifth Republic.

The Gaullist networks were greatly weakened during the period
between 1953 and 1958 and they could not have survived much
longer as an effective political instrument. Social contact between
men who had known each other for a long time, visits to General de
Gaulle in retirement at Colombey-les-deux-Eglises and membership
of the party, the *Républicains Sociaux*, composed of those who did
not wish to lose their Gaullist identity, helped to keep these networks
in being. In this period the Gaullists had no strategic direction and
de Gaulle seems to have encouraged his visitors at Colombey to
pursue a variety of tactics. These five years were the heyday of the
gaullistes de combinaison as Jacques Soustelle described them, the
masters of 'maintaining an unstable equilibrium, at the same time
inside and outside the system':[1] the main practitioners of this art
were Frey, Chalandon, Baumel and, above all, Chaban-Delmas.
The *Républicains Sociaux* became a ministerial party, little more
cohesive than the first group of apostates from the RPF, the ARS led
by Edmond Barrachin. Even on the Algerian question they were
almost as divided as members of other parties: most took a hard line
but there were progressives among them such as Jacques Debû-
Bridel who lost his Senate seat in 1958 as a consequence of his
attitude over Algeria. Like most small ministerial parties, the Gaullists
were split on electoral tactics. In 1956, Chaban-Delmas joined the
Republican Front combination headed by Mendès-France and Mollet, whilst most of his colleagues made alliances with the Right.

The *Républicains Sociaux* supported the Mollet government of
1956–7, in which Chaban-Delmas was a Minister. After initial
support for subsequent governments, most Gaullist Deputies withdrew into disorderly and aggressive opposition. How far they were
committed, or became committed between 1956 and 1958, to the
overthrow of the Fourth Republic varied from individual to individual. Chaban-Delmas built on the Gaullist heritage with his slogan
for the *Républicains Sociaux* '*Plus nationaux que la droite, plus
sociaux que la gauche*'.[2] But he was absorbed by 'the system' in the
last two years of the Fourth Republic, as Minister of Defence in the
Bourgès-Maunoury and Gaillard governments. Michel Debré was
feverishly working to overthrow the regime by denouncing all

[1] J. Soustelle, *L'Espérance trahie*, 1962, p. 18.
[2] Centre National des Républicains Sociaux, *1er Congrès National, Asnières,
18–20 novembre 1955*, 'discours d'ouverture'.

governments and all their works, by publishing a vituperative newsletter, *le Courrier de la colère*, in 1957–8, and by spreading subversive ideas among senior civil servants.[1] The degree of trust placed by de Gaulle in the two men after 1958 is revealing: Chaban-Delmas was President of the National Assembly but never held ministerial office whilst de Gaulle remained President of the Republic, whereas Debré was placed in charge of drafting the new constitution and was the first Prime Minister of the Fifth Republic. But de Gaulle also distrusted those who had been deeply involved in clandestine activity, such as Delbecque and Soustelle. Soustelle's case was complicated: the circumstances surrounding the break-up of the RPF and his total involvement in the cause of *Algérie française* must also have influenced de Gaulle's attitude towards him. The Gaullists who became involved in conspiracies against the Fourth Republic were very much more likely to adopt hard-line positions on Algeria than those who remained relatively aloof from the plotting. But despite the differences between Gaullists, Gaullism survived in 1958 as a loosely knit clan on the basis of which a government and, subsequently, a large political party were assembled.

The Union pour la Nouvelle République
The three Gaullist parties of the Fourth Republic were very different in character. The *Union Gaulliste* was a small band of devotees preparing a comeback, the RPF was a mass membership party which aspired to be highly disciplined and the *Républicains Sociaux* were a cadre party grouping Gaullist notables with strong personal positions in their constituencies. The *Union pour la Nouvelle République* organised in October 1958 in the offices of Jacques Soustelle was different again, although its centralised and authoritarian structure bore the marks of the heritage of the RPF. Established to support the action of General de Gaulle, he refused to give it any public acknowledgement and vainly forbade the use of his name 'even as an adjective' in the election campaign of November 1958. It possessed only a rudimentary organisation when 200 Gaullist Deputies were elected to the National Assembly. This success was mainly based on the desire to support the action of General de Gaulle after the approval of the constitution by a massive majority of thirteen million in the referendum of September 1958. When a sample of the Gaullist electorate was asked to give two reasons why so many people voted for the UNR, the following replies were received:[2]

---

[1] See especially O. Rudelle, *Le Sénateur M. Michel Debré*, unpublished *mémoire*, 1967.

[2] J. Charlot, op. cit., pp. 216–18 for other polls' evidence of a similar character.

	True per cent	False per cent
Support the action of General de Gaulle	93	0
Desire for national unity	31	2
Fight against Communism	23	9
Vote for new men	25	2
Political misunderstanding	0	29
To favour the integration of Algeria into France	16	8
Political ignorance	1	50
To beat the candidates of the old parties	9	19
Lack of awareness of the danger of a single political party	1	31

In the first year of the Fifth Republic all leading Gaullists, with the notable exceptions of Léon Delbecque and Jacques Soustelle, were or became convinced of three simple theses. Firstly, in the very tense political situation following the collapse of the Fourth Republic, the major policy options would be the personal decisions of de Gaulle. These options might run counter to the wishes and aspirations of his most loyal supporters: the personal preferences of Gaullists would, in Roger Frey's words, be submerged in the desire 'to be above all, an efficacious aid for General de Gaulle'.[1] Secondly, de Gaulle was unwilling to lead or lend his prestige to a Gaullist party. Thirdly, there was little point in calling oneself a Gaullist and disagreeing on major policy matters with the President, and it was also electorally disastrous to do so. Soustelle and Delbecque disagreed because they felt that their crucial role in the return of de Gaulle to power was not sufficiently recognised by him and because de Gaulle was not pursuing the policy of saving the honour of the army by keeping Algeria French. In their view he was supported by the army, the Europeans in Algeria and the French nation on the understanding that he adhered to that policy. Soustelle behaved as though he believed that de Gaulle could be captured by the *Algérie française* faction of the Gaullist party.[2]

The potential threat represented by Soustelle was realised at an early stage by de Gaulle who, despite his public show of indifference, did not hesitate to intervene in the affairs of the UNR behind the scenes. Soustelle wanted to be Secretary General of the new organisation but his appointment was apparently vetoed by de Gaulle. Soustelle also wanted to establish a national electoral alliance with

[1] R. Frey, *L'UNR, sa victoire, son avenir*, 1958.
[2] See especially J. Charlot, *L'UNR. Etude du pouvoir au sein d'un parti politique*, 1967, pp. 45–105.

Morice, Bidault and Duchet on a platform of *Algérie française* to fight the parliamentary elections of November 1958; after agreement had been reached on candidates in about a third of the *départements*, de Gaulle again intervened with a veto. Although de Gaulle was not ready at this stage to appear as a party leader, he was not prepared to allow the UNR to become the instrument of any faction among his followers. It was, however, eighteen months before the threat from the *Algérie française* lobby within the UNR was nullified. In the circumstances of 1958, it looked a dangerous challenge because of the prevailing mood of nationalist euphoria and the apparent weakness of the forces favourably disposed towards a negotiated solution to the Algerian War.

The quarrel between the 'orthodox' Gaullists and the Soustelle-Delbecque faction commenced as soon as the UNR was founded. It continued in the controversy over whether the party should seek a mass membership (Soustelle's view) or should remain a cadre party, and, in June 1959, reached bitter proportions in a quarrel over endorsement by the UNR of a list of candidates in the Algerian *départements* for the Senate elections. Compromise always seemed possible whilst Debré appeared to have at least residual sympathy for the French Algeria faction. In June 1959, after no agreement was reached on a UNR list of candidates for Algeria, a committee was set up, containing Delbecque and Picard (a Soustelle supporter), to work with Chalandon, the Secretary General of the UNR, and a liberal on the Algerian question.[1] By July 1959 Debré was so incensed by Chalandon, who complained that the policy of the government was at variance with President de Gaulle's stated views that he resumed relations with the Soustelle-Delbecque group in order to plot the removal of Chalandon from office.[2]

If the dissidents had been engaged in conventional intra-party manoeuvres, they were in a reasonably strong position from which to make a bid for some of the leading posts in the party. They were, however, totally committed to a cause and nothing less than complete victory was a satisfactory outcome for them. The declaration of 16 September 1959 in which de Gaulle promised self-determination for Algeria provoked them to precipitate action. Four UNR Deputies joined the newly formed *Rassemblement de l'Algérie Française*. In October, when the UNR parliamentary group would not vote a motion in favour of what de Gaulle had described as 'the most French solution', nine Deputies resigned – Arrighi, Battesti, Biaggi, Brice, Cathala, Delbecque, Grasset, Souchal and Thomazo. Although

[1] *Le Monde*, 26 June 1959.
[2] *ibid.*, 16 July 1959.

four realised their tactical mistake, and tried to return to the party, the bureau of the party expelled them. Soustelle was gravely weakened by this: he disapproved of the resignations and regretted that such a severe attitude was adopted by the party. He went on to take a decisive defeat at the Bordeaux *Assises* of the UNR in November 1959.[1] At this conference Chaban-Delmas defined his doctrine of the *domaine réservé* comprising the affairs of the Community, Algeria and foreign policy which were the President's preserve and in which the party should not interfere. Michel Habib-Deloncle went even further and stated that the party owed General de Gaulle unconditional loyalty. The conference then expressed complete confidence in de Gaulle and voted a compromise motion on Algeria. There was a good deal of behind-the-scenes bargaining on this motion which included opposition to any kind of secession of Algeria and support for 'a close union' between Algeria and France. Observers thought that a majority of the delegates agreed with Soustelle on Algeria. He tried hard to emphasise the importance of Algeria to France and to the Gaullist movement, but the other major figures of the party kept out of the public debate. A procedural motion was successful in removing the debate from the floor to a special commission headed by Lucien Neuwirth, with all the Ministers present at the conference as members. The outcome was a defeat for the *Algérie française* lobby. Soustelle was personally defeated when he was not elected to the central committee of the party.

The purge, begun when Delbecque left the party, was resumed after Soustelle was dismissed from the government by de Gaulle in February 1960, allegedly for sympathising with the participants in the Barricades affair of the previous month. He was subsequently expelled from the UNR: five Deputies resigned in sympathy and eight federations broke away from the party.[2] Another ten Deputies signed an integrationist manifesto in December 1960: two resigned from the party and various disciplinary measures were taken against the others. The national council did not meet for a twelve-month period in 1960–1, because of the difficult and tense situation within the party. The great unease within the UNR was shown by the rapid turnover of leading officers: there were six chairmen of the National Assembly group and six Secretaries General of the UNR between 1958 and 1962. De Gaulle's behaviour added to the uncertainties – it was sometimes construed as being conciliatory towards the *ultras* and his words as late as March 1960 during his famous *tournée des*

[1] Union pour la Nouvelle République, *1ères Assises nationales, Bordeaux, 13–15 novembre 1959. Rapports et discours*, n.d.
[2] *Le Monde*, 19 October 1960.

popotes (tour of the messes) in Algeria were variously interpreted as a basic agreement with the cause of French Algeria or as reliance on ultra support.[1] After his declaration in favour of self-determination for Algeria in September 1959, his life was in danger from terrorist action, his authority in the army was insecure and some members of the administration were engaged in subversion in the interests of the *Algérie française* lobby. This situation was deeply troubling for members of the UNR and the jettisoning of the *Algérie française* element of the party was a painful and arduous process. The break with de Gaulle was very difficult for men like Dronne and Soustelle who felt a deep sense of loss and betrayal. For others, such as Colonel Thomazo, with only a very superficial attachment to the Gaullist cause, it was a matter of little moment. The exclusion of the extreme *Algérie française* wing of the parliamentary group was a necessary step towards establishing the UNR as a majority party of government. The dissidents represented a style of political action which could not be integrated into a party whose vocation was loyal support for a President and his team of Ministers.

The clash between Delbecque and Soustelle, on the one hand, and Debré, Chaban-Delmas, Frey on the other, was the only leadership struggle in the Gaullist Party which took place in public whilst de Gaulle was President of the Republic. Other politicians subsequently represented tendencies within the Gaullist Party but Soustelle and Delbecque, like the *Gaullistes de gauche* who later excluded themselves from the UDR, were unusual in leading organised factions. The contrast in the way the crisis was resolved with the way in which the CNIP handled disputes between factions could not have been more marked. The sharp disciplinary action taken against those who rebelled was more like the behaviour of parties of the Left than previous parliamentary parties of the Right. Although it was estimated that Soustelle supporters at one time totalled nearly half the national membership, the parliamentary group lost only about twenty members, not counting those such as Souchal who subsequently returned. The UNR *Assises* of Strasbourg in March 1961 demonstrated the loyalty of the rank and file to the leadership. That congress showed that the crisis was over. There was no clash between the militants and the platform, no attempt to dictate policy to the government, and unequivocal support was given for the principle of self-determination for Algeria. The great achievement of the leadership was to emerge from the crisis without having made any compromise which mortgaged the future.

[1] De Gaulle remarked acidly on the 'faculty for invention and interpretation of the press', *Memoirs of Hope*, 1971, p. 86.

The Algerian War, however, permanently alienated some militants from the Gaullist movement and left some scars within the Gaullist Party, particularly in the form of unsavoury entanglements with the security services. These caused the government great, though temporary, embarrassment in the Ben Barka affair in 1965 when the internationally known Moroccan Left-wing leader was kidnapped in the streets of Paris with the collusion of members and ex-members of the security police.[1] Despite a public undertaking by President de Gaulle that the truth would be uncovered no matter whose reputation might suffer, the precise fate of the victim was never established. One Gaullist Deputy, Maître Pierre Lemarchand, friend of Jacques Foccart, a member of de Gaulle's staff, was deeply implicated. Lemarchand had been responsible for recruiting *barbouzes*, or irregulars, in Algiers in 1962 to fight the OAS; he was elected the Deputy for Yonne a week after the only serious candidate of the opposition had been arrested on charges dropped immediately after the election. He was the lawyer and friend of the central figure of the affair, a small-time crook called Georges Figon who conveniently committed suicide as the police were closing in on him. How far Lemarchand was directly involved in the kidnapping never became clear but the old *barbouze* network certainly existed. The UNR Deputies refused to dissociate themselves from Lemarchand. After he had been disbarred, an amendment to add his name to the general amnesty bill for offences connected with the Algerian War was proposed; despite the opposition of the government, the Independent Republicans, the Gaullist Left and all opposition parties, the motion attracted the votes of 90 per cent of the UNR Deputies. The purge of the main security service, the SDECE (*Service de Documentation Extérieure et de Contre-Espionnage*), which followed the Ben Barka affair did not put an end to the trouble. In 1971 the arrest in New York of a former employee of the SDECE for smuggling heroin again exposed some of the seamier side of the Gaullist government and the Gaullist movement. Although the Minister of Defence, Michel Debré, tried to dismiss the affair as trivial, some Gaullist Deputies, particularly General Billotte who had prepared a government report on the SDECE in 1970, took it very seriously. The allegation that the heroin was supplied by a member of the SDECE, Colonel Fournier, was supported by the Gaullist, Colonel Barberot, head of a government agency for agricultural development suspected of being a front for intelligence work. The scandal developed into typical allegations concerning improper relations

[1] P. M. Williams, 'The Ben Barka Affair', *Wars, Plots and Scandals*, 1970, pp. 78–125.

between politicians and security forces, corruption, treason and penetration of SDECE by the CIA and the KGB. The Senate showed its disgust on 2 December 1971 by cutting the Secret Service budget in half. However, neither this nor any other part of the legacy of the Algerian War, such as the difficult problems raised by the *rapatriés* and the amnesty for offenders, harmed the cohesion and electoral appeal of the Gaullist Party.

From 1962 President de Gaulle had a loyal and fairly well-disciplined political instrument at his disposal. The electoral success of the Gaullist Party was remarkable and unprecedented. In the referendum of October 1962, against the combined opposition of the main government parties of the Fourth Republic – the CNIP, Radicals, Socialists and MRP (forming the *Cartel des Non*) and the Communist Party – de Gaulle won a majority for his constitutional proposal to introduce direct election for the Presidency of the Republic. The UNR put up candidates against all those Deputies who, on 5 October, had voted the successful motion of censure against the Pompidou government on the issue of constitutional reform. In the election campaign, de Gaulle took an important step towards assuming the role of a party leader. As he subsequently wrote, 'I was induced to enter the electoral fray myself'.[1] In a television broadcast, he strongly urged the electorate to vote only for those candidates who supported the Fifth Republic and sharply attacked the opposition:

'Frenchwomen and Frenchmen, on 28 October [the date of the referendum] you put the seal on the condemnation of the disastrous regime of the parties and marked your desire to see the new Republic continue its task of progress, of development and of grandeur. On the 18 to the 25 November you are going to elect the Deputies. It is my earnest wish that you ensure that this second consultation does not contradict the results of the first.'

The UNR and the Independent Republicans emerged victorious with an absolute majority in the National Assembly. Gaullist discipline played an important part in this because the UNR and its allies received only 37 per cent of the votes at the first ballot and 43 per cent at the second. The victory was mainly at the expense of the Right, of the CNIP (which lost seventy-eight seats) and the MRP, neither of whom returned enough Deputies to form an independent parliamentary group.

The achievement of an absolute majority in 1962 was confirmed by the very narrow majority of two in the 1967 election, after

[1] C. de Gaulle, *Memoirs of Hope*, p. 333.

President de Gaulle had intervened vigorously in the election campaign, in a television broadcast on 7 February:

'From every point of view, it is right and extremely desirable that the [Gaullist] majority is victorious. And, in present conditions, it is absolutely necessary. The three electoral formations which are attempting to replace it and impose their policies on the Republic through victory in the elections, cannot, either separately or by a coalition of any two of them, achieve anything except disastrous ruin . . . they will be incapable in the future, as they were in the past, of constructing anything. . . . Next month, the Fifth Republic itself is at stake.'

Whilst denying that it was a party of the Right, the Gaullist Party transformed the whole pattern of Right-wing electoral politics. The loosely structured party dominated by notables who could not be effectively disciplined by national political organisations, which had been the typical form of Right-wing electoral organisation since the beginning of the twentieth century was replaced by a centralised, disciplined and well-financed party with the declared aim of consistent support for the government. The Gaullist surge either incorporated, destroyed or pushed to one side all the other moderate or Right-wing electoral forces.

The manner of the Gaullist achievement is uncomplicated but the reasons for it are obscure. The tactics of the old parties were poor because they considered Gaullism a transitory movement. They failed to recognise its originality and appeal. Jean Charlot argues that there were important and long-term tendencies of public opinion, which only the Gaullists could use successfully.[1] These were basically three: the desire for national independence, expressed in vague neutralist and anti-American sentiments; the desire for stability of government, even at the expense of parliamentary influence; and the wish to participate in the choice of the chief of government made impossible by the multi-party system and *gouvernement d'assemblée* of the previous two Republics. After the settling of the immediate problem which had brought him back to power, de Gaulle was in a position to satisfy these other aspirations. In doing so, the nature of the appeal of de Gaulle and of the Gaullist Party inevitably changed.

The extent of General de Gaulle's appeal was, according to the evidence of the public opinion polls, much the same at the beginning of the Fifth Republic as it was in the Liberation period. From the beginning of 1959 to the middle of 1961, through seventeen opinion

[1] J. Charlot, *The Gaullist Phenomenon*, 1971, ch. 2.

surveys, between 60 and 70 per cent of the French people said that they were satisfied with de Gaulle as President of the Republic: the same percentage of the French people, occasionally rising as high as 80 per cent, wanted de Gaulle to remain as *Président du Conseil* in the months from July to October 1945. But there were differences in the way he was regarded because of the different circumstances. In 1945 he had been thought of as 'the best qualified man', 'the necessary arbitrator', 'the irreplaceable man' faced by a generally difficult situation and a variety of problems.[1] In 1958, the problem of Algeria was overriding: constitutional reform and international affairs were secondary matters. Public attitudes towards parties had also changed considerably. Although de Gaulle would almost certainly have won a presidential election by universal suffrage in 1945–6, the balance of opinion was very much in favour of the Left-wing parties: the majority of French people believed both that there should be an agreement between the Communist and Socialist parties and that these parties had an important role in the future of the country. In October 1945 the 'Marxist' parties succeeded in winning an absolute majority of the votes in the country and of seats in the Constituent Assembly. De Gaulle did not sympathise with them: he effectively broke with the Communist Party in November 1945 and relations between himself and the Socialist Party were strained. The twelve years of the Fourth Republic greatly diminished the standing of the parties in public opinion: on the Left, the vote for the Socialist Party declined sharply and, as the 1958 election showed, the voters for the Communist Party were not unshakable in their loyalty. Whereas in 1944, 72 per cent of a sample of the electorate said that they would vote for a programme rather than a man, in 1959 (before de Gaulle was returned to power), 52 per cent said that they would vote for a man rather than a party. After de Gaulle came to power, according to a survey of September 1958, 46 per cent said that they would consider voting for a Gaullist Party, against only 19 per cent who said that they would certainly not vote for such a party.[2] This was a real change from the days of the *Rassemblement du Peuple Français* which, according to the polls, was never accepted by much more than a third of the electorate.

The clientele of the *Union pour la Nouvelle République* was drawn from mainly moderate and Right-wing milieux. Alain Girard and Jean Stoetzel concluded after the elections of 1958 that most of the Gaullist electorate had previously voted for candidates of the CNIP or the MRP: the numbers of converts from the Radical Party and

[1] J. Charlot, *Les Français et de Gaulle*, 1971, p. 33.
[2] ibid., 34–9.

parties further to the Left were relatively modest.[1] In this respect the UNR followed the pattern of the RPF which had attracted MRP and PRL votes but made little inroads in the Left-wing vote. Jean Charlot has persuasively argued that the Independents and MRP continued to lose votes to the Gaullist parties in the 1962 and 1967 elections and the followers of the parties of the Left tended to remain loyal to them. The evidence of the opinion polls on this point is not, however, conclusive: it is possible that respondents who voted Gaullist were unwilling to admit having voted for Left-wing parties on previous occasions.[2] The votes for candidates of the Left (Radicals to Communists) between 1945 and 1956 were never less than half the total votes cast: after 1958 they never reached 45 per cent. In some sense, the expansion of the Gaullist vote was at the expense of the Left and the extreme Left, and it is not entirely convincing to suggest that new voters accounted for all, or even most, of the relative decline of these parties.

The 15 per cent increase in the Gaullist vote between 1967 and 1968 hardly modified the sociological characteristics of the Gaullist electorate. The highest social category (liberal professions, employers in commerce and industry) showed a greater tendency to vote Gaullist – 51 per cent in 1968 against 45 per cent in 1967 – and thus became the only social category over a half of whose members voted for the Gaullist Party. The Gaullist electorate was closest of all the parties to matching a profile of the nation in age distribution and socio-professional status.[3] It was slightly unbalanced in some respects: proportionately fewer members of the working class voted for the Gaullist Party (the divergence from the national profile was not great – 3 per cent in 1967 and 6 per cent in 1968); slightly more women than men were attracted by the Gaullist Party, although fewer than for de Gaulle himself in the presidential election. There were no parallels to the specialised clientèle of the other parties such as the high proportion of men among Radical Party voters, of the old among the CNIP or of Peasants among the *Centre Démocrate*. The only milieu in which there were proportionately many fewer Gaullist Party voters was amongst the well-educated young.

[1] Association Française de Science Politique, *Le Référendum de septembre et les élections de novembre 1958*, 1960, p. 165.

[2] There was a considerable Left-wing vote for de Gaulle personally. One estimate gives 2,700,000 to 3,000,000 electors who voted for Left-wing parties in 1956, voted for de Gaulle in the Presidential election of 1965. See F. Goguel, 'Combien y a-t-il eu électeurs de gauche parmi ceux qui ont voté le 5 décembre 1965 pour le général de Gaulle', *Revue française de science politique*, vol. 17, 1967, pp. 65–9.

[3] J. Charlot, *The Gaullist Phenomenon*, pp. 66–75.

The characteristics of Gaullist support in the country have been simplified in the course of the Fifth Republic. The 'presidential' vote was far bigger than the vote for the party in the early years of the Fifth Republic, and it had different characteristics. The UNR was camped uneasily between the clienteles of the MRP and the CNIP. From 1968, the vote for the leader was scarcely larger than that of the party and had a similar social and geographical distribution. Gaullism obtained the great majority of Right-wing votes, at least in national elections. Personal and local factors allowed fragments of the old Right to survive, but they were relatively insignificant. This success, however, was achieved partly by allowing an independent and more conservative Gaullist formation to establish itself on the Right of the Gaullist Party of strict obedience.

Jean Charlot, without claiming to be exhaustive, has listed thirty Gaullist organisations which have existed during the Fifth Republic.[1] There have been parties which have had a continuous existence like the UNR; organisations which have been intermittently active such as the *Association Nationale pour le Soutien du Général de Gaulle* to support de Gaulle during referenda campaigns; and specialist organisations such as the *Service d'Action Civique*, a union of stewards who maintain order at meetings, and the *Comités de Défense de la République* formed during the events of 1968 to support the cause of law and order throughout the country. Gaullist movements have been of three political types: the Gaullist Left, individualistic and divided; the moderate Right, Gaullist in many cases only because it is the regime in place; and the Gaullism of the most faithful followers of de Gaulle and most of the Gaullist electorate. The moderate Right supported the regime and Gaullist governments for tactical reasons rather than on grounds of political principle or personal loyalty. As de Gaulle himself put it: '[they] pledged their support in order to get elected'.[2] These Independent Republicans were more in the tradition of the CNIP than the *compagnonage* and are discussed elsewhere.

The Gaullist Left was of insignificant weight in government, in parliament and in elections, but has some importance in understanding the success of the Gaullist movement and the attraction de Gaulle exercised on some intellectuals.[3] The Left gave a radical, reforming aspect to Gaullism, quite different in style to the technocratic reformism of Michel Debré. The desire for social justice,

[1] J. Charlot, *The Gaullist Phenomenon*, p. 133.
[2] C. de Gaulle, *Memoirs of Hope*, p. 335.
[3] B. Cahen, *Les Gaullistes de gauche, 1958–1962*, unpublished *mémoire*, 1962. J. F. Carrez, P. A. Wiltzer, *Le Gaullisme de gauche*, unpublished *mémoire*, 1962.

typified by the 'Vallon amendment' to give workers a share in the profits of the firms in which they worked, was more important to the Gaullist Left than improvements in the efficiency of the economy.[1] For the Left, the most important role of Gaullism was to reintegrate the working class in the nation and wean it from its attachment to the Moscow-dominated Communist Party. The main Left-wing group was the *Union Démocratique du Travail* founded by Louis Vallon in April 1959 to bring together Gaullists who were favourable to a liberal policy in Algeria and a progressive social policy. Although most *Gaullistes de gauche* united with the UNR in 1962, break-away movements soon appeared. At the end of the 1960s a federation was formed, the *Convention de la Gauche Vème République*, but only three out of the five *Gaullistes de gauche* groups came together. They all behaved like typical splinter groups of the French Left, their only distinguishing feature being an apparently eccentric loyalty to the person of de Gaulle. The excessive importance of personal rivalries and absence of consensus on basic issues became even more prominent when the main Gaullist party established itself as a force independent of de Gaulle. The refusal of leading Left-wing Gaullists to go to the *Assises* of Lille in 1967 and their very disunited response to the events of May 1968 condemned them to the political 'fringe'. Some were able and widely publicised propagandists for a particular political position. Those who remained within the main Gaullist party until after the departure of de Gaulle, such as Louis Vallon and René Capitant, had some influence over policy. But they were not the principal actors in the great structural change of French politics in the 1960s.

The Union des Démocrates pour la République
The change centred on the main Gaullist party called the *Union pour la Nouvelle République* (UNR) until 1967, *Union des Démocrates pour la Vème République* (UDVᵉ) in 1967 and 1968, and, after 1968, the *Union des Démocrates pour la République* (UDR). The frequent changes of name were symptomatic of the painful process of evolving a new party of government. At the beginning of the Fifth Republic, the building of a mass-membership party in the country seemed fraught with dangerous political consequences. Progress was fairly slow in transforming the Gaullists from a collection of the followers of one man, supported by a virtually unorganised mass of voters, into a modern political party. From 1962 the Gaullist group in parliament had a fairly well-structured organisation and relatively lively internal

[1] J. C. Casanova, 'L'Amendment Vallon', *Revue française de science politique*, vol. 17, 1067, pp. 97–109.

life. It was not, however, until 1967 that an integrated set of relationships was established between the government, the National Assembly
and Senate groups, and the party. In March 1967, the Prime Minister,
Georges Pompidou, proposed that the Secretary General of the
UNR be replaced by five national secretaries to meet weekly with the
Minister of State for Relations with Parliament and, occasionally,
the chairmen of the groups of the Senate and National Assembly
under the Prime Minister's chairmanship. He also proposed that
a new executive committee of twenty-six members representing the
government, the parliamentary groups and the party, should meet
fortnightly. These committees were intended to bring reciprocal
benefits: the party would gain influence at the highest levels of
government whilst the Prime Minister would acquire more direct
control over the day-to-day business of the party. The next step in
party building, the reform of the party statutes prepared by Michel
Habib-Deloncle, encountered difficulties.

To the general surprise of political commentators, the *Assises*
of Lille in November 1967, the fourth party conference, was marked
by a genuine revolt from the floor, headed off only by a conciliatory
attitude and concessions by the leadership. There were two main
reasons for this controversy within the party: firstly some sections
of the party were suspicious of the intentions of the party managers;
secondly, there was a conflict of generations made virtually inevitable by the history of the Gaullist movement.[1] Georges Pompidou,
aided by the *gaullistes de combinaison* of the inner circle such as
Chaban-Delmas and Roger Frey, was preparing the party for
après-Gaullisme, the time when de Gaulle was no longer in office.
For some Gaullists the notion of Gaullism without de Gaulle was
inconceivable whilst, among those who admitted the desirability of
a Gaullist party after de Gaulle, some refused to accept that Pompidou's cautious conservatism represented the true spirit of Gaullism.
The new blood injected into the party as a result of electoral successes
in the Fifth Republic added another dimension to the tensions.
Until 1967 the inner circle of Gaullism has been composed almost
exclusively of men who had been in the Resistance, although
Pompidou himself was a rather late recruit. The *gaullistes historiques*
had, however, been in a minority in the National Assembly group in
the 1962–7 parliament. Only 36 per cent had played a part in the
Resistance and 40 per cent had neither been in the Resistance, nor
held office in the RPF and the *Républicains Sociaux*. The process of
rejuvenation was gradually reaching the top leadership of the
movement. The Secretary General of the UDVᵉ appointed in 1967,

[1] J. Charlot, op. cit., pp. 87–100.

Robert Poujade, was too young to have fought in the war and made his political debut in 1947 at the age of nineteen, in the RPF.[1] By the time of the Couve de Murville government of 1968 only half the members of the government held wartime decorations. Pompidou himself seemed to be encouraging this process by favouring rising young men such as Jacques Chirac. For rather different reasons both the old guard and the new men felt insecure in this situation.

At the 1967 conference, some members of the old guard resisted the change in the party's name, from *Union pour la Nouvelle République* to *Union des Démocrates pour la Vème République*. If there was to be a change, they asked for a specific reference to Gaullism in the new title. Behind this apparently trivial discussion lay the fear that, by broadening the appeal of the party and increasing the membership, many elements would be attracted who were not 'true Gaullists'. The younger generation, on the other hand, could see that the majority of the most important posts were still held by the wartime Gaullists who commanded an influence far in excess of their numbers. The rejuvenation process was not going quickly enough for the young men. Suspicious that the inner circle were a self-perpetuating oligarchy, they demanded more democracy within the movement. The platform made concessions. It dropped the idea of a collegiate national secretariat and accepted a single Secretary General but resisted the proposal that the Secretary General should be elected by the conference. Another concession by the leadership was that the majority of members on all senior committees of the party, including the central committee, were to be elected.

Opening the top levels of the party to new men was complemented by an increase in party activity in the provinces and a membership drive, especially among young people. The youth movement, the *Union des Jeunes pour le Progrès* (UJP), under the Presidency of Robert Grossman had considerable success although the conformist enthusiasm manifest at its Strasbourg conference of 1969 was reported to have disquieted Pompidou. Other organisations such as the *Clubs Vᵉ République, Université Réforme* and the *Centre Féminin d'Etudes et d'Information* were not particularly successful and the attempt early in the Fifth Republic to establish social and professional sections within the UNR similar to those of the RPF was a failure. Regional study days, organised by the UDR from 1968, demonstrated the strength of the party at the regional level and were an adjunct of the theme of 'participation' launched by de Gaulle in May 1968 and part of the party platform for the elections of June 1968. An internal party newspaper, *Démocrates*, appeared in April 1968 in

[1] ibid., p. 129.

order to encourage the ordinary members to take an interest in party affairs.

Before de Gaulle's resignation in 1969, the party had assumed the shape which allowed it to survive the shock. With 292 Deputies, it had a commanding majority in parliament, even without the support of its Centrist and Independent Republican allies. This majority was perhaps too large for good party discipline and some of its members showed signs of insecurity because they had been elected in circumstances which were unlikely to be repeated. In the elections of June 1968, the UDR, representing itself as the defender of order and democratic institutions, received massive support because of the widespread alarm caused by the 'events of May', particularly the violence in the streets, the occupation of public buildings and factories, and the general strike. On 30 May de Gaulle, when he announced the dissolution of the National Assembly, provided the keynote of the election campaign:

> '[The elections will take place] unless the French people are gagged, are prevented from making their voices heard, from leading a normal existence by those same elements which are preventing the students from studying, the workers from working – that is to say by intimidation, intoxication and tyranny organised within and by a party, the Communist Party, which is the extension of a totalitarian enterprise.'

De Gaulle thus revived the virulent anti-Communism of the RPF period. The charges against the Communist Party had little foundation. The Communists had not organised the student agitation and, even at the height of the crisis, had given it only very equivocal support. The Communist-led trade unions had played an important part in keeping order during workers' demonstrations and in maintaining electricity and good supplies. But the propaganda thrust was successful and anti-Communism remained one of the main UDR themes after de Gaulle's departure.

The UDR outside parliament was a mass membership party (having about 160,000 members) with a well-articulated structure and a fairly strong regional organisation. It had a forward-looking, if rather vague, programme calling for 'participation' and modernisation of the country, and stressing individual well-being and family happiness.[1] Even before May 1968 the main symbols of the Gaullist tradition, the Cross of Lorraine and the portrait of de Gaulle, were being phased out of party propaganda, although they were discreetly

[1] See particularly, *Elections législatives de mars 1967. Ve République. Dossier du candidat.*

re-emphasised in the referendum campaign of 1969. The reformulation of the appeal of the party was not popular with all Gaullists. It was one reason for the formation of new Gaullist associations immediately after de Gaulle's retirement: in May 1969 Michel Debré, Louis Joxe and Pierre Messmer founded *Action et Présence du Gaullisme* to defend the heritage of de Gaulle; two months later, Jacques Vendroux, de Gaulle's brother-in-law, established another *groupe amical, Actualité et Influence du Gaullisme*. The more conservative Gaullists were also to be found in associations established before de Gaulle's resignation such as the *Comités de Défense de la République* which came into being after the appeal of de Gaulle on 30 May 1968 for action to defend the Republic against Left-wing subversion, and in the *Association Nationale pour le Soutien de l'Action du Général de Gaulle* which was entirely independent of the UDR. The *Comités de Défense de la République*, in particular, represented the *ancien combattant* element of Gaullism, more sentimental and 'Bonapartist' than the Gaullism of Georges Pompidou. The establishment of these groups caused rumours of schism in the Gaullist movement but they proved to be unfounded. The groups were not very active and sometimes changed their objectives – the *Association Nationale pour le Soutien du Général de Gaulle* was transformed in 1971 into a documentation centre. The Gaullist inner circle prevented the groups organising dissidence within the Gaullist movement after the departure of President de Gaulle. The most loyal and authoritarian representative of the old guard, Michel Debré, repeatedly preached the duty of loyalty to President Pompidou and to Prime Minister Chaban-Delmas, although his previous differences with the two men was common knowledge.

In the first two years of Pompidou's term there were abundant rumours of divisions and desertions. The strains of transition were certainly present.[1] The broadening of the basis of the parliamentary majority and the inclusion of 'Centrist' ministers in the government, the *ouverture* proclaimed by Pompidou and Chaban-Delmas, was not well received by members of the UDR who saw no good reason why, with an overall parliamentary majority, they should concede seats in the cabinet to other parties. The national council of the UDR held on 25 to 27 June 1970 was the occasion of some sharp criticism of the leadership, especially from members of the group *Action et Présence du Gaullisme*. Pierre Messmer remarked sharply: 'The government today is not homogeneous and our allies are not slow to suggest and even, occasionally, propose that they will take it over. Whilst giving our loyal support to the government, we have no reason

[1] P. Viannson-Ponté, 'Les Gaullismes', *le Monde*, 11 April 1970.

to be identified with it, and still less to feel identified with the other parties of the majority'. Many Gaullist Deputies had reservations about the reforms of the Chaban-Delmas government, in particular the Faure bill for higher education. This gave substance to the criticism of Left-wing Gaullists, such as the Paris Deputy David Rousset, that the UDR was the party of inertia and status quo. Debré's blunt assertion at the 1970 national council meeting, 'Gaullism is the enemy of conservatism' carried respect but not conviction.

There were some notable departures from the UDR between the 1969 presidential election and the 1971 party conference. The Left-wing Gaullist, Louis Vallon, was excluded from the party, probably to the relief of the leadership because of his notorious hostility to Pompidou; David Rousset, unsurprisingly, resigned. The defections on the Right caused more alarm, especially those of Jacques Vendroux and Christian Fouchet (one of the few politicians to be received at Colombey-les-Deux-Eglises after the 1969 resignation) during the municipal election campaign of 1971. They resigned because they considered members of the UDR were engaging in the same kind of corrupt tactics as the despised parties of the Fourth Republic. The acceptance by the Lyons Gaullists of places on the broadly-based list of Louis Pradel, the out-going mayor, in which Jacques Soustelle was also participating, particularly irritated them. The party secretariat subsequently admitted that the resignation of Jacques Vendroux, General de Gaulle's brother-in-law, caused anxious speculation. Neither his resignation nor subsequently that of another influential conservative Gaullist, Jean-Marcel Jeanneney, caused much trouble in the party. The defections were, in effect, personal protests: none tried to organise splinter groups, although the political atmosphere in 1969–70 which Chaban-Delmas described as *morosité* seemed to give encouragement to factionalism.[1]

The unease within the party gradually subsided. The coolness with which Chaban-Delmas was received at the National Council of the UDR in June 1970 was transformed into moderate enthusiasm at the UDR study days held at Chamonix in September 1970. There were complaints about the lack of influence of parliament at a conference of Gaullist MPs at Hyères in September 1971 but there were no expressions of grass-roots discontent at the *Assises* of Strasbourg of the UDR in November 1971.[2] Rumours circulated that the elections for the central committee at the Strasbourg conference

[1] *Année politique, 1971*, pp. 39–40.
[2] *5èmes Assises, Strasbourg, discours, rapports, motions.* N. Copin, 'La Famille gaulliste après Strasbourg: conserver l'héritage'; J. P. Roux, 'L'UDR: ses options et ses objectifs', *Revue politique et parlementaire*, vol. 73, 1971, pp. 21–32, 33–44.

would upset the leadership but, in the event, they consolidated the position of the men in place. All the members of the government were elected and the Secretary General of the UDR, René Tomasini, came head of the poll. The delegates to the conference showed by their behaviour that they wanted party unity: spokesmen of all the various tendencies within the party were applauded equally and Chaban-Delmas received a very enthusiastic reception when he called for party unity for the general election of 1973. The peroration of the Prime Minister was taken as the keynote of the conference: 'Behind Georges Pompidou and with Chaban-Delmas, the UDR is bringing about for France and for the French, the destiny conceived and embarked upon by General de Gaulle'. The memory of General de Gaulle helped to seal the unity necessary to win parliamentary elections. As with most conservative parties it was much easier to define what the party was against rather than what the party stood for. The enemy against whom the party was uniting was clearly identified by Michel Debré:

'[The enemy] has changed its name but we know it well. It is called the Union of the Left . . . it is not the Union of the Left of grand-papa, with reassuring beards and comforting discussions about the future of humanity concluded by the division of jobs, subsidies and decorations among friends. The Union of the Left is henceforth the mechanism designed to allow the Communists to enter the government in strength.'[1]

The confusion about what the party was for was increased by the resignation of Chaban-Delmas and the appointment of one of his sternest critics, Pierre Messmer, as Prime Minister in July 1972. Although Messmer hardly changed the composition of the government the contrast between the liberal reformist, Chaban-Delmas and the dull authoritarianism of his successor could not have been more marked. Messmer did little to stem the tide of opinion running against the Gaullists. The coalition, the *Union des Républicains pour le Progrès* (UDR, FNRI and *Centre Démocratie et Progrès* of Duhamel and Pleven) won the elections of March 1973. However, the UDR share of the votes on the first ballot was over 10 per cent down compared with the election of 1968 and 3 per cent down on 1967. Losing eighty-nine seats, the party no longer commanded an absolute majority in the Assembly.

The nature of UDR
Since the days of the Free French movement, there has been a cult

[1] Quoted N. Copin, op. cit., p. 25.

within Gaullism of *rassemblement*, of gathering together various groups, interests and traditions to form a great national movement. This contrasts with the view which prevails in most of the other political parties, including the Independent Republicans, that the multi-party system is based on inescapable sociological realities. The presence of various tendencies and groups within the Gaullist Party is often regarded as a cause of self-congratulation. Albin Chalandon, just before the opening of the 1971 conference, said that it was a highly desirable state of affairs that there were as many conservatives as reformers within the UDR: he regarded this as a guarantee of progress because the reformers would only advance when they were on sure ground. He might have added that the reformers were divided between liberal *anti-étatistes* like himself and interventionist neo-Socialists, usually found the Left of the party although Michel Debré could be included amongst their number. This division weakened the reformist elements within the UDR but at least it gave a Gaullist government the possibility of alternative strategies. Chaban-Delmas was referring to both doctrinal and social divisions when he remarked at the Strasbourg conference in 1971:

> 'The role of our movement is not to divide but to unite. This is why we do not clamour for the particular support of specific categories of people but seek the support of all Frenchwomen and all Frenchmen. More precisely, we do not appeal to the Left, or the Right, or the Centre but seek to express from each of these families of thought all that is best for the interests of France and for the happiness of Frenchmen.'[1]

Ordinary members, members of parliament and leaders of the UDR had been recruited from the Radical Party, the Socialist Party, the MRP, the CNIP and minor parties; the electoral profile of the UDR showed that the party gathered votes from all sections of the community.

The rather curious discussions about whether the UNR was, and the UDR is, a party or a movement, is a very cloudy debate although it has specific practical implications. It is linked to the question about whether there should be a chairman of the party and an elected Secretary General. The problem posed by Soustelle's ambition to be Secretary General at the beginning of the Fifth Republic was revived in a slightly different form in the debate over the office of Secretary General at the Lille conference in 1967, and was raised again when, in 1971, André Sanguinetti suggested that the party ought to have a chairman. The memory of Soustelle's behaviour as Secretary General

[1] Quoted by N. Copin, op. cit., p. 27.

of the RPF, and the fear that powerful party officials backed by a large number of militants would force the government's hand on sensitive policy matters, caused de Gaulle and, subsequently, Pompidou to reject the notion of a party chairman. Sanguinetti, when he sent his proposal to committee at the Strasbourg conference, was careful to explain that the creation of a chairmanship would not transform the movement into a party like the other parties and that the chairman should normally be the Prime Minister. The very word 'party' in the minds of some Gaullist leaders implied an organisation, with a specific programme of a rather doctrinaire kind, whose unity was built around its programme.[1]

The desire not to be regarded as a party, based on the Gaullist tradition going back to the Second World War and the RPF, did not prevent the emergence of structures and attitudes typical of political parties. After Roger Frey's Asnières speech in February 1965, calling for a broadly-based Gaullist political formation, a new party of the 'Centre', it became a widely held view among Gaullists that the party should play a more positive and independent role. The duty of 'unconditional' support for General de Gaulle during the struggle against the supporters of French Algeria was felt to be an inadequate permanent basis for a large government party. The young and ambitious men joining the party in the early and middle 1960s were not satisfied with the function of being part either of a malleable instrument in the hands of the government or of a passive channel of communication – in Jacques Baumel's words at the 1963 *Assises* 'a permanent two-way liaison between the government and opinion'. Most members of the UNR and UDR accepted that the government was not a Gaullist party government but the government of the President of the Republic. But this situation was sometimes regarded as giving the party the opportunity for a greater degree of freedom of action than was possible, for example, in the British Conservative Party when its leaders formed the government. Members of the Gaullist National Assembly group were always restive over their relations with the government: many felt personally and collectively diminished by their lack of influence over important policy decisions. Gaullist Deputies were sometimes very obstructive over government legislation in the 1962–7 parliament and in subsequent parliaments. Whilst the government could get unconditional support in times of crisis, in 'normal' conditions the Deputies expected to exercise

---

[1] In conversation with members of the *bureau politique* of the UDR M. Pompidou said that the Gaullist movement should not become a party because this would encourage a return to the habits of the Fourth Republic. *Le Monde*, 19 November 1971.

influence through recognised channels. When certain views commanded wide support in the party, the Deputies expected the
government to take account of this.

After Pompidou's appointment as Prime Minister, the government
was usually prepared to listen sympathetically to the expressions of
views by the parliamentary party. From time to time it made concessions following opposition and criticisms in party meetings. The
party occasionally expressed the views of a coalition of interests and
successfully opposed the will of the government; the first major
example of this was over the government's proposals on value added
tax in 1965.[1] Usually Gaullist Deputies were allowed virtually
complete freedom of expression but decisions on policy were often
imposed by the government. The government had to impose discipline fairly frequently because of the heterogeneity of the parliamentary party. The original basis of the discipline within the party
was respect for de Gaulle's leadership, fortified by his massive
support in the country, and the knowledge that exclusion from the
party would probably lead to electoral defeat. The convergence of
the levels of support in the country for de Gaulle and the Gaullist
party eroded to some extent the presidential basis of party discipline
but it remained a very powerful factor whilst de Gaulle remained in
office. His departure in 1969 necessarily involved a reappraisal.

There was no apostolic succession: Pompidou imposed his
candidature for the Presidency of the Republic on the Gaullist
movement by a statement calling for its support on 29 April 1969.
He received neither the blessing nor the public support of de Gaulle
when he became President. His authority was derived from victory
at the second ballot of the presidential election and he was soon
rivalled in popularity in the country by the Prime Minister, Jacques
Chaban-Delmas. Pompidou tried to shore up his authority by
appealing again to the people in the referendum of April 1972
on the issue of the enlargement of the European Communities but,
because of the low turn-out, he only partially succeeded. He followed
this by changing the Prime Minister, replacing the 'usé et désabusé'[2]
Chaban-Delmas by the more conservative and less popular Pierre
Messmer. Pompidou's skill helps to keep the UDR united but in the
years following 1969, Gaullists at all levels of the party have shown
that they realise the importance of maintaining the cohesion of the
movement. The will to maintain discipline comes from below as well
as from above – from the electorate and the militants quite as much
as from the President of the Republic.

[1] P. M. Williams, *The French Parliament, 1958–1967*, 1968, pp. 93–5.
[2] *Le Monde*, 6 July 1972.

Gaullist party members clearly believe that the only way of maintaining a presidential and a parliamentary majority is to conserve a disciplined unity. But some justification, other than the maintenance of the status quo, is required to keep the various tendencies within Gaullism together. The search for a common fund of principles contains risks because, if precisely expressed, they are divisive and, if vague (such as Chaban-Delmas's *nouvelle société*) they are ineffective in mobilising enthusiasm and uniting the party. The Gaullists under Pompidou are plagued by the fear of 'neo-Radicalism', of being an alliance of convenience for the division of the spoils of office, and having no other *raison d'être*. The dependence on allies both on their Right and their Left, forced upon the Gaullists by the results of the 1973 elections, increases this apprehension.[1] There have also been signs that some of the Gaullists have conformed to the perennial *mœurs* of French parliamentary democracy, associated with the Radical Party of the Third Republic. In elections this has taken the form of administrative pressure and promises of material rewards for the constituencies. A startling example of this were the methods used by the most puritanical of Gaullists, Michel Debré, in his constituency of Réunion. Chaban-Delmas in Bordeaux had, during the Fourth Republic, used hints that his position in Paris could bring important benefits to his town and he continued this practice in the Fifth Republic.[2] In a by-election which he fought in September 1970 against the Radical leader, Jean-Jacques Servan-Schreiber, he was accused of having used his position to obtain the relocation of a new Ford factory in Bordeaux, overriding a previous decision to place it in Lorraine.

In government and in parliament, relationships and practices have been revealed which at least border on the corrupt. The charges made against officials of the State broadcasting service, the ORTF, in 1972 of allowing clandestine advertising in return for payments was perhaps a peripheral matter but the property scandals revealed in the summer of 1971 tarnished the reputation of the Gaullist parliamentary party. André Rives-Henrys, Deputy for the XIXth *arrondissement* of Paris, André Roulland, ex-Deputy and formerly member of Georges Pompidou's personal staff, and Maître Victor Rochenoir, a Gaullist parliamentary candidate, were involved in the

[1] On the question of 'radicalisation' of the UDR, see G. Martinet, *Le Système Pompidou*, 1973, and M. Kesselman, 'Systèmes de pouvoir et cultures politiques au sein des partis politiques français', *Revue française de sociologie*, vol. 13, 1972, pp. 485–518.

[2] B. Pacteau, *Analyse des rapports entre la carrière nationale et la carrière locale de M. Chaban-Delmas*, unpublished *mémoire*, 1968.

336 CONSERVATIVE POLITICS IN FRANCE

collapse of two property companies, La Garantie Foncière and Le Patrimoine Foncier. They were charged with fraud and, in the case of Rives-Henrÿs, with abuse of his position as Deputy. Rives-Henrÿs used his parliamentary privilege to give a speech on 26 November 1971, implicating as many public figures as he could. Although the Gaullist leadership dissociated itself from the business practices of Rives-Henrÿs and his friends, the affair cast a shadow of scandal over the regime. The revelation by *le Canard enchaîné* in January 1972 that the Prime Minister, Chaban-Delmas, had not paid any direct taxation for some years and that another minister, Jacques Chirac, might have misrepresented the financial details about the purchase of a chateau, served only to increase suspicions of malpractice at the highest levels of the Gaullist movement. Although the Prime Minister justified his tax position and seems to have acted within the law, he lost popularity and set off a barrage of criticism against a tax system weighted in favour of the better-off. These and other scandals involving administrators and politicians lent substance to the opinion that the Gaullists had been in government too long.

The difficult problems concerning the authority system within the party, the justification for holding office and the maintaining of high standards of personal conduct gave rise to occasional hints of a desire for a credible alternative to Gaullist government. A real opponent, rather than the straw enemy of the Communist Party, would help the cohesion of the Gaullists. The alliance of the Socialist and Communist parties announced in June 1972, based on an agreed 'programme of government' was probably welcomed in private by the Gaullist leadership as a threat which would help preserve the unity of the Gaullist coalition. As Chaban-Delmas put it, the Gaullists had 'the extraordinary responsibilities towards the country' of representing both 'order' and 'movement' because of their long period in office and the prospect of remaining in power for many years.[1] Short-term tactical reasons for encouraging divisions within a fragmented opposition have usually been much stronger than any desire to create a credible alternative party of government.

The long-term cohesion of the Gaullist Party has been constantly questioned, and is constantly at risk, because of the interplay of personal ambitions within the party. Whilst the FNRI of Giscard d'Estaing continues to thrive and the CDP of Duhamel remains a necessary ally, they provide havens for dissident Gaullists. The desire for unity is strong and the interest which the Gaullist Party has in maintaining discipline is clearly perceived but an unpredictable crisis could intervene to destroy that unity. In 1973, however, the

[1] *Le Monde*, 10 July 1972.

Gaullists seem unlikely to wither away like the Bonapartists at the beginning of the Third Republic or to become impotent through deep divisions over the succession, like the Orleanists and Legitimists of the same period. A new and original movement has been created similar in some respects to parties in other countries whose vote is twice as large as their nearest competitor.[1]

Describing the UDR as a party of the Right, associates it with other parties such as the *Centre National des Indépendants et des Paysans* and the *Fédération Républicaine*, which had quite different characteristics. Some of these characteristics, such as ill-discipline and defence of sectional interests, the Gaullists specifically rejected. But traces of the old Right – clericalism nationalism and 'social defence' – are present in the Gaullist Party. It is well-disposed towards the Church. De Gaulle attended mass, sometimes ostentatiously. Ecclesiastical dignatories are invited to many State ceremonies. Most of the Catholic votes go to the Gaullists. The schools question was virtually solved by the Debré law of 1959 which gave State aid to Catholic schools. It is not, however, a confessional party or, like the *Mouvement Républicain Populaire*, a party of Catholic inspiration. It contains Jews, Protestants and free-thinkers, as well as Catholics, and no one seems to have been preferred or discriminated against because of his religious affiliations. The UDR also expresses a nationalist tradition without being a nationalist party in the rather narrow and exclusive sense given to that term in the Third Republic. By placing 'the interest of France above that of Frenchmen', de Gaulle and his followers have not necessarily implied that their opponents are traitors. Although the most obvious embodiment of Gaullist nationalism, foreign policy, seems to have undergone a profound change since 1969, *le fait national* continues to be the explicit assumption on which that policy is based. The commitment to 'bourgeois' social and economic policies was not always clear in de Gaulle's case. He was willing, if necessary, to nationalise industries and impose profit-sharing and workers' participation in management. However, the defence of the franc in the Fifth Republic made him appear a fiscal and monetary conservative and, in the case of his support for the gold standard in the middle 1960s, a reactionary. If de Gaulle was, from time to time, willing to envisage great structural reforms, this is not the case for his successor, Georges Pompidou, and the majority of UDR members of parliament. The inequitable distribution of income in France, one of the worst in highly industrialised countries, is unlikely to be changed under Gaullist government.

[1] For a discussion of the notion of the dominant party see J. Charlot, op. cit., ch. 3.

Paradoxically, the electoral success of Gaullism has been greatly helped by social change. The position of the old provincial notables, the backbone of *la droite classique*, has been whittled away by the erosion of the particularism of local social systems. Urbanisation, economic growth, increased geographic and social mobility have all had a part in this process. The Gaullists are a national elite and a national party, only possible in the more integrated national economy and society which has developed since the demise of the *Rassemblement du Peuple Français*. But social changes are continuing. There are signs of new regional identities emerging which could have the effect of creating a new kind of notable. The new notables would probably have more in common with big city mayors such as Chaban-Delmas in Bordeaux, Pflimlin in Strasbourg and Pradel in Lyons, than with the conservative notables of the small towns and countryside during the Third and Fourth Republics. They would naturally have a keen interest in access to, and perhaps the control of, central government. The kind of national leadership and national appeal provided by the Gaullists could meet their needs.

Prior to the Fifth Republic conservative leaders with a genuinely national appeal were very rare. The cult of the heroic figure and the search for the great national leader contrasted oddly with the absence of specific heroes who were universally admired on the Right. There was no leader of the parliamentary Right during the Third Republic around whose memory broad sections of the Right could unite in veneration. Clemenceau who, during his lifetime, despised most of the Right gained more contemporary and posthumous admiration than any politician clearly identified with them. If the memory of a Right-wing leader, such as Marshal Pétain, was cherished by a fairly large group, it was usually bitterly rejected by other sections of the Right. During the Fourth Republic Pinay was widely admired, although combated by the nationalist Right. He did not, however, follow his 'miracle' by any other notable success. The record of de Gaulle during the Second World War, in solving the Algerian problem in achieving stability in government and in re-establishing the international prestige of France is without precedent. Members of the UDR and the Gaullist electorate were and are united in respect for this record. The men who helped and collaborated with de Gaulle are accorded some respect for these achievements. Glory, as well as the benefits of office, have been the fruits of loyalty to the Gaullist cause. An heroic figure, a record of political success and a political interest have come together to form a combination which has always been sought by the Right, but never before achieved.

Conclusion

A simple prejudice has been widely shared among French politicians, since the failure to restore the monarchy in the 1870s, that to be of the Right implies association with the forces of the past and this leads almost inevitably to electoral defeat. Conservative groups and parties have often tried to escape the label of Right-wing by including in their names progressive sounding words such as democratic, liberal, popular, progressist and social. Although politicians, journalists and scholars have frequently used the categories of Right and Left to describe political groups, many have denied either the value or the usefulness of the distinction. These have included all those who have sought a realignment in French politics, such as the would-be regenerators of France after the First World War, those involved in the *complot des Acacias* in 1933 or the *rendez-vous de Saint-Denis* in 1936 and, above all, the Gaullists. The groups with an interest in political fragmentation like the CNIP at the beginning of the Fifth Republic or contemporary 'Centrist' politicians such as Jean Lecanuet have tended to see the party system as a multiplicity, indeed a confusion, of political forces in which the terms Right and Left have little meaning. Some scholars such as Raymond Aron have held a similar view. Maurice Duverger argues that the 'Centre' has as much continuity in terms of attitudes and of cohesion as the Right and the Left and that it has been in power for most of the last century and a half.[1]

There is little dispute that the moderates of Right and Left have had more in common with each other than they have had with their own extremists. This is not unusual even in two-party systems but the frequency with which the moderate Right and the moderate Left, facing opposition from both extremes, have formed coalition governments, gives a certain plausibility to the notion of the Centre.

[1] M. Duverger, 'L'Eternel marais', *Revue française de science politique*, vol. 14, 1964, pp. 33–51.

The division between Right and Left has seldom been clear because Right and Left have not alternated in government. Some parliamentary groups, such as the Radicals and the MRP in the last two parliaments of the Fourth Republic, and some individuals, such as Poincaré in the years before the First World War and Laval in the 1920s, are impossible to classify in terms of Right and Left. Nevertheless, from the 1880s, there have always been aspirations to form 'blocs' of the Right and of the Left in order to bring stability to the political system. The great simplicities of the *élections de lutte* seemed to divide the country into two sides, Catholics and clericals or 'liberals' and 'Marxists' although these sides were translated into a confusing multiplicity of groups in parliament. One of the tenuous threads of continuity in the Right, since the beginning of the Third Republic, is the belief that a genuine 'national' party existed in the country, the *pays réel*, but the formal framework of representation and government, the *pays légal*, prevented this party emerging. The electoral system, the personal ambitions of politicians and the machinations of political enemies have been blamed for this.

The sentiment that, beneath the turbulence and confusion of the multiparty system down to 1962, there was in the country a 'party' of social conservatism, the *parti de l'ordre établi*, is the basis of the notion of the Right.[1] It is inevitably a cloudy notion because, whatever perspective is adopted, the content of this conservatism is very diffuse. There is no permanent irreducible element because, as René Rémond has written, 'excepting the counter-revolutionary Right which was, from the beginning, in the camp opposed to change, no tendency originates on the Right: tendencies become of the Right by the effect of time which displaces strands of thought in the ideological spectrum. . . . '[2] Groups accrete to the Right as a result of changing circumstances.

No issue or theme defines the Right for any extended period of time but there nevertheless have been threads running through the politics of the Right since the late nineteenth century. These are clericalism, nationalism, regionalism and the defence of property. Jacques Laurent exaggerated when he wrote: 'All that one can be certain of is that the Right has been clerical when it has not been Voltairean, defeatist when it has not been jingoist.'[3] At any time

[1] For an analysis of the politics of the Third Republic using the notions of the *parti de l'ordre établi* and the *parti de mouvement*, see F. Goguel, *La Politique des partis sous la Troisième République*, 3rd edition, 2 vols, 1958.

[2] R. Rémond, *La Droite en France*, 2nd edition 1963, p. 258.

[3] J. Laurent, *Au Contraire*, 1967.

during the last century, men of the Right have been more likely than men of the Left to believe in the existence of God, in the innate wickedness of man and in the non-rational, if not divinely ordained, basis of authority. Although there have been significant numbers of pious Catholics on the Left, at least since the turn of the twentieth century, and anti-clericalism in sections of the Right, particularly after the papal condemnation of *Action Française* in 1926 and during the Algerian War, all organised attacks on the interests of the Church have come from the Left and all concerted defence of them has come from the Right. The significance of religion in politics has greatly changed between the first years of the twentieth century and the 1960s, when matters touching religion were rarely raised in French politics. Religious allegiance no longer defines the Right and the Left but it remains an important undercurrent in political cleavages. There is still a positive correlation between voting patterns and religious practice. The commitment in the 1972 joint programme of the Communist and Socialist parties to integrate private schools in the public education system illustrates that, in policy matters, the interests of the Church can still divide Right and Left.

Nationalism has also been common ground among members of the Right. The beautifully expressed and eclectic nationalist sentiments of Maurice Barrès have been very widely held. Many of his ideas were typical of a European wide intellectual climate of the 1890s. The sense of decadence, hostility to liberal democracy and big city civilisation, and condemnation of corrupt and unheroic modern society were attitudes which he shared with Drumont, Bourget and Lemaître as well as with contemporaries in other European countries. These ideas reached their apotheosis in the Vichy regime. But Barrèsian thought was not systematised and could be modified without loss of coherence and appeal. Barrès gave an account, very similar to the first two pages of de Gaulle's war memoirs, of the origins of his political views:

'In politics, I have held deeply only to one thing: the reconquest of Strasbourg and Metz. Everything else has been subordinated to this principal aim . . . my ideas derive from my earliest memories of a grandfather who was an officer in the *Grande Armée*, from the images of war which were imprinted in my mind in Alsace when I was eight years old'.[1]

An exalted patriotism, a veneration of past glories and a sense of shame about national setbacks were shared by Barrès, de Gaulle and most of the French Right in the twentieth century. The nation-

[1] M. Barrès, 'Vingt cinq années de vie litteraire', *le Matin*, 1 March 1908.

alism of Barrès and de Gaulle, linked to the desire for a strong State and stable government, was essentially defensive, directed at preserving French interests and maintaining the influence of France in the international community. Imperialism, the desire for domination of other peoples, has had a curious history and has been a less influential strand in French political thought.

Defence of regionalism and localism has been mainly, though not exclusively, a Right-wing theme between the first part of the Third Republic and the early 1960s. Decentralisation has always been, to an extent, an opposition platform espoused, for example, by the Legitimists and the Republicans during the Second Empire, by the Right in the Third Republic and by the 'Centrists' and some of the Left in the Fifth Republic. But the type of regionalism associated with the renaissance of interest in local languages and cultures in the late nineteenth century, the reactions to urbanisation and hostility to some of the forms of political and economic dominance exercised by the capital, was predominantly Right-wing. It was associated with heavily sentimental feelings for *la France charnelle* and has, to varying degrees, been in the counter-revolutionary tradition. The two main regionalist organisations,[1] founded at the beginning of the twentieth century, were dominated by the Right and men of the moderate Left who supported measures of decentralisation, were always careful to explain that they were not attacking the Republican tradition and the sovereignty of the people.

Regionalism is another element common to Barrèsian and Gaullist thought.[2] Although there was something factitious about the Lorrain patriotism of Barrès – a Parisian by adoption with the chateau Mirabeau in Vaucluse as his country home – it was nevertheless deeply felt. De Gaulle's more tacit support of the regionalist cause in the reforms of 1964, made much more explicit in the 1969 referendum proposal, was a vague but genuine commitment. In the years between the Barrèsian statements of the 1890s and 1969, a considerable range of views and proposals on the regional question were produced by men of the Right. Right-wing men have usually exaggerated their attachment to the nation, the region and the *petite patrie* by contrast to an allegedly *apatride* Left. Strong local and national patriotism has been expressed by men of the Left who have rejected the rhetoric of nationalism and traditionalism. On

---

[1] *Fédération Nationale de Décentralisation, Fédération Régionaliste Française.* The latter contained members of the moderate Left, as well as prominent politicians of the Right.

[2] Z. Sternhell, *Les Idées politiques et sociales de Maurice Barrès, 1884–1902*, unpublished thesis, 1969, vol. 2, pp. 180 ff.

the Right there have been those, particularly Gaullists such as Debré and Sanguinetti, who have had no sympathy with regionalism, regarding it as a threat to the unity of the French State.

Indeed clericalism, nationalism and regionalism have been areas of fierce sectarian controversy on the Right. There have been many differences and few charitable feelings between 'clericals' as diverse as agnostic defenders of the Church, modernists, *intégristes* and *ultra* Catholics, socially conforming but privately sceptical Catholic notables in predominantly Catholic regions, pious militants of Catholic Action and progressive Catholics who have been from time to time the target of the disciplinary authority of the Church. Decentralisers have fought over various approaches to the regional question and autonomists from the frontier provinces have condemned those who have worked for modest measures of devolution of activities from the capital as being quite unable to understand the nature of Parisian domination. Nationalists have been divided over doctrinal and policy issues. For some 'integral' nationalism led logically to acceptance of the necessity of monarchist restoration whilst others claimed the Jacobin Republican tradition of the France of Valmy. The ideology of nationalism has never provided a common programme in foreign policy. Nationalists have chosen widely differing options, particularly in the late 1930s and early 1940s when a deep gulf emerged between those in favour of appeasement, *attentisme* and collaboration and those who opted for diplomatic and military resistance to the Axis dictators. Decolonisation after the Second World War also caused divisions among nationalists depending on the time at which they accepted its inevitability; a minority never genuinely accepted it.

The defence of private property has not been a matter about which there have been bitter sectarian disputes among members of the Right. This has been partly because it has been based on primitive prejudices and not on clear, well-defined economic doctrines. At the end of the nineteenth century, there were well known *laissez-faire* economists such as Léon Say and Paul Leroy-Beaulieu and, in the middle of the twentieth century, Jacques Rueff has carried the banner of economic 'liberalism' as well as the defence of the gold standard. There have been notable free-traders and opponents of State intervention in the economy among the parliamentary Right. But, in the twentieth century, there have probably been as many politics of the Right who have espoused vague corporatist doctrines as they have been doctrinaire economic liberals. The level of economic intelligence has always been very low on the Right; unorthodox economic ideas of men like Tardieu have scarcely been understood or genuinely supported by more than small minorities. Ignorance of economics was partly wilful on the part of Deputies of the *droite classique* engaged in the defence of special economic interests, which no general economic theory could justify.

The long-standing prejudices of the majority of the Right have been in favour of a balanced budget, economies in government expenditure, low taxation, defence of the value of the currency and of credit, and hostility to collectivism. The Right-wing ministers who have successfully managed the finances of the State, Poincaré in the period 1926–9, Pinay in 1952–3 and to a lesser extent Giscard d'Estaing in the Fifth Republic, have put into effect policies which were in line with these prejudices. Although de Gaulle's own support for a return to the gold standard is a striking illustration of the survival of old ideas, the Gaullists have, to some extent, broken away from the old prejudices in the direction of modernisation, expansion and planning. There is a fairly broad acceptance among Gaullists of a large public sector of the economy, government promotion of technologically advanced industry and sophisticated techniques of management of the economy. But there is no real commitment, except by the Gaullist Left, to use taxation and the social security system to achieve a more equitable distribution of income. The general position of the main Gaullist party, especially during the period of 'Pompidolien' Gaullism, can be represented as the politics of 'bourgeois defence' in a manner not unlike that of the *Bloc National* majority of 1919.

There are other continuities of attitude on the Right as, for example, on the constitutional question. Views about the constitution deriving from the Legitimist, Orleanist and Bonapartist regimes in the nineteenth century have survived and been synthesised in various ways in the twentieth century. The extreme Right has had its own themes expressed continuously but with varying degrees of vociferousness since the end of the nineteenth century. These have related mainly to various conspiratorial views of politics involving Jews, Freemasons, foreigners, bankers and the 'two hundred families'. *Anti-Etatisme* has been a common platform, at various times, of groups threatened by economic change and the fiscal policy of the State. But all the continuities are vague and tenuous. The content of the common attitudes or traditions has been so ill-defined and so much disputed that they have not provided symbols around which durable political organisations could be built. Discontinuity, particularly discontinuity of political organisations, has been a most obvious feature of the history of the Right.

There have been barriers or divisions between different generations of the Right since early in the Third Republic. Although prominent leaders of the parliamentary Right, such as Albert de Mun, Louis Marin, Paul Reynaud and Antoine Pinay have had long political careers and some families such as Aillières, Baudry d'Asson, Flandin, La Ferronays, Grandmaison and Roulleaux-Dugage have sent representatives to parliamentary assemblies for several generations, there has been strangely little sentimental unity between generations. Parties and groups of the Right have seldom lasted as effective organisations for more than one generation. The influence of experiences at the beginning of maturity has often been noticed and successive generations have experienced crises which were genuinely traumatic. Those who participated in the battles arising out of the Dreyfus affair, or who survived the bloody holocaust of 1914–18, or who were involved in either Vichy or the Resistance, or who fought for the preservation of French Algeria were deeply marked by these events, sometimes to the extent of manifesting paranoid political attitudes. They found it difficult to explain to younger people what these events had meant and to convey their feelings about them. Younger people, for their part, could not share the perspectives and the passions of their elders; often they could barely understand and had little sympathy for their feelings. The *glissement à gauche* of the parliamentary Right during the Third Republic represented, in part, a disavowal by the younger generation of their elders.

The failure of successive generations of the Right to achieve the most important and the best known of their political objectives meant that there were few heroes or achievement for younger people to admire. The monarchist of 1900 could only have qualified admiration for his father's generation who had, in the favourable circumstances of the 1870s, failed to achieve a restoration. The Christian Democrat of the inter-war period, a member of the *Parti Démocrate Populaire*, could not wholeheartedly admire the achievement of the previous generation who had carried through the *Ralliement* but failed to win acceptance for themselves as Republicans. The moderate Republicans of the post Second World War generation could perhaps understand the cruel dilemma which faced members of his parent's generation in 1940 but could not entirely forgive the unfortunate choice which most of them made. The rising generation of the moderate Right in the Giscardian party or the UDR can consider the 'second *Ralliement*' to the Republic, made by their predecessors after the Second World War, as unfortunate because the discredit of the Fourth Republic tarnished an important section of the parliamentary Right.

The Gaullists have broken this cycle of disillusionment. Although cleavages between different generations of Gaullists occasionally cause difficulties, they can look back on a history of considerable political achievement, marred only by the RPF episode. The old Right-wing themes can be linked to specific triumphs – nationalism with the Resistance and the foreign policy of the Fifth Republic, the strong State with the Constitution and the practice of government of the Fifth Republic, accommodation of the interests of the Church with the Debré law of 1959, the defence of the social hierarchy with the maintenance of a tax system in which the better off need pay very little direct tax. In addition, the Gaullist party has won elections and been in office for almost a decade and a half. It is now the Left which looks back to a series of political debacles in the Fourth and Fifth Republics.

The great interest of the French Right for the student of politics is the complex relationship between the values and doctrines expressed by its members, the interests which they represented and the political organisations they have established. Occasionally there are obvious relationships between doctrines, interests and organisations but the examples involve minority groups and transitory situations. Authoritarian and neo-Fascist doctrines, and the leagues of the inter-war period appealed to groups threatened by inflation, recession and the revolutionary Left. The *colons* of Algeria became susceptible to the extremist doctrines of organisations such as *Jeune Nation* and to the counter-revolutionaries of MP 13 because of the threat posed by Algerian independence. But the connections are seldom so easy to identify and only the broadest generalisations are possible. There is, for example, a certain parallelism between the profound social changes in the agricultural milieu and the disengagement of the Church from the political forces of the Right. However, in the context of a declining rural population and the breaking down of old social hierarchies, priests and Catholic laymen have been variously encouraging, ignoring and actively hindering social change. There is an even more complex set of relationships between the conservative notables, who dominated the electoral politics of the Right during the Third and Fourth Republics, and social change in both urban and rural communities. The notables occupied different social positions in different parts of the country and these have changed in the course of time; for example, in Brittany the aristocratic notables were largely replaced by bourgeois notables between 1919 and the end of the Second World War. Any generalisation about the notables is hazardous because their political attitudes and the organisations in which they participated were so diverse. The decline in their position since the beginning of the Fifth Republic is, however, incontestable. Old styles of political dominance and representation linger on at the local government level and in some Independent Republican, even UDR, constituencies but the notables of the *droite classique* are unlikely to reacquire their former position in national politics. Their partial demise is attributable to involvement of many of them in the disastrous episodes of Vichy and the Algerian War. But economic and social change has made increasingly difficult the establishment of the personal following and local political position which were the hallmarks of their political style.

Gaullism is an expression of the breakdown of the old localism of conservative politics in France, based on local social systems of considerable complexity. There has been a simplification of the party system but Gaullism is not the same phenomenon wherever one looks. Within the UDR there are many different types of politician and the ways in which Gaullist electoral success has been achieved vary from region to region. The sociological basis of Gaullism is multi-faceted as any local study of French politics quickly reveals. But there is a certain parallelism between the modernisation of the economy and Gaullist political success. The Gaullists have desired this modernisation and implemented policies designed to encourage it. The contention that the Gaullists are the instrument of the 'monopolies' which have taken over or pushed to one side the smaller enterprises characteristic of the old capitalism is too simple. But the Gaullists have been intimately and deliberately associated with the economic development of the country since the beginning of the Fifth Republic.

Despite their political successes and association with economic development and concomitant social change, there remains doubt about the political future of the Gaullist Party. The kind of circumstances which in the past have destroyed political organisations such as those surrounding the collapse of the Third and Fourth Republics are unlikely to be repeated in the future. But the Gaullist leadership has to contend with a long tradition of political practice on the Right in which men and issues have been considered more important than the survival of party organisations. The survival of the Gaullist Party may depend as much on contingencies and accidents as on structural factors. Since the departure of de Gaulle, the UDR has come to resemble conservative parties in other advanced countries because it is difficult to identify positive elements in its doctrines and programmes. But it will have to survive electoral defeat and a period of poor leadership to acquire the aura of permanence possessed by some other conservative parties.

BIBLIOGRAPHY

Party documents cited
Action Libérale Populaire
  Programme et statuts, 1903
  Projet d'une constitution libérale, 1907
  Compte-rendu du congrès général de 1907, 1908

Croix de Feu. Parti Social Français
  Tracts politiques, 1934–1939, n.d.
  Parti Social Français et la semaine de 40 heures, n.d.
  Le PSF après quatre années d'ostracisme et de persécutions, 1945

Centre National des Indépendants et des Paysans
  Statuts du Centre National des Indépendants, 1949
  1er Congrès national, Paris, 7–9 décembre 1954 – rapports divers
  Le Centre national des indépendants: son histoire, n.d.
  4ème Congrès national, Paris, 30 novembre–2 décembre 1960 – rapports et motions

Centre National des Républicains Sociaux
  1er Congrès national, Asnières, 18–20 novembre 1955

Fédération Républicaine
  Programme et statuts, 1904
  Compte-rendu du congrès national, 1909 n.d.

Jeunesses Patriotes
  Bulletin de liaison

Patri National Breton
  Notre lutte pour la Bretagne, notre histoire, nos idées, nos buts, 1941

Rassemblement du Peuple Français
  2èmes Assises de Lille, 1–12 février, 1941 – discours, motions, rapports
  Allocation-éducation, 1950
  Association capital-travail, 1950

Union Gaulliste pour la IVème République
  Programme et statuts, 1946

Union pour la Nouvelle République
  1ères Assises nationales, Bordeaux, 13–15 novembre 1959, rapports et discours
  2èmes Assises nationales, Strasbourg, 17–19 mars 1961, rapports et discours
  4èmes Assises nationales, Lille 24–26 novembre 1967 – discours, rapports, motions

Union pour la Vème République
  Elections législatives de mars 1967 – dossier du candidat

Union des Démocrates pour la République
    5èmes *Assises nationales, 17–19 novembre 1971, Strasbourg – discours,
    rapports, motions*

Newspapers and political reviews referred to

Action française, Action française agricole, l'Ami du peuple, Aspects de la France, l'Association catholique, l'Autorité, la Bretagne, le Brin de houx, Cahiers de Centre d'Étutes politiques et civiques, Cahiers de la nouvelle journée, Cahiers de la révolution européenne, Carrefour, le Combat, le Combattant européen, le Crapouillot, le Courrier du Centre d'Études politiques et civiques, le Cri du sol, la Croix, Défense de l'occident, le Document, les Documents politiques, économiques et financiers, l'Écho de Paris, l'Écho des syndicats agricoles du nord, les Écrits de Paris, l'Esprit public, Europe-action, l'Express, le Figaro, le Flambeau, la France catholique, la France indépendante, la France moderne, la France rurales et indépendante, la Gazette agricole, le Gerbe, l'Heure bretonne, l'Humanité, les Idées et les faits, Jeune nation, le Jour, Journal des indépendants, la Liberté, le Matin, Minute, le Monde, le Monde économique, le National, la Nation française, le Nouveau siècle, la Nouvelliste de Bretagne, le Nouvel Observateur, l'Ordre, Paroles françaises, la Patrie, le Petit démocrate, Politique, Pour le Victoire, la Presse de Paris, le Progrès agricole, le Rassemblement, Réaction, Réponses, la République française, la Revue des jeunes, la Revue de Paris, la Revue des vivants, Sept, le Temps, T-V Demain, Unité paysanne, Verbe, la Vie catholique, la Vie intellectuelle, la Voix de la terre.

Works on the Right
All general studies of the French political system contain some account of Right-wing politics but very few works are specifically devoted to an analysis of the Right. Recent writings which contain attempts to define the essence of the Right are not of outstanding quality although they contain interesting insights. The most notable of these works are: J. Jaélic, *La Droite – cette inconnue*, 1963; R. Lasierra, J. Plumyène, *Le Complexe de droite*, 1969; P. Sérant, *Ou va la droite?*, 1958.

A number of attempted definitions of the Right and the Left are contained in: M. Duverger, *Constitutions et documents politiques*, 1957, pp. 207–16. A stimulating essay on the Right is to be found in: R. Aron, *Espoir et peur du siècle*, 1957.

Some of the books, published in the inter-war period, which attempt to relate traditions, political activity and social structure are still of considerable interest, although they are often superficial in their approach: L. Fourcade, *La République de province*, 1936; P. Frédérix, *État des forces en France*, 1935; P. de Pressac, *Les Forces historiques de la France*, 1928; A. Thibaudet, *Les Idées politiques de la France*, 1932.

All these works are, however, overshadowed by a book which contains many subtle judgements on groups and traditions of the Right, from 1815 to the Fifth Republic, as well as many useful bibliographical references: R. Rémond, *La Droite en France*, 3rd edition, 2 vols 1968, 2nd American edition 1969.

Works cited

L. Aertz, L. Moulin, 'Les classes moyennes; essai de bibliographie critique', *Revue d'histoire économique et sociale*, 1954, pp. 161–81, 293–309.

P. Allard, *Les Dessous de la grande guerre révélés par les comités secrets*, 1932.

J. S. Ambler, *The French Army in Politics, 1945–1962*, 1966.

'Les Anciens combattants et la nation', *Défense de l'occident*, Nos 56–7, 1958.

M. Anderson 'The Right and the Social Question in Parliament, 1905–1919', in D. Shapiro (ed.), *The Right in France, 1880–1919*, St Antony's Papers, No. 13, 1962, pp. 85–134. 'The Myth of the Two Hundred Families', *Political Studies*, vol. 13, 1965, pp. 163–78. 'Regional Identity and Political Change: the Case of Alsace from the Third to the Fifth Republic', *Political Studies*, vol. 20, pp. 17–30.

P. Andreu, 'Le Complot des acacias', *la Science historique*, February–August 1955, pp. 97–9.

S. Arbellot, 'La Cagoule', *le Document*, February 1938.

Capitain d'Arbeux, *L'Officier contemporaine; la démocratisation de l'armée*, 1911.

Marquis d'Argenson, *Pétain et pétinisme* [*sic*], 1953.

P. Ariès, *Histoire des populations françaises*, 1971.

R. Aron, *L'Histoire de Vichy*, 2 vols, 1954, English edition 1958. *L'Histoire de l'épuration*, 2 vols, 1967–9.

Association Française de Science Politique, *Le Référendum de septembre et les élections de novembre 1958*, 1960. *Paris et sa région*, 1966.

M. Aucouturier, *Au Service des Croix de Feu*, 1936.

M. Augé-Laribé, *Syndicats et coopératives agricoles*, 2nd edition, 1938. *La Politique agricole de la France de 1880 à 1940*, 1950.

H. Azeau, *Révolte militaire, Alger 22 avril 1961*, 1961.

M. Bal, 'Les Indépendants', *Revue française de science politique*, vol. 15, 1965, pp. 537–55.

B. C. F. Bankowitz, 'Paris on 6 February 1934' in B. D. Gooch (ed.), *Interpreting European History*, 1967. *Maxime Weygand and Civil Military Relations in France*, 1967.

Baron Barclay de Lautour, *Paradoxes de la noblesse française*, 1967.

M. Bardèche, *Lettre à François Mauriac*, 1947. *Nurnberg ou la terre promise*, 1948. *Qu'est-ce que le fascisme?*, 1961.

R. Barillon, 'Le RPF', in M. Duverger (ed.), *Partis politiques et classes sociales*, 1955.

P. Barral, *Les Agrariens français de Méline à Pisani*, 1968.

M. Barrès, *Scènes et doctrines du nationalisme*, n.d. *La Grande pitié des églises de la France*, 1914. *Mes Cahiers*, 12 vols, 1929–49. *Chroniques de la grande guerre*, 13 vols, 1924–39. With C. M. P. Maurras, *La République ou le roi*, 1970.

P. Barret, J. Senger, *Le Problème scolaire en Alsace-Lorraine*, 1948.

M. Bassi, *Valéry Giscard d'Estaing*, 1968.

M. Baudot, *L'Opinion publique sous l'occupation. L'exemple d'un département français, 1939–1945*, 1960.

C. Baussan, *La Tour du Pin*, 1931.

E. Beau de Loménie, *Les Responsabilités des dynasties bourgeoises*, 4 vols, 1943–63.

S. de Beauvoir, *La Force de l'âge*, 1960.

F. Bédarida, 'L'Armée et la République', *Revue historique*, vol. 232, 1964, pp. 119–64.

M. Beloff, 'The Sixth of February', St Antony's Papers, No. 5, 1956, pp. 9–35.

J. Berger, *L'Industrie cotonnière alsacienne*, 1952.

S. Berger, *Peasants against Politics*, 1972.

G. Berry, *Un Page d'histoire. La Séparation des églises et de l'état à la Chambre des Députés*, 1905.

G. Berthier de Sauvigny, *La Restauration*, 2nd edition, 1962.

R. Binion, *Defeated Leaders. The Political fate of Caillaux, Jouvenel and Tardieu*, 1960.

P. Bois, *Les Paysans de l'ouest*, 1971.

A. Bonafous, *Les Royalistes du nord et le ralliement*, unpublished *mémoire*, Lille, 1963. 'Les Royalistes du nord et le ralliement', *Revue du nord*, vol. 57, 1965, pp. 29–48.

G. Bonet-Maury, R. Samuel, *Annuaire du parlement*, 1899–1912.

E. and G. Bonnefous, *Histoire politique de la Troisième République*, 7 vols, 2nd edition, 1965–7.

L. Bonnevay, *Les Journées sanglantes de février 1934*, 1935.

M. J. Bopp, *L'Alsace sous l'occupation allemande*, 1945.

E. Borne, 'Du Côté de la droite classique', *la Vie intellectuelle*, June 1955.

W. Bosworth, *Catholicism and Crisis in Modern France*, 1962.

J. Bourdin, 'La Crise des indépendants', *Revue française de science politique*, vol. 13, 1963, pp. 443–50. With R. Rémond, 'Les Forces adverses', in *Léon Blum, chef de gouvernement*, 1967.

P. Bourdrel, *La Cagoule: 30 ans de complots*, 1970.

L. Boudrier, *Le Comte de Paris: un cas politique*, 1965.

J. Bouvier, *Le Krach de l'Union générale, 1878–1885*, 1960.

M. Braibant, *D'Abord la terre*, 1935.

P. Brisson, *Vingt ans du Figaro, 1938–1958*, n.d.

M. and S. Bromberger, *Les Treize complots du treize mai*, 1959. With J. F. Chauvel, G. Elgey, *Barricades et colonels*, 1960.

R. Brunois, *Le Groupe pour l'Unité de la République et ses séquelles*, unpublished *mémoire*, Paris, 1962.

P. Brunot, *La Droite traditionaliste dans les Basses-Pyrénées*, unpublished *mémoire*, Bordeaux, 1969.

P. Bruyelle, 'L'Industrie cotonnière à Lille-Roubaix-Tourcoing', *Revue du nord*, vol. 36, 1954, pp. 21–40.

P. Buttin, *Le Procès Pucheu*, 1947.

R. Caerléon, *Complots pour une république bretonne*, 1967. *La Révolution bretonne permanente*, 1969. *Au village des condamnés au mort*, 1970.

B. Cahen, *Les Gaullistes de gauche, 1958–1962*, unpublished *mémoire*, Paris, 1962.

J. C. Cairns, 'Politics and Foreign Policy, 1911–1914', *Canadian Historical Journal*, September 1953.

I. R. Campbell, *Political Attitudes in France to the Algerian Question, 1954–1962*, unpublished thesis, Oxford, 1972.

L. Capéran, *L'Anticléricalisme et l'affaire Dreyfus*, 1948.

F. Carreras, *L'Accord FLN-OAS*, 1967.

F. Carrez, P. A. Wiltzer, *Le Gaullisme de Gauche*, unpublished *mémoire*, Paris, 1962.

H. Cartier, H. de Kérillis, *Faisons le point*, 1931.

J. Casanova, 'L'Amendment Vallon', *Revue française de science politique*, vol. 17, 1967, pp. 97–109.

M. Cépède, *Agriculture et alimentation en France durant la deuxième guerre mondiale*, 1961.

P. Chalmin, 'Crises morales de l'armée française au 19ème siècle', *Revue de défense nationale*, vol. 6, 1950, pp. 554–70.

G. Chapman, *The Dreyfus Case*, 1955. *The Dreyfus Trials*, 1972.

H. Charbonneau, *Les Mémoires de Porthos*, 1967. *Le Roman noir de la droite française*, 1969.

J. Charlot, *L'UNR, étude du pouvoir au sein d'un parti politique*, 1967. *Le Gaullisme*, 1970. 'Les Préparatifs de la majorité', *Les Elections législatives de 1967*, 1970. *Les Français et de Gaulle*, 1971. *The Gaullist phenomenon*, 1971.

G. Charpenay, *Les Banques régionales, leur vie et leur mort*, 1939.

J. Chastenet, *La France de M. Fallières*, 1949.

L. Chevallier, *Les Parisiens*, 1967.

J. P. Chevènement, *La Droite nationaliste devant l'Allemagne*, unpublished *mémoire*, Paris, 1960.

P. Chopine, *Le Colonel de La Rocque, veut-il la guerre civile ?*, 1937. *La Verité sur le PSF et le comte de La Rocque*, n.d.

A. Christnacht, *Aspects de la campagne présidentielle de M. Tixier-Vignancour*, unpublished *mémoire*, Paris, 1967.

J. C. Colliard, *Les Républicains Indépendants*, 1971.

E. Combes, *Mon Ministère, 1902–1905*, 1956.

Y. Congar, 'La Mentalité de droite et l'intégrisme', 'Documents sur l'intégrisme', *La Vie intellectuelle*, June 1950, September 1952.

N. Copin, 'La Famille gaulliste après Strasbourg: conserver l'héritage', *Revue politique et parlementaire*, vol. 73, 1971, pp. 21–32.

R. Cornilleau, *Le Ralliement a-t-il échoué ?*, 1927. *Du Bloc national au front populaire, 1939*.

F. Coront-Ducluzeau, *La Formation de l'espace économique français*, 1959.

F. Costa, *L'Extrême droite et les élections de 1965*, unpublished *mémoire*, Paris, 1966.

H. Coston, *Le Retour des deux cents familles*, 1960. *Partis, journaux et hommes politiques d'hier et d'aujourd'hui*, 1960.

M. Cotta, *Les Idéologies de la collaboration à travers de la presse*, thesis, Paris, published in abridged form, *La Collaboration*, 1964.

P. Dabry, *Les Catholiques républicains. Histoire et souvenirs, 1980–1903*, 1905.

A. Dansette, *L'Histoire religieuse de la France contemporaine*, 2nd edition, 1965, English edition 1961. *Destin du catholicisme français*, 1957. *L'Affaire Wilson et la chute du Président Grévy*, 1936. *Le Boulangisme*, 1886–90, 1947.

J. M. Darboise, *et al.*, *Officiers en Algérie*, 1960.

G. Dargnies, *L'Action régionale et l'opinion en Bretagne*, unpublished thesis, Paris, 1966.

J. L. Davant, *Histoire du Pays Basque*, 1972.

Dazelle, *De l'Union nationale à la révolution nationale*, unpublished *mémoire*, Paris, 1958.

M. Déat, *Le Parti unique*, 1942.

J. Debû-Bridel, *L'Agonie de la Troisième République*, 1948.

J. Delahaye, *La Reprise des relations avec le Vatican*, 1921.

J. Delperrie de Bayac, *Histoire de la milice*, 1969.

J. Delumeau (ed.), *Histoire de Bretagne*, 1969.

J. Denais, *Jacques Piou*, 1959.

H. Descamp de Bragelonge, *La Vie politique des Basses-Pyrénées*, 1958.

J. Désert, *Toute la verité sur l'affaire de la Cagoule*, 1940.

Dictionnaire des vanités, Documentation sociale contemporaine, cahier no. 1, 1970.

'Les Directeurs', *Annales d'histoire économique et sociale*, vol. 8, 1936.

La Doctrine du Maréchal, classée par thèmes, 3rd edition, 1943.

M. Dogan, 'Les Officiers dans la carrière politique: du Maréchal Mac-Mahon au Général de Gaulle', *Revue française de sociologie*, vol. 2, 1961, pp. 88–99.

P. Dollinger (ed.), *Histoire de l'Alsace*, 1970.

J. Domenach, 'Le Regroupement de droite et l'intégrisme', *Synthèse*, December 1953, pp. 107–16.

H. Dorgères, *Haut les fourches*, 1935. *Au XXème siècle, dix ans de jacquerie*, 1959.

J. Doriot, *La France avec nous*, 1937.

F. G. Dreyfus, *La Vie politique en Alsace, 1919–1936*, 1969.

P. Drieu La Rochelle, *Socialisme fasciste*, 1934. *Doriot ou la vie d'un ouvrier français*, 1936. *Chronique politique, 1934–1942*, 1943.

R. Duchet, 'Le Mouvement des Indépendants, son histoire', *la France indépendante*, 12 September 1953. *Pour le Salut public*, 1958.

L. Ducloux, *Du Chantage à la trahaison*, 1955, English edition, 1958.

G. Dupeux, *Le Front populaire et les elections de 1936*, 1959. *La Société française, 1789–1960*, 1964.

F. Duprat, *Les Mouvements d'extrême droite en France depuis 1945*, 1972.

M. Duverger et al., *Les Elections du 2 janvier 1956*, 1957. 'L'Eternel marais', *Revue française de science politique*, vol. 14, 1964, pp. 33–51.

H. Ehrmann, *Organised Business in France*, 1957, French edition, 1959.

G. Elgey, *La République des illusions, 1945–1951*, 1965.

A. Fabre-Luce, *Au Nom des silencieux*, 1946.

E. Faguet, *Problèmes politiques du temps présent*, 1900.

L. Fatoux, *Les Coulisses du nationalisme*, 1903.

M. Faure, *Les Paysans dans la société française*, 1966.

J. Fauvet, *Les Partis politiques dans la France actuelle*, 1947. *La Quatrième République*, 1959. With H. Mendras, *Les Paysans et la politique*, 1958. With J. Planchais, *La Fronde des généraux*, 1961.

P. E. Flandin, *Politique française, 1919–1940*, 1947.

E. Flornoy, *La Lutte par l'association*, 2nd edition, 1907.

J. Folliet, *Pacificisme de droite? Bellicisme de gauche?*, 1938.

J. Fonlupt, 'Notre Administration et la crise alsacienne', *La Revue des vivants*, October 1928.

H. Fontanille, *L'Œuvre sociale d'Albert de Mun*, 1926.

Y. Fouéré, *La Bretagne écartelée. Essai pour servir à l'histoire de dix ans, 1938–1948*, 1962.

E. Fournol, *Le Plutarque moderne*, 1923.

R. Frey, *L'UNR, sa victoire, son avenir*, 1958.

R. Fruit, *L'Agriculture dans la région du nord*, 1958.

L. Gabriel-Robinet, *Dorgères et le Front Paysan*, 1937.

J. Gadille, *La Pensée et l'action politique des évêques français au début de la IIIème République, 1870–1883*, 2 vols, 1957.

R. Garric, *Albert de Mun*, 1935.

M. Garrigou-Legrange, 'L'Intégrisme et national-catholicisme', *Esprit*, November 1958.

O. Gaudry, *Henri de Kérillis*, unpublished *mémoire*, Paris, 1966.

C. de Gaulle, *Discours de guerre*, 3 vols, 1944–45. *Mémoires de guerre*, 3 vols, 1954–9. *Memoirs of Hope*, 1971.

R. Gendarme, *La Région du nord*, 1954.

L. Giard, *Les Elections à Paris, 1871–1939*, unpublished *mémoire*, Paris, 2 vols, n.d.

Y. Gicquel, *Le Comité consultatif breton*, 1960.

R. Girardet, *La Sociéteé militaire, 1814–1940*, 1953. *La Crise militaire, 1945–1962*, 1964. *L'Idée coloniale en France*, 1965–6. *Le Nationalisme français, 1871–1914*, 1966. 'Pour une introduction à l'histoire du nationalisme français', *Revue française de science politique*, vol. 8, 1958, pp. 505–28. 'Pouvoir civil et pouvoir militaire dans la France contemporaine', ibid., vol. 10, 1950, pp. 5–38.

F. Goguel, *La Politique des partis sous la Troisième République*, 3rd edition, 2 vols, 1958. 'Structure sociale et repartition des votes dans les élections du 17 juin 1951', *Revue française de science politique*, vol. 1, 1951, pp. 326–33. 'Combien y a-t-il en électeurs de gauche parmi ceux qui ont voté le 5 décembre 1965 pour le général de Gaulle?', ibid., vol. 17, 1967, 65–9.

D. B. Goldey, *The Disintegration of the Cartel des Gauches and the Politics of French Government Finance, 1924–1928*, unpublished thesis, Oxford, 1962.

L. Gorny, *Les Economies régionales de la France*, 1958.

B. Gourdon, 'Les Grands commis et le mythe de l'intérêt général', *Cahiers de la République*, vol. 1, 1956, pp. 78–90.

R. Grand, *La Force paysanne*, 1931.

P. Gratton, *Les Luttes de classes dans les compagnes*, 1971.

F. Grover, *Drieu La Rochelle*, 1962.

P. Grover, *Histoire de la Restauration Nationale*, unpublished *mémoire*, Aix, 1970.

J. Guegan, *Un Exemple d'expansion économique régionale: l'Alsace de 1944 à 1961*, 1961.

R. Guespin, *L'Action républicaine et sociale, mouvement politique*, 1953.

C. Guignebert, *Le Problème religieux dans la France d'aujourd'hui*, 1922.

V. Guiraud, *Un Grand français. Albert de Mun*, 1920. *Le Général de Castelnau*, 1928.

J. Guitton, *La Vie ardente et féconde de Léon Harmel*, 1929.

D. Halèvy, *La Fin des notables*, 1930. *La République des ducs*, 1937.

A. Hamon, *Les Maîtres de la France*, 3 vols, 1936–8.

F. de Hautecloque, *Grandeur et décadence des Croix des Feu*, 1937.

J. E. S. Hayward, 'From Functional Regionalism to Functional Representation in France: the Battle for Brittany', *Political Studies*, vol. 17, 1969, pp. 48–75.

P. Henry, *Mouvement patronal catholique français*, 1936.

F. Hoffet, *Psychoanalyse d'Alsace*, 1951.

S. Hoffman, *Le Mouvement poujade*, 1956. (ed.) *France: Change and Tradition*, 1963. 'Quelques aspects du régime de Vichy', *Revue française de science politique*, vol. 6, 1956, pp. 46–69. 'Collaboration in France during World War II', *Journal of Modern History*, vol. 40, 1968, pp. 375–95.

S. Hugonnier, 'Tempéraments politiques et géographie électorale des deux grandes vallées des Alpes du Nord: Maurienne et Tarentaise', *Revue de géographie alpine*, vol. 42, 1954, pp. 45–80.

J. Huret, *Enquête sur la question sociale en Europe*, 1897.

W. D. Irvine, *The Republican Federation of France during the 1930s*, unpublished thesis, Princeton, 1972.

R. E. M. Irving, *The MRP and French Policy in Indo-China*, unpublished thesis, Oxford, 1968. *Christian Democracy in France*, 1972.

L. Jacques, *Les Partis politiques*, 1913.

D. Johnson, *France and the Dreyfus Affair*, 1966.

E. Judet, *Ma Politique, 1905–1917*, 1923.

E. Juillard, *Problèmes alsaciens vus par un géographe*, 1958.

G. A. Kelly, 'The French Army re-enters politics', *American Political Science Review*, vol. 76, 1961, pp. 354–67.

H. de Kérillis, *Français, voici la verité*, 1942. See also H. Cartier.

M. Kesselman, 'Systèmes de pouvoir et cultures politiques au sein des partis politiques français', *Revue française de sociologie*, vol. 13, 1972, pp. 485–518.

M. C. Kessler, 'M. Valéry Giscard d'Estaing et les Républicains Indépendants', *Revue française de science politique*, vol. 18, 1968, pp. 77–93.

J. Klatzmann, 'Géographie électorale de l'agriculture française' in J. Fauvet, H. Mendras, *Les Paysans et la politique*, 1958.

R. Kovar *Les Idées politiques d'André Tardien*, unpublished *mémoire*, Paris, 1959.

A. Kupferman, *François Coty, journaliste et homme politique*, unpublished thesis, Paris, 1965.

G. Lachapelle, *Le Ministère Méline*, 1928. *L'Alliance démocratique*, 1935.

P. G. La Chesnais, *Statistique des élections législatives de 1914*, 1914.

J. Lacouture, *De Gaulle*, 1965, English edition, 1970.

P. M. de La Gorce, *La République et son armée*, 1963, English edition 1963.

G. de Lamarzelle, *Démocratie politique, démocratie sociale, démocratie chrétienne*, 1907.

J. Lambert-Dansette, J. A. Roy, 'Origines et évolution d'une bourgeoisie. Le patronat textile du bassin lillois, 1789–1914', *Revue du nord*, vol. 40, 1958, pp. 46–9, vol. 41, 1959, pp. 23–8.

M. T. Lancelot, *L'Organisation de l'Armée Secrète*, 2 vols, 1963.

J. Laniel, 'Le Parti Républicain de la Liberté', *Revue de Paris*, May 1946.

M. J. M. Larkin, *French Catholics and the Question of the Separation of the Churches and the State*, unpublished thesis, Cambridge, 1958. 'President Loubet's visit to Rome', *The Historical Journal*, vol. 4, 1961, pp. 97–103. 'The Church and the French Concordat, 1891–1902', *English Historical Review*, vol. 81, 1966, pp. 117–38.

Colonel de La Rocque, *Service public*, 1934. *Le PSF devant la cour d'appel. Plaidorie de Me Andriot, déclaration de La Rocque*, n.d.

E. and G. Le Rocque, *Le Rocque, tel qu'il était*, 1962.

E. de Las Cases, *Les Autorités sociales dans une démocratie*, 1903.

R. Lasierra, J. Plumyène, *Les Fascismes français, 1923–1963*, 1963.

R. de la Tour du Pin, 'Crise agricole ou crise agraire', *L'Association catholique*, 15 August 1886.

L. Lauga, *Le Centre National des Jeunes Agriculteurs*, 1971.

J. de Launay, *Les Carnets secrets de Louis Loucheur*, 1962. *Le Dossier de Vichy*, 1967.

L. de Lavergne, *Economie rurale de la France*, 2nd edition 1861.

M. Lebesque, *Comment peut-on être breton?* 1971.

M. A. Leblond, *Litterature sociale. La Société française sous la Troisième République*, 1905.

H. Le Boeterf, *La Bretagne dans la guerre*, 1969.

G. Lebras, 'Nuances régionales du catholicisme en France', *Revue de psychologie des peuples*, vol. 8, 1953, pp. 12–23.

L. J. Lebret, *La France en transition*, 1957.

E. Lecanuet, *L'Eglise de France sous la Troisième République, 1870–1910*, 4 vols, 1910–30.

G. Leclerc, *Le Mouvement breton de 1914 à nos jours*, 1968.

G. Lecordier, *Les Classes moyennes en marche*, 1950.

C. Le Goffic, *L'Ame bretonne*, 1902.

G. Le Guen, 'L'Evolution conservatrice', in J. Delumeau, *Histoire de Bretagne*, 1969.

J. Lemaître, *Opinions à repandre*, 1901.

Duc de Lévis-Mirepoix, *Que Signifie 'le parti des ducs' à l'Académie?*, 1964.

R. Livet, *Avenir des régions agricoles*, 1965.

J. L. Loubet del Bayle, *Les Non-conformistes des années trente*, 1969.

Commandant G. Loustaunau-Lacau, *Mémoires d'un français rebelle*, 1948.

J. Mabire, *Drieu parmi nous*, 1963. *Histoire d'un français, Tixier-Vignancour*, 1965.

P. Machefer, 'L'Union des droites: le PSF et le Front de la Liberté', *Revue d'histoire moderne et contemporaine*, vol. 17, 1970, pp. 112–26.

J. MacManners, *Church and State in France, 1870–1914*, 1972.

D. Macrae, *Parliament, Parties and Society in France, 1946–1958*, 1967.

Y. Madiot, *L'Extrême droite et l'élection présidentielles de décembre 1965*, Poitiers, unpublished *mémoire*, 1966.

J. Madiran, *L'Intégrisme: histoire d'histoire*, 1964.

A. Mahé, 'La Cagoule', *Le Crapouillot*, No. 20, 1963.

J. Maître, 'Catholicisme d'extrême droite et croisade anti-subversive', *Revue française de sociologie*, vol. 2, 1961, pp. 107–17.

R. Mallet, *Nécessités d'un retour à la terre*, 1941.

P. Marabuto, *Les Partis politiques et les mouvements sociaux sous la IVème République*, 1948.

B. Marienne, *Sociologie électorale de la Somme de 1919 à 1939*, unpublished *mémoire*, 1962.

P. Marion, *Programme du Parti Populaire Français*, 1938.

P. Marquer, *Contribution à l'étude anthropologique du peuple basque*, 1963.

E. Martin-Saint-Léon, *Le Problème des classes moyennes en France*, 1903. *Les Sociétés de la nation*, 1930.

G. Martin, *Les Banques régionales*, 1922.

G. Martinet, *Le Système Pompidou*, 1971.

J. Martinez, 'Les Elections législatives de 1958 à 1967 dans la vie politique des Basses-Pyrénées', in *Trois études sur le sud-ouest*, 1968.

R. Maspétiol, *L'Ordre éternel des champs*, 1945.

P. Maugé, *Le Particularisme alsacien*, 1972.

C. M. P. Maurras, *Dictionnaire politique et critique*, definitive edition, 5 vols, 1932–4. See also M. Barrès.

J. P. Maxence, *Histoire de dix ans, 1927–1937*, 1939.

J. M. Mayeur, 'Les Congrès nationaux de la démocratie chrétienne (1896–97–98)', *Revue d'histoire moderne et contemporaine*, vol. 9, 1962, pp. 171–206.

F. Médine, *L'Armée qui souffre*, 1908.

L. V. Méjan, *La Séparation des églises et l'état*, 1959.

H. Mendras, 'Structures écologiques et sociales', *Economie rurale*, July 1956, pp. 17–19. See also J. Fauvet.

M. Merle, 'Les Modérés', in M. Duverger (ed.), *Les Partis politiques et classes sociales*, 1955, pp. 241–76.

Mermeix, *Les Coulisses du boulangisme*, 1890. *Au sein des commission. Fragments d'histoire*, 1924.

H. de la Messelière, *Filiations bretonnes*, 1913, reprinted 1965.

C. Micaud, *The French Right and Nazi Germany*, 1943.

H. Michel, *Les Courants de la pensée de la résistance*, 1962.

J. Micheu-Puyou, *Histoire électorale du département des Basses-Pyrenées sous la Troisième et la Quatrième Republique*, 1958.

G. Michon, *La Préparation à la guerre, 1910–1914*, 1935.

P. Miguel, *L'Affaire Dreyfus*, 1961. *Poincaré*, 1961.

A. Millerand, *Le Retour de l'Alsace-Lorraine à la France*, 1923.

A. Mirambel, *La Comédie du nationalisme intégral*, 1947.

J. Molinier, *Le Parti Démocrate Populaire et la réforme de l'état*, unpublished *mémoire*, Paris, 1966.

J. Mollin, *La Verité sur l'affaire des fiches*, 1905.

Count G. de Morant, *La Noblesse française au champ de l'honneur*, 1918.

R. Moreau, *Histoire de l'âme basque*, 1970.

Morland, Barangé, Martinez, *Histoire de l'Organisation de l'Armée Secrète*, 1964.

G. Mosse, 'The French Right and the Working Classes: les Jaunes', *Journal of Contemporary History*, vol. 7, 1972, pp. 185–208.

H. du Moulin de Labarthète, *Les Temps des illusions*, 1946.

L. Moulin, see L. Aertz.

A. de Mun, *Ma Vocation sociale*, 1908.

A. Mutter, *L'Alsace à l'heure de l'Europe*, 1968.

R. Nanteuil, *Le Dossier de M. Guyot de Villeneuve*, 1906.

Count de Neufbourg, *Les Paysans*, 1945.

M. Nicolas, *Le MRP en Alsace de 1947 à 1956*, unpublished *mémoire*, Strasbourg, 1969.

G. Noblemaire, *Concordat ou séparation*, 1905.

L. Noel, *Notre dernière chance*, 1956.

H. Noilhan, *La République des paysans*, 1932.

J. Ollé-Laprune, *La Stabilité des ministres sous la Troisième République, 1879–1940*, 1962.

S. M. Osgood, *French Royalism since 1970*, 1971. 'The Front Populaire: Views from the Right', *International Review of Social History*, vol. 9, 1964, pp. 189–201.

B. Pacteau, *Analyse des rapports entre la carrière nationale et la carrière locale de M. Chaban-Delmas*, unpublished *mémoire*, Bordeaux, 1968.

R. O. Paxton, *Politics and Parades at Vichy*, 1966.

F. Payen, *Raymond Poincaré*, 1936.

Monseigneur Perrin, 'Un Exemple de géographie religieuse: les vocations sacerdotales en Ille-et-Vilaine', *Economie et humanisme*, 1947, pp. 523–9.

E. Pezet, 'La Fédération Nationale Catholique', *la Vie catholique*, 22 February 1925.

P. Pflimlin, R. Uhrlich, *L'Alsace, destin et volonté*, 1963.

J. Philippet, *Les Jeunesses patriotes et Pierre Taittinger*, unpublished *mémoire*, Paris, 1967.

M. Phlipponeau, *Debout la Bretagne!*, 1970.

D. Pickles, *French Politics: the First Years of the Fourth Republic*, 1953.

C. Pineau, *La Simple verité, 1940–1945*, 1961.

J. Piou, *Le Comte Albert de Mun*, n.d. *Le Ralliement*, 1928. *D'Une Guerre à l'autre*, 1932.

J. Planchais, *see* J. Fauvet.

P. Pleven, *L'Avenir de Bretagne*, 1961.

J. Plumyène, *Pétain*, 1964. See also, R. Lasierra.

M. Prélot, 'Histoire et doctrine du Parti Démocrate Populaire', *Politique*, July–December 1962, pp. 307–40.

R. Priouret, *La République des partis*, 1947.

M. Pujo, *Comment La Rocque a trahi*, n.d.

C. Purtschet, *Le Rassemblement du Peuple Français, 1947–1953*, 1965.

Count A. de Puységur, *De l'Epée au tango*, 1914. *Les Maquéraux légitimes: du coursier des croisades au bidet de Rebecca*, 1938.

P. Rambeaud, *Economie et sociologie de la montagne: Albiez-le-vieux en Maurienne*, 1964.

Raymond-Laurent, *Le Parti Démocrate Populaire; un effort de dix ans, 1924–1934*, 1935. *Le Parti Démocrate Populaire*, 1965.

R. Rémond, *La Droite en France*, 3rd edition, 1968, 2nd American edition 1969. *Le Gouvernement de Vichy, 1940–1942*, 1972. With A. Coutrot, *Les Catholiques, le communisme et les crises, 1929–1939*, 1960. 'Les Anciens combattants et la politique', *Revue française de science politique*, vol. 5, 1955, pp. 267–90. 'Explications du 6 février', *Politique*, July–September 1959, pp. 218–30. See also J. Bourdin.

H. Rollet, *Albert de Mun et le parti catholique*, 1947. *L'Action sociale des catholiques en France, 1871–1914*, 2 vols, 1948–58.

P. Rouanet, *Mendès-France au pouvoir*, 1965.

G. Roupnel, *L'Histoire de la campaigne française*, 1932.

J. P. Roux, 'L'UDR: ses options et ses objectifs', *Revue politique et parlementaire*, vol. 73, 1971, pp. 33–44.

J. A. Roy, *Histoire du Jockey club de Paris*, 1958. *Histoire de la famille Schneider et du Creusot*, 1962. See also J. Lambert-Dansette.

P. Rudeaux, *Les Croix de Feu et le PSF*, 1967.

O. Rudelle, *Le Sénateur M. Michel Debré*, unpublished *mémoire*, Paris, 1967.

L. Rudloff, *La Carrière politique d'un homme politique local: André Bord*, unpublished *mémoire*, Strasbourg, 1969.

Saint-Paulien (pseudonym of M. I. Sicard), *Histoire de la Collaboration*, 1964. *Doriot et la guerre du Rif*, 1943.

L. Salleron, *Un Régime corporatif pour l'agriculture*, 1937.

R. Samuel, see G. Bonet-Maury.

P. de Sarcus, *De L'Elite. Essai sur la restauration d'une noblesse nouvelle*, 1966.

P. Sauvage, *Le Poujadisme de 1958 à 1968*, unpublished *mémoire*, Paris, 1970.

A. Sauvy, *Mouvement économique de 1929 à 1939*, 1941. *Histoire économique de la France l'entre les deux guerres*, 2 vols, 1965–7.

E. Schaeffer, *L'Alsace et Lorraine, 1940–1945*, 1953.

F. H. Seager, *The Boulanger Affair*, 1969.

A. Sedgwick, *The 'Ralliement' in French Politics*, 1965.

R. Sédillot, *La Maison de Wendel de mil sept cent quatre à nos jours*, 1968.

P. Semart, *La Guerre du Rif*, 1926.

J. Senger, *see* P. Barret.

P. Sérant, *Le Romanticisme fasciste*, 1959. *La France des minorités*, 1965. *Le Bretagne et la France*, 1971.

E. Seuillard, *Les Groupements de l'extrême droite actuelle en France*, unpublished *mémoire*, Paris, 1960.

D. Shapiro, 'The *Ralliement* in the Politics of the 1890s' in D. Shapiro (ed.), *The Right in France 1890–1919*, St Antony's Papers, No. 13, 1962, pp. 13–48.

J. Sherwood, *Georges Mandel and the Third Republic*, 1971, and St Antony's Papers, No. 5, 1959, pp. 86–125.

J. P. Sicre, 'Les Allemands à la conquete de l'Alsace', *Revue politique et parlementaire*, vol. 71, 1969, pp. 38–55.

A. Siegfried, *Tableau politique de la France de l'ouest*, 1913. *Tableau des partis en France*, 1930. *De la Troisième à la Quatrième République*, 1956. 'Le Vichy de Pétain, le Vichy de Laval', *Revue française de science politique*, vol. 6, 1956, pp. 737–49.

Y. Simon, *La Campagne d'Ethiopie et la pensée politique française*, 1936.

T. A. Smith, 'Algeria and the French Modérés: the Politics of Immoderation?', *Western Political Quarterly*, vol. 18, 1965, pp. 116–34.

P. Sorlin, *Waldeck-Rousseau*, 1966. *'La Croix' et les juifs, 1880–1899*, 1967. *La Société française, 1840–1968*, 2 vols, 1969–71.

J. Soustelle, *L'Espérance trahie*, 1962. *La Page n'est pas tournée*, 1965.

General E. L. Spears, *Assignment to Catastrophe*, 2 vols, 1954.

Z. Sternhell, *Les Idées politiques et sociales de Maurice Barrès, 1884–1902*, unpublished thesis, Paris, 1969, 2 vols.

G. Suarez, *La Grande peur du 6 février au Palais Bourbon*, 1934.

J. Susini, *Histoire de l'OAS*, 1963.

R. Talmy, *Un Forme hybride du catholicisme social en France. L'Association catholique des patrons du nord, 1884–1895*, 1962.

E. Tannenbaum, *Action Française*, 1962.

A. Tardieu, *La Révolution à refaire*, 2 vols, 1936–7. *L'Epreuve du pouvoir*, 1931.

L. Teste, *L'Anatomie de la Troisième République, 1870–1910*, 1910.

R. Thabault, *Mon Village*, 1944.

G. M. Thomas, *The Political Career and Ideas of Paul Marion*, unpublished thesis, Oxford, 1969.

M. Thomas, *L'Affaire sans Dreyfus*, 1961.

J. L. Tixier-Vignancour, *La France trahie*, 1956. *J'ai choisi la défense*, 1964.

H. Torres, *De Clemencau à de Gaulle*, 1958.

J. Touchard, 'L'Esprit des années trente', *Cahiers de la civilisation*, No. 1, 1960, pp. 89–120.

'Les transformations des sociétés rurales française', special number, *Revue française de sociologie*, 1965.

Abbé Trochu, *Trente-cinq ans de politique religieuse*, 1936.

W. R. Tucker, 'The New look of the Extreme Right in France', *Western Political Quarterly*, vol. 21, 1968, pp. 86–97.

R. Uhrlich, see P. Pflimlin.

X. Vallat, 'Souvenirs sur le général de Castelnau', *Revue de Rouergue*, 1954, pp. 405–12. 'La Fédération Nationale Catholique', *Ecrits de Paris*, November 1954, pp. 65–74.

C. Vallin, 'Le Parti Social Français', *Sciences politiques*, August 1937.

F. Veuillot, *La Rocque et son parti comme je les ai vus*, 1938.

G. Warner, *Pierre Laval and the Eclipse of France*, 1968.

P. K. Warner, *The Winegrowers of France and the Government since 1875*, 1960.

D. R. Watson, 'The Nationalist Movement in Paris, 1900–1906', in D. Shapiro (ed.), *The Right in France 1890–1919*, St Antony's Papers, No. 13, 1962, pp. 49–84.

E. Weber, *The Nationalist revival in France*, 1959. *Action Française*, 1962.

S. Weil, *L'Enracinement*, 1949.

General M. Weygand, *Mémoires*, 3 vols, 1950–57. *L'Armée à l'Académie*, 1963.

P. M. Williams, *Crisis and Compromise: the Politics of the Fourth French Republic*, 1964. *The French Parliament, 1958–67*, 1968. *Wars, Plots and Scandals in Post-War France*, 1970. *French Politicians and Elections, 1951–1969*, 1970.

J. G. S. Wilson, *French Banking Structure and Credit Policy*, 1951.

P. A. Wiltzer, see J. F. Carrez.

D. Wolf, *Doriot: du communisme à la collaboration*, 1969. German edition 1967.

R. Wolff, *Economie et finances de la France*, 1943.

G. Wright, *Raymond Poincaré and the French Presidency*, 1942. *The Rural Revolution in France*, 1964.

V. Wright, *The Basses Pyrénées from 1848 to 1870 – a Study in Departmental Politics*, unpublished thesis, London, 1965.

Index